THE ARCTIC
p 123

GERMANY &
THE ALPINE STATES
pp 42-43

THE LOW
COUNTRIES
pp 34-35

NORTHERN EUROPE
pp 32-33

nd
3

RUSSIA & KAZAKHSTAN
pp 60-61

EUROPEAN RUSSIA
pp 52-53

THE BRITISH
ISLES
pp 36-37

CENTRAL
EUROPE
pp 46-47

EUROPE
pp 28-55

ASIA
pp 56-75

FRANCE
pp 38-39

EASTERN
EUROPE
pp 50-51

ITALY
pp 44-45

SOUTHEAST
EUROPE
pp 48-49

TURKEY &
THE CAUCASUS
pp 62-63

CENTRAL
ASIA
pp 66-67

EAST
ASIA
pp 70-71

JAPAN &
KOREA
pp 68-69

SPAIN &
PORTUGAL
pp 40-41

Gibraltar
p 41

Malta
p 54

THE
MEDITERRANEAN
pp 54-55

Cyprus
p 54

Israel
p 65

SOUTHWEST
ASIA
pp 64-65

Ryukyu
Islands
p 69

PACIFIC

OCEAN

NORTH AFRICA
pp 106-107

SOUTH
ASIA
pp 72-73

WEST AFRICA
pp 108-109

EAST
AFRICA
pp 110-111

Andaman
& Nicobar
Islands
p 73

SOUTHEAST
ASIA
pp 74-75

AFRICA
pp 102-113

SOUTHWEST
PACIFIC
pp 120-121

SOUTHERN
AFRICA
pp 112-113

INDIAN

OCEAN

AUSTRALASIA
& OCEANIA
pp 114-121

Samoa
p 120

AUSTRALIA
pp 116-117

NEW ZEALAND
pp 118-119

ANTARCTICA

p 122

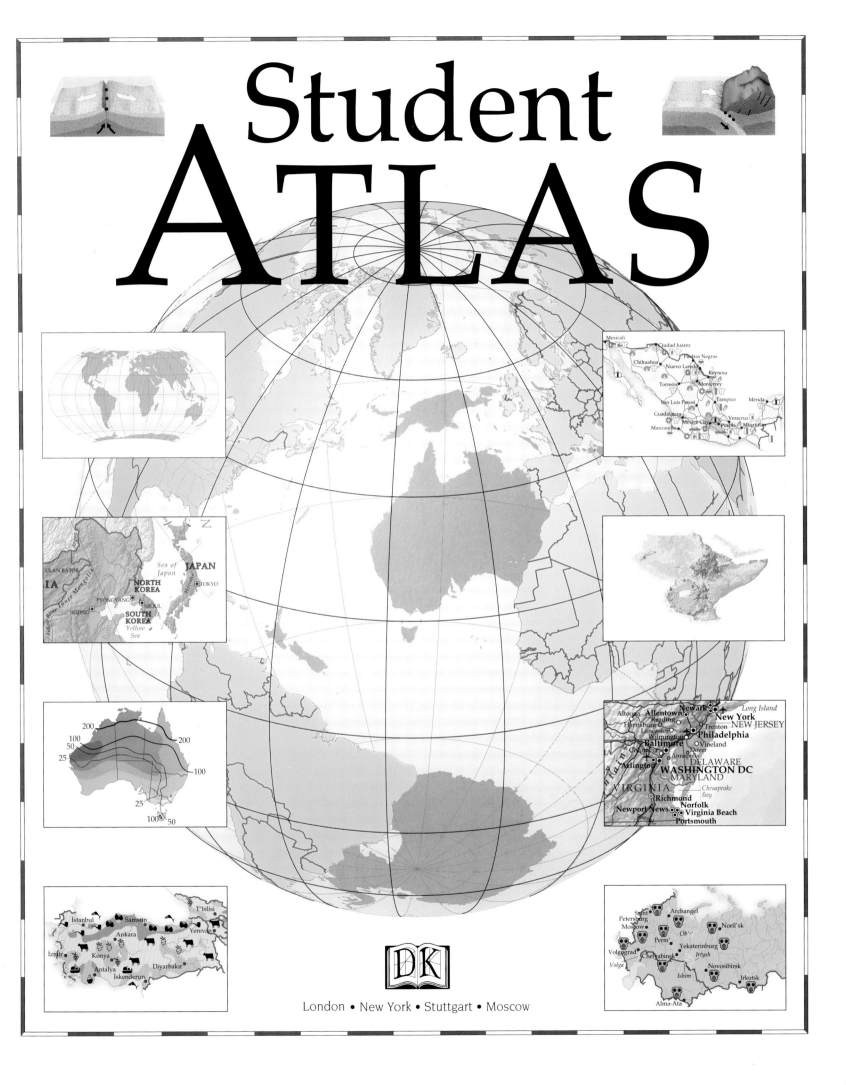

Student
ATLAS

DK

London • New York • Stuttgart • Moscow

A DORLING KINDERSLEY BOOK

EDUCATIONAL CONSULTANT
David Lambert, Department of Education, University of London

MAP SKILLS CONSULTANT
David R Wright, BA MA

TEACHER REVIEWERS
Kevin Ball, Langdon School, London, Pat Barber, Poynton County High School, Cheshire
Stewart Marson, Guilsborough School, Northampton

ACKNOWLEDGEMENTS
Geography students at Poynton County High School, Cheshire

DORLING KINDERSLEY CARTOGRAPHY

MANAGING EDITOR   MANAGING ART EDITOR
Lisa Thomas   Philip Lord

PROJECT EDITORS   PROJECT DESIGNERS
Debra Clapson, Wim Jenkins   Rhonda Fisher, Karen Gregory

EDITORIAL CONTRIBUTORS   DESIGNERS
Thomas Heath, Kevin McRae, Constance Novis,   Carol Ann Davis, David Douglas
Siobhan Ryan   Nicola Liddiard

MANAGING CARTOGRAPHER   SENIOR CARTOGRAPHIC EDITOR
David Roberts   Roger Bullen

CARTOGRAPHERS
Pamela Alford, James Anderson, Sarah Baker-Ede, Dale Buckton,
Tony Chambers, Ian Clark, Martin Darlison, Sally Gable, Jeremy Hepworth,
Michael Martin, Simon Mumford, John Plumer, Jane Voss, Peter Winfield

DATABASE MANAGER   DIGITAL MAPS CREATED IN DK CARTOPIA BY
Simon Lewis   Phil Rowles, Rob Stokes

PLACENAMES DATABASE TEAM   PICTURE RESEARCH
Julia Lynch, Natalie Clarkson, Margaret Stevenson   Louise Thomas

EDITORIAL DIRECTION   PRODUCTION
Andrew Heritage   David Proffit

First published in Great Britain in 1998 by Dorling Kindersley Limited,
9 Henrietta Street, London WC2E 8PS
Visit us on the World Wide Web at http://www.dk.com

A CIP catalogue record for this book is available from the British Library

ISBN 0 7513 0699 1

Reproduction by Colourscan, Singapore, and The Printed Word, London
Printed and bound in China by L.Rex Printing Co., Ltd.

ACKNOWLEDGEMENTS
The publishers are grateful for permission to reproduce the following photographs:
t=top, b=bottom, a=above, l=left, r=right, c=centre

Axiom: J Spaull 74br. **Bridgeman Art Library**: Hereford Cathedral, Trustees of the Hereford Mappa Mundi 8tr.
J Allan Cash: 120cr. **Bruce Coleman Ltd**: C Ott 92cr (below); Dr E Pott 4bc; H Reinhard 19cr; J Murray 130bl; Peter Terry
19crr. **Colourific**: Black Star/R Rogers 111br; Frank Herrmann 119bc. **Comstock**: 17tc. **James Davis Travel Photography**:
26cr (above), 27bl, 44tr, 119tr. **Robert Harding Picture Library**: 6tr (below), 21c, 21br, 22br, 74cr (above), 92bl, 94cr, 94br,
95bl, 118bl; A Tovy 120br; Adam Woolfitt 44br; C Bowman 110tr; Charcrit Boonson 72cr (below); David Lomax 20tr; Franz
Joseph Land 19tr; G Boutin 120cl (below); G Renner 17c, 118cr(above); Gavin Hellier 95tr; H P Merten 23tl; Jane Sweeney
23bl; Louise Murray 75tr; Peter Scholey 73tr; Philip Craven 28cl; Robert Francis 23cr; Schuster/Keine 44cr (above); Simon
Westcott 72br. **Hutchison Library**: A Zvoznikov 19cl; J Nowell 75bl; R Ian Lloyd 10cl. **Image Bank**: Carlos Navajas 17bl; M
Isy-Schwart 17bc; P Grumann 46cr (below); Steve Proehl 94cr (below); Terje Rakke 17br. **Images Colour Library**: 19c, 26br,
44cr (below), 118br. **Impact**: Bruce Stephens 26cr (below); Jeremy Nicholl 121cl (below); Mark Henley 20bl; Paul O'Driscoll
45cr; Robin Lubbock 118br. **Frank Lane Picture Agency**: D Smith 19bc; W Wisniewsli 17cr. **Magnum**: Chris Steele Perking
120tr (below); Ian Berry 46br; Jean Gaumy 47cr. **N.A.S.A**: 9tc. **N.H.P.A**: M Wendler 4cl, 108bl. **Oxford Scientific Films**:
Konrad Wothe 19tc; L Gould 4tr; Nobert Rosing 92cl. **Panos Pictures**: Alain le Garsheur 75cr; Alain le Garsmeur 95cl
(below); Alberto Arzoz 45tr; Bruce Paton 121bl; Jeremy Hartley 120bl; Maria Luiza M Cavalho 110cl (below); Paul Smith
109cr; Rhodri Jones 111bl; Ron Gilling 119cr; Trygve Bolstad 22bl. **Edward Parker**: 17cr (above). **Pictor International**: 4tc,
10bc, 18tr, 20br, 26tr, 26bl, 29bc. **Planet Earth Pictures**: I Waters 111bc. **South American Pictures**: Robert Francis 92br;
Tony Morrison 108cr, 109cl. **Spectrum Colour Library**: 93br. **Frank Spooner Pictures**: Gamma/E Baitel 73cl. **Still Pictures**:
J Frebet 111cr; R Seitre 72cr (above). **Tony Stone Images**: 17tr, 110cl; A Sacks 92cr; Alan Levenson 74cr; D Austen 131cr; D
Hanson 17cl; Donald Johnson 44bc; Earth Imaging 6tr (above); G Johnson 72bl; H Strand 111tr; J Jangoux 19bcr; J Warden
108bc; John Garrett 121br; L Resnick 121tr; P Chesley 130tr; Randy Wells 19br; Robert Frerck 47tr; Tony Craddock 47cr.
Telegraph Colour Library: 93tr. **Travel Ink**: Colin Marshall 22bc; Ian Booth 27cl. **Trip**: A Kuznetsov 74bc;
H Rogers 72cr; M Barlow 110bl; N Ray 10tr; Robert Belbin 74bl; V Kolpakov 75cr (below); V Sidoropolev 46cr; W Jacobs 130c.
World Pictures: 131tr. **ZEFA Picture Library**: 19bcl, 19cll, 45bc; Bramaz 94bl; Damm 119c; Heilman 108cr (below);
K Siewert 108cl; Kitchen 19bll; Sunak 73cr; Surpress 109tr.
Jacket: Robert Harding Picture Library: T Gervis front bl; Louise Murray back tr; G Renner back tl.
Tony Stone Images: Tony Craddock front bc; Donald Johnson back br.

CONTENTS

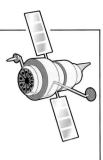

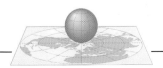

AMAZING EARTH

Earth is unique among the nine planets that circle the Sun. It is the only one that can support life, because it has enough oxygen in its atmosphere and plentiful water. In fact, seen from space, the Earth looks almost entirely blue. This is because about 70% of its surface is under water, submerged beneath four huge oceans: the Pacific, Atlantic, Indian and Arctic oceans. Land makes up about 30% of the Earth's surface. It is divided into seven landmasses of varying shapes and sizes called continents. These are, from largest to smallest: Asia, Africa, North America, South America, Antarctica, Europe and Australia.

WATERY WORLD

The Earth's oceans and seas cover more than 367 million sq km – that is twice the surface of Mars and nine times the surface of the moon.

Beneath the ocean waves lies the biggest and most unexplored landscape on Earth. Here are coral reefs, enormous, open plains, deep canyons, and the longest mountain range on Earth – the Mid-Atlantic Ridge – which stretches almost from pole to pole.

THE SHAPE OF THE EARTH

Photographs taken from space by astronauts in the 1960s, and more recently from orbiting satellites, have proven beyond doubt what humans had already worked out long ago – that the Earth is shaped like a ball. But it is not perfectly round. The force of the Earth's rotation makes the world bulge very slightly at the Equator and go a little flat at the North and South poles. So the Earth is actually a flattened sphere, or a 'geoid'.

 HEIGHTS AND DEPTHS

The Pacific Ocean contains the deepest places on the Earth's surface – the ocean trenches. The very deepest is Challenger Deep in the Mariana Trench which plunges 10,990 m into the Earth's crust. If Mount Everest, the highest point on land at 8,848 m, was dropped into the trench, its peak wouldn't even reach the surface of the Pacific.

☐ WATER

Over 97% of the Earth's water is salt water. The total amount of salt in the world's oceans and seas would cover the whole of Europe to a depth of five km. Less than 3% of the Earth's water is fresh. Of this, 2.24% is frozen in ice sheets and about 0.6% is stored underground as groundwater. The remainder is in lakes and rivers.

☐ COASTS

The total length of the Earth's coastlines is more than 500,000 km – that is the equivalent of 12 times around the globe. A high percentage of the world's people live in coastal zones: of the ten most populated cities on Earth, eight are situated on estuaries or the coast.

☐ BIODIVERSITY

Today, almost six hundred million humans, approximately one million animal species and 355,000 known plant species depend on the air, water and land of planet Earth.

WET EARTH

Tropical rainforests grow in areas close to the Equator, where it is wet and warm all year round. Although they cover just 7% of the Earth's land, these thick, damp forests form the richest ecosystems on the planet. More plant and animal species are found here than anywhere else on Earth.

DRY EARTH

Deserts are among the most inhospitable places on the planet. Some deserts are scorching hot, others are freezing cold, but they have one thing in common – they are all dry. Very few plant and animal species can survive in these harsh conditions. The world's coldest and driest continent, Antarctica (*left*), is a cold desert.

☐ VANISHING FORESTS

10,000 years ago, thick forests covered about half of the Earth's land surface. Today, 33% of those forests no longer exist, and more than half of what remains has been dramatically altered. During the 20th century, more than 50% of the Earth's rainforests have been felled.

DIFFERENT WORLD VIEWS

Because the Earth is round, we can only see half of it at any one time. This half is called a hemisphere, which means 'half a sphere'. There are always two hemispheres – the half that you see and the other half that you don't see. Two hemispheres placed together will always make a complete sphere.

PLANET WATER, PLANET LAND

The Earth can also be divided into land and water hemispheres. The land hemisphere shows most of the land on the Earth's surface. The water hemisphere is dominated by the vast Pacific Ocean – from this view, the Earth appears to be almost entirely covered by water.

Equator 0°

NORTH AND SOUTH

The Equator is an imaginary line drawn around the middle of the Earth, where its circumference is greatest. If we cut along the Equator, the Earth separates into two hemispheres: the northern and southern hemispheres. Most of the Earth's land is the northern hemisphere. Europe and North America are the only continents which lie entirely in the northern hemisphere. Australia and Antarctica are the only continents that lie wholly in the southern hemisphere.

The southern hemisphere contains three of the Earth's four great oceans: the Pacific, Indian and Arctic oceans.

EAST AND WEST

The Earth can also be divided along two other imaginary lines – the Prime Meridian (0°) and 180° – which run opposite each other between the North and South poles. This creates eastern and western hemispheres. The continents in the eastern hemisphere are traditionally called the Old World while those in the western hemisphere – the Americas – were named the New World by the Europeans who explored them in the 15th century.

Prime Meridian (0°)

North Pole

180°

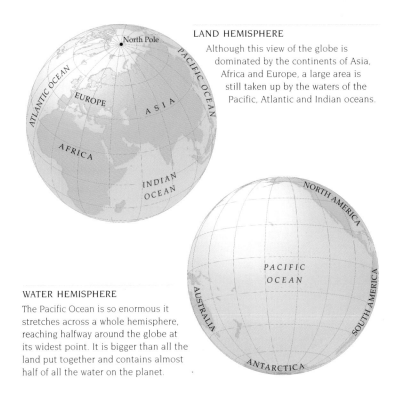

LAND HEMISPHERE

Although this view of the globe is dominated by the continents of Asia, Africa and Europe, a large area is still taken up by the waters of the Pacific, Atlantic and Indian oceans.

WATER HEMISPHERE

The Pacific Ocean is so enormous it stretches across a whole hemisphere, reaching halfway around the globe at its widest point. It is bigger than all the land put together and contains almost half of all the water on the planet.

THE SEASONS

As the Earth orbits the Sun, it is also spinning around an imaginary line called its axis, which joins the north and south poles. The Earth's axis is not quite at right angles to the Sun, but tilts over at an angle of 23.5°. As a result, each place gradually moves closer to the Sun and then further away from it again. Summer in the northern hemisphere is when the north is closest to the Sun. In winter, the northern hemisphere tilts away from the Sun, receiving far less heat and light. In the southern hemisphere the seasons are reversed, with summer in December and winter in June.

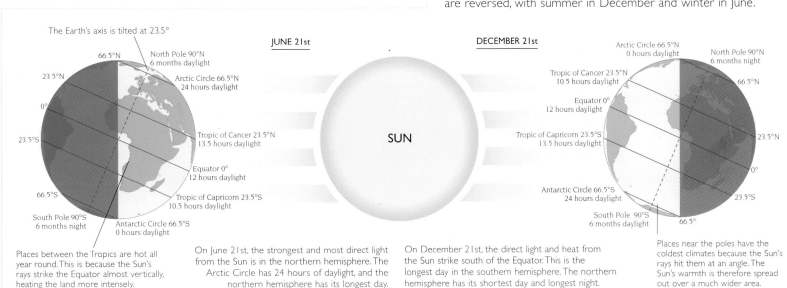

The Earth's axis is tilted at 23.5°

66.5°N

23.5°N

North Pole 90°N
6 months daylight

Arctic Circle 66.5°N
24 hours daylight

0°

Tropic of Cancer 23.5°N
13.5 hours daylight

23.5°S

Equator 0°
12 hours daylight

66.5°S

Tropic of Capricorn 23.5°S
10.5 hours daylight

South Pole 90°S
6 months night

Antarctic Circle 66.5°S
0 hours daylight

JUNE 21st

SUN

DECEMBER 21st

Arctic Circle 66.5°N
0 hours daylight

North Pole 90°N
6 months night

Tropic of Cancer 23.5°N
10.5 hours daylight

66.5°N

Equator 0°
12 hours daylight

Tropic of Capricorn 23.5°S
13.5 hours daylight

23.5°N

Antarctic Circle 66.5°S
24 hours daylight

0°

South Pole 90°S
6 months daylight

23.5°S

66.5°

Places between the Tropics are hot all year round. This is because the Sun's rays strike the Equator almost vertically, heating the land more intensely.

On June 21st, the strongest and most direct light from the Sun is in the northern hemisphere. The Arctic Circle has 24 hours of daylight, and the northern hemisphere has its longest day.

On December 21st, the direct light and heat from the Sun strike south of the Equator. This is the longest day in the southern hemisphere. The northern hemisphere has its shortest day and longest night.

Places near the poles have the coldest climates because the Sun's rays hit them at an angle. The Sun's warmth is therefore spread out over a much wider area.

MAPPING THE WORLD

The main purpose of a map is to show, or locate, where things are. The only truly accurate map of the whole world is a globe – a round model of the Earth. But a globe is impractical to carry around, so map-makers (cartographers) produce flat paper maps instead. Changing the globe into a flat map is not simple. Imagine cutting a globe in half and trying to flatten the two hemispheres. They would be stretched in some places, and squashed in others. In fact, it is impossible to make a map of the round Earth on flat paper without some distortion of area, distance or direction.

MODELS OF THE WORLD

Satellite images can show the whole world as it appears from space. However, this image shows only one half of the world, and is distorted at the edges.

A globe (*right*) is the only way to illustrate the shape of the Earth accurately. A globe also shows the correct positions of the continents and oceans and how large they are in relation to one another.

LATITUDE

We can find out exactly how far north or south, east or west any place is on Earth by drawing two sets of imaginary lines around the world to make a grid. The horizontal lines on the globe below are called lines of latitude. They run from east to west. The most important is the Equator, which is given the value 0°. All other lines of latitude run parallel to the Equator. and are numbered in degrees either north or south of the Equator.

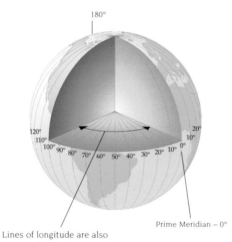

North Pole – 90°N

The value of each line of latitude increases from 0° to 90° as you move towards the North or South poles.

90° 80° 70° 60° 50° 40° 30° 20° 10° 0° 10° 20° 30° 40° 50° 60°

Equator 0°

South Pole – 90°S

Lines of latitude are measured from the centre of the Earth. An angle is then measured from here in relation to the Equator.

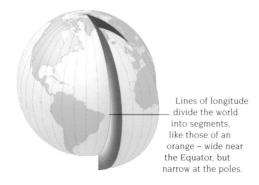

One degree of latitude is approximately 113 km.

Lines of latitude divide the world into 'slices' of equal thickness on either side of the Equator.

LONGITUDE

The vertical lines on the globe below run from north to south between the poles. They are called lines of longitude. The most important passes through Greenwich, London and is numbered 0°. It is called the Prime Meridian. All other lines of longitude are numbered in degrees either east or west of the Prime Meridian. The line directly opposite the Prime Meridian is numbered 180°.

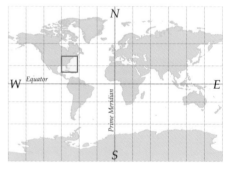

180°

120° 110° 100° 90° 80° 70° 60° 50° 40° 30° 20° 10° 0° 10° 20°

Prime Meridian – 0°

Lines of longitude are also measured from the centre of the Earth. This time, the angle is taken in relation to the Prime Meridian.

Lines of longitude divide the world into segments, like those of an orange – wide near the Equator, but narrow at the poles.

WHERE ON EARTH?

When lines of latitude and longitude are combined on a globe, or as here, on a flat map, they form a grid. Using this grid, we can locate any place on land, or at sea, by referring to the point where its line of latitude intersects with its line of longitude. Even when a place is not located exactly where the lines cross, you can still find its approximate position.

The map above is of the eastern USA. It is too small to show all the lines of latitude and longitude, so they are given at intervals of 5° Miami is located at about 26° north of the Equator and 80° west of the Prime Meridian. We write its location like this: 26°N 80°W.

MAKING A FLAT MAP FROM A GLOBE

Cartographers use a technique called projection to show the Earth's curved surface on a flat map. Many different map projections have been designed. The distortion of one feature – either area, distance, or direction – can be minimized, while other features become more distorted. Cartographers must choose which of these things it is most important to show correctly for each map that they make. Three major families of projections can be used to solve these questions.

To make a globe, the Earth is divided into segments or 'gores' along lines of longitude.

1 CYLINDRICAL PROJECTIONS

These projections are 'cylindrical' because the surface of the globe is transferred onto a surrounding cylinder. This cylinder is then cut from top to bottom and 'rolled out' to give a flat map. These maps are very useful for showing the whole world.

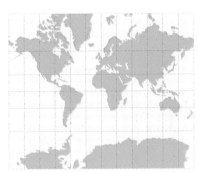

The cylinder touches the globe at the Equator. Here, the scale on the map will be exactly the same as it is on the globe. At the northern and southern edges of the cylinder, which are furthest away from the surface of the globe, the map is most distorted. The Mercator projection (*above*), created in the 16th century, is a good example of a cylindrical projection.

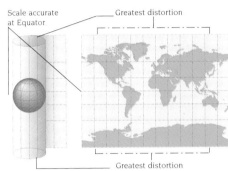

Scale accurate at Equator

Greatest distortion

Greatest distortion

2 AZIMUTHAL PROJECTIONS

North Pole

New Delhi

Azimuthal projections put the surface of the globe onto a flat circle. 'Azimuthal' means that the direction or 'azimuth' of any line coming from the centre point of that circle is correct. Azimuthal maps are useful for viewing hemispheres, continents and the polar regions. Mapping any area larger than a hemisphere gives great distortion at the outer edges of the map.

Accurate scale at central point

Greatest distortion

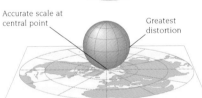

The circle only touches the globe's surface at one central point. The scale is only accurate at this point and becomes less and less accurate the further away the circle is from the globe. This kind of projection is good for maps centreing on a major city or on one of the poles.

3 CONIC PROJECTIONS

Conic projections are best used for smaller areas of the world, such as country maps. The surface of the globe is projected onto a cone which rests on top of it. After cutting from the point to the bottom of the cone, a flat map in the shape of a fan is left behind.

The conic projection touches the globe's surface at one latitude. This is where the scale of the map will be most accurate. The parts of the cone furthest from the globe will be the most distorted and are usually omitted from the map itself.

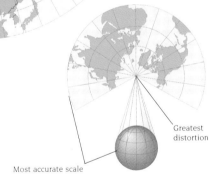

Greatest distortion

Most accurate scale

PROJECTIONS USED IN THIS ATLAS

The projections which are appropriate for showing maps at a world, continental or country scale are quite different. The projections for this atlas have been carefully chosen. They are ones that show areas as familiar shapes and ensure that they are distorted as little as possible.

1 World Maps

The Wagner VII projection is used for our world maps as it shows all the countries at their correct sizes relative to one another.

2 Continents

The Lambert Azimuthal Equal Area is used for continental maps. The shape distortion is relatively small and countries retain their correct sizes relative to one another.

3 Countries

The Lambert Conformal Conic shows countries with as little distortion as possible. The angles from any point on the map are the same as they would be on the surface of the globe.

HOW MAPS ARE MADE

New technologies have revolutionized map making. Computers and information from satellites have replaced drawing boards and drafting pens, and the process of creating new maps is now far easier. But map making is still a skilled and often time-consuming process. Information about the World must be gathered, sorted and checked. The cartographer must make decisions about the function of the map and what information to select in order to make it as clear as possible.

Maps have been made for thousands of years. The 13th century Mappa Mundi, meaning 'known world' shows the Mediterranean Sea and the Don and Nile rivers. Asia is at the top, with Europe on the left, and Africa to the right. The oceans are shown as a ring surrounding the land. The map reflects a number of biblical stories.

HISTORICAL MAP MAKING

This detailed hand-drawn map of the southern coast of Spain was made in about 1750. The mountains are illustrated as small hills and the labels have been hand lettered.

For centuries, maps were drawn by hand. Very early maps were no more than a pictorial representation of what the surface of the ground looked like. Where there were hills, pictures were drawn to represent them. Later maps were drawn using information gathered by survey teams. They would carefully mark out and calculate the height of the land, the positions of towns and other geographical features. As knowledge and techniques improved, maps became more accurate.

NEW TECHNIQUES

Computers make it easier to change map information and styles quickly. This map of the southern coast of Spain, made in 1997 has been made using digital terrain modelling (see below) and traditional cartography.

Today, cartographers have access to far more data about the Earth than in the past. Satellites collect and process information about its surface. This is called remote-sensed data. Further information may be drafted in the traditional way. Locations can be verified by GPS (Global Positioning Systems) linked to satellites. Computers are now widely used to combine different sorts of map information. Any computerized map is produced using a GIS (Geographical Information System).

MODERN MAP MAKING

1 **Measuring the Earth's surface**
The surface of the Earth is divided up into squares. Satellites take measurements of the height of the land in each square. The data collected can then be manipulated on a computer to produce a digital terrain model (DTM).

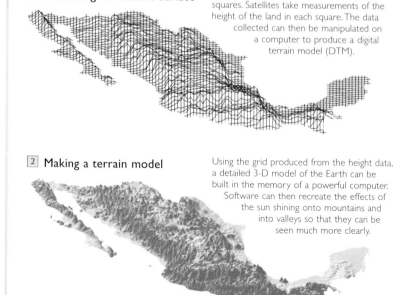

3 **Adding detail to the land surface**
The height of the land can be shown using bands of colour, or by contour lines, which are applied to the digitally-created surface of the Earth. Colour can also be used to show different kinds of vegetation, such as deserts, forests and grasslands.

2 **Making a terrain model**
Using the grid produced from the height data, a detailed 3-D model of the Earth can be built in the memory of a powerful computer. Software can then recreate the effects of the sun shining onto mountains and into valleys so that they can be seen much more clearly.

4 **Adding map detail**
Features such as roads, rivers, towns and cities can now be added to the map. They are selected, and compiled and scanned digitally into the computer. The information can then be 'draped' on top of the terrain model to create a map.

SHOWING INFORMATION ON A MAP

A map is a **selective diagram** of a place. It is the cartographer's job to decide what kind of information to show on a map. They can choose to highlight certain kinds of features – such as roads, rivers and land height. They can also show other features such as sea depth, place names, and borders which would be impossible to see either on the ground or from a photograph. The information that can be shown in a map is influenced by a number of factors, most notably by its scale.

This is a satellite photograph of the harbour area of Rio de Janeiro in Brazil. Although you can see the bay and where most of the housing is, it is impossible to see roads or get any sense of the position of places relative to one another.

This is a map of the same area as you can see in the photograph. Much of the detail has been greatly simplified. Towns are named and marked; contours indicate the height of the land; and roads, railways and borders between districts have been added.

SCALE

To make a map of an area it needs to be greatly reduced in size. This is known as drawing to scale. The scale of the map shows us by how much the area has been reduced. The smaller the scale, the greater the area of land that can be shown on the map. There will be far less detail and the map will not be as accurate. The maps below show the different kinds of information that can be shown on maps of varying scales.

WAYS TO SHOW SCALE

When using a map to work out what areas or distances are in reality, we need to refer to the scale of that particular map. Map scales can be shown in several ways.

1 Representative fraction
One unit on the map would be equal to 1,000,0000 units on the ground.

1:1,000,000

2 Linear scale
The line is marked off in units which represent the real distances of the map, given in both miles and kilometres.

SCALE BAR

0 km   10   20

0 miles   10   20

3 Statement of scale
It means that 1 mm on the map represents 1 km on the ground.

1 mm represents 1 km

LONDON 1:21,000,000

This small-scale map shows the position of London in relation to Europe. Very little detail can be seen at this scale – only the names of countries and the largest towns.

LONDON 1:5,500,000

At a scale of 1 to 5,500,000 you can see the major road network in the southeast of the UK. Many towns are named and you can see the difference in size and status.

LONDON 1:900,000

This map is at a much larger scale. You can see the major roads that lead out from London and the names of many suburbs, places of interest and airports.

LONDON 1:12,500

This is a street map of central London. The streets are named, as are places of interest, train and underground stations. The scale is large enough to show plenty of detail.

9

READING MAPS

Maps use a unique visual language to convey a great deal of detailed information in a relatively simple form. Different features are marked out using special symbols and styles of print. These symbols are explained in the key to the map and you should always read a map alongside its key or legend. This page explains how to look for different features on the map and how to unravel the different layers of information that you can find on it.

PHYSICAL FEATURES

All the regional and country maps in this atlas are based on a model of the Earth's surface. The computer-generated relief gives an accurate picture of the surface of the land. Colours are used to show the relative heights of the land; green is for low-lying land, and yellows, browns and greys are for higher land. Water features like streams, rivers and lakes are also shown.

1 WATER FEATURES

On this map extract, the blue lines show a number of rivers, including the Salween and the Irrawaddy. The Irrawaddy forms a huge delta, splitting into many streams as it reaches the sea.

2 RELIEF

These mountains are in the north of Southeast Asia. The underlying relief on the map and the coloured bands help you to see the height of the land.

HUMAN FEATURES

Maps also reveal a great deal about the human geography of an area. As well as showing where towns and roads are, different symbols can tell you more about the size of towns and the importance of a road. Borders between countries or regions can only be seen on a map.

3 BORDERS

Borders on the map are marked by a thick purple line. The boundary between Laos and Vietnam is in sparsely populated mountainous terrain, with the border generally running along a mountain range.

KEY TO MAP SYMBOLS

BOUNDARIES

▬▬▬	Full international border
▬ ▬ ▬	Disputed border

COMMUNICATION FEATURES

▬▬▬	Major road
▬▬▬	Minor road
✈	Railway
	International airport

DRAINAGE FEATURES

	Major river
	Minor river
⬭	Lake
▭	Wetland

NAMES

BURMA	Country
PARACEL ISLANDS (disputed by China, Taiwan & Vietnam)	Dependent territory
JAKARTA	Capital city
Sarawak	Cultural region
Chin Hills	Landscape feature
Puncak Jaya 5040m	Mountain/pass
Red River	River/lake
Java Sea	Sea feature

LANDSCAPE FEATURES

△	Mountain

POPULATED PLACES

○	Less than 50,000
○	50,000–100,000
◉	100,000–500,000
◼	Greater than 500,000
●	Capital city

4 SETTLEMENTS

The symbol for a settlement can tell you its position, population and political status. Most towns are shown by a circle or a square. These represent the size of their population. Where a town is coloured red, this shows that it is a capital city such as Kuala Lumpur in Malaysia.

FINDING PLACES

Alphanumeric grid references

All the maps in this book are indexed using their alphanumeric grid reference – for example, G4. To find a place you must first look up its page number and then its grid reference. Read the letters and numbers off the bottom and side of the grid. Using rulers held at right angles to one another you will find the point where the lines meet. The place will be located within this square.

Latitude and longitude references

The lines of latitude and longitude are known as graticules. They are shown on the map as thin blue lines with the value of their latitude or longitude given as a blue number at the edge of the map.

LAND HEIGHT

Above 4000 m
2000–4000 m
1000–2000 m
500–1000 m
250–500 m
100–250 m
0–100 m

SEA DEPTH

0–250 m
250–500 m
500–1000 m
1000–2000 m
2000–3000 m
3000–4000 m
Below 4000 m

CITIES AND TOWNS

◼	Over 500,000 people
◉	100,000–500,000
○	50,000–100,000
○	Less than 50,000

5 ROADS AND RAILWAYS

a The major road and railway links between Hue and Nha Trang hug the Vietnamese coast. A string of coastal towns is often connected by road and rail in this manner.

Chiang Mai, in northern **b** Thailand, is linked to the capital Bangkok to the south by railway and road. At Chiang Mai, the mountains are too high for the railway to continue, and only roads go north into Burma.

USING THE ATLAS

This Atlas has been designed to develop map-reading skills and to introduce readers to a wide range of different maps. It also provides a wealth of detailed geographic information about the world today. The Atlas is divided into four sections: Learning Map Skills; The World About Us, covering global geographic patterns; the World Atlas, dealing with the world's regions, and an Index-Gazetteer.

LEARNING MAP SKILLS

Maps show the Earth – which is three-dimensional – in just two dimensions. This section shows how maps are made; how different kinds of information are shown on maps; how to choose what to put on a map and the best way to show it. It also explains how to read the maps in this Atlas.

THE WORLD ABOUT US

These pages contain a series of world maps which show important themes, such as physical features, climate, life zones, population and the world economy, at a global scale. They give a worldwide picture of concepts which are explored in more detail later in the book.

Text introduces themes and concepts in each spread.

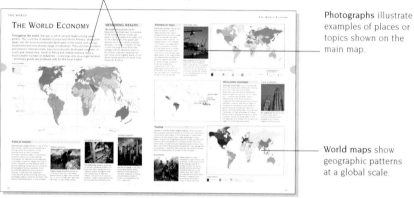

Photographs illustrate examples of places or topics shown on the main map.

World maps show geographic patterns at a global scale.

Introduction to projections: different projections and how they work.

Choosing the best projections: the map projections used in this book.

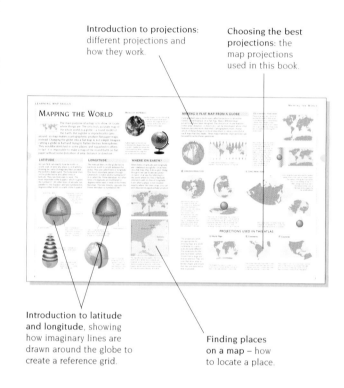

Introduction to latitude and longitude, showing how imaginary lines are drawn around the globe to create a reference grid.

Finding places on a map – how to locate a place.

CONTINENTAL MAPS

A cross-section through the continent shows the relative height of certain features.

A detailed physical map of the continent shows major natural geographic features, including mountains, lakes and rivers.

Photographs and locator maps illustrate the main geographic regions and show you where they are.

The industry map shows the main industrial towns and cities and the main industries in each continent. It also shows the wealth of each country relative to the rest of the world.

CONTINENTAL GEOGRAPHY PAGES

Humans have colonized and changed all the continents except Antarctica. These pages show the factors which have affected this process: climate, the availability of resources such as coal, oil, and minerals, and varying patterns of land use. Mineral resources are directly linked to many industries, and most agriculture is governed both by the quality of the land and the climate.

CONTINENTAL PAGES

These pages show the physical shape of each continent and the impact that humans have made on the natural landscape – building towns and roads and creating borders between countries. They show where natural features such as mountain ranges and rivers have created physical boundaries, and where humans have created their own political boundaries between states.

The political map of the continent shows country boundaries and country names.

The climate map shows the main types of climates across the continent and where the hottest and coldest, wettest and driest places are.

The mineral resources map shows where the most important reserves of minerals, including coal and precious metals, are found.

The land use map shows different types of land and the main kinds of farming that take place in each area.

REGIONAL MAPS

The main part of the Atlas contains detailed maps of countries and regions. Each of these is accompanied by a series of small thematic maps, models and charts, which give information about the climate, where people live, how they use the land, the different kinds of industry, and important environmental issues.

TERRAIN MODEL

A computer-generated landscape model shows what the land really looks like. There are no roads or towns to mask the physical geography of the country or region. Mountain ranges, plains and river basins can be easily seen.

COLOURED THUMB TAGS

Each section has its own colour code.

- Learning Map Skills
- The World About Us
- Europe
- Asia
- North America
- South America
- Africa
- Australasia and Oceania
- Antarctica and the Arctic

CLIMATE MAPS

These maps show the temperature and rainfall patterns in January and July. Coloured bands indicate temperatures: blue for low temperatures, orange for high ones. Rainfall is represented by black lines with a number giving the average amount of rain. These are called isohyets.

Isohyets show the rainfall patterns in millimetres per year. The areas between the lines are either over or under the figures shown on the ishohyets.

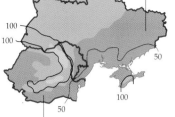

JULY

The hottest areas are coloured orange.

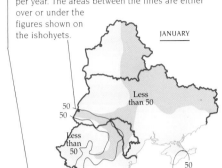

JANUARY

Here the rainfall is between 50 and 100 mm per year.

LOCATOR GLOBE

This shows the location of the country or region both within its continent, and in relation to the rest of the world.

MAP GRID

Each main map has a grid. Using the grid will help you to find a place on the map. Grid references are expressed as letters (running from left to right across the frame), and numbers (running from the top to the bottom of the frame), for example, A 4, G 6. Everything on the map is referenced in the **Index-Gazetteer** at the back of the book.

REGIONAL MAPS

The main map on each regional page shows the main topographical features of the area: the height of the land, the major roads, the rivers and lakes. It also shows the main cities and towns in the region – represented by different symbols.

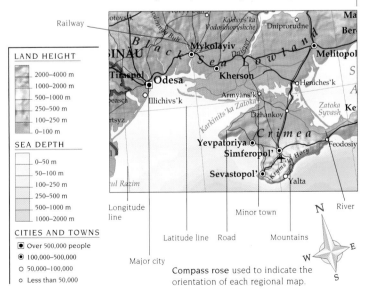

Railway

LAND HEIGHT
- 2000–4000 m
- 1000–2000 m
- 500–1000 m
- 250–500 m
- 100–250 m
- 0–100 m

SEA DEPTH
- 0–50 m
- 50–100 m
- 100–250 m
- 250–500 m
- 500–1000 m
- 1000–2000 m

CITIES AND TOWNS
- Over 500,000 people
- 100,000–500,000
- 50,000–100,000
- Less than 50,000

Longitude line

Latitude line Road

Minor town

Mountains

River

Major city

Compass rose used to indicate the orientation of each regional map.

THEMATIC MAPS

These small maps show various aspects of the geography of the country or region. The environment maps cover topics such as the effects of pollution. Industry, land use and population maps locate the major industries, types of agriculture and the distribution of population.

Diagrams are used to show the geographic information on the map statistically.

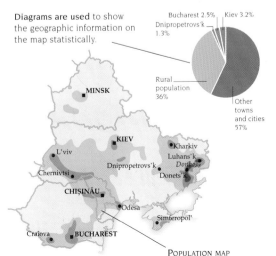

Bucharest 2.5% Kiev 3.2%
Dnipropetrovs'k 1.3%

Rural population 36%

Other towns and cities 57%

POPULATION MAP

INDUSTRY MAP

LAND USE MAP

ENVIRONMENT MAP

THE PHYSICAL WORLD

This map shows the main physical features of the world: the mountain ranges, the great rivers and lakes, deserts, grassland plains, seas and oceans. No human settlements are named on this map – only the physical or landscape features.

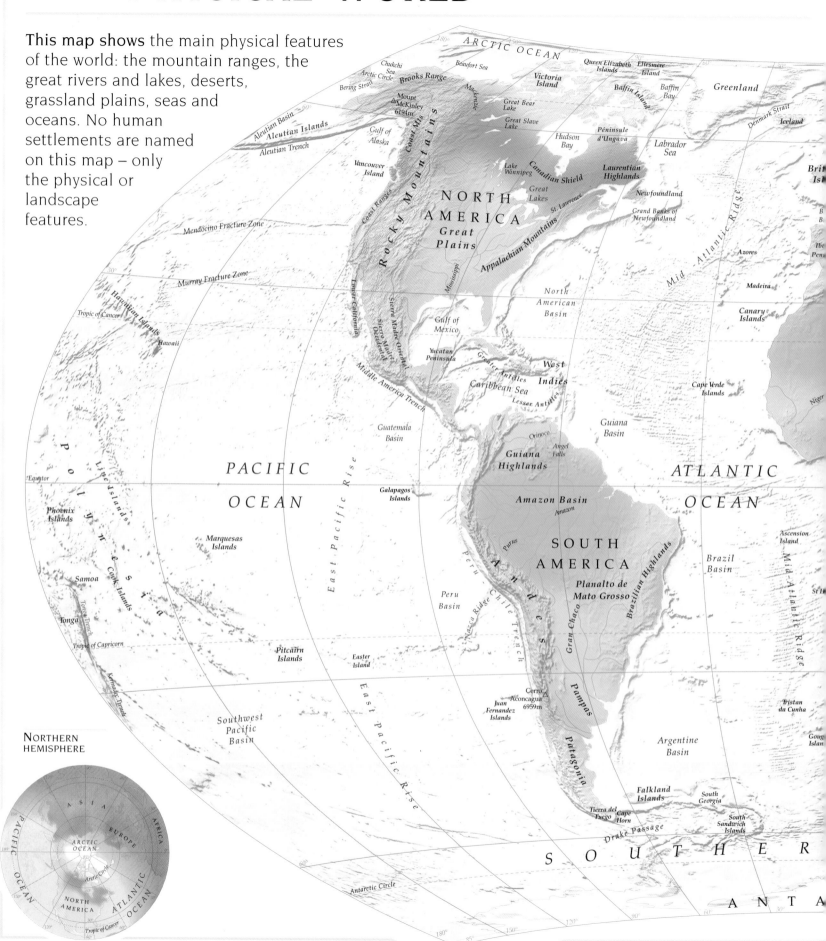

ARCTIC OCEAN

Chukchi Sea
Beaufort Sea
Arctic Circle
Bering Strait
Brooks Range
Mackenzie
Victoria Island
Queen Elizabeth Islands
Ellesmere Island
Baffin Island
Baffin Bay
Greenland
Denmark Strait
Iceland

Aleutian Basin
Aleutian Islands
Aleutian Trench
Gulf of Alaska
Mount McKinley 6194m
Great Bear Lake
Great Slave Lake
Hudson Bay
Péninsule d'Ungava
Labrador Sea

Vancouver Island
Coast Ranges
Lake Winnipeg
Canadian Shield
Laurentian Highlands
Newfoundland
Grand Banks of Newfoundland

Rocky Mountains
NORTH AMERICA
Great Plains
Great Lakes
St. Lawrence
Appalachian Mountains

Mendocino Fracture Zone
Mississippi
North American Basin

Murray Fracture Zone

Hawaiian Islands
Tropic of Cancer
Hawaii

Lower California
Sierra Madre Occidental
Sierra Madre Oriental
Gulf of Mexico
Yucatan Peninsula
Greater Antilles
West Indies
Caribbean Sea
Lesser Antilles

Azores
Madeira
Canary Islands
Cape Verde Islands
Niger

Middle America Trench

Guatemala Basin

Guiana Basin

PACIFIC OCEAN

Polynesia

Equator
Phoenix Islands

Line Islands
Cook Islands

Marquesas Islands

Samoa
Tonga
Tonga Trench

Tropic of Capricorn

Kermadec Trench

Pitcairn Islands

Easter Island

Galapagos Islands

Orinoco
Guiana Highlands
Angel Falls

Amazon Basin
Amazon

SOUTH AMERICA

Purus

Peru Basin

Nazca Ridge

Andes
Peru-Chile Trench

Cerro Aconcagua 6959m
Juan Fernandez Islands

East Pacific Rise

East Pacific Rise

Southwest Pacific Basin

Planalto de Mato Grosso
Gran Chaco

Brazilian Highlands

Pampas

Patagonia

ATLANTIC OCEAN

Ascension Island

Brazil Basin

Mid-Atlantic Ridge

Argentine Basin

Tristan da Cunha

Falkland Islands
Tierra del Fuego
Cape Horn
Drake Passage

South Georgia

South Sandwich Islands

SOUTHERN

Antarctic Circle

ANTA

NORTHERN HEMISPHERE

ASIA
EUROPE
AFRICA
PACIFIC OCEAN
ARCTIC OCEAN
Arctic Circle
ATLANTIC OCEAN
NORTH AMERICA
Tropic of Cancer

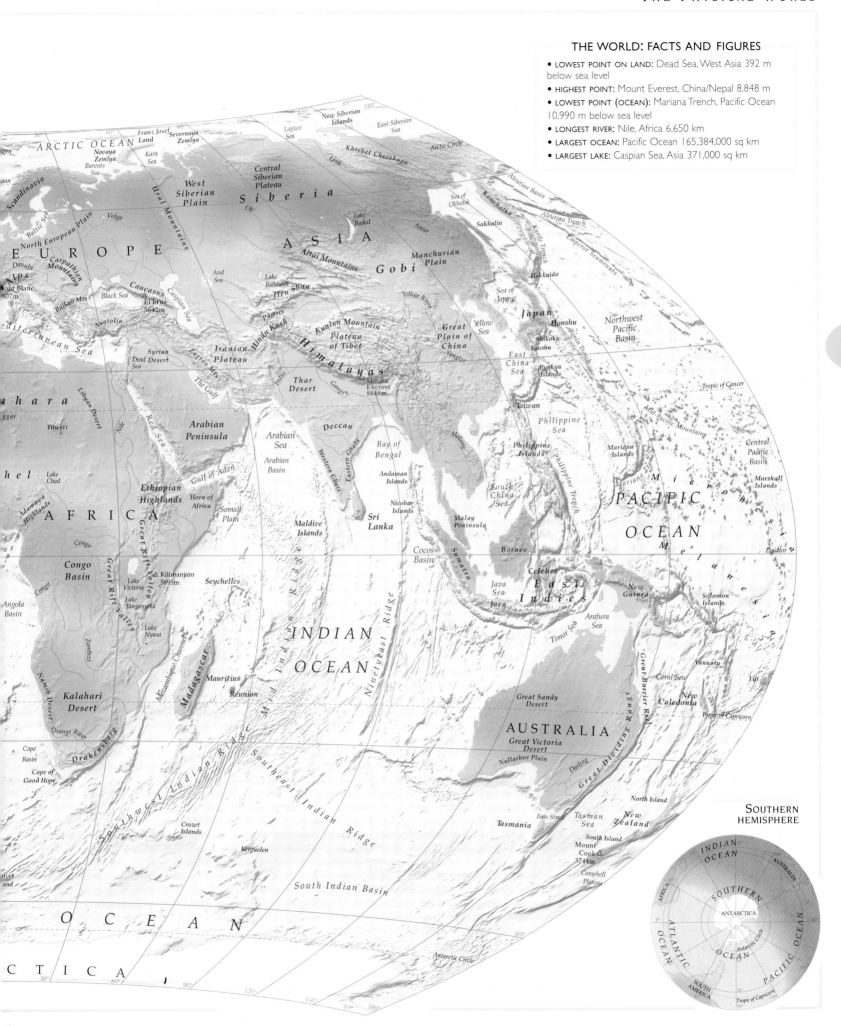

THE WORLD: FACTS AND FIGURES

- **LOWEST POINT ON LAND:** Dead Sea, West Asia 392 m below sea level
- **HIGHEST POINT:** Mount Everest, China/Nepal 8,848 m
- **LOWEST POINT (OCEAN):** Mariana Trench, Pacific Ocean 10,990 m below sea level
- **LONGEST RIVER:** Nile, Africa 6,650 km
- **LARGEST OCEAN:** Pacific Ocean 165,384,000 sq km
- **LARGEST LAKE:** Caspian Sea, Asia 371,000 sq km

ARCTIC OCEAN
Franz Josef Land
Novaya Zemlya
Severnaya Zemlya
New Siberian Islands
East Siberian Sea
Laptev Sea
Kara Sea
Barents Sea
Baltic Sea
North European Plain
Volga
Ural Mountains
West Siberian Plain
Siberia
Central Siberian Plateau
Lena
Khrebet Cherskogo
Arctic Circle
Sea of Okhotsk
Kamchatka
Aleutian Basin
Aleutian Trench
EUROPE
Danube
Carpathian Mountains
ALPS
Mont Blanc
4807m
Balkan Mts
Black Sea
Caucasus
El'brus 5642m
Caspian Sea
Aral Sea
Lake Balkhash
Altai Mountains
Tien Shan
ASIA
Gobi
Manchurian Plain
Amur
Lake Baikal
Ob
Sakhalin
Kuril Trench
Hokkaido
Sea of Japan
Japan
Honshu
Shikoku
Kyushu
Northwest Pacific Basin
Emperor Seamounts
Mediterranean Sea
Anatolia
Syrian Desert
Dead Sea
Iranian Plateau
Zagros Mts
Pamirs
Hindu Kush
Kunlun Mountain
Plateau of Tibet
Himalayas
Great Plain of China
Yangtze
Yellow River
Yellow Sea
East China Sea
Taiwan
Ryukyu Islands
Bonin Trench
Sahara
Ahaggar
Tibesti
Libyan Desert
Nile
Red Sea
Arabian Peninsula
Thar Desert
Indus
Ganges
Mount Everest 8848m
Deccan
Mekong
Philippine Sea
Mid-Pacific Mountains
Tropic of Cancer
Sahel
Lake Chad
Adamawa Highlands
Gulf of Aden
Ethiopian Highlands
Horn of Africa
Somali Plain
Arabian Sea
Arabian Basin
Western Ghats
Eastern Ghats
Bay of Bengal
Andaman Islands
Nicobar Islands
Maldive Islands
Sri Lanka
South China Sea
Philippine Islands
Mariana Islands
Philippine Trench
Mariana Trench
Central Pacific Basin
Marshall Islands
AFRICA
Congo
Congo Basin
Great Rift Valley
Lake Victoria
Kilimanjaro 5895m
Seychelles
Malay Peninsula
Cocos Basin
Borneo
Celebes
PACIFIC OCEAN
Micronesia
Melanesia
Equator
Angola Basin
Congo
Lake Tanganyika
Lake Nyasa
Zambezi
INDIAN OCEAN
Ninetyeast Ridge
Mid Indian Ridge
Sumatra
Java Sea
Java
East Indies
New Guinea
Solomon Islands
Namib Desert
Zambezi
Mozambique Channel
Madagascar
Mauritius
Réunion
Arafura Sea
Timor Sea
Vanuatu
Coral Sea
New Caledonia
Fiji
Kalahari Desert
Orange River
Cape Basin
Cape of Good Hope
Drakensberg
Southwest Indian Ridge
Southeast Indian Ridge
Great Sandy Desert
Great Barrier Reef
AUSTRALIA
Great Victoria Desert
Nullarbor Plain
Darling
Great Dividing Range
Tropic of Capricorn
Crozet Islands
Kerguelen
South Indian Basin
North Island
Bass Strait
Tasmania
Tasman Sea
New Zealand
South Island
Mount Cook 3744m
Campbell Plateau
OCEAN
ANTARCTICA
Antarctic Circle

SOUTHERN HEMISPHERE

INDIAN OCEAN
AUSTRALIA
AFRICA
SOUTHERN OCEAN
ANTARCTICA
Antarctic Circle
ATLANTIC OCEAN
PACIFIC OCEAN
SOUTH AMERICA
Tropic of Capricorn

THE EARTH'S STRUCTURE

The shape and position of the Earth's oceans and continents form a familiar pattern. This is just the latest in a series of forms which the Earth has taken over the hundreds of millions of years since its formation. Massive forces from inside the Earth cause the continents and oceans to move apart and together again, forming larger landmasses and then breaking them apart again. The movement is slow – only a few centimetres a year – but over millions of years, the changes can be enormous.

DYNAMIC EARTH

The heart of the Earth is a solid core of iron surrounded by several layers of very hot – sometimes liquid – rock. The crust is relatively thin and is made up of a series of 'plates' which fit closely together. Movement of the molten rock deep within the mantle of the Earth causes the plates to move, creating changes in the surface features of the Earth.

THE EARTH'S PLATES

Continental plate

Continental and oceanic plates are tectonic plates – made from crustal rock on which continents or oceans float

Oceanic plate

Plate boundary or margin

INSIDE THE EARTH

Rocky crust

Lithosphere

Outer core – liquid iron and nickel

Mesosphere

Inner core – made of iron

Mantle – made from solid and molten rock

Asthenosphere

TECTONIC PLATES, VOLCANOES AND EARTHQUAKES

▲ Volcanic zone

Earthquake zone on land

⇨ Direction of plate movement

⌄⌄⌄⌄⌄ Rift valley

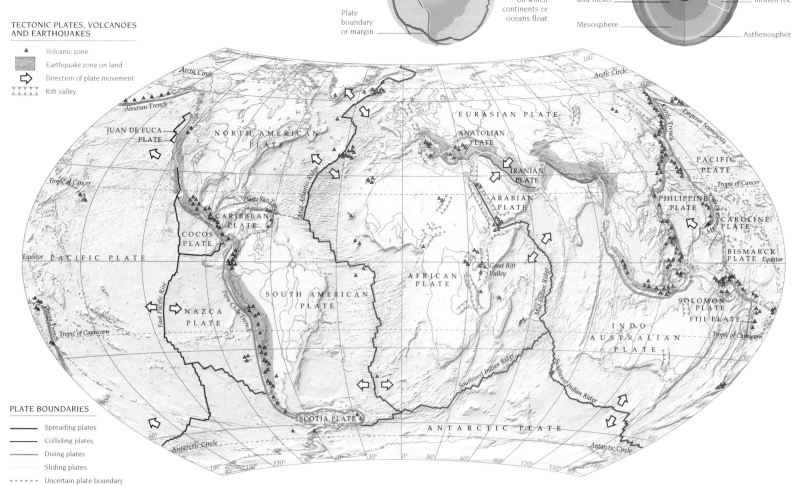

PLATE BOUNDARIES

——— Spreading plates

——— Colliding plates

——— Diving plates

——— Sliding plates

- - - - - Uncertain plate boundary

PLATE BOUNDARIES

As the Earth's plates move together or apart or slide alongside one another, the great forces created can literally cause the Earth to move. At these plate boundaries, mountains are created, earthquakes occur and there are frequent volcanic eruptions. Little activity occurs at the centre of the plates.

SPREADING PLATES

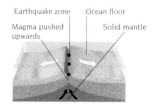

Earthquake zone   Ocean floor

Magma pushed upwards   Solid mantle

As plates move apart, magma rises through the outer mantle. When it cools, it forms new crust. The Mid-Atlantic Ridge is caused by spreading plates.

COLLIDING PLATES

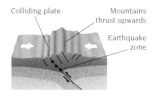

Colliding plate   Mountains thrust upwards

Earthquake zone

When two plates bearing landmasses collide with one another, the land is crumpled upwards into high mountain peaks such as the Alps, and the Himalayas.

DIVING PLATES

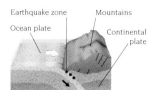

Earthquake zone   Mountains

Ocean plate   Continental plate

When an ocean-bearing plate collides with a continental plate it is forced downwards under the other plate and into the mantle. Volcanoes occur along these boundaries.

SLIDING PLATES

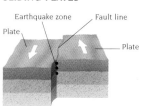

Earthquake zone   Fault line

Plate   Plate

As two plates slide past each other, great friction is set up along the fault line which lies between them. This can lead to powerful earthquakes.

SHAPING THE LANDSCAPE

The Earth's surface is made from solid rock or water. The land is constantly re-shaped by external forces. Water flowing as rivers or in the oceans erodes and deposits material to create valleys, lakes and changes the shape of coastlines. When it is compressed into solid sheets of ice, water erodes more deeply, creating deeper, wider valleys. Wind also has a powerful effect; stripping away vegetation and transporting rock particles vast distances.

RIVERS

Most rivers have their sources in mountain areas. They flow fast through the mountains, eroding deep V-shaped valleys. As they reach flatter areas they begin to meander in great loops, both eroding and depositing rock particles before reaching the sea.

GLACIERS

In cold areas close to the poles or on mountain tops, snow is built up into rivers of ice called glaciers. They move slowly carrying a load of rocks which erode deep valleys. When the glacier melts, ridges called moraines are left at the sides and end of the glacier.

SEA ACTION

The oceans change the landscape in two major ways. They batter cliffs, causing rock to break away and the land to retreat, and they carry eroded material further down the coast, to make beaches and sand bars.

WIND

Desert sand dunes are shaped by the force of the wind. Small particles of sand are built up into dunes, which can be narrow surface ripples, or hills up to 200 m high. The amount of sand affects dune shape.

LANDSLIDES

Heavy rain loosens soil and rock beneath the surface of slopes. As this moves, the top layers slip forward, to form heaps of rubble at the base of the slope.

THE WORLD'S OCEANS

Just over two-thirds of the Earth's surface is covered by water and more than 98% of this water is contained in the oceans. Movements within the Earth shape the ocean floor in the same way as they do the land surface, creating mountain ranges, trenches and plateaus, and changing the shape and size of the oceans. The difference between an ocean and a sea is simply its size; oceans are much bigger.

SOUTHERN OCEAN

A vast iceberg, broken off from the Antarctic ice shelf, floats in the freezing Southern Ocean.

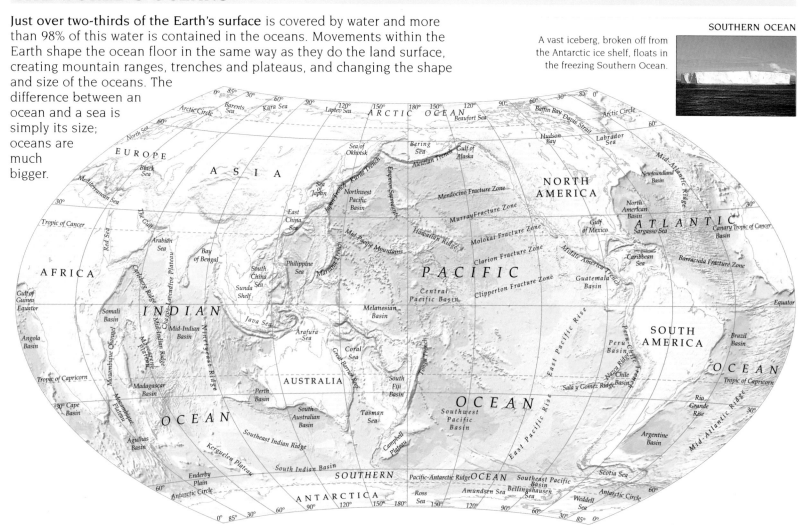

INDIAN OCEAN

The Indian Ocean covers about 20% of the world's surface. Ocean swells, starting deep in the Southern Ocean, often cause flooding in Sri Lanka and the Maldives.

PACIFIC OCEAN

The Pacific is the largest and deepest ocean in the world. It is surrounded by an arc of volcanic islands, including Japan, Indonesia and New Guinea, known as the 'Ring of Fire'.

ATLANTIC OCEAN

The Atlantic Ocean was formed about 180 million years ago. The land which is now Europe and Africa pulled apart from the Americas forming an ocean 3,000 km wide.

CLIMATE AND LIFE ZONES

This map shows the different climates found around the world. Climates are particular combinations of temperature and humidity. Climates are affected by latitude, the height of the land, winds and ocean currents. Climates can change, but not overnight. Weather is local and consists of short-term events such as thunderstorms, hurricanes and blizzards.

HURRICANES

Hurricanes are violent cyclonic windstorms, driven by heat energy gathered from tropical seas. The Caribbean islands and the east coast of the USA are particularly prone to hurricanes.

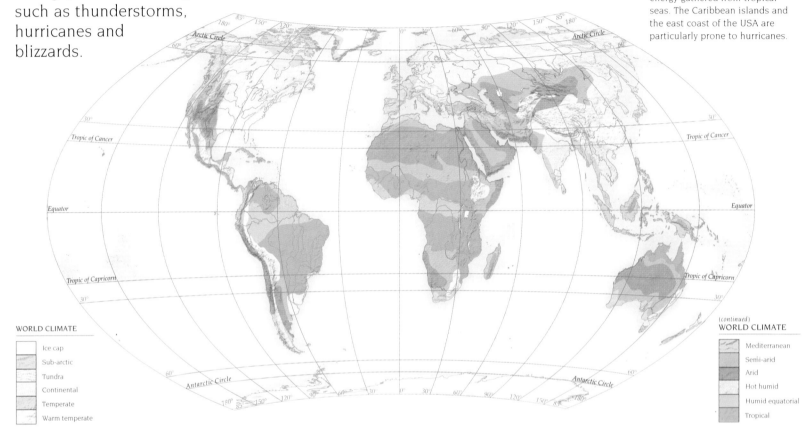

WORLD CLIMATE

- Ice cap
- Sub-arctic
- Tundra
- Continental
- Temperate
- Warm temperate

(continued) WORLD CLIMATE

- Mediterranean
- Semi-arid
- Arid
- Hot humid
- Humid equatorial
- Tropical

WINDS

All over the Earth there are a series of large-scale wind patterns called prevailing winds which have a direct effect on weather and climate. The direction of the wind depends on global air pressure. Winds travel from areas of high pressure to areas of low pressure. The westerlies, polar easterlies, and the northeast and southeast trade winds are all prevailing winds. The Equator is known for its light winds – known as the Doldrums. Changes in the direction of the prevailing winds can have a serious impact on the weather all over the planet.

WINDS

- Cool wind
- Warm wind

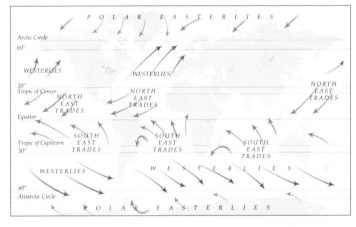

OCEAN CURRENTS

Ocean currents help to distribute heat around the Earth and have a great influence on climate. Convection currents circulate massive amounts of warm and cold water around the oceans. Warm water is moved away from the tropics to higher latitudes and cold water is moved toward the tropics.

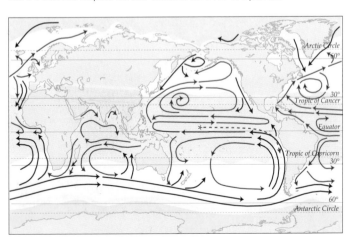

OCEAN CURRENTS AND SURFACE TEMPERATURES

- Cold currents
- Warm currents
- El Niño
- 20 – 30°C
- 10 – 20°C
- 0 – 10°C
- Sea-water −2° – 0°C
- Sea-ice (average) below −2°C

LIFE ZONES

The map below shows the Earth divided into different biomes – also called biogeographical regions. The combination of climate, the type of landscape, and the plants and animals that live there, are used to classify a region. Similar biomes are found in very different places around the world.

POLAR REGIONS
The North and South poles are permanently covered by ice. Only a few plants and animals can live here.

TUNDRA
Tundra is flat, cold and dry with few trees. Plants such as mosses and lichens grow close to the ground.

DESERTS
Very little rain falls in desert areas, whether they are hot deserts such as the Sahara or cold deserts like the Gobi.

NEEDLELEAF FORESTS
Tall coniferous trees such as pine and spruce, with spines or needles instead of leaves, grow in the far north of Scandinavia, Canada and the Russian Federation.

BROADLEAF FORESTS
Broadleaf or deciduous forests once covered temperate regions over most of the northern hemisphere. They contain trees of many varieties – all of which shed their leaves every year.

TEMPERATE RAINFORESTS
Evergreen, broadleaved trees need a warmer, wetter climate than deciduous trees. They are known as temperate rainforests.

MEDITERRANEAN
Close to the shores of the Mediterranean Sea, the vegetation consists mainly of herbs, shrubs and drought-resistant trees.

BIOME TYPES

- Mountains
- Polar regions
- Tundra
- Tropical rain forests
- Dry woodlands
- Savanna
- Temperate grasslands

(continued)
BIOME TYPES

- Mediterranean
- Needleleaf forest
- Temperate rainforest
- Broadleaf forest
- Cold desert
- Hot desert
- Wetlands

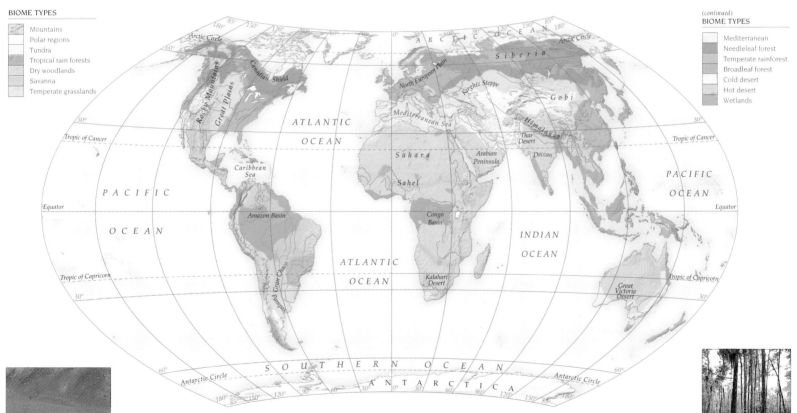

TEMPERATE GRASSLANDS
Grasslands cover the central areas of the continents. They are known in the middle latitudes as prairies, steppe and pampas.

SAVANNAH
The savannah consists of woodland, interspersed with grassland. These regions lie between the tropical rainforest and hot desert regions.

DRY WOODLANDS
Dry woodlands are found at the edge of grasslands. They contain small trees and shrubs adapted to dry conditions.

TROPICAL RAINFORESTS
Around the Equator, where temperatures are high and there is plenty of rain, tropical rainforests can flourish. Trees grow continuously and are tall with huge, broad leaves.

WETLANDS
Low-lying swamps and marshes are known as wetlands. They are often home to a rich variety of animal, plant and bird species.

WORLD POPULATION

There are now nearly six thousand million people on Earth. The population has increased more than three times since 1900. Before that date, the number of people increased slowly as people were born and died at similar rates. With improved living conditions, better medical care and more efficient food production, more people survived to adulthood and the population began to grow much faster. If growth continues at the present rate, the world's population is likely to reach 8.5 billion by the year 2020.

Favelas – or shanty towns – have grown up many South American cities because of overcrowding.

POPULATION STRUCTURES

Measuring the numbers of old and young people gives the age structure of a country or continent. If there are large numbers of young people and a high birth rate, the population is said to be youthful – as is the case in many African, Asian and South American countries. If the birth rate is low but many people survive into old age, the population distribution is said to be ageing – this is true of much of Europe, Japan, Canada and the USA. Extreme events like wars can distort the population, leading to a loss of population in certain age groups.

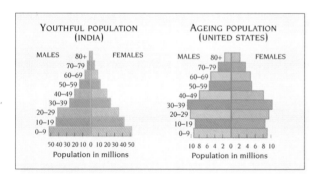

POPULATION DENSITY

The main map (centre) and the map below both show population density – the number of people who live in a given area. The map below shows the average population density per country. You can see that European countries and parts of Asia are very densely populated. The large map shows where people actually live. While the average population density in Brazil and Egypt is quite low, the coasts of Brazil and the areas close to the River Nile in Egypt are very densely populated.

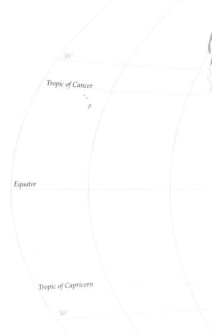

DENSE POPULATION

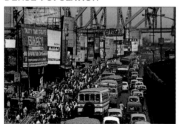

Huge crowds near the Haora Bridge in Calcutta, India – one of the world's most densely populated cities.

POPULATION DENSITY

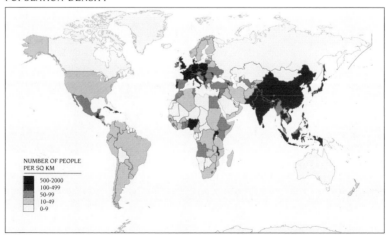

NUMBER OF PEOPLE
PER SQ KM

- 500-2000
- 100-499
- 50-99
- 10-49
- 0-9

SPARSE POPULATION

The cold north of Canada has one of the lowest population densities in the world. Some people live in extreme isolation, separated from others by lakes and forests.

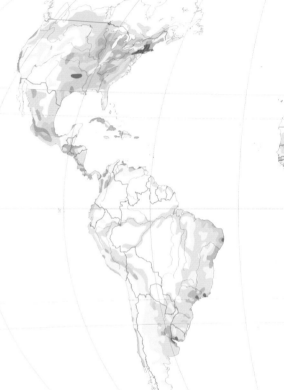

URBAN GROWTH

The 20th century has seen a huge increase in the number of people living in cities. This has led to more large cities and the development of some 'super cities' such as Mexico City and Tokyo, each with more than 20 million people. In 1900, only about 10% of the population lived in cities. Now it is closer to 50% and soon the figure may be nearer two in three people. Some continents are far more 'urbanized' than others: in South America nearly 80% of people live in cities, whereas in Africa the figure is only about 30%.

LEVELS OF URBANIZATION

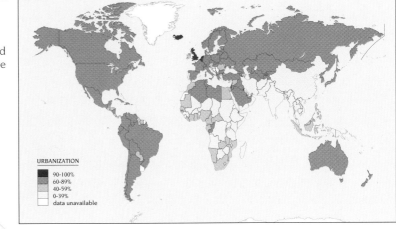

URBANIZATION
- 90-100%
- 60-89%
- 40-59%
- 0-39%
- data unavailable

POPULATION GROWTH

The rate of population growth varies dramatically between the continents. Europe has a large population but it is increasing slowly. Africa is still sparsely populated, but in some countries such as Kenya, the population is growing very rapidly, increasing pressure on the land. China and India have the world's largest populations. Both countries now have laws to try and curb the birth rate.

CONTROLLING GROWTH

In 1980, fewer than 25% of women in less developed countries used birth control. Education programmes and more widely available contraceptives are thought to have doubled this figure. But many families still have no access to contraception.

AN AGEING POPULATION

In some countries, a low birth rate, and an increasingly long-lived elderly population has greatly increased the ratio of old people to younger people, putting a strain on health and social services. For example, in Japan, most people can now expect to live to at least 80 years of age.

POPULATION DENSITY
(People per sq km)
- Below 1
- 1–5
- 6–10
- 11–20
- 21–50
- 51–100
- 101–200
- Above 200

Arctic Circle
Tropic of Cancer
Equator
Tropic of Capricorn
Antarctic Circle

BIRTH RATE

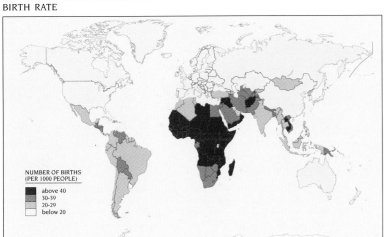

NUMBER OF BIRTHS
(PER 1000 PEOPLE)
- above 40
- 30-39
- 20-29
- below 20

LIFE EXPECTANCY

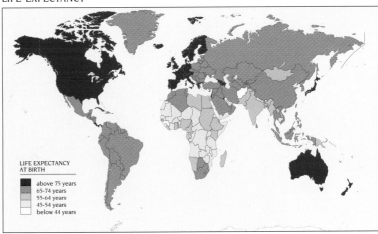

LIFE EXPECTANCY AT BIRTH
- above 75 years
- 65-74 years
- 55-64 years
- 45-54 years
- below 44 years

21

THE WORLD ECONOMY

MEASURING WEALTH

The wealth of a country can be measured in several ways: for example, by the average annual income per person; by the volume of its trade; and by the total value of the goods and services that the country produces annually – its Gross Domestic Product or GDP. The map below shows the average GDP per person for each of the world's countries, expressed in $US. Most of the highest levels of GDP are in Europe and the US; most of the lowest are in Africa.

Throughout the world, the way in which people make a living varies greatly. The countries of western Europe and North America, along with Japan, are the most economically developed in the world, with a long-established and very diverse range of industries. They sell their products and services internationally. Less economically developed countries in south and central Asia, much of Africa, and Central America have a much smaller number of industries – some may rely on a single product – and many goods are produced only for the local market.

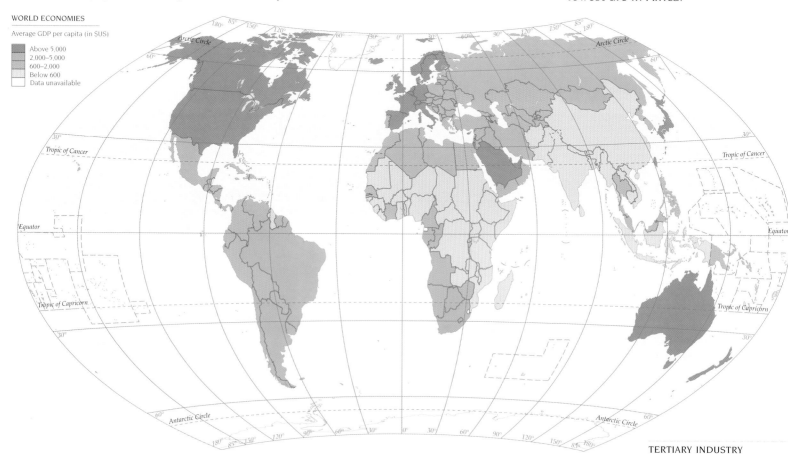

WORLD ECONOMIES

Average GDP per capita (in $US)

- Above 5,000
- 2,000–5,000
- 600–2,000
- Below 600
- Data unavailable

TYPES OF INDUSTRY

Industries are usually defined in one of three ways. Primary industries such as farming or mining involve the production of raw materials such as food or minerals. Secondary industries make or manufacture finished products out of raw materials: clothing and car manufacture are examples of secondary industries. People who work in tertiary industries provide different kinds of services. Banking, insurance and tourism are all examples of tertiary industries. Some economically advanced nations such as Germany or USA now have quaternary industries such as biotechnology which are knowledge-creation industries, devoted to the research and development of new products.

PRIMARY INDUSTRY

Tobacco leaves are picked and laid out for drying in Cuba, one of the world's great producers of cigars. Many countries rely on one or two high-value 'cash crops' like tobacco to earn foreign currency.

SECONDARY INDUSTRY

This skilled Thai weaver is producing an intricately patterned silk fabric on a hand loom. Fabric manufacture is an important industry throughout South and Southeast Asia. In India and Pakistan, vast quantities of cotton are produced in highly mechanized factories, but many fabrics are still hand woven.

TERTIARY INDUSTRY

The City of London is one of the world's great finance centres. Branches of many banks and insurance companies, including the world famous Lloyds of London, are clustered into the City's 'square mile'.

PATTERNS OF TRADE

Almost all countries trade goods with one another in order to obtain products they cannot produce themselves, and to make money from goods they have produced. Some countries – for example those in the Caribbean – rely mainly on a single export, usually a foodstuff or mineral, and can suffer a loss of income when world prices drop. Other countries, such as Germany and Japan, export a vast range of both raw materials and manufactured goods throughout the world. A number of huge companies, known as transnational corporations or TNCs, are responsible for more than 70% of world trade, with divisions all over the world. They include firms like BP, Coca Cola and IBM.

CONTAINER SHIPS

Many products are transported around the world on container ships. Containers are of a standard size so that they can be efficiently transported to their destinations. Some ships are specially designed to carry perishable goods such as fruit and vegetables.

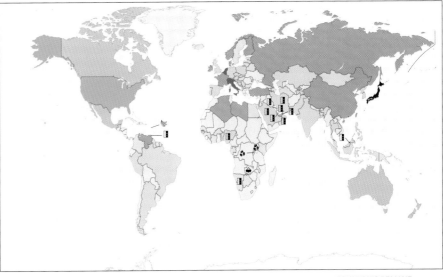

BALANCE OF TRADE (MILLIONS $US)

Surplus		Deficit		
Over 30,000	1,000–9,999	0–999	10,000–29,999	Data unavailable
10,000–29,000	0–999	1,000–9,999	Below 30,000	

COUNTRIES RELIANT ON ONE EXPORT

- oil/petroleum
- bananas
- coffee
- copper

DEVELOPING ECONOMIES

Although world trade is still dominated by the more economically developed countries, since the 1970s, less economically developed countries have increased their share of world trade from less than 10% to nearly 20%. Countries such as Brazil, Mexico, Malaysia and South Korea, aided by investment from their governments or from wealthier countries, were able to begin to manufacture and export a wide variety of goods. Products include cars, electronic goods, clothing and footwear. Multinational companies can take advantage of cheaper labour costs to manufacture goods in these countries. Moves are being made to limit the exploitation of workers who are paid low wages for producing luxury goods.

ASIAN 'TIGER' ECONOMIES

The economies of Malaysia, Taiwan and South Korea, boomed in the late 1980s, attracting investment for buildings such as the Petronas Towers.

TOURISM

Tourism is now the world's largest industry. More than 500 million people travel both abroad and in their own countries as tourists each year. People in more developed countries have more money and leisure time to travel. Tourism can bring large amounts of cash into the local economy, but local people do not always benefit. They may have to take low-paid jobs and experience great intrusions into their lives. Tourist development and pollution may damage the environment – sometimes destroying the very attractions that led to the development of tourism in the first place.

ECOTOURISM

These tourists are being introduced to a giant tortoise, one of the many unique animals found in the Galapagos Islands. A number of places with special animals and ecosystems have introduced schemes to teach visitors about them. This not only educates more people about the need to safeguard these environments, but brings in money to help protect them.

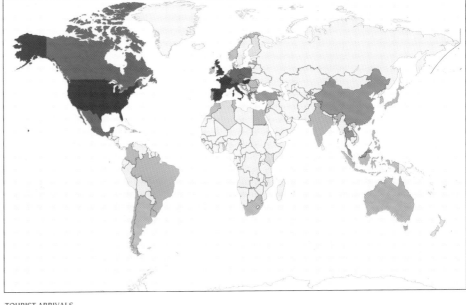

TOURIST ARRIVALS

Over 20 million	5–10 million	1–2.5 million	Under 700,000
10–20 million	2.5–5 million	700,000–1 million	Data unavailable

BORDERS AND BOUNDARIES

There are more countries in the world today than ever before – over 190 – whereas in 1950, there were only 82. Since then, many former European colonies and Soviet states have become independent. The establishment of borders for each of these countries has often been the subject of disagreement.

Military borders

At the end of wars, new borders are often drawn up between the countries – frequently along ceasefire lines. They may remain there for many years. At the end of the Korean War in 1953, North and South Korea were divided close to the 38° line of latitude. This border has remained heavily fortified.

The longest border

The border between the USA and Canada is the longest continuous border in the world. It cuts through the centre of the Great Lakes. To the west of the Great Lakes, the border runs along the 49° line of latitude.

Enclaves

If part of a country's territory has become separated from the rest of the country, and is surrounded by foreign territory, it is called an enclave. Kaliningrad is part of the Russian Federation, but is cut off from it by Lithuania and Belorussia.

River borders

Over one-sixth of the world's national borders are formed by rivers. Long stretches of the Danube form natural borders in southeastern Europe.

Mountain borders

Mountain ranges such as the Pyrenees, Alps and Himalayas form natural borders between many countries. In the Andes, border disputes between Chile and Argentina centred on finding the highest point in the mountain range which divided them.

Straight line borders

The borders of many countries in Africa and other former colonial territories are straight lines. This was the simplest solution for colonial administrators, who often knew little of the country's geography or population.

Lake boundaries

Countries which lie next to lakes usually fix their borders in the middle of the lake. Complicated agreements between colonial powers led to the awkward division of Lake Nyasa in Africa.

Territorial disputes

There are still many disputed territories and borders. One of the most serious territorial disputes is between India and Pakistan over Jammu and Kashmir, which has led to three wars since 1947.

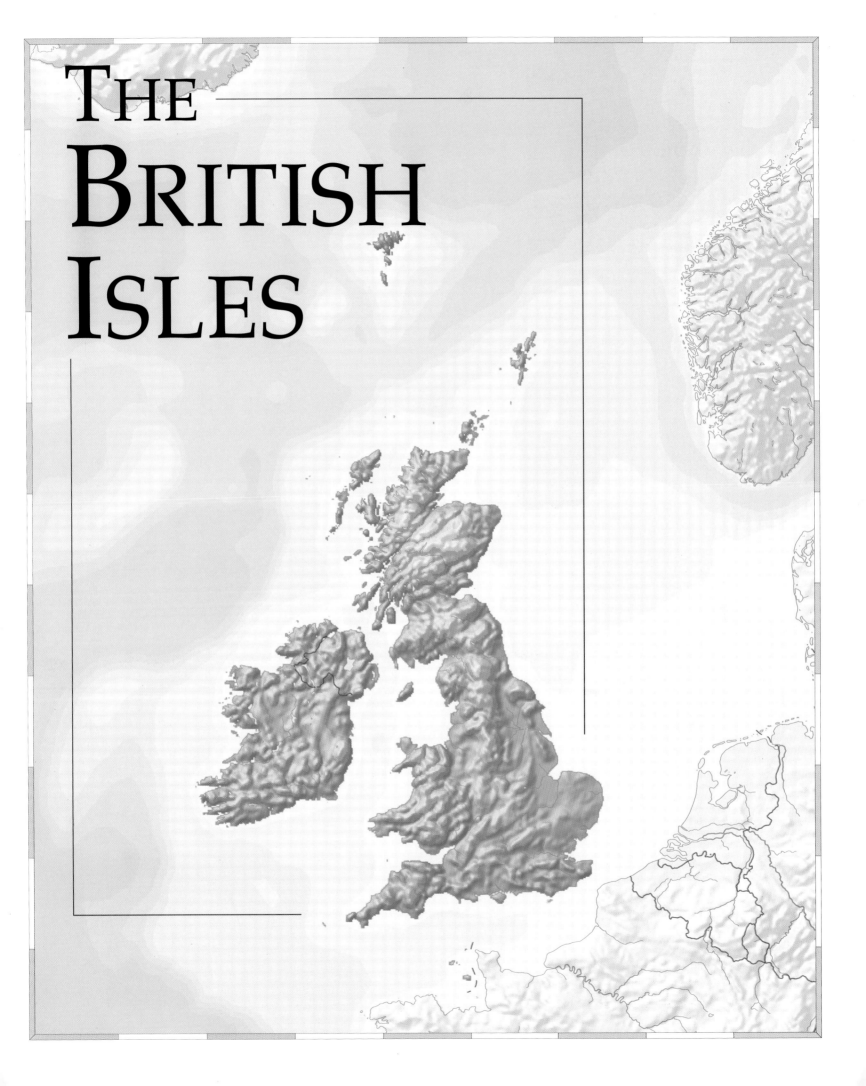

THE
BRITISH
ISLES

PHYSICAL BRITISH ISLES

The British Isles contain two of the largest islands in Europe and numerous smaller ones. They lie to the northwest of the continent. The rugged north and west of the British Isles is an extension of the mountain range that runs through western Scandinavia. The movement of continents and oceans over millions of years has given the British Isles a very interesting and complicated geological structure, with some of the world's oldest rocks – more than 2,500 million years old, found in both England and southeast Ireland.

LANDSCAPE OF THE BRITISH ISLES

Much of the landscape of the British Isles has been shaped by the ice which covered the Britain and northern Europe for almost 8,000 years during the last ice age, until about 10,000 years ago. The ice scoured and eroded the highlands, smoothing the peaks but deepening valleys and depositing piles of rock and clay in the lowlands. The coastline is indented and constantly changing. Drowned glaciated valleys or fjords are found on the west coast of Scotland. In the southwest of England long inlets called rias are drowned river valleys

5 HIGHLANDS

The British Isles have no true mountains to compare with the Alps of mainland Europe. The highest peaks are found in the highlands of Scotland, in southwest Ireland, Wales and northern England.

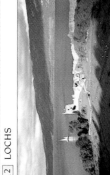

1 ISLANDS

Thousands of small islands lie off the coast of the British Isles – the majority of Scotland. These Scottish islands – the Shetlands, Orkneys and the Hebrides – are part of the same mountain chain that runs through Scandinavia.

2 LOCHS

Up until about 10,000 years ago, most of Britain was covered by ice. Glaciers carved deep, wide valleys in the highlands of Scotland and northern England. Where water has accumulated in glacial valleys, huge long lakes, known in Scotland as lochs, have been formed.

3 COASTAL DEPOSITION

Along the east coast of England there are many large sand dunes, sand bars and spits which have been formed by erosion and deposition along the coast.

4 LOWLANDS

The Fens of eastern England are some of the flattest parts of the British Isles. Some of the land lies below sea level and areas close to the sea are at risk from flooding. Artificial drainage helps to prevent flooding.

Herma Ness
Unst
Yell
Mainland **Shetland Islands**
Sumburgh Head

Westray
Sanday
Stronsay
Hoy
Orkney Islands Mainland
Pentland Firth
Dunnet Head

Cape Wrath
Butt of Lewis
Isle of Lewis
Harris
The Little Minch
North Uist
South Uist
Outer Hebrides
Barra Head
Sea of the Hebrides
Isle of Skye
Rhum
Coll
Tiree
Colonsay
Jura
Tiree
Inner Hebrides
Islay

The Minch
Sound of Jura
Firth of Lorn
Isle of Mull
Loch Awe

Moray Firth
Loch Ness
Loch Eil
Ben Nevis 1343m
Beinn Dearg 1084m
North West Highlands
Loch Ericht
Loch Rannoch
Grampian Mountains
Cairngorm Mountains
Ben Macdui 1309m

Dee
Buchan Ness
Loch Tay
Loch Lomond
Clyde
Ochil Hills
Sidlaw Hills
Firth of Tay
Firth of Forth
St Abb's Head
Holy Island
Firth of

N O
C E A N
O

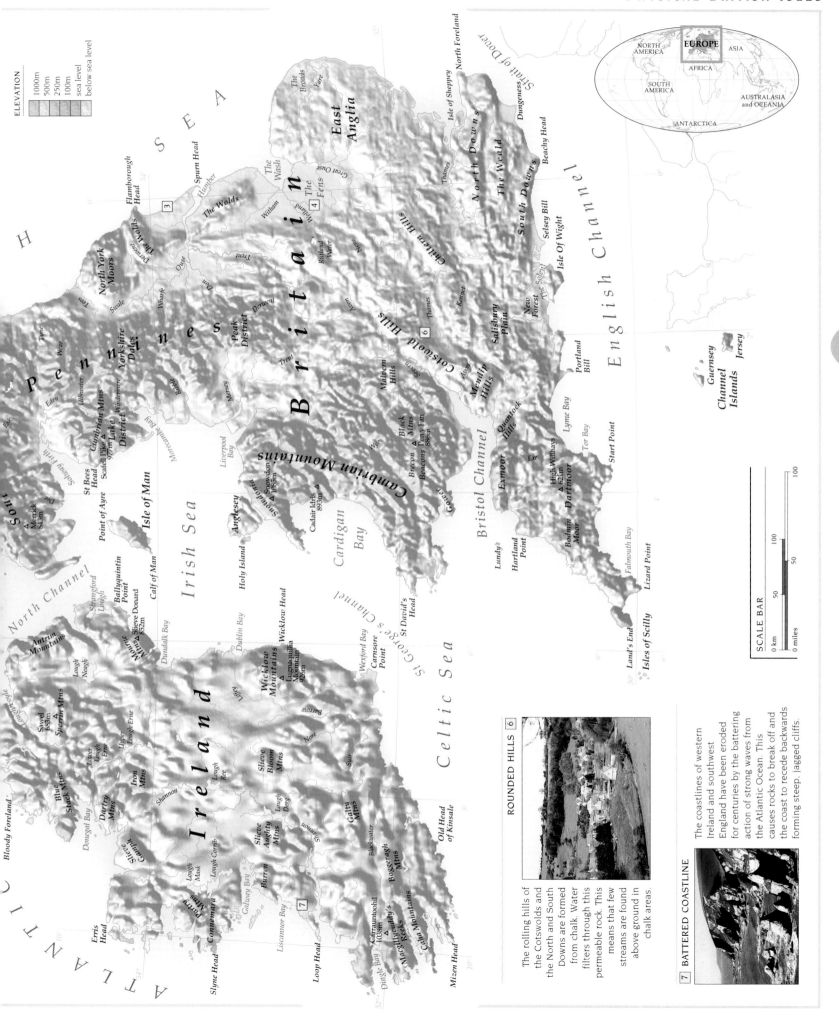

ELEVATION

1000m
500m
250m
100m
sea level
below sea level

NORTH AMERICA
EUROPE
ASIA
AFRICA
SOUTH AMERICA
AUSTRALASIA and Oceania
ANTARCTICA

NORTH SEA

East Anglia

Strait of Dover

The Broads
Yare
Isle of Sheppey
North Foreland
Spurn Head
Flamborough Head
The Wash
Great Ouse
The Wolds
Humber
Welland
The Fens
Witham
Nene
Rutland Water

North Downs
The Weald
Beachy Head
Dungeness
South Downs
Selsey Bill

Chiltern Hills

Selsey Bill
Isle Of Wight
The Solent
New Forest
Salisbury Plain
Kennet
Thames

English Channel

Guernsey
Jersey
Channel Islands

Cotswold Hills

Portland Bill

North York Moors
Tees
Swale
Ure
Wharfe
The Wolds
Derwent

B r i t a i n

Tyne
Wear
Pennines
Yorkshire Dales
Peak District
Don
Trent
Ouse
Derwent

Eden
Ullswater
Cumbrian Mtns
Scafell Pike 977m
Lake District
Windermere
Ribble

Malvern Hills
Avon
Wye
Mendip Hills

Lyme Bay
Tor Bay
Start Point

Quantock Hills
Exe
Exmoor

Esk
St Bees Head
Point of Ayre
Isle of Man
Calf of Man
Morecambe Bay
Liverpool Bay

Severn
Brecon Beacons
Black Mtns
Pen-y-Fan 886m

High Willhays 621m
Dartmoor
Bodmin Moor

Hartland Point
Lundy

Merrick 843m
Nith

North Channel

Mersey
Anglesey
Holy Island

Snowdon 1085m
Snowdonia
Cambrian Mountains
Cadair Idris 893m

Irish Sea

Cardigan Bay

Bristol Channel

Falmouth Bay
Lizard Point
Land's End
Isles of Scilly

St David's Head

St George's Channel

Carnsore Point
Wexford Bay

Wicklow Head
Wicklow Mountains
Lugnaquillia Mountain 926m

Dublin Bay
Liffey

Strangford Lough
Ballyquintin Point
Slieve Donard 852m
Mourne Mtns
Dundalk Bay

Antrim Mountains
Lough Neagh

Bloody Foreland

Sperrin Mtns
Sawel 683m
Lower Lough Erne
Upper Lough Erne

Foyle
Bann

Blue Stack Mtns
Derry Mtns
Donegal Bay
Erne

Slieve Bloom Mtns
Barrow
Nore
Suir

I r e l a n d

Shannon

Galty Mtns

Iron Mtns
Shannon
Lough Ree
Lough Derg
Slieve Aughty Mtns
Blackwater
Comeragh Mtns
Old Head of Kinsale

Lough Conn
Lough Mask
Lough Corrib
Galway Bay
Burren
Corrib
Slieve Mts
Liscannor Bay

Celtic Sea

Nephin 806m

Twelve Bens
Slyne Head
Errisbeg Head
Connemara
Dingle Bay
Loop Head
Carrauntoohil 1038m
MacGillycuddy's Reeks
Macroom Mountains
Mizen Head

A T L A N T I C

ROUNDED HILLS 6

The rolling hills of the Cotswolds and the North and South Downs are formed from chalk. Water filters through this permeable rock. This means that few streams are found above ground in chalk areas.

BATTERED COASTLINE 7

The coastlines of western Ireland and southwest England have been eroded for centuries by the battering action of strong waves from the Atlantic Ocean. This causes rocks to break off and the coast to recede backwards forming steep, jagged cliffs.

27

POLITICAL BRITISH ISLES

The British Isles contain two separate countries: the United Kingdom – including the nations of England, Scotland, Wales and the province of Northern Ireland – and the Republic of Ireland. The United Kingdom has one of the longest-lasting systems of government in the world. The Queen is the head of state. There are two Houses of Parliament: the House of Lords, and the more important House of Commons, whose representatives are elected by the people. The issue of the reunification of Northern Ireland with the Republic has led to bloodshed – particularly since 1969.

LOCAL GOVERNMENT

The map below shows the counties and administrative districts of the United Kingdom. The boundaries have changed greatly since the mid-1990s. In densely populated regions – such as the conurbations of London, and Greater Manchester, all aspects of local government are dealt with by single bodies known as unitary authorities. In more rural areas there is a two-tiered system. The county administers services such as schools and the local councils administer services such as refuse collection.

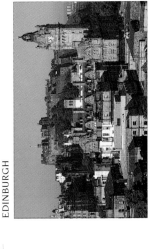

EDINBURGH

Edinburgh is the capital of Scotland. Until 1603, Scotland was a separate country. It became part of the United Kingdom when James VI of Scotland became James I of England.

2 THE NORTHEAST

NORTH TYNESIDE
SOUTH TYNESIDE
NEWCASTLE UPON TYNE
GATESHEAD
SUNDERLAND

3 TEESSIDE

HARTLEPOOL
STOCKTON-ON-TEES
MIDDLES-BROUGH
REDCAR AND CLEVELAND
DARLINGTON

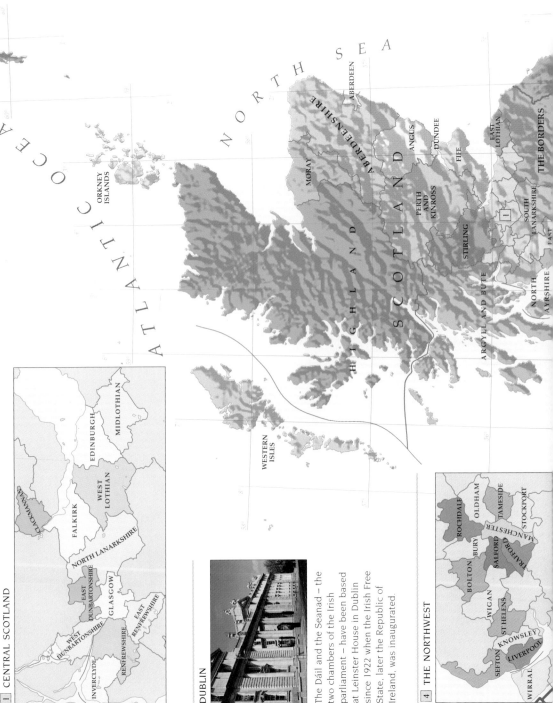

NORTH SEA
ATLANTIC OCEAN

SHETLAND ISLANDS
ORKNEY ISLANDS
WESTERN ISLES

HIGHLAND
SCOTLAND
ABERDEENSHIRE
MORAY
ABERDEEN
ANGUS
DUNDEE
PERTH AND KINROSS
FIFE
STIRLING
EAST LOTHIAN
THE BORDERS
SOUTH LANARKSHIRE
NORTH LANARKSHIRE
ARGYLL AND BUTE
NORTH AYRSHIRE
EAST

1 CENTRAL SCOTLAND

CLACKMANNAN
FALKIRK
EDINBURGH
MIDLOTHIAN
WEST LOTHIAN
NORTH LANARKSHIRE
EAST DUNBARTONSHIRE
GLASGOW
WEST DUNBARTONSHIRE
INVERCLYDE
RENFREWSHIRE
EAST RENFREWSHIRE

DUBLIN

The Dáil and the Seanad – the two chambers of the Irish parliament – have been based at Leinster House in Dublin since 1922 when the Irish Free State, later the Republic of Ireland, was inaugurated

4 THE NORTHWEST

ROCHDALE
OLDHAM
TAMESIDE
STOCKPORT
BURY
MANCHESTER
SALFORD
TRAFFORD
BOLTON
WIGAN
ST HELENS
KNOWSLEY
SEFTON
LIVERPOOL
WIRRAL

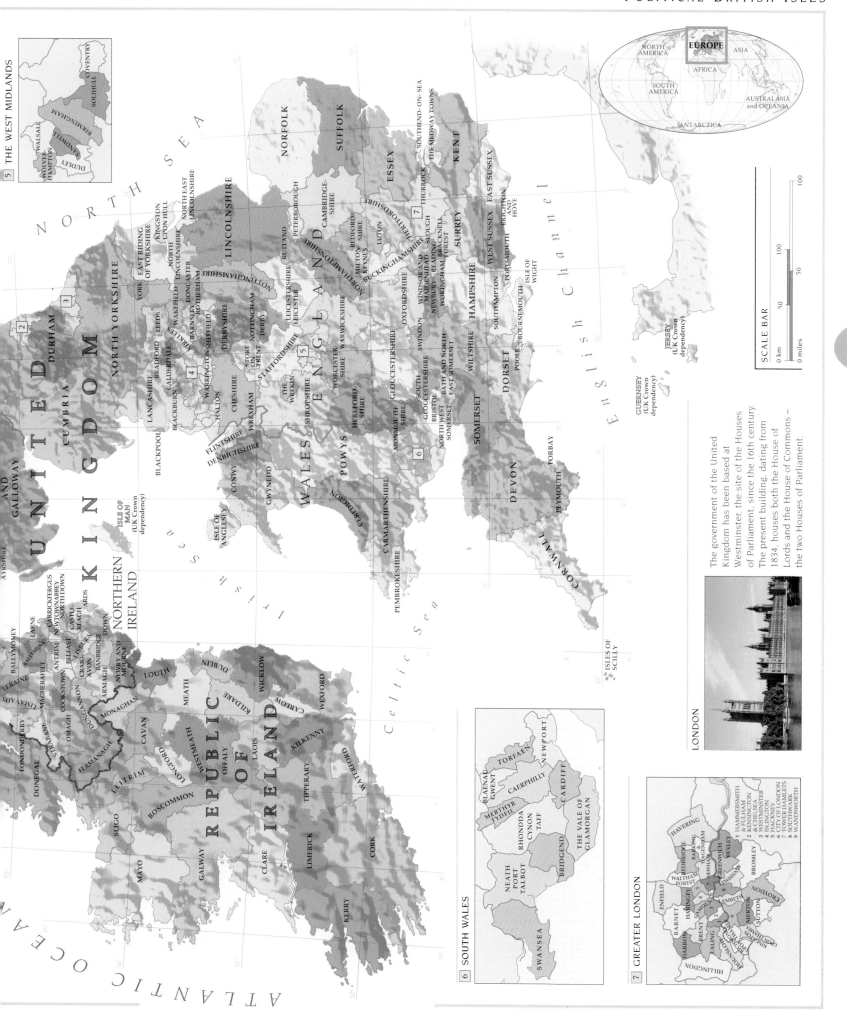

WOLVERHAMPTON
WALSALL
DUDLEY
SANDWELL
BIRMINGHAM
SOLIHULL
COVENTRY

NORTH SEA

EUROPE
NORTH AMERICA
ASIA
AFRICA
SOUTH AMERICA
AUSTRALASIA and OCEANIA
ANTARCTICA

SCALE BAR

0 km   50   100
0 miles   50   100

UNITED

KINGDOM

AND GALLOWAY
AYRSHIRE

DURHAM
CUMBRIA

2

3

NORTH YORKSHIRE
EAST RIDING OF YORKSHIRE
KINGSTON UPON HULL
NORTH EAST LINCOLNSHIRE
NORTH LINCOLNSHIRE

YORK
BRADFORD
LEEDS
WAKEFIELD
KIRKLESS
BARNSLEY
DONCASTER
ROTHERHAM
SHEFFIELD

LANCASHIRE
CALDERDALE
BLACKBURN

BLACKPOOL

LINCOLNSHIRE

NORFOLK
SUFFOLK

SOUTHEND-ON-SEA
THE MEDWAY TOWNS

ESSEX

THURROCK

KENT

PETERBOROUGH
CAMBRIDGESHIRE
HERTFORDSHIRE

EAST SUSSEX
WEST SUSSEX
BRIGHTON AND HOVE

SURREY

RUTLAND
LEICESTERSHIRE
LEICESTER
NORTHAMPTONSHIRE
BEDFORDSHIRE
MILTON KEYNES
LUTON

7

WARRINGTON
HALTON
CHESHIRE

4

STOKE ON TRENT
DERBYSHIRE
DERBY
NOTTINGHAMSHIRE
NOTTINGHAM

STAFFORDSHIRE
THE WREKIN

5

WARWICKSHIRE
WORCESTERSHIRE

OXFORDSHIRE
BUCKINGHAMSHIRE

SWINDON
WINDSOR AND MAIDENHEAD
NEWBURY
WOKINGHAM
READING
SLOUGH
BRACKNELL FOREST

HAMPSHIRE

SOUTHAMPTON
PORTSMOUTH
ISLE OF WIGHT

BOURNEMOUTH
POOLE

WILTSHIRE

ENGLAND

SHROPSHIRE

HEREFORDSHIRE

GLOUCESTERSHIRE
SOUTH GLOUCESTERSHIRE
BRISTOL
BATH AND NORTH EAST SOMERSET
NORTH WEST SOMERSET

6

WALES

POWYS

MONMOUTHSHIRE

SOMERSET

DORSET

WREXHAM
FLINTSHIRE
DENBIGHSHIRE
CONWY
GWYNEDD

ISLE OF MAN
(UK Crown dependency)

CEREDIGION

CARMARTHENSHIRE

ISLE OF ANGLESEY

PEMBROKESHIRE

DEVON

TORBAY

PLYMOUTH

CORNWALL

Irish Sea

NORTHERN IRELAND

BALLYMONEY
LARNE
CARRICKFERGUS
NEWTOWNABBEY
NORTHDOWN
ANTRIM
BELFAST
LISBURN
CASTLEREAGH
CRAIGAVON
ARDS

COLERAINE
BALLYMENA
MAGHERAFELT
COOKSTOWN
DUNGANNON
OMAGH
ARMAGH
BANBRIDGE
NEWRY AND MOURNE
DOWN

STRABANE
LONDONDERRY
DONEGAL
LIMAVADY

FERMANAGH

English Channel

JERSEY
(UK Crown dependency)

GUERNSEY
(UK Crown dependency)

ATLANTIC OCEAN

REPUBLIC

OF

IRELAND

SLIGO
MAYO
ROSCOMMON
LEITRIM
CAVAN
MONAGHAN
LONGFORD
WESTMEATH
MEATH
LOUTH
DUBLIN
KILDARE
WICKLOW
CARLOW
WEXFORD
KILKENNY
LAOIS
OFFALY
TIPPERARY
LIMERICK
CLARE
GALWAY
KERRY
CORK

Celtic Sea

ISLES OF SCILLY

The government of the United Kingdom has been based at Westminster, the site of the Houses of Parliament, since the 16th century. The present building, dating from 1834, houses both the House of Lords and the House of Commons – the two Houses of Parliament.

LONDON

BLAENAU GWENT
TORFAEN
NEWPORT
MERTHYR TYDFIL
CAERPHILLY
CARDIFF
RHONDDA CYNON TAFF
BRIDGEND
THE VALE OF GLAMORGAN
NEATH PORT TALBOT
SWANSEA

1 HAMMERSMITH & FULHAM
2 KENSINGTON & CHELSEA
3 WESTMINSTER
4 ISLINGTON
5 HACKNEY
6 CITY OF LONDON
7 TOWER HAMLETS
8 SOUTHWARK
9 WANDSWORTH

HAVERING
BARKING & DAGENHAM
NEWHAM
GREENWICH
BEXLEY
REDBRIDGE
WALTHAM FOREST
HARINGEY
LEWISHAM
BROMLEY
ENFIELD
BARNET
BRENT
CAMDEN
LAMBETH
CROYDON
MERTON
SUTTON
HARROW
HILLINGDON
EALING
HOUNSLOW
RICHMOND UPON THAMES
KINGSTON UPON THAMES

29

IRELAND

NORTHERN IRELAND, REPUBLIC OF IRELAND

Ireland faces the north Atlantic Ocean and is one of the remotest parts of the European Union. Since 1921 the island has been divided into two separate states: Northern Ireland, which is part of the United Kingdom, and the Republic of Ireland, which has its own government in Dublin. The eastern side of the island has more people and industry. In the west, traditional ways of life based on farming remain strong and the native Irish language is still spoken by some people.

INDUSTRY

Ireland has few mineral resources and much of its electricity is produced by burning peat. In the last 20 years the European Union has given money to help the Irish economy and many new factories have been set up, mainly in the area around Dublin. Hi-tech industries are expanding fast, as a result of low set-up costs and tax benefits.

INDUSTRY

- ✈ Aerospace
- 🍺 Brewing
- ⚗ Chemicals
- ⚙ Engineering
- 🗗 Food processing
- 🧵 Textiles
- 🖥 Hi-tech industry
- ⓘ Tourism
- ▣ Major industrial centre / area
- — Major road

POPULATION

The population of Ireland has actually fallen over the last century as a result of mass emigration, mainly to North America. The rate of people leaving the country to live abroad is still one of the highest in Europe, although a very high birth rate is finally causing the population to rise again, with one person in every three being less than 20 years old.

INHABITANTS PER SQ KM

- More than 250
- 100–250
- 50–100
- Less than 50
- ■ Capital city
- ● Major city

FARMING AND LAND USE

Potatoes are the traditional staple food of the Irish and potato fields are found throughout the country. The climate is too wet for many types of crop, particularly in the west, where the soils are thin and the land is mostly used for sheep grazing. In bog areas a type of soil called peat is cut from the ground and dried to be burned as fuel.

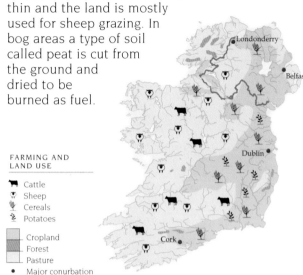

FARMING AND LAND USE

- 🐂 Cattle
- 🐑 Sheep
- 🌾 Cereals
- 🥔 Potatoes
- Cropland
- Forest
- Pasture
- ● Major conurbation

THE LANDSCAPE

Ireland's mountains are nearly all close to the sea. They form a ring of high ground – broken in only a few places – encircling a lower lying plain which fills the central areas. Hundreds of lakes, large areas of bogland and low, grassy hills cover this central plain. The west coast follows an extremely irregular line, with many long bays and headlands.

High cliffs (C2)
The cliffs of Donegal are some of the highest in Europe. Slieve League has been half cut away by sea erosion, so that the cliff rises vertically, all the way up from the shore to its 670 m summit.

Lakes made by glaciers
The central plain is covered with lakes of many different sizes. Most of these lakes were formed by huge blocks of ice which remained lying around as the last Ice Age came to an end, slowly melting over hundreds of years to leave sunken pits in the land surface.

Flooded river valleys (A6)
Dingle Bay extends deep inland. Rising seas have flooded the old river valley. Bays formed when the sea floods a river valley are known as rias.

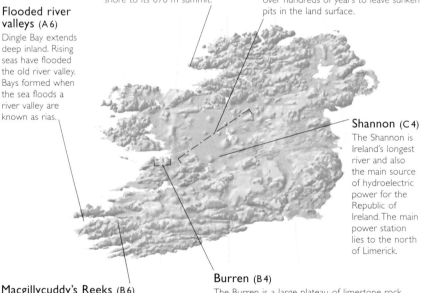

Shannon (C4)
The Shannon is Ireland's longest river and also the main source of hydroelectric power for the Republic of Ireland. The main power station lies to the north of Limerick.

Macgillycuddy's Reeks (B6)
This is the highest mountain range in Ireland. The jagged peaks and steep-sided valleys were cut from the highly resistant rocks by glacial erosion, during the last Ice Age.

Burren (B4)
The Burren is a large plateau of limestone rock. Limestone is permeable, which means that water sinks below the surface and flows underground. The bare rock is visible at the surface in many places, where it is called a limestone pavement.

BRITISH ISLES

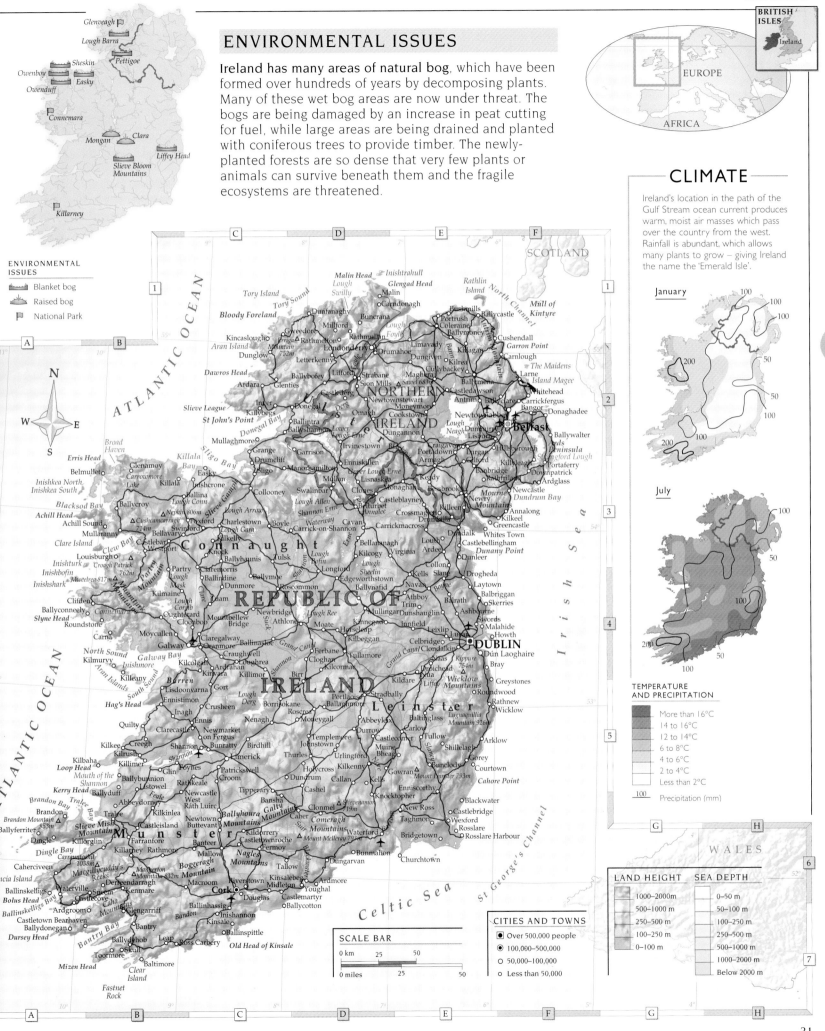

ENVIRONMENTAL ISSUES

Ireland has many areas of natural bog, which have been formed over hundreds of years by decomposing plants. Many of these wet bog areas are now under threat. The bogs are being damaged by an increase in peat cutting for fuel, while large areas are being drained and planted with coniferous trees to provide timber. The newly-planted forests are so dense that very few plants or animals can survive beneath them and the fragile ecosystems are threatened.

CLIMATE

Ireland's location in the path of the Gulf Stream ocean current produces warm, moist air masses which pass over the country from the west. Rainfall is abundant, which allows many plants to grow – giving Ireland the name the 'Emerald Isle'.

January

July

TEMPERATURE AND PRECIPITATION
- More than 16°C
- 14 to 16°C
- 12 to 14°C
- 6 to 8°C
- 4 to 6°C
- 2 to 4°C
- Less than 2°C
- 100 — Precipitation (mm)

ENVIRONMENTAL ISSUES
- Blanket bog
- Raised bog
- National Park

CITIES AND TOWNS
- ⬛ Over 500,000 people
- ◉ 100,000–500,000
- ○ 50,000–100,000
- ○ Less than 50,000

SCALE BAR
0 km 25 50
0 miles 25 50

LAND HEIGHT
- 1000–2000m
- 500–1000 m
- 250–500 m
- 100–250 m
- 0–100 m

SEA DEPTH
- 0–50 m
- 50–100 m
- 100–250 m
- 250–500 m
- 500–1000 m
- 1000–2000 m
- Below 2000m

SCOTLAND

Scotland occupies the northern third of Britain and has three main regions: the northern highlands and islands, the Southern Uplands and, between these two mountain areas, the central lowlands, where around three quarters of the population live and work. Scotland was once an independent country and, after nearly 300 years of union with England, is likely to regain some form of self-government in the near future. Scotland's economy has been boosted over the last 20 years by the North Sea oil industry.

INDUSTRY

A century ago, the area around the River Clyde was one of the great industrial regions of the world. The old heavy industries have since declined and been replaced by hi-tech and electronics industries, earning the area the name of 'Silicon Glen'. North Sea oil has brought many jobs and attracted new, oil-based industries such as chemicals and plastics production to the east coast.

INDUSTRY

✈ Aerospace	◊ Oil and gas
♦ Brewing	▭ Hi-tech industry
♦ Chemicals	▨ Printing and publishing
✿ Engineering	
◢ Fish processing	● Major industrial centre / area
◗ Food processing	
♉ Textiles	— Major road

ENVIRONMENTAL ISSUES

During a storm in January 1993, the Braer oil tanker struck the cliffs of southern Shetland. The ship broke up, shedding its entire load of crude oil into the sea. Although the oil was washed away within weeks, the long-term effects are not yet known. Scotland's fledgling skiing industry in the highlands is continually expanding, causing mild environmental damage.

ENVIRONMENTAL ISSUES

◣ Major oil spill

✦ Skiing resort

Braer – 1993

Aviemore

Cairngorms

Glen Coe

FARMING AND LAND USE

The eastern side of Scotland has a drier climate than the west and is suitable for growing cereal crops and vegetables. Most of the mountain areas are too wet and barren for arable farming and are put to a variety of uses, which include sheep and deer farming, game-keeping, forestry, tourism and recreation. Scottish fishermen currently land about two-thirds of all the fish caught by the UK.

FARMING AND LAND USE

🐂 Cattle	
🦌 Deer	
🐟 Fishing	
🐑 Sheep	
Cereals	
Root crops	
Timber	

▨ Cropland

▨ Forest

▨ Mountains

▢ Pasture

● Major conurbation

Aberdeen

Dundee

Glasgow

Edinburgh

THE LANDSCAPE

Much of Scotland is rugged and mountainous. During the last Ice Age, around 18,000 years ago, glaciers and great sheets of ice attacked Scotland's hard, ancient rocks, leaving behind a landscape of high moorlands and steep-sided mountains separated by deep valleys, often filled by lakes known as lochs.

Glen Mor (D 3)
Glen Mor is a deep valley which runs right across Scotland. It marks a major line of rock fracture, known as a fault. Much of the fault line is filled by Loch Ness (D 3) and Loch Linnhe (C 4).

Grampians (D 4)
The Grampians are Britain's largest and highest mountain region. They include the spectacular Cairngorm range (E 3) and, to the west, Ben Nevis (D 4), the highest point in the British Isles, at 1,343 m.

Hebrides (A 2), (B 6)
The Inner and Outer Hebrides comprise several large islands and hundreds of small ones. Many of these were formed following the last Ice Age, as the sea level rose, cutting off parts of the mountainous landscape from the mainland.

Firth of Forth (E 5)
The Firth of Forth is one of several great sea inlets, known as firths, along the Scottish coast. They include the Firths of Clyde (D 6), Tay (F 5) and Moray (E 3).

Lochs (D 5)
The many sea lochs (fjords) of the west coast were formed as the sea level rose after the last Ice Age, flooding the deep valleys that had been cut by glaciers. The sea lochs cause the coast to follow a highly irregular line.

Rannoch Moor (D 5)
Rannoch Moor is the largest wild moorland in Scotland. A great ice sheet covered the area during the last Ice Age, leaving behind a vast expanse of bleak, bare ground, pitted with small depressions.

Wick

Stornoway

Banff

Inverness

Peterhead

Aberdeen

Fort William

Perth

Dundee

Glasgow

Dunfermline

Edinburgh

Greenock

Paisley

Kilmarnock

East Kilbride

Ayr

Prestwick

Dumfries

Lerwick

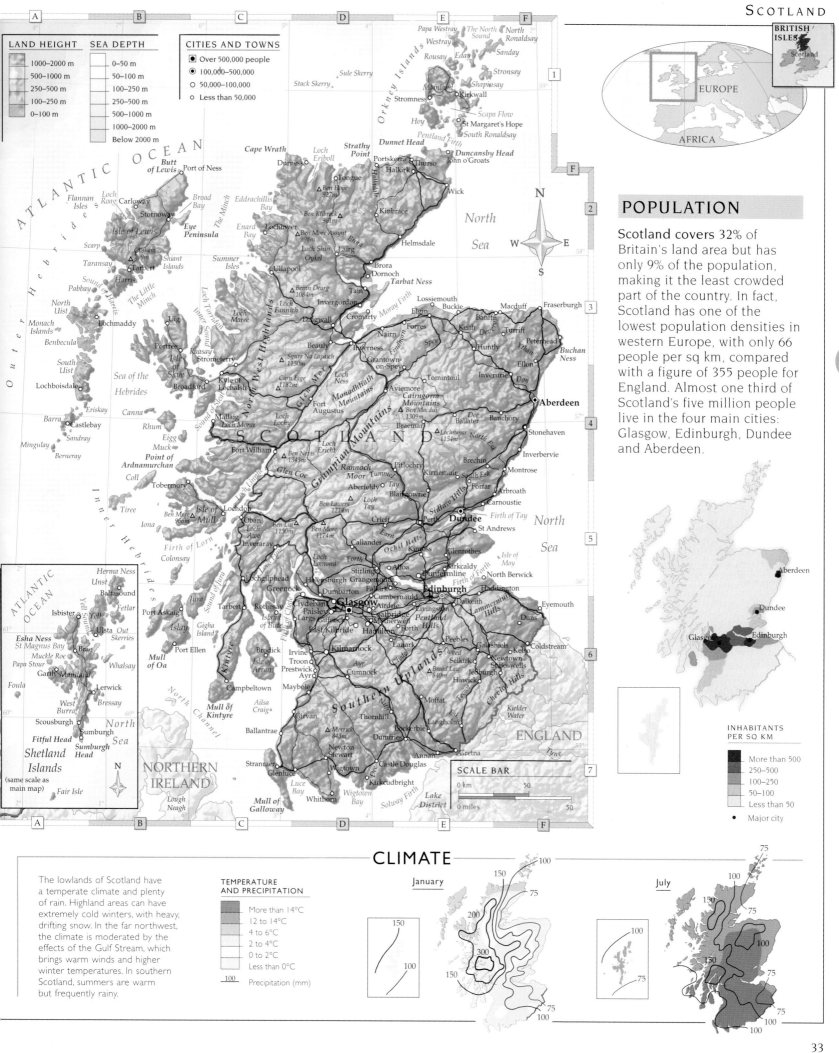

LAND HEIGHT
- 1000–2000 m
- 500–1000 m
- 250–500 m
- 100–250 m
- 0–100 m

SEA DEPTH
- 0–50 m
- 50–100 m
- 100–250 m
- 250–500 m
- 500–1000 m
- 1000–2000 m
- Below 2000 m

CITIES AND TOWNS
- ■ Over 500,000 people
- ◉ 100,000–500,000
- ○ 50,000–100,000
- ○ Less than 50,000

POPULATION

Scotland covers 32% of Britain's land area but has only 9% of the population, making it the least crowded part of the country. In fact, Scotland has one of the lowest population densities in western Europe, with only 66 people per sq km, compared with a figure of 355 people for England. Almost one third of Scotland's five million people live in the four main cities: Glasgow, Edinburgh, Dundee and Aberdeen.

INHABITANTS PER SQ KM
- More than 500
- 250–500
- 100–250
- 50–100
- Less than 50
- ● Major city

CLIMATE

The lowlands of Scotland have a temperate climate and plenty of rain. Highland areas can have extremely cold winters, with heavy, drifting snow. In the far northwest, the climate is moderated by the effects of the Gulf Stream, which brings warm winds and higher winter temperatures. In southern Scotland, summers are warm but frequently rainy.

TEMPERATURE AND PRECIPITATION
- More than 14°C
- 12 to 14°C
- 4 to 6°C
- 2 to 4°C
- 0 to 2°C
- Less than 0°C
- 100 Precipitation (mm)

January

July

SCALE BAR
0 km 50
0 miles 50

33

NORTHERN ENGLAND

The **Industrial Revolution** of the 18th and 19th centuries began in northern England. Rich coalfields and new developments in iron and steel and textile production started a new era of mass production – encouraging the growth of cities such as Liverpool and Manchester. Today, these industries have declined, but despite a number of difficult years, northern England is becoming more prosperous again. The magnificent scenery is attracting many tourists and new service industries are thriving.

INDUSTRY

Traditional industries such as iron and steel, coal-mining and textiles have been declining in northern England for over half a century. The region is still the industrial heartland of the UK, although the type of industries have changed. New light engineering and car production plants have developed in and around the region's cities, alongside hi-tech industries producing microchips and computers, and service industries such as insurance and retailing, printing and publishing.

INDUSTRY

✈ Aerospace	⊞ Food processing	▦ Printing and publishing
⚗ Brewing	⚒ Iron & steel	① Tourism
🚗 Car manufacture	△ Metal refining	
⚗ Ceramics	⚗ Pharmaceuticals	⊡ Major industrial centre / area
⚗ Chemicals	⚓ Shipbuilding	
⚙ Engineering	👕 Textiles	— Major road
🐟 Fish processing	🖥 Hi-tech industry	

ENVIRONMENTAL ISSUES

Some of England's most dramatic scenery is found in northern England, and National Parks have long been established to protect the environment. The National Parks have proved so popular that in some places tourists are in danger of destroying the environment. Coal-fired power stations in the region power the large cities, but also contribute to acid rain in the UK and Scandinavia.

ENVIRONMENTAL ISSUES

🏭 Coal-fired power station

🚩 National Park

● Major industrial city

FARMING AND LAND USE

The eastern lowlands have an ideal climate for arable crops, while oats and potatoes grow in the north and west. Market gardening is concentrated along the Humber and Mersey estuaries. The southwest is used mainly for grazing cattle and sheep, which also graze rough in upland areas such as the Pennines.

FARMING AND LAND USE

🐂 Cattle		▨ Cropland
🐑 Sheep		▦ Forest
🌾 Cereals		□ Pasture
🧺 Market gardening		● Major conurbation
🌱 Root crops		

THE LANDSCAPE

Northern England has a higher and more rugged landscape than the south, dominated by the bleak hills and moors of the Pennines. The Aire and Ouse rivers have cut a broad flood plain between the Pennines and the North York Moors. In the far northwest, Cumbria's Lake District has many long, deep lakes, which were formed during the last Ice Age.

Limestone pavements
Bare 'pavements' of weathered limestone are also known as karst scenery. They have a block-like appearance, with deep cracks between the blocks which have been dissolved by rainwater.

Spurn Head (F 4)
Spurn Head is a long sand bar at the mouth of the Humber estuary called a spit. It was formed by waves which deposited sand across the mouth of the bay. Recent heavy storms have made Spurn Head almost inaccessible from the mainland.

Kielder Water (C 2)
Kielder Water lies close to the Scottish border. With a perimeter of 44 km, it is the largest man-made lake in Europe.

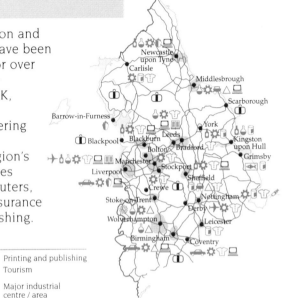

Isle of Man (A 3)
The Isle of Man is about 50 km long. It has a deeply indented coastline eroded by strong waves in the Irish Sea.

Morecambe Bay (B 4)
The bay is renowned for its tides which rise and fall rapidly. A barrage scheme has been proposed to harness this tidal energy.

North York Moors (D 3)

Lake District (B 3)
The Lake District covers a small area of the Cumbrian Mountains. The 15 lakes here form a radial pattern, spreading out from a central zone of volcanic rock.

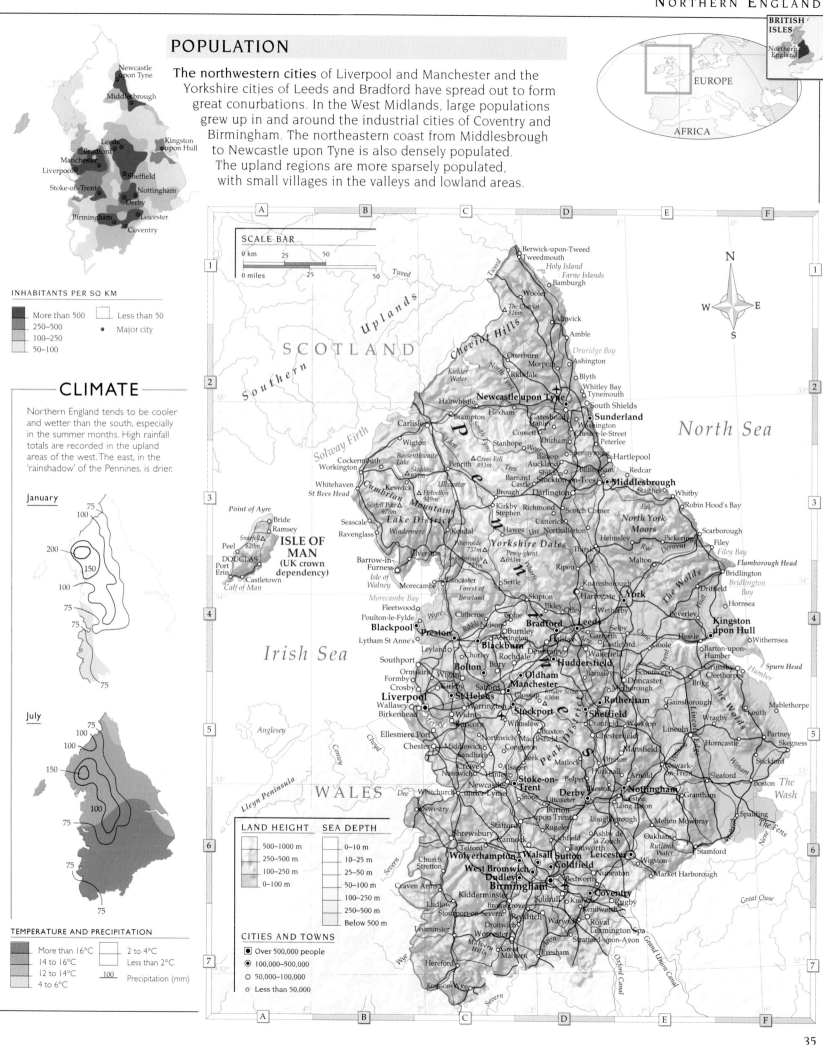

POPULATION

The northwestern cities of Liverpool and Manchester and the Yorkshire cities of Leeds and Bradford have spread out to form great conurbations. In the West Midlands, large populations grew up in and around the industrial cities of Coventry and Birmingham. The northeastern coast from Middlesbrough to Newcastle upon Tyne is also densely populated. The upland regions are more sparsely populated, with small villages in the valleys and lowland areas.

BRITISH ISLES
Northern England

EUROPE

AFRICA

INHABITANTS PER SQ KM

- More than 500
- 250–500
- 100–250
- 50–100
- Less than 50
- • Major city

CLIMATE

Northern England tends to be cooler and wetter than the south, especially in the summer months. High rainfall totals are recorded in the upland areas of the west. The east, in the 'rainshadow' of the Pennines, is drier.

January

July

TEMPERATURE AND PRECIPITATION

More than 16°C	2 to 4°C
14 to 16°C	Less than 2°C
12 to 14°C	100 Precipitation (mm)
4 to 6°C	

SCALE BAR

0 km 25 50

0 miles 25 50

LAND HEIGHT
- 500–1000 m
- 250–500 m
- 100–250 m
- 0–100 m

SEA DEPTH
- 0–10 m
- 10–25 m
- 25–50 m
- 50–100 m
- 100–250 m
- 250–500 m
- Below 500 m

CITIES AND TOWNS
- ⊙ Over 500,000 people
- ● 100,000–500,000
- ○ 50,000–100,000
- ○ Less than 50,000

SCOTLAND

Southern Uplands

Cheviot Hills

The Cheviot 816m

Berwick-upon-Tweed
Tweedmouth
Holy Island
Farne Islands
Bamburgh
Wooler
Alnwick
Amble
Druridge Bay
Ashington
Blyth
Whitley Bay
Tynemouth
South Shields

Otterburn
Morpeth
Ridsdale
Kielder Water
North Tyne

Haltwhistle
Brampton
Hexham
Newcastle upon Tyne
Gateshead
Stanley
Sunderland
Washington
Consett
Chester-le-Street
Peterlee

Carlisle
Wigton
Eden
Penrith
Cross Fell 893m
Bishop Auckland
Spennymoor
Hartlepool
Billingham
Redcar

Cockermouth
Workington
Bassenthwaite Lake
Skiddaw 931m
Stanhope
Wear
Durham

Whitehaven
St Bees Head
Keswick
Helvellyn 949m
Ullswater
Barnard Castle
Stockton-on-Tees
Middlesbrough
Staithes
Whitby

Seascale
Scafell Pike 978m
Lake District
Kirkby Stephen
Richmond
Scotch Corner
Northallerton
North York Moors
Robin Hood's Bay

Ravenglass
Windermere
Kendal
Hawes
Helmsley
Scarborough
Filey
Filey Bay

Barrow-in-Furness
Isle of Walney
Whernside 737m
Ingleborough 723m
Pen-y-ghent 693m
Ripon
Malton
Flamborough Head
Bridlington
Bridlington Bay

Morecambe
Lancaster
Settle
Knaresborough
Harrogate
York
The Wolds
Driffield
Hornsea

Fleetwood
Forest of Bowland
Skipton
Ilkley
Otley
Wetherby
Beverley

Poulton-le-Fylde
Wyre
Clitheroe
Colne
Bradford
Leeds
Selby
Kingston upon Hull
Withernsea

Blackpool
Preston
Burnley
Halifax
Garforth
Castleford
Hessle
Barton-upon-Humber
Spurn Head

Lytham St Anne's
Leyland
Chorley
Rochdale
Dewsbury
Wakefield
Goole
Grimsby
Cleethorpes

Southport
Ormskirk
Wigan
Bury
Huddersfield
Barnsley
Scunthorpe
Doncaster
Brigg
Louth
Mablethorpe

Formby
Crosby
Kirkby
Bolton
Oldham
Manchester
Glossop
Rotherham
Gainsborough
The Wolds

Liverpool
Wallasey
St Helens
Salford
Kinder Scout 636m
Sheffield
Wragby
Partney
Skegness

Birkenhead
Widnes
Warrington
Stockport
Dronfield
Worksop
Lincoln
Horncastle

Ellesmere Port
Runcorn
Wilmslow
Buxton
Chesterfield
Stickford

Chester
Northwich
Macclesfield
Peak District
Matlock
Mansfield
Sleaford

Sandbach
Congleton
Alfreton
Newark-on-Trent

Crewe
Leek
Belper
Hucknall
Arnold
Grantham

Nantwich
Alsager
Hanley
Stoke-on-Trent
Stone
Derby
Ilkeston
Nottingham
Long Eaton
Boston

Newcastle-under-Lyme
Uttoxeter
Burton upon Trent
Loughborough
Melton Mowbray
Spalding

Whitchurch
Stafford
Rugeley
Ashby de la Zouch
Oakham
Rutland Water
Stamford

Oswestry
Cannock
Lichfield
Tamworth
Bedworth
Market Harborough

Shrewsbury
Telford
Wolverhampton
Walsall
Sutton Coldfield
Leicester
Wigston

Church Stretton
West Bromwich
Dudley
Birmingham
Nuneaton

Craven Arms
Kidderminster
Solihull
Knowle
Coventry
Rugby
Kenilworth

Ludlow
Bromsgrove
Redditch
Warwick
Royal Leamington Spa

Leominster
Stourport-on-Severn
Droitwich
Worcester
Stratford-upon-Avon

Malvern Hills
Great Malvern
Evesham

Hereford
Ross-on-Wye

North Sea

Irish Sea

Anglesey

WALES

Lleyn Peninsula

Conwy
Clwyd
Dee

The Wash

The Fens

Nene
Great Ouse
Oxford Canal
Grand Union Canal

ISLE OF MAN (UK crown dependency)

Point of Ayre
Bride
Ramsey
Peel
Snaefell 620m
DOUGLAS
Port Erin
Castletown
Calf of Man

Solway Firth

Cumbrian Mountains

Yorkshire Dales

Pennines

Severn
Wye

SOUTHERN ENGLAND

The southern counties of England, and particularly Greater London, are the most densely populated part of the British Isles. There are more industries and more jobs here than anywhere else in the UK. In contrast, the counties of the far west and east are much less heavily populated and more rural, although towns in the eastern counties have been growing rapidly since the 1980s. Following the completion of the Channel Tunnel, the UK has had a direct rail link to Europe.

INDUSTRY

London is one of the world's top financial centres and is also a leading centre for other service industries including insurance, the media and publishing. Many car manufacturers are based in southern England, though the numbers of people employed have greatly decreased. Several cities, including Cambridge and Swindon are centres for hi-tech industry. Thousands of tourists visit the historic and cultural centres in southern England every year.

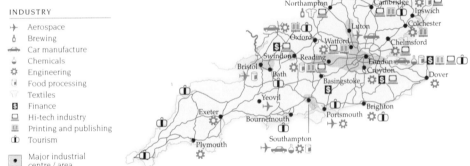

INDUSTRY

- ✈ Aerospace
- ♦ Brewing
- ⚙ Car manufacture
- ⚗ Chemicals
- ✿ Engineering
- 🗋 Food processing
- 🖈 Textiles
- ⑤ Finance
- 💻 Hi-tech industry
- ▥ Printing and publishing
- ① Tourism
- ▣ Major industrial centre / area
- — Major road

ENVIRONMENTAL ISSUES

The large population has put pressure on existing 'green belt' land – parts of which are now being used for new houses and roads. People have very different opinions about roads – some see them as necessary for the ever-growing number of cars; others are worried about the damage that cars and pollution are doing to the environment.

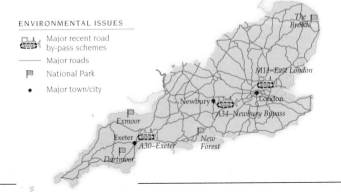

ENVIRONMENTAL ISSUES

- 🚐 Major recent road by-pass schemes
- — Major roads
- ⚑ National Park
- • Major town/city

FARMING AND LAND USE

Fertile soils and reliable rainfall mean that a wide range of crops can be grown in southern England. Large arable farms growing wheat and barley are found in the flat eastern counties, and a great variety of soft and orchard fruits and vegetables are grown in market gardens in the far southeast. Beef and dairy cattle and large flocks of sheep are grazed throughout the south.

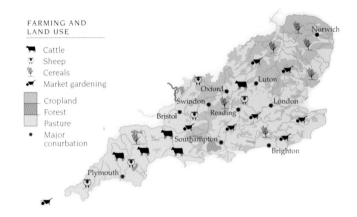

FARMING AND LAND USE

- 🐂 Cattle
- 🐑 Sheep
- 🌾 Cereals
- 🥕 Market gardening
- ▨ Cropland
- ▧ Forest
- ▢ Pasture
- • Major conurbation

THE LANDSCAPE

The landscape of southern England is very varied. Cornwall in the far west has craggy hills, and a jagged coastline shaped by the Atlantic Ocean. The Cotswolds and the North and South Downs are gentle hills, while towards the east, the land becomes flatter. Near the east coast, low-lying areas are occasionally prone to flooding.

Chalk hills The rounded hills of the Chilterns (F 3) are made from chalk. Because chalk is a porous rock, water quickly seeps through it, so few rivers can be seen in chalk areas.

The Broads (H 2) The Broads in Norfolk are a series of wide waterways flowing across flat meadows. The channels were cut by peat cutters and are not 'natural'. They then flooded, forming shallow inland lakes.

Steep cliffs The coasts of north Devon and Cornwall are battered by great waves from the Atlantic Ocean. The force of the waves weakens the rock at the foot of the cliffs, causing them to be 'undercut'. The top layer of rock breaks off and the cliffs recede.

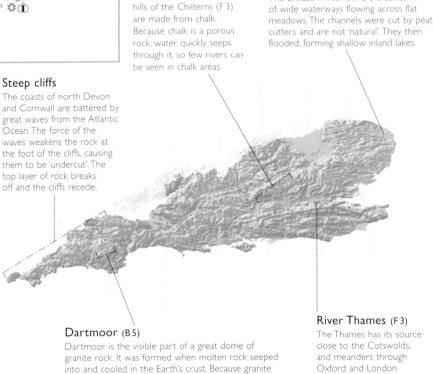

Dartmoor (B 5) Dartmoor is the visible part of a great dome of granite rock. It was formed when molten rock seeped into and cooled in the Earth's crust. Because granite is so hard it erodes very slowly, so outcrops of rock known as tors can be seen all over Dartmoor.

River Thames (F 3) The Thames has its source close to the Cotswolds, and meanders through Oxford and London before reaching the North Sea in a wide estuary.

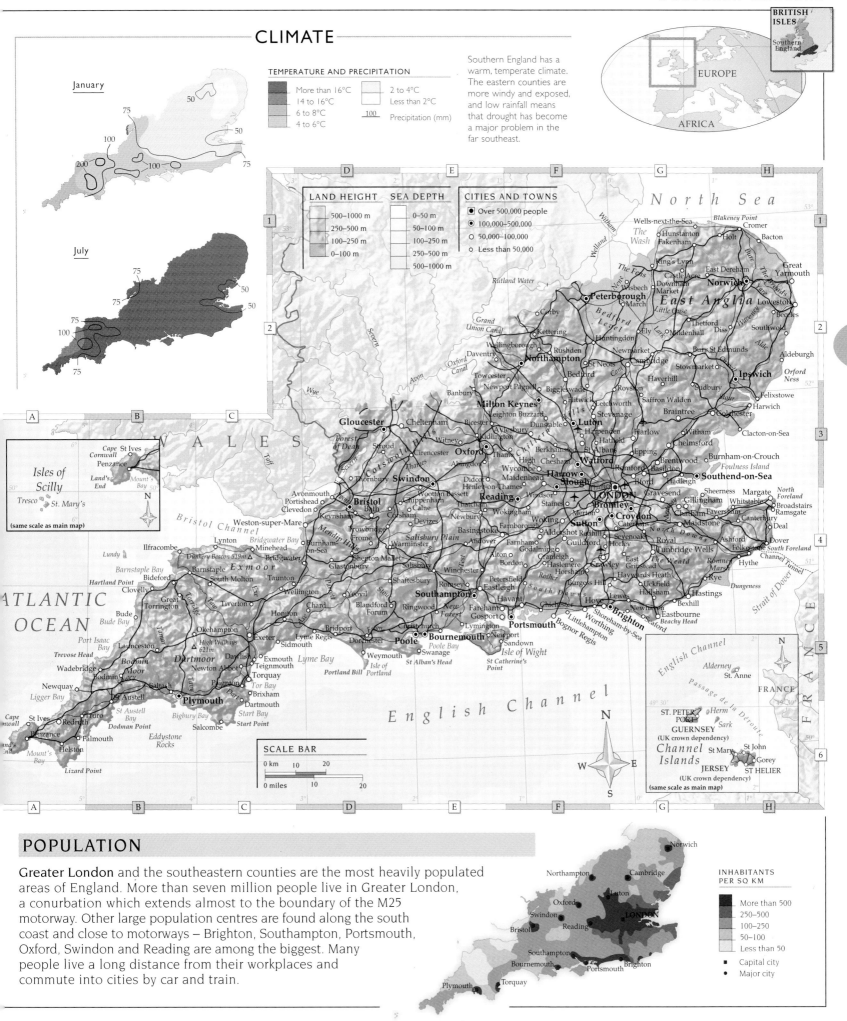

CLIMATE

TEMPERATURE AND PRECIPITATION

More than 16°C
14 to 16°C
6 to 8°C
4 to 6°C
2 to 4°C
Less than 2°C

100 Precipitation (mm)

January

July

Southern England has a warm, temperate climate. The eastern counties are more windy and exposed, and low rainfall means that drought has become a major problem in the far southeast.

BRITISH ISLES

EUROPE

AFRICA

Southern England

LAND HEIGHT

500–1000 m
250–500 m
100–250 m
0–100 m

SEA DEPTH

0–50 m
50–100 m
100–250 m
250–500 m
500–1000 m

CITIES AND TOWNS

Over 500,000 people
100,000–500,000
50,000–100,000
Less than 50,000

North Sea

Isles of Scilly
(same scale as main map)

Bristol Channel

ATLANTIC OCEAN

English Channel

SCALE BAR
0 km 10 20
0 miles 10 20

English Channel

FRANCE

ST. PETER PORT
GUERNSEY
(UK crown dependency)

Channel Islands
JERSEY
ST HELIER
(UK crown dependency)
(same scale as main map)

POPULATION

Greater London and the southeastern counties are the most heavily populated areas of England. More than seven million people live in Greater London, a conurbation which extends almost to the boundary of the M25 motorway. Other large population centres are found along the south coast and close to motorways – Brighton, Southampton, Portsmouth, Oxford, Swindon and Reading are among the biggest. Many people live a long distance from their workplaces and commute into cities by car and train.

INHABITANTS PER SQ KM

More than 500
250–500
100–250
50–100
Less than 50
■ Capital city
● Major city

WALES

Wales has been governed by England since 1535, yet it remains a distinctly different nation. Over a fifth of the people speak the native Welsh language of their Celtic ancestors. Wales has a strong artistic and musical tradition, celebrated in events such as the Eisteddfod festival. Large areas of the country are sparsely populated, with small and often isolated hill farming communities. South Wales is the main urban area and was once a major coal-mining and heavy industrial region. Wales's wild mountain scenery attracts many tourists and outdoor enthusiasts.

INDUSTRY

Vast quantities of slate, coal and other minerals were mined from the Cambrian Mountains during the Industrial Revolution, supplying the factories of south Wales. Very little mining takes place today but new hi-tech and service industries have grown rapidly in the south. Government assistance has helped these industries to spread into more rural places. Tourism is important in Wales, and large numbers of people visit its National Parks each year.

INDUSTRY

- 🚗 Car manufacture
- ⚙ Engineering
- 🚂 Iron and steel
- △ Metal refining
- ▯ Oil refining
- ▭ Hi-tech industry
- ⓘ Tourism
- ▪ Major industrial centre / area
- — Major road

POPULATION

The area around Newport, Cardiff and Swansea is home to more than 60% of the 2.9 million people living in Wales. Rising numbers of people have been moving into rural areas in north and central Wales over the last ten years. In old mining and industrial towns such as Merthyr Tydfil and Port Talbot, the population has fallen.

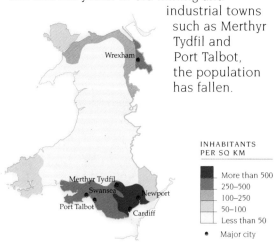

INHABITANTS PER SQ KM

- More than 500
- 250–500
- 100–250
- 50–100
- Less than 50
- • Major city

FARMING AND LAND USE

More land is used for farming in Wales than in England, yet only a few parts of Wales, such as the Conwy and Clwyd river valleys, are suitable for growing crops. The main land use is pastoral farming, with dairy cattle in more sheltered areas and sheep farmed on the more exposed uplands. Coniferous forests are now being planted in many mountain areas.

FARMING AND LAND USE

- 🐄 Cattle
- 🐑 Sheep
- 🌰 Root crops
- Cropland
- Forest
- Mountains
- Pasture
- • Major conurbation

THE LANDSCAPE

Mountains, plateaus and hills make up most of the Welsh landscape. The only lowland areas are the river valleys and parts of the coast and the English border. The Cambrian mountain range forms the backbone of the country and includes the rugged peaks of Snowdonia in the north, the rounded uplands of mid-Wales and the Brecon Beacons in the south.

The Brecon Beacons (D6) and the Black Mountains (E5)

These mountains are less steep than the jagged peaks of Snowdonia. This is due to the softer sandstone rock from which they were formed.

Sandy beaches

The coastline of mid and north Wales has large sandy beaches, many with sand dunes. Most of the sand was originally formed from the erosion of cliffs further south along the coast. The beach material is then carried north by longshore drift.

Anglesey (C1)

The flat, low island of Anglesey is separated from the mainland by the Menai Strait. The flat land surface is believed to be a wave-cut platform, eroded by the sea. It is now exposed because the land has risen since the end of the Ice Age.

Snowdonia (C2)

These spectacular mountains include Snowdon, the highest point in England and Wales, at 1,085 m. The spectacular sheer sides and jagged ridges were carved by glaciers during the last Ice Age.

Cambrian Mountains (D5)

The Cambrian range runs the whole length of the country and contains some of the oldest rocks in Britain. The rock is rich in minerals. Slate was also once mined in great quantities in northern and central areas.

Plynlimon (D4)

This mountain in central Wales is the source for two of the country's most important rivers: the Severn and the Wye.

The Vale of Glamorgan (D7)

The Vale of Glamorgan is a fertile coastal plateau, dissected by a number of streams which have cut down into the land surface. The plateau ends abruptly at the coast, with sheer cliffs 33 m high.

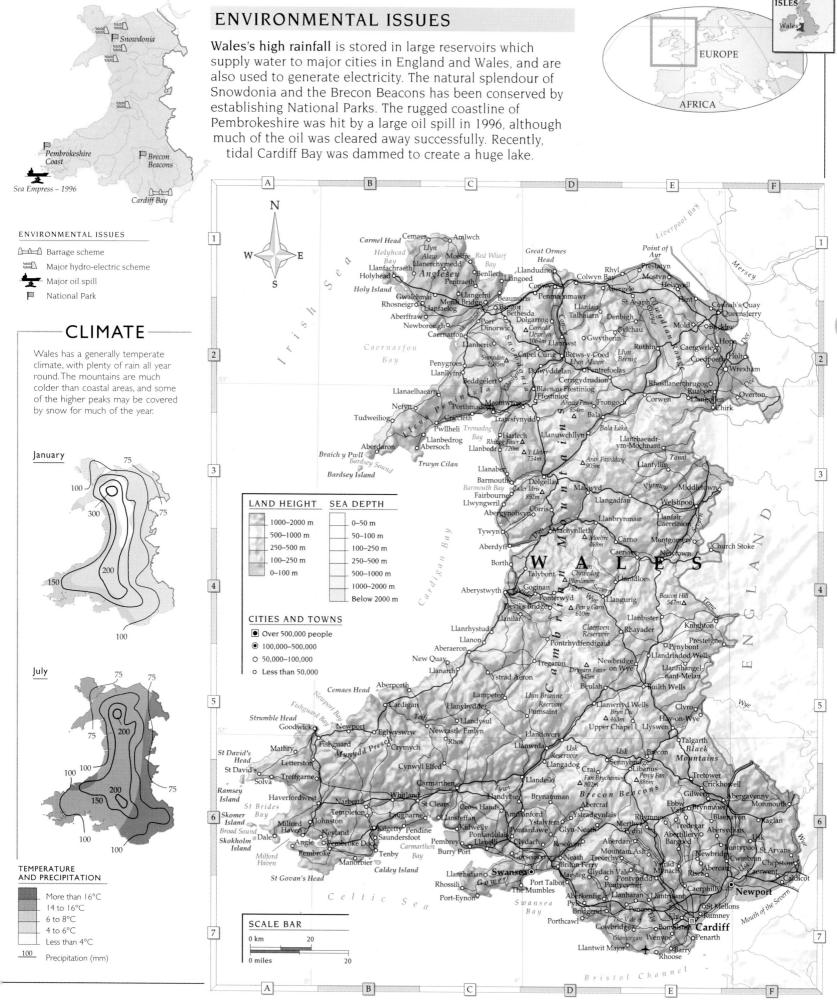

BRITISH ISLES
Wales
EUROPE
AFRICA

ENVIRONMENTAL ISSUES

Wales's high rainfall is stored in large reservoirs which supply water to major cities in England and Wales, and are also used to generate electricity. The natural splendour of Snowdonia and the Brecon Beacons has been conserved by establishing National Parks. The rugged coastline of Pembrokeshire was hit by a large oil spill in 1996, although much of the oil was cleared away successfully. Recently, tidal Cardiff Bay was dammed to create a huge lake.

Snowdonia
Pembrokeshire Coast
Brecon Beacons
Cardiff Bay
Sea Empress – 1996

ENVIRONMENTAL ISSUES
- Barrage scheme
- Major hydro-electric scheme
- Major oil spill
- National Park

CLIMATE

Wales has a generally temperate climate, with plenty of rain all year round. The mountains are much colder than coastal areas, and some of the higher peaks may be covered by snow for much of the year.

January

July

TEMPERATURE AND PRECIPITATION
- More than 16°C
- 14 to 16°C
- 6 to 8°C
- 4 to 6°C
- Less than 4°C
- 100 Precipitation (mm)

LAND HEIGHT
- 1000–2000 m
- 500–1000 m
- 250–500 m
- 100–250 m
- 0–100 m

SEA DEPTH
- 0–50 m
- 50–100 m
- 100–250 m
- 250–500 m
- 500–1000 m
- 1000–2000 m
- Below 2000 m

CITIES AND TOWNS
- Over 500,000 people
- 100,000–500,000
- 50,000–100,000
- Less than 50,000

SCALE BAR
0 km   20
0 miles   20

WALES

UK OVERSEAS TERRITORIES

The UK has the largest number of overseas territories in the world. They still exist for a variety of reasons: some are of strategic or economic importance; others are considered too small or remote to be able to survive as independent countries. UK overseas territories are split between Crown colonies, Crown dependencies and dependent territories but, regardless of their status, most have a high degree of local responsibility for government.

BRITISH INDIAN OCEAN TERRITORY

These islands are also known as the Chagos Archipelago. Most are uninhabited except for the US–UK military base on Diego Garcia. The islands will become part of Mauritius when no longer required by the UK.

TURKS AND CAICOS ISLANDS

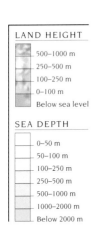

LAND HEIGHT
- 500–1000 m
- 250–500 m
- 100–250 m
- 0–100 m
- Below sea level

SEA DEPTH
- 0–50 m
- 50–100 m
- 100–250 m
- 250–500 m
- 500–1000 m
- 1000–2000 m
- Below 2000 m

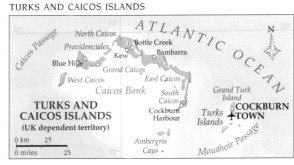

The Turks and Caicos Islands lie to the southeast of the Bahamas. Eight of the 30 islands are inhabited. Tourism and offshore banking are the most important economic activities, but many skilled islanders seek work in the Bahamas.

BERMUDA

Bermuda consists of more than 150 coral islands in the Atlantic. The most important industry is tourism but Bermuda is also an international insurance market.

FALKLAND ISLANDS

Just over 2,000 British citizens live in these windswept islands in the South Atlantic. Since the Argentine invasion of 1982, the British army has maintained a military presence here.

BRITISH VIRGIN ISLANDS

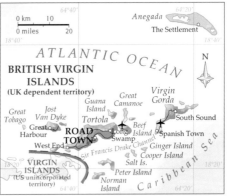

There are 40 islands in the British Virgin Islands; 15 of them are inhabited. Tourism is now the main economic activity, and the government has developed the Virgin Islands as an offshore tax haven.

MONTSERRAT

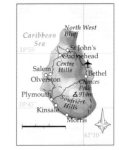

The southern part of Montserrat, including the capital, Plymouth, was devastated by the eruption of the Soufriére Hills volcano in the mid-1990s. The capital is currently at Olverston.

CAYMAN ISLANDS

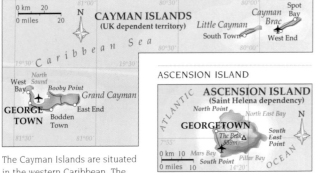

The Cayman Islands are situated in the western Caribbean. The islanders are keen to retain links with the UK and the Caymans are one of the world's largest offshore finance centres.

ASCENSION ISLAND

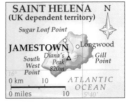

Ascension Island operates mainly as a military base and communications centre. It has a permanent resident population of around 250 people.

SAINT HELENA

Saint Helena is a small island in the South Atlantic. Its economy is unable to support the population, so many people are forced to seek work elsewhere. Ascension and Tristan da Cunha are part of Saint Helena.

TRISTAN DA CUNHA

Tristan da Cunha is a volcanic island, 2,000 km to the south of Saint Helena. It has a small, close-knit farming community.

GIBRALTAR

Gibraltar guards the western entrance to the Mediterranean. Some local people want independence, and Spain also claims control of the territory.

THE ATLAS
OF THE
WORLD

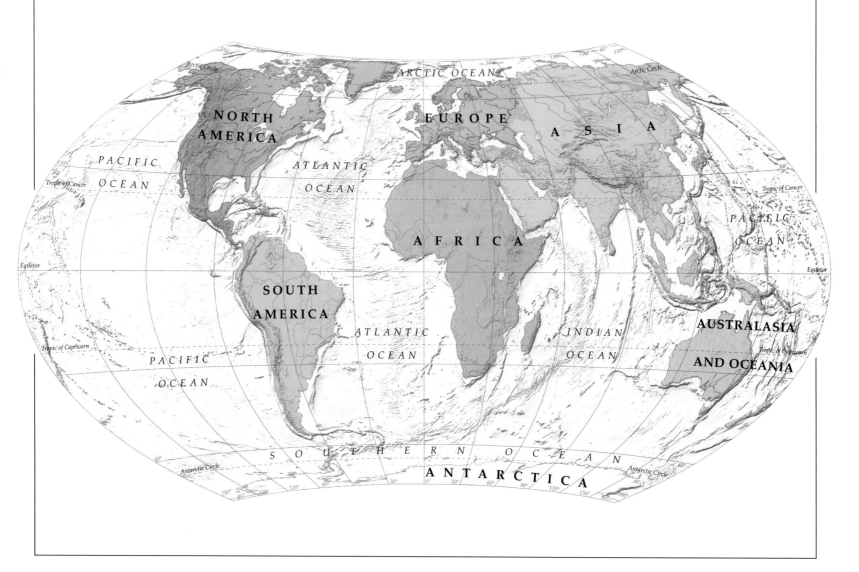

THE NATIONS OF THE WORLD

The world is divided into 192 independent countries, and about 60 overseas territories or dependencies. The largest country is the Russian Federation covering 17,075,400 sq km; the smallest is Vatican City in Rome, with an area of 0.44 sq km.

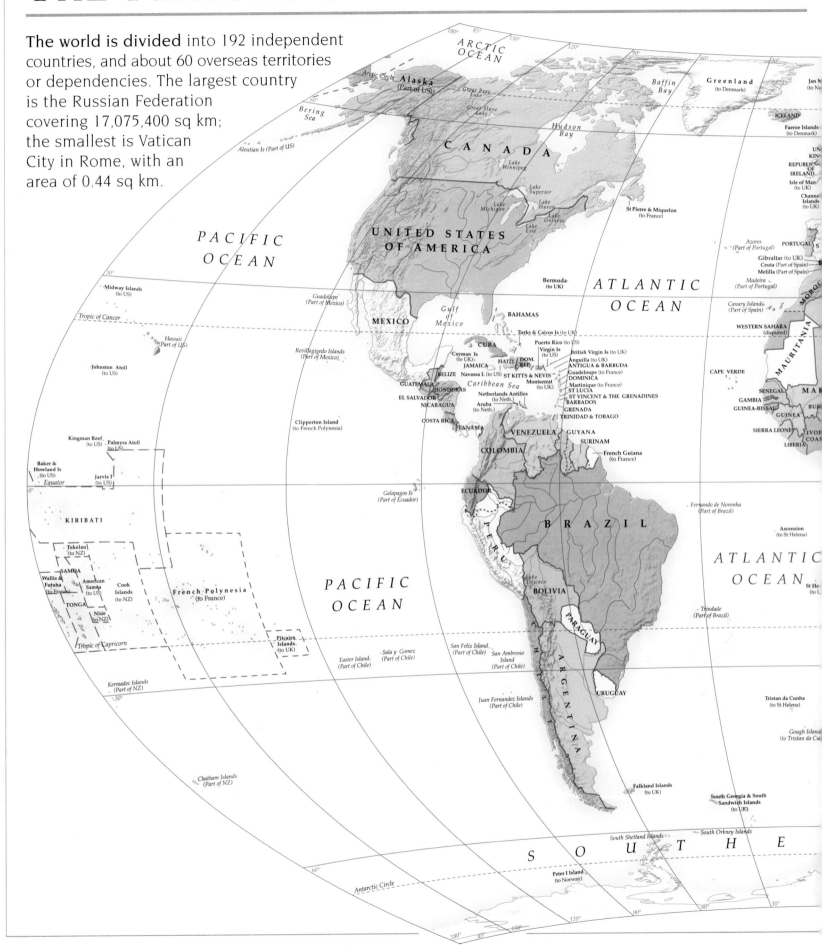

ARCTIC OCEAN

Arctic Circle

Alaska (Part of US)

Bering Sea

Aleutian Is (Part of US)

Great Bear Lake

Great Slave Lake

Hudson Bay

Baffin Bay

Greenland (to Denmark)

Jan M (to Ne)

ICELAND

Faeroe Islands (to Denmark)

CANADA

Lake Winnipeg

Lake Superior

Lake Michigan

Lake Huron

Lake Ontario

Lake Erie

UNITED STATES OF AMERICA

St Pierre & Miquelon (to France)

UN KING

REPUBLIC OF IRELAND

Isle of Man (to UK)

Channel Islands (to UK)

PACIFIC OCEAN

Midway Islands (to US)

Tropic of Cancer

Hawaii (Part of US)

Johnston Atoll (to US)

Bermuda (to UK)

ATLANTIC OCEAN

Azores (Part of Portugal)

PORTUGAL

Gibraltar (to UK)
Ceuta (Part of Spain)
Melilla (Part of Spain)

Madeira (Part of Portugal)

MOROC

Guadalupe (Part of Mexico)

MEXICO

Gulf of Mexico

BAHAMAS

Turks & Caicos Is (to UK)

Canary Islands (Part of Spain)

WESTERN SAHARA (disputed)

MAURITANIA

Revillagigedo Islands (Part of Mexico)

Cayman Is (to UK)

CUBA

JAMAICA

HAITI

DOM. REP.

Puerto Rico (to US)
Virgin Is (to US)

British Virgin Is (to UK)
Anguilla (to UK)
ANTIGUA & BARBUDA
Guadeloupe (to France)
DOMINICA
Martinique (to France)
ST LUCIA
ST VINCENT & THE GRENADINES
BARBADOS
GRENADA
TRINIDAD & TOBAGO

CAPE VERDE

SENEGAL

GAMBIA

GUINEA-BISSAU

MAL

BELIZE

Navassa I. (to US)

ST KITTS & NEVIS
Montserrat (to UK)

GUATEMALA

HONDURAS

EL SALVADOR

NICARAGUA

Caribbean Sea

Netherlands Antilles (to Neth.)

Aruba (to Neth.)

GUINEA

SIERRA LEONE

IVO COAS

LIBERIA

Clipperton Island (to French Polynesia)

COSTA RICA

PANAMA

VENEZUELA

GUYANA

SURINAM

COLOMBIA

French Guiana (to France)

Kingman Reef (to US)

Palmyra Atoll (to US)

Baker & Howland Is (to US)

Jarvis I (to US)

Equator

Galapagos Is (Part of Ecuador)

ECUADOR

Fernando de Noronha (Part of Brazil)

Ascension (to St Helena)

KIRIBATI

PERU

BRAZIL

ATLANTIC

OCEAN

St He (to U

Tokelau (to NZ)

SAMOA

Wallis & Futuna (to France)

American Samoa (to US)

Cook Islands (to NZ)

TONGA

Niue (to NZ)

French Polynesia (to France)

Lake Titicaca

BOLIVIA

Trindade (Part of Brazil)

PACIFIC OCEAN

Tropic of Capricorn

PARAGUAY

CHILE

San Felix Island (Part of Chile)

San Ambrosio Island (Part of Chile)

Sala y Gomez (Part of Chile)

Pitcairn Islands (to UK)

Easter Island (Part of Chile)

ARGENTINA

Kermadec Islands (Part of NZ)

Juan Fernandez Islands (Part of Chile)

URUGUAY

Tristan da Cunha (to St Helena)

Gough Island (to Tristan da Cu)

Chatham Islands (Part of NZ)

Falkland Islands (to UK)

South Georgia & South Sandwich Islands (to UK)

South Shetland Islands

South Orkney Islands

SOUTHE

E

Peter I Island (to Norway)

Antarctic Circle

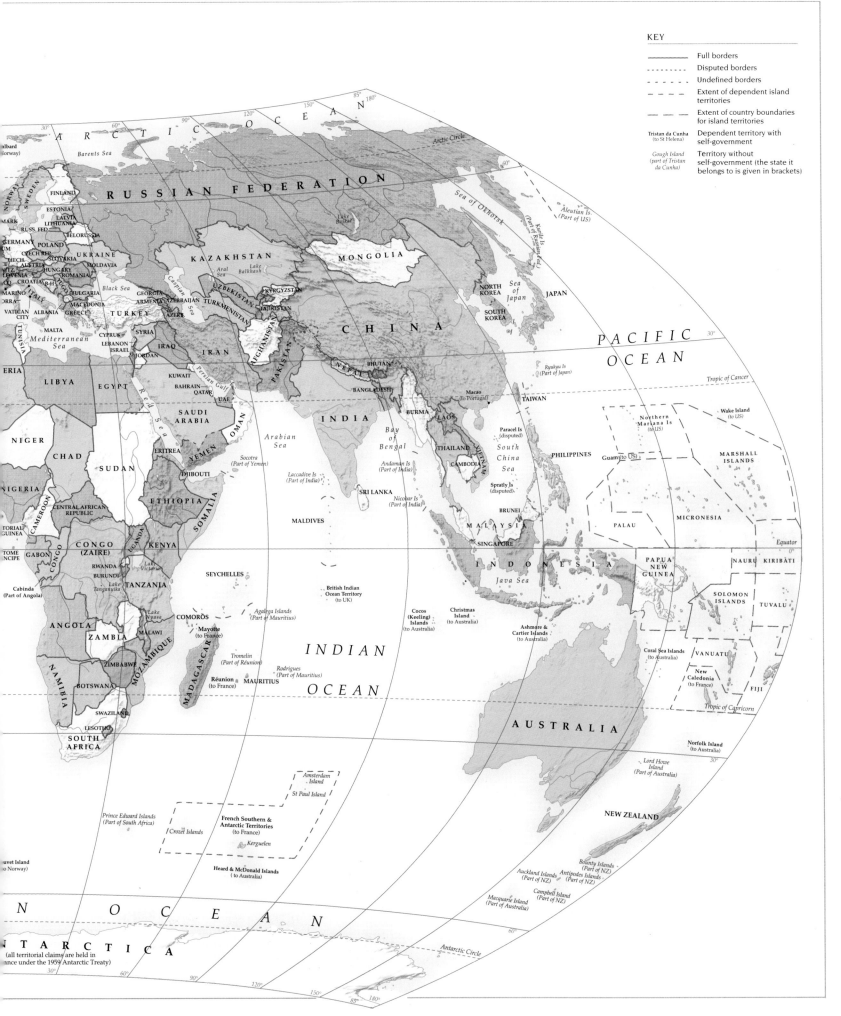

CONTINENTAL EUROPE

Europe is the world's second smallest continent, occupying the western tip of the vast Eurasian landmass. To the north and west are old highlands, with the high peaks of the Alps in the south. Most people live on the densely populated North European Plain, which runs from southern England, through northern France, across Germany into Russia.

CROSS-SECTION THROUGH EUROPE

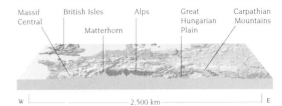

Massif Central | British Isles | Matterhorn | Alps | Great Hungarian Plain | Carpathian Mountains

W ⊢──────── 2,500 km ────────⊣ E

In the west, the land rises up from the Atlantic coast towards the Massif Central in France, and the high peaks of the Alps. Between the Alps and the Carpathian Mountains is the Great Hungarian Plain, where the River Danube flows on its way to the Black Sea.

PHYSICAL EUROPE

The ancient mountains of northwest Europe were scoured and smoothed by glaciers in the last Ice Age. The Alps are newer and more jagged – pushed up when Africa collided with Europe. In between is the North European Plain, where thick layers of fertile soils allow many different crops to be grown.

1 THE FROZEN NORTH

Europe's northern coastline stretches deep into the Arctic Circle. Here in Norway, icebergs drift into the deep, wide-bottomed fjords.

THE NORTH EUROPEAN PLAIN 2

The North European Plain has low, rolling hills and plains. Much of the area is cultivated and used for growing crops like wheat and sugar beet.

3 ANCIENT HIGHLANDS

Some of the world's oldest rocks are found in northwest Europe. Erosion by glaciers in the last Ice Age created smoothed hills such as the mountains of Wales.

4 THE ATLANTIC COAST

On Europe's Atlantic coast, the force of waves and winds has created striking landforms like this huge sand dune in southwest France.

THE ALPS 5

The Alps are Europe's major mountain chain. They formed about 65 million years ago. The Matterhorn is one of the most dramatic peaks.

Novaya Zemlya

Barents Sea

Ostrov Kolguyev

Arctic Circle

Iceland

Norwegian Sea

Faeroe Islands

Shetland Islands

Outer Hebrides

Galdhøpiggen 2469m

Ben Nevis 1343m

British Isles

North Sea

Jutland

English Channel

Seine

Loire

Rhine

Ardennes

Bay of Biscay

Massif Central

Pyrenees

Ebro

Iberian Peninsula

Corsica

Balearic Islands

Sardinia

Mediterranean Sea

AFRICA

Kölen

Gulf of Bothnia

White Sea

Lake Vänern

Lake Ladoga

Lake Onega

Baltic Sea

Elbe

Vistula

Danube

Dinaric Alps

Adriatic Sea

Tyrrhenian Sea

Vesuvius 1171m

Sicily

Etna 3265m

Malta

Ionian Sea

Peloponnese

Aegean Sea

Crete

Kola Peninsula

Northern Dvina

Western Dvina

Pripet Marshes

Dnieper

Carpathian Mountains

Gerlachovskij Štít 2655m

Great Hungarian Plain

Balkan Mountains

North European Plain

Central Russian Upland

Volga

Volga Upland

Lowest point ▽ Volga Delta -28m

Don

Sea of Azov

Crimea

Black Sea

Caucasus △ Highest point El'brus 5642m

Caspian Sea

Ural Mountains

A S I A

Gora Narodnaya △ 1895m

Arctic Circle

A L P S

Matterhorn 4478m

Mt Blanc 4807m

Apennines

Po

ATLANTIC OCEAN

ASIA

ELEVATION
5000m
4000m
3000m
2000m
1000m
500m
250m
100m
sea level
below sea level
⋈ cross-section

SCALE 1:31,000,000
0 km   300   600
0 miles   300   600

POLITICAL EUROPE

Europe's population increased rapidly during the 18th and 19th centuries, following the Industrial Revolution. In the 20th century, Europe suffered a series of wars which redrew the political map. From 1989–1991, communist governments in eastern Europe and the former Soviet Union collapsed, as political reform swept through the countries behind the 'Iron Curtain'. In western Europe, the 15 countries of the European Union are discussing closer political and economic ties.

POPULATION
Capital cities
⊙ Above 500,000
⊙ 100,000 to 500,000
• 50,000 to 100,000

SCALE 1:27,500,000
0 km   300   600
0 miles   300   600

REGIONAL IDENTITY

Throughout Europe, there is a growing call to recognize regional cultural identity. The Basque region, bordering southwest France and Spain, is one example.

RURAL LIFE

Away from Europe's bustling cities, traditional rural lifestyles survive. Here in the Republic of Ireland, a winter shelter is being made for cattle.

STANDARDS OF LIVING

Living standards are generally much lower in eastern Europe than in the wealthier west. Homelessness and unemployment are still problems, even in the most prosperous countries.

POPULATION

More than 700 million people live in Europe, and its population is highly urbanized. In Belgium and the Netherlands, almost 90% of people live in cities. In the south and east, more people still live in rural areas. The northern countries have the smallest populations, because much of the land is too cold to be habitable.

POPULATION DENSITY
(People per sq km)
Below 49
50–99
100–149
150–199
200–299
Above 300

SPREADING CITIES

Rotterdam, in the Netherlands is part of a conurbation, a large built-up area where several towns or cities have merged together to form a single urban area.

● Largest city
MOSCOW
9.4 million people

STANDARD OF LIVING
(UN Human Development Index)
low   high

European Geography

Europe is blessed with a temperate climate, ample mineral reserves, and good transport links. During the 18th and 19th centuries the continent was transformed, as new methods of production made industry and farming more efficient and productive. Today, in many countries, 'heavy' industries have been replaced by hi-tech and service industries. Agriculture is still important and many crops thrive on Europe's fertile plains.

Industry

Western Europe has some of the world's wealthiest countries. In countries such as France, Germany and the UK, traditional industries like iron and steel-making are now being replaced by light industries such as electronics, and services like finance and insurance. In Eastern Europe, industry was subsidized by the communist governments for years. Many factories are old fashioned and need investment to improve their equipment and production methods.

ECONOMIC ACTIVITY

- Aerospace
- Car/vehicle manufacture
- Chemicals
- Coal
- Defence
- Electronics
- Engineering
- Finance
- Food processing
- Hi-tech industry
- Iron & steel
- Oil and gas
- Printing & publishing
- Textiles
- Timber processing

ICELAND
Barents Sea
Norwegian Sea
NORWAY
SWEDEN
FINLAND
RUSSIAN FEDERATION
ASIA
Perm'
Ufa
North Sea
UNITED KINGDOM
Glasgow
Newcastle upon Tyne
REPUBLIC OF IRELAND
Manchester
Birmingham
London
Oslo
Stockholm
Gothenburg
Helsinki
St Petersburg
ESTONIA
LATVIA
LITHUANIA
DENMARK
Baltic Sea
Kaliningrad (part of Russ. Fed.)
Yaroslavl'
Moscow
Nizhniy Novgorod
Samara
Tula
Saratov
Hamburg
Amsterdam
NETH.
GERMANY
Berlin
Cologne
Brussels
BELG.
LUX.
Frankfurt am Main
Prague
Stuttgart
CZECH REP.
POLAND
Warsaw
Kraków
BELORUSSIA
Kiev
UKRAINE
Dnipropetrovs'k
Volgograd
Rostov-on-Don
Kryvyy Rih
MOLDAVIA
SLOVAKIA
Paris
FRANCE
LIECH.
Munich
Zürich
SWITZ.
AUSTRIA
HUNGARY
ROMANIA
Bucharest
Black Sea
Lyon
Milan
Turin
SLVN.
CROATIA
BOSNIA AND HERZ.
SAN MARINO
YUGOSLAVIA
BULGARIA
Sofia
Istanbul
TURKEY
MACED.
ALBANIA
GREECE
Athens
ITALY
Naples
Bilbao
Toulouse
ANDORRA
Barcelona
SPAIN
Madrid
PORTUGAL
Lisbon
ATLANTIC OCEAN
Mediterranean Sea
MALTA
AFRICA
ASIA

GNP per capita (US$)

- Below 1999
- 2000-4999
- 5000-9999
- 10,000-19,999
- 20,000-24,999
- Above 25,000
- • Industrial centre

Mineral Resources

Europe has few sizeable reserves of metallic minerals; most were used up by industry during the last century. Oil, gas and coal are found in large quantities – gas in the North Sea and oil in the Volga basin. Coal, though abundant, is being steadily depleted.

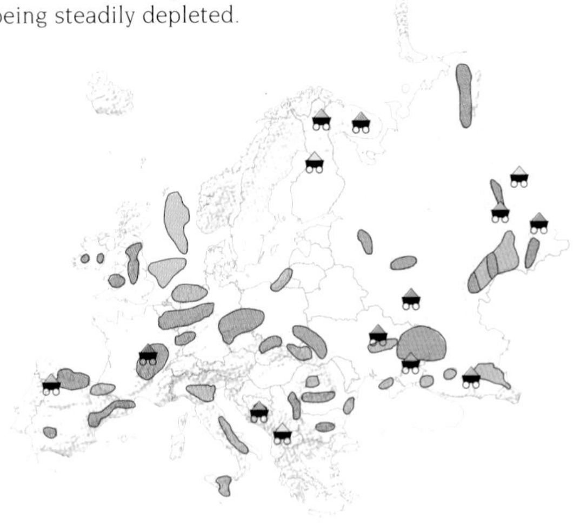

MINERAL RESOURCES

- Bauxite
- Chromium
- Iron
- Manganese
- Nickel
- Uranium
- Oil/gas field
- Coal field

OIL AND GAS

Oil and gas reserves are plentiful in the Russian Federation. South of Rostov-on-Don, oil is pumped from the ground and piped to nearby refineries.

CAR MANUFACTURE

Germany is one of the world's largest manufacturers of cars. Companies like BMW, Mercedes-Benz and Volkswagen export cars across the world.

FINANCE

London is one of the most important financial centres in the world. Many banks and financial institutions have their headquarters here. At the London Stock Exchange, people buy and sell stocks and shares.

CLIMATE

Europe's climate is temperate with few climatic extremes. In the far north, Europe extends into the Arctic Circle and the climate is so cold that in the winter, the Baltic Sea freezes over. Towards the Atlantic coast in the west, the climate becomes wetter and warmer because of a warm ocean current, known as the Gulf Stream. Countries such as Italy and Spain which border the Mediterranean Sea, have long, hot summers and low rainfall, which can sometimes lead to problems such as drought.

EXTREME WEATHER EVENTS

Symbols indicate climatic extremes

CLIMATE
- Tundra
- Subarctic
- Cool continental
- Temperate/humid
- Mediterranean
- Semi-arid

Arctic Circle

Coldest place
UST' SHCHUGOR (Russ. Fed.)
Temp. -55°C

Driest place
ASTRAKHAN' (Russ. Fed.)
Annual rainfall 160 mm

Hottest place
SEVILLE (Spain)
Temp. 50°C

Wettest place
CRKVICE (Bos. & Herz.)
Annual rainfall 4650 mm

THE MEDITERRANEAN CLIMATE

The mild, warm climate around the Mediterranean Sea allows olives, citrus fruits and grapes to thrive. Long, sunny days also help the fruits ripen. Grapes are harvested and crushed to make many different wines.

LAND USE AND AGRICULTURE

Europe's agricultural heart is the North European Plain, where fertile soils and ample rainfall mean that a variety of crops can be grown. Wheat is the main grain crop, and a wide range of fruit and vegetables are also grown. Dairy and beef cattle are raised for their milk and meat throughout Europe. In the south, the Mediterranean climate allows citrus fruits and olives to grow. Forests cover much of northern Scandinavia, while in the hills of the British Isles, sheep farming is common.

CROPLANDS

Many different crops are grown on the North European Plain. Sunflowers, wheat, and sugar beet – used to make sugar – are amongst the main crops grown there.

FISHING

The north Atlantic Ocean provides a rich marine harvest for fishermen. High-quality cod and mackerel are caught in the cold, nutrient-rich waters.

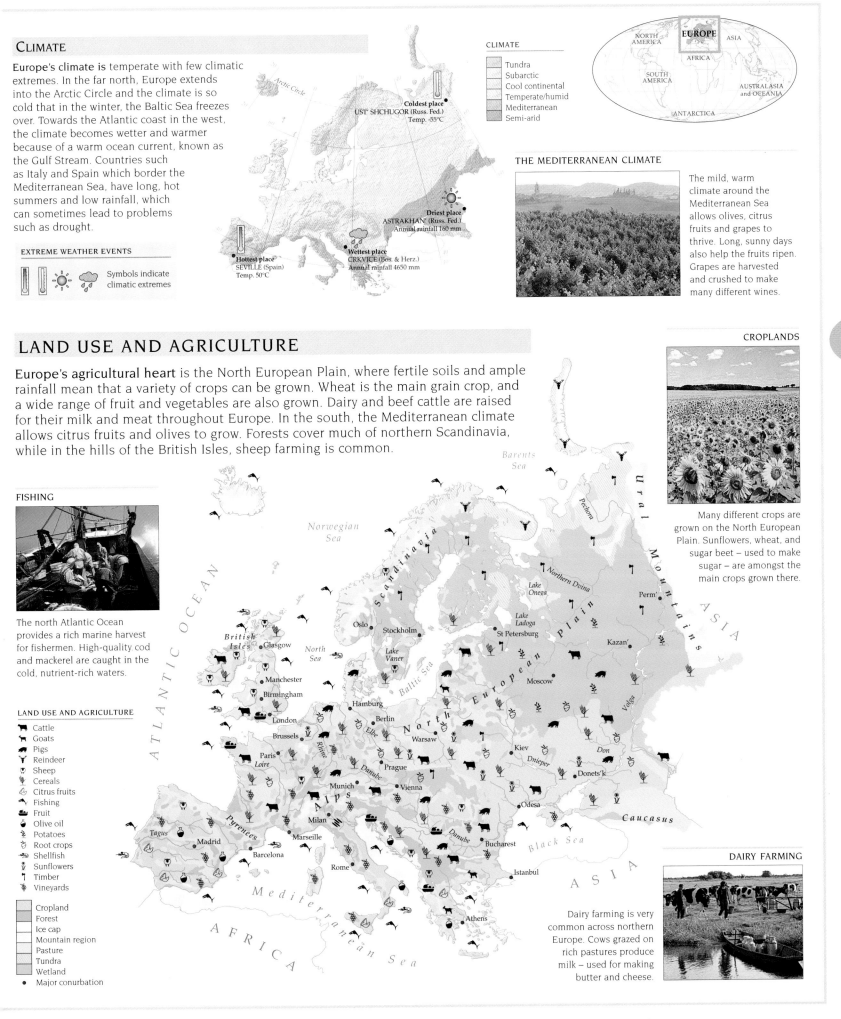

LAND USE AND AGRICULTURE
- 🐂 Cattle
- 🐐 Goats
- 🐖 Pigs
- Reindeer
- 🐑 Sheep
- Cereals
- Citrus fruits
- Fishing
- Fruit
- Olive oil
- Potatoes
- Root crops
- Shellfish
- Sunflowers
- Timber
- Vineyards

- Cropland
- Forest
- Ice cap
- Mountain region
- Pasture
- Tundra
- Wetland
- • Major conurbation

DAIRY FARMING

Dairy farming is very common across northern Europe. Cows grazed on rich pastures produce milk – used for making butter and cheese.

NORTHERN EUROPE

DENMARK, ESTONIA, FINLAND, ICELAND, LATVIA, LITHUANIA, NORWAY, SWEDEN

Denmark, Sweden and Norway are together known as Scandinavia. These countries, along with the North Atlantic island of Iceland, have similar languages and cultures. Finland has a very different language and a separate identity from its Scandinavian neighbours. Estonia, Latvia and Lithuania, known as the Baltic states, were part of the Soviet Union until 1989, when each became an independent country.

INDUSTRY

In Scandinavia, many natural resources are used in industry: timber for paper and furniture; iron ore for steel and cars; and fish and natural gas from the seas. Hydro-electric power is generated by water flowing down steep mountain slopes. The Baltic states still rely on Russia to supply their raw materials and energy.

INDUSTRY

- 🚗 Car manufacture
- ⚗ Chemicals
- ⚙ Engineering
- 🐟 Fish processing
- ⊣ Hydro-electric power
- ⚓ Shipbuilding
- 🌲 Timber processing
- 🏛 Tourism
- ▪ Major industrial centre / area
- — Major road

STRUCTURE OF INDUSTRY

Primary 4%
Services 65%
Manufacturing 31%

POPULATION

The population is distributed mainly along the warmer and flatter southern and coastal areas. Population totals and densities are low for all of the countries, and Iceland has the lowest population density in Europe, with just three people per sq km. Many Scandinavians have holiday homes on the islands, along the lake shores, or in coastal areas.

INHABITANTS PER SQ KM

- More than 200
- 100–200
- 50–100
- Less than 50
- ▪ Capital city
- ▪ Major city

URBAN/RURAL POPULATION DIVIDE

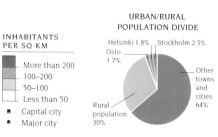

Helsinki 1.8%   Stockholm 2.5%
Oslo 1.7%
Other towns and cities 64%
Rural population 30%

FARMING AND LAND USE

Southern Denmark and Sweden are the most productive areas, with pig farming, dairy-farming and crops such as wheat, barley and potatoes. Sheep farming is important in southern Norway and Iceland. In the Baltic states, cereals, potatoes and sugar beet are the main crops and cattle graze on damp pasture.

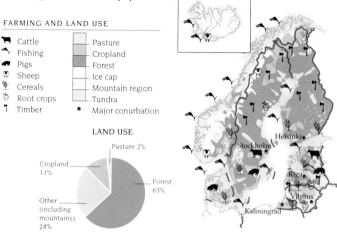

FARMING AND LAND USE

- 🐄 Cattle
- 🐟 Fishing
- 🐖 Pigs
- 🐑 Sheep
- 🌾 Cereals
- 🌱 Root crops
- 🌲 Timber
- ▨ Pasture
- ▨ Cropland
- ▨ Forest
- ☐ Ice cap
- ☐ Mountain region
- ☐ Tundra
- • Major conurbation

LAND USE

Pasture 2%
Cropland 11%
Other (including mountains) 24%
Forest 63%

THE LANDSCAPE

The north and west of Scandinavia is extremely rugged and mountainous, with landscapes eroded by ice. In the south of Scandinavia the land is flatter, with fertile soils deposited by glaciers. Much of Finland, Norway and Sweden is covered by dense forests. The Baltic states are much lower, with rounded hills and many lakes and marshes.

The land of ice and fire.
Iceland is one of the world's most active volcanic areas. There are about 200 volcanoes on the island, along with bubbling hot springs, mud-holes, and geysers which spurt boiling water and steam high into the air.

Fjords
Norway has many fjords: deep, wide valleys, drowned by seawater when the ice melted at the end of the last Ice Age.

Baltic Sea (D 7)
Ships from Finland, Sweden and the Baltic states use the Baltic Sea as their route to the north Atlantic Ocean. In winter, much of the sea is frozen.

Glacial lakes
Finland and Sweden have many thousands of lakes. During the last Ice Age, glaciers scoured hollows which filled with water when the ice melted.

Courland Spit (D 7)
This wide sandspit runs for 100 km along the Baltic coast of Lithuania and the Russian enclave of Kaliningrad. It encloses a huge lagoon.

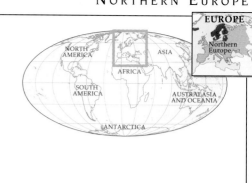

EUROPE
Northern Europe

Vatnajökull 1996
Surtsey 1963

Stockholm
Helsinki
Tallinn
Riga
Copenhagen

ENVIRONMENTAL ISSUES

- Major dams
- Urban air pollution
- Volcanic eruption
- Affected by acid rain / Sea pollution
- Major industrial centre

CLIMATE

Warm ocean currents flowing north along the coasts of Norway and Iceland make the climate mild and wet. Away from the sea, the climate is generally colder, and drier.

January

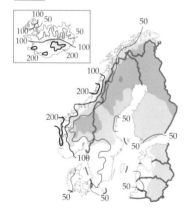

July

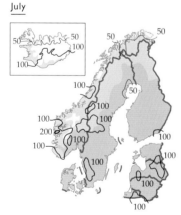

TEMPERATURE AND PRECIPITATION

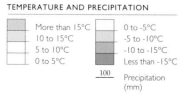

More than 15°C	0 to -5°C
10 to 15°C	-5 to -10°C
5 to 10°C	-10 to -15°C
0 to 5°C	Less than -15°C

100 Precipitation (mm)

ENVIRONMENTAL ISSUES

Northern Europe has been badly affected by industrial pollution from other parts of Europe. Polluted air moves north, and mixes with the rain to create acid rain. This poisons forests and lakes, destroying the plants and animals living in them. In Norway and Sweden, electricity is produced by dams that obtain power from the plentiful water supply. Hydro-electric power is a clean, alternative energy source.

ICELAND

Bolungarvík, Siglufjórdhur, Raufarhöfn, Ísafjördur, Húsavík, Akureyri, Stykkishólmur, Seydhisfjördhur, REYKJAVÍK, Neskaupstadhur, Selfoss, Djúpivogur, Thorlákshöfn, Hvannadalshnúkur 2119m, Vestmannaeyjar, Surtsey, Faxaflói

Norwegian Sea
Arctic Circle
ATLANTIC OCEAN

SCALE BAR
0 km 100 200
0 miles 100 200

LAND HEIGHT
- 2000–4000 m
- 1000–2000 m
- 500–1000 m
- 250–500 m
- 100–250 m
- 0–100 m

SEA DEPTH
- 0–50 m
- 50–100 m
- 100–250 m
- 250–500 m
- 500–1000 m
- 1000–2000 m
- Below 2000 m

CITIES AND TOWNS
- Over 500,000 people
- 100,000–500,000
- 50,000–100,000
- Less than 50,000

NORWAY
SWEDEN
FINLAND
DENMARK
ESTONIA
LATVIA
LITHUANIA
RUSSIAN FEDERATION
GERMANY
POLAND
BELORUSSIA

OSLO, STOCKHOLM, HELSINKI, COPENHAGEN, TALLINN, RIGA, VILNIUS, KALININGRAD, Bergen, Stavanger, Trondheim, Gothenburg, Malmö, Turku, Tampere, Espoo, Vantaa

North Sea, Norwegian Sea, Baltic Sea, Gulf of Bothnia, Gulf of Finland, Gulf of Riga, Skagerrak, Kattegat, Barents Sea

THE LOW COUNTRIES

BELGIUM, LUXEMBOURG, NETHERLANDS

Belgium, Luxembourg and the Netherlands are called the Low Countries because most of their land is flat and low-lying. Much of the Netherlands lies below sea level, and over hundreds of years the Dutch have built dykes and dams to prevent flooding, and have pumped water off large areas of land to reclaim them from the sea. The Low Countries are Europe's most densely populated countries, but most of their people have a high living standard.

ENVIRONMENTAL ISSUES

Huge land reclamation projects in the Netherlands, such as the IJsselmeer project, have created some new land for agricultural use, and also for houses, roads and open spaces. Heavy industry has caused serious air pollution in cities such as Amsterdam and Rotterdam, and added to Europe's acid rain problem.

ENVIRONMENTAL ISSUES

- Urban air pollution
- Built-up areas
- Reclaimed land
- Polluted river
- Major industrial centre

CLIMATE

The Low Countries share a similar climate, with mild winters and warm summers. Only in the upland Ardennes region does rainfall increase and temperatures decrease.

TEMPERATURE AND PRECIPITATION

- More than 15°C
- 10 to 15°C
- 5 to 10°C
- 0 to 5°C
- Less than 0°C

100 Precipitation (mm)

January

July

Less than 50

Less than 50

100

100

NETHERLANDS' TWO CAPITALS
AMSTERDAM - capital
THE HAGUE - seat of government

LAND HEIGHT

- 500–1000 m
- 250–500 m
- 100–250 m
- 0–100 m
- Below sea level

SEA DEPTH

- 0–100 m

CITIES AND TOWNS

- Over 500,000 people
- 100,000–500,000
- 50,000–100,000
- Less than 50,000

SCALE BAR

0 km   50   100

0 miles   50   100

EUROPE
Low Countries

POPULATION

More than 25 million people live in the Low Countries and nine out of every ten people live in a town or city. The largest urban area – known as the *Randstad Holland* – is in the Netherlands. It runs in an unbroken line from Rotterdam in the south, to Amsterdam in the west. Even most rural areas in the Low Countries are densely populated.

INHABITANTS PER SQ KM

- More than 200
- 100–200
- 50–100
- 0–50
- ■ Capital city
- ● Major city

Groningen
AMSTERDAM
THE HAGUE
Utrecht
Rotterdam
Arnhem
Ghent
Antwerp
BRUSSELS
Liège
Charleroi
LUXEMBOURG

URBAN/RURAL POPULATION DIVIDE

Amsterdam 2.8%
Brussels 3.9%
Rotterdam 2.3%
Rural population 8%
Other towns and cities 83%

FARMING AND LAND USE

The Low Countries' fertile soils and flat plains provide excellent conditions for farming. The main crops grown are barley, potatoes, and flax for making linen. In the Netherlands, much farmland is used for dairy-farming. The country is also famous for growing flowers, which are exported around the world. Flowers and vegetables are grown either in open fields or in enormous greenhouses, which allow production all year round.

Amsterdam
The Hague
Rotterdam
Brussels

LAND USE

Forest 16%
Other (including urban) 29%
Pasture 26%
Cropland 29%

FARMING AND LAND USE

- 🐂 Cattle
- 🐖 Pigs
- 🌾 Cereals
- 🌷 Flowers
- Sugar beet
- Pasture
- Cropland
- Forest
- Wetland
- ● Major conurbation

THE LANDSCAPE

The Low Countries are largely flat and low-lying. The ancient hills of the Ardennes, in the far southeast, are the only higher region. They rise to heights of more than 500 m. Two major rivers – the Meuse and the Rhine – flow across the Low Countries to their mouths in the North Sea. At the coast, the River Rhine deposits large quantities of sediment to form a delta.

Polders

In the Netherlands, land has been reclaimed from the sea since the Middle Ages by building dykes and drainage ditches. These areas of land are called polders. They are very fertile.

The River Rhine (E4)

The River Rhine erodes and carries large amounts of sediment along its course. When it reaches the Netherlands it divides into three rivers. As they approach the North Sea, the rivers slow down, depositing the sediment to form a delta.

Low-lying Netherlands

Over two-thirds of the Netherlands lies at or below sea level. This makes flooding a constant threat in coastal areas.

INDUSTRY

The Low Countries are an important centre for the hi-tech and electronics industries. Good transport links to the rest of Europe allow them to sell their products in other countries. The built-up area stretching from Amsterdam in the Netherlands to Antwerp in Belgium has the greatest number of factories. Luxembourg is also an important banking centre; many international banks have their headquarters in its capital city.

STRUCTURE OF INDUSTRY

Primary 3%
Services 68%
Manufacturing 29%

Groningen
Amsterdam
Enschede
The Hague
Utrecht
Rotterdam
Nijmegen
Breda
Tilburg
Eindhoven
Bruges
Ghent
Antwerp
Brussels
Kortrijk
Liège
Charleroi
Namur
Luxembourg

INDUSTRY

- ✈ Aerospace
- Chemicals
- ⚙ Engineering
- Pharmaceuticals
- 👕 Textiles
- S Finance
- 💻 Hi-tech industry
- Tourism
- ● Major industrial centre / area
- — Major road

Flanders (B 6)

The plains of Flanders in western Belgium have fertile soils which were deposited by glaciers during the last Ice Age. They provide excellent land for growing crops.

Heathlands

The heathlands on the Dutch-Belgian border have thin, sandy soils. The only plants which grow well here are heathers and gorse.

The Ardennes (D 8)

The hills of the Ardennes were formed over 300 million years ago. They have many deep valleys, which have been eroded by rivers like the Meuse.

51

THE BRITISH ISLES

UNITED KINGDOM, REPUBLIC OF IRELAND

The British Isles lie off the northwest coast of mainland Europe. They are made up of two large islands and over 5,000 smaller ones. Politically, the region is divided into two countries: the United Kingdom – England, Wales, Scotland and Northern Ireland – and the Republic of Ireland. Geographically, the British Isles are divided between highlands to the north and west, and lowlands to the south and east.

THE LANDSCAPE

Low rolling hills, high moorlands, and small fields with high hedges are all typical of the British Isles. Ireland is known as the Emerald Isle, because heavy rainfall gives it a lush, green appearance. Scotland and Wales are mountainous; the rocks forming the mountains there are some of the oldest in the world.

Indented coastlines
The west coast of the British Isles faces the Atlantic Ocean, and over 3,000 km of open sea to the North American continent. Storms and high waves constantly batter the hard, rocky coastline, giving it a jagged outline.

Ben Nevis (C 4)
This mountain is the highest point in the British Isles. It is 1,343 m above sea level.

The Lake District (D 5)
The Lake District National Park has England's highest peak, Scafell Pike, at 978 m (E4), its deepest lake, Wast Water (80 m), and its largest lake, Windermere (16 km long).

The Pennines (D 6)
The Pennines are a chain of high hills, topped by moorland. They run for over 400 km, and are known as the 'backbone of England'.

The Burren (A 6)
The Burren is a large area of limestone rock in the west of Ireland. Its flat surfaces are known as limestone 'pavements'. There are also many caves and sinkholes in the area.

Rias
Rias are river valleys that have been drowned by rising sea levels. The southern coast of southwest England has many good examples.

The Fens (E 6)
This is the flattest area in England. Much of the land here has been reclaimed from the sea.

FARMING AND LAND USE

The English lowlands and the wide, flat stretches of land in East Anglia are the agricultural heartland of the United Kingdom. The country is no longer self-sufficient in food, but wheat, potatoes and other vegetables, and fruits, are widely grown. In Ireland, and in central and southern England, dairy and beef cattle feed off grassy pastures. In the hilly and mountainous areas, sheep farming is more usual.

FARMING AND LAND USE

- 🐄 Cattle
- 🐑 Sheep
- 🌾 Cereals
- 🐂 Market gardening
- 🌱 Root crops
- ▢ Pasture
- ▨ Cropland
- ▨ Forest
- ▢ Mountain region
- ● Major conurbation

LAND USE

- Cropland 24%
- Pasture 50%
- Other (including urban) 17%
- Forest 9%

INDUSTRY

The United Kingdom's traditional industries, such as coal mining, iron and steel-making, and textiles, have declined in recent years. Today, newer industries make cars, chemicals, electronic and hi-tech goods. Service industries, especially banking and insurance, have grown in importance. The country's most valuable natural resource is its large North Sea oil and gas fields.

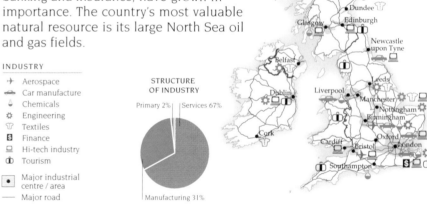

INDUSTRY

- ✈ Aerospace
- 🚗 Car manufacture
- 🧪 Chemicals
- ⚙ Engineering
- 👕 Textiles
- Finance
- 💻 Hi-tech industry
- Tourism
- ● Major industrial centre / area
- — Major road

STRUCTURE OF INDUSTRY

- Primary 2%
- Services 67%
- Manufacturing 31%

POPULATION

The United Kingdom is densely populated, with most of the people living in urban areas. The southeast is the most crowded part of the country. The Scottish Highlands are less populated today than they were 200 years ago. Ireland is still mainly rural, with many Irish people making their living from farming.

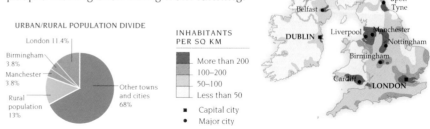

URBAN/RURAL POPULATION DIVIDE

- London 11.4%
- Birmingham 3.8%
- Manchester 3.8%
- Rural population 13%
- Other towns and cities 68%

INHABITANTS PER SQ KM

- ▨ More than 200
- ▨ 100–200
- ▨ 50–100
- ▢ Less than 50
- ■ Capital city
- ● Major city

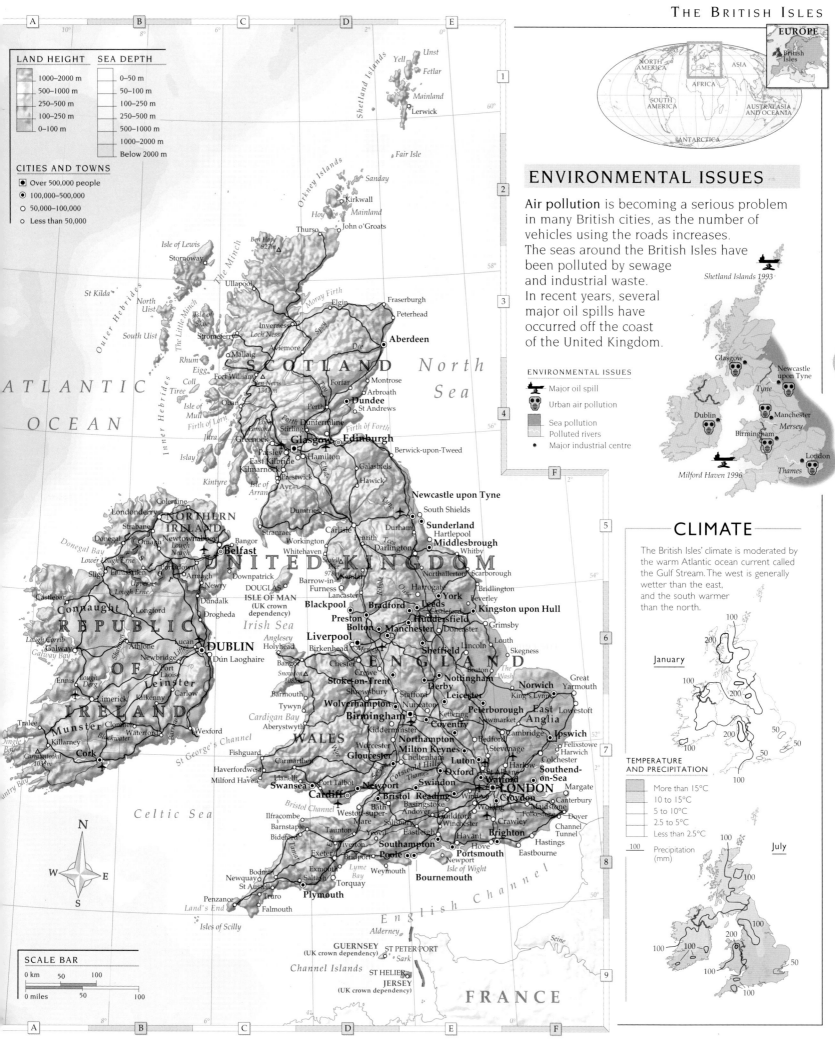

LAND HEIGHT / SEA DEPTH

LAND HEIGHT
- 1000–2000 m
- 500–1000 m
- 250–500 m
- 100–250 m
- 0–100 m

SEA DEPTH
- 0–50 m
- 50–100 m
- 100–250 m
- 250–500 m
- 500–1000 m
- 1000–2000 m
- Below 2000 m

CITIES AND TOWNS
- Over 500,000 people
- 100,000–500,000
- 50,000–100,000
- Less than 50,000

ENVIRONMENTAL ISSUES

Air pollution is becoming a serious problem in many British cities, as the number of vehicles using the roads increases.
The seas around the British Isles have been polluted by sewage and industrial waste.
In recent years, several major oil spills have occurred off the coast of the United Kingdom.

Shetland Islands 1993

Milford Haven 1996

ENVIRONMENTAL ISSUES
- Major oil spill
- Urban air pollution
- Sea pollution
- Polluted rivers
- Major industrial centre

Glasgow
Newcastle upon Tyne
Tyne
Dublin
Manchester
Mersey
Birmingham
London
Thames

CLIMATE

The British Isles' climate is moderated by the warm Atlantic ocean current called the Gulf Stream. The west is generally wetter than the east, and the south warmer than the north.

January

July

TEMPERATURE AND PRECIPITATION
- More than 15°C
- 10 to 15°C
- 5 to 10°C
- 2.5 to 5°C
- Less than 2.5°C

100 Precipitation (mm)

SCALE BAR
0 km   50   100
0 miles   50   100

ATLANTIC OCEAN

North Sea

SCOTLAND

Shetland Islands
Yell
Unst
Fetlar
Mainland
Lerwick

Orkney Islands
Sanday
Kirkwall
Hoy
Mainland
John o'Groats
Thurso

Fair Isle

Isle of Lewis
Stornoway
St Kilda
North Uist
South Uist
Outer Hebrides
The Minch
The Little Minch
Isle of Skye
Ullapool
Ben Hope 927 m
Stromeferry
Loch Ness
Inverness
Moray Firth
Elgin
Fraserburgh
Peterhead
Aviemore
Dee
Aberdeen
Rhum
Eigg
Coll
Tiree
Mallaig
Fort William
Ben Nevis 1344 m
Loch Lomond
Spey
Forfar
Montrose
Arbroath
Isle of Mull
Oban
Perth
Dundee
St Andrews
Jura
Loch Fyne
Firth of Lorn
Forth
Dunfermline
Stirling
Islay
Greenock
Glasgow
Edinburgh
Paisley
East Kilbride
Hamilton
Kilmarnock
Prestwick
Galashiels
Berwick-upon-Tweed
Isle of Arran
Ayr
Hawick
Kintyre

NORTHERN IRELAND
Coleraine
Londonderry
Strabane
Newtownabbey
Bangor
Omagh
Lough Neagh
Belfast
Donegal
Dumfries
Carlisle
Newcastle upon Tyne
South Shields
Sunderland
Hartlepool
Middlesbrough
Whitby
Stranraer
Workington
Whitehaven
Penrith
Durham
Darlington
Tees
Northallerton
Scarborough
Armagh
Downpatrick
Newry
Barrow-in-Furness
Lancaster
Bridlington
Beverley

DOUGLAS
ISLE OF MAN
(UK crown dependency)

REPUBLIC OF IRELAND

Donegal Bay
Sligo
Enniskillen
Lower Lough Erne
Upper Lough Erne
Castlebar
Connaught
Longford
Dundalk
Drogheda
Lough Corrib
Galway
Galway Bay
Athlone
Shannon
Lucan
DUBLIN
Dún Laoghaire
Ennis
Lough Derg
Limerick
Leinster
Newbridge
Port Laoise
Carlow
Kilkenny
Tralee
Munster
Killarney
Carrauntoohil 1036 m
Dingle Bay
Bantry Bay
Cork
Waterford
Wexford
Blackwater

UNITED KINGDOM
ENGLAND
WALES

Blackpool
Preston
Bolton
Bradford
Leeds
York
Huddersfield
Halifax
Castleford
Doncaster
Grimsby
Liverpool
Birkenhead
Manchester
Sheffield
Lincoln
Louth
Skegness
Holyhead
Anglesey
Bangor
Chester
Crewe
Nottingham
Derby
The Wash
Boston
King's Lynn
Snowdon 1085 m
Stoke-on-Trent
Shrewsbury
Stafford
Leicester
Norwich
Great Yarmouth
Barmouth
Wolverhampton
Nuneaton
Peterborough
East Anglia
Lowestoft
Tywyn
Birmingham
Coventry
Kettering
Newmarket
Cardigan Bay
Kidderminster
Northampton
Cambridge
Ipswich
Aberystwyth
Worcester
Milton Keynes
Bedford
Stevenage
Felixstowe
Harwich
Gloucester
Cheltenham
Cotswold Hills
Luton
Harlow
Colchester
Fishguard
Carmarthen
Wye
Oxford
St Albans
Southend-on-Sea
Haverfordwest
Llanelli
Swindon
Watford
LONDON
Margate
Milford Haven
Port Talbot
Swansea
Cardiff
Newport
Bristol
Reading
Croydon
Canterbury
Bath
Basingstoke
Woking
Maidstone
Folkestone
Dover
Ilfracombe
Weston-super-Mare
Andover
Guildford
Crawley
Channel Tunnel
Barnstaple
Taunton
Salisbury
Winchester
Bideford
Tiverton
Yeovil
Eastleigh
Havant
Brighton
Hove
Hastings
Exeter
Southampton
Portsmouth
Eastbourne
Bridport
Poole
Newport
Bournemouth
Exmouth
Lyme Bay
Weymouth
Isle of Wight
Bodmin
Newquay
St Austell
Saltash
Torquay
Penzance
Truro
Plymouth
Land's End
Falmouth
Isles of Scilly

Irish Sea
St George's Channel
Celtic Sea
Bristol Channel
English Channel

Alderney
Seine
GUERNSEY
(UK crown dependency)
ST PETER PORT
Sark
Channel Islands
ST HELIER
JERSEY
(UK crown dependency)

FRANCE

N
W   E
S

FRANCE

ANDORRA, MONACO, FRANCE

France has helped to shape the history and culture of Europe for centuries. Today, as a founder-member of the European Union, France is a keen supporter of the eventual political and economic integration of Europe's different countries. France is Western Europe's leading farming nation, and one of the world's top industrial powers. Its cultural attractions and scenery draw tourists from around the world.

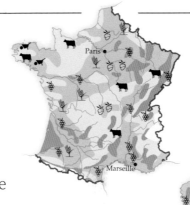

FARMING AND LAND USE

France is able to produce a variety of crops because of its rich soils and mild climate. Wheat is grown in many parts of the north, along with potatoes and other vegetables. Fields of maize and sunflowers and fruit orchards, are found in the south, while grapes for the famous wine industry are grown across the country. Beef and dairy cattle are grazed on low-lying pasture.

FARMING AND LAND USE

- 🐄 Cattle
- 🌾 Cereals
- 🥬 Market gardening
- 🌿 Root crops
- 🍇 Vineyards
- Pasture
- Cropland
- Forest
- Mountain region
- Wetland
- • Major conurbation

LAND USE

- Cropland 35%
- Pasture 20%
- Forest 27%
- Other (including urban) 18%

THE LANDSCAPE

The north and west of France is made up of mainly flat, grassy plains or low hills. Wooded mountains line the country's borders in the south and east, and much of central France is taken up by the Massif Central, an enormous plateau, cut by deep river valleys and scattered with extinct volcanoes. Three major rivers, the Loire, Seine and Garonne drain the lowland basins.

Paris Basin
The Paris Basin is a saucer-shaped hollow made up of layers of hard and soft rock, covered with very fertile soils. It runs across about 100,000 sq km of northern France.

Alps (E 5)
The western end of the European Alpine mountain chain stretches into southeast France. The French Alps can be crossed by several passes, which give access to Italy and Switzerland.

Normandy
The coast of Normandy is lined with high chalk cliffs.

INDUSTRY

France is one of the world's top manufacturing nations, with a variety of both traditional and hi-tech industries. Cars, machinery and electronic products are exported worldwide, along with luxury goods such as perfumes, fashions and fine wines. Fossil fuels provide some energy, but France is currently the world's second-biggest producer of nuclear power.

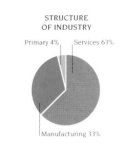

STRUCTURE OF INDUSTRY

- Primary 4%
- Services 63%
- Manufacturing 33%

INDUSTRY

- ✈ Aerospace
- 🚗 Car manufacture
- ⚗ Chemicals
- ⚙ Engineering
- 👕 Textiles
- 💻 Hi-tech industry
- 🧳 Tourism
- • Major industrial centre / area
- — Major road

POPULATION

In the past 50 years, most people have moved from the countryside into urban areas. Paris and its suburbs, the industrial cities, and the Côte d'Azur in the southeast are the most economically developed parts of France and now have the biggest populations.

URBAN/RURAL POPULATION DIVIDE

- Paris 16.6%
- Lyon 2.3%
- Marseille 1.5%
- Rural population 26%
- Other towns and cities 53.6%

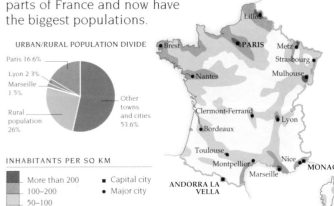

INHABITANTS PER SQ KM

- More than 200
- 100–200
- 50–100
- Less than 50
- ■ Capital city
- • Major city

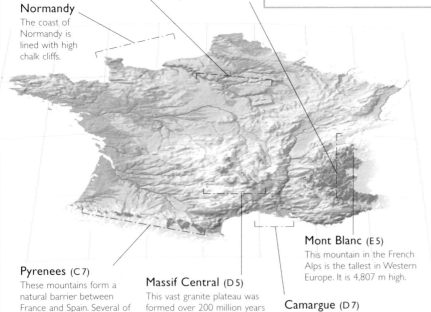

Pyrenees (C 7)
These mountains form a natural barrier between France and Spain. Several of their peaks reach heights of over 3,000 m. The Pyrenees are difficult to cross, due to their height, and because they have few low passes.

Massif Central (D 5)
This vast granite plateau was formed over 200 million years ago. Volcanic activity here only stopped within the last 10,000 years and the region's rounded hills are the worn down remains of volcanic mountains.

Mont Blanc (E 5)
This mountain in the French Alps is the tallest in Western Europe. It is 4,807 m high.

Camargue (D 7)
The Camargue is an area of marshes, pastures, sand dunes and salt flats at the mouth of the River Rhône. Rare animal and plant species are found there.

ENVIRONMENTAL ISSUES

Many of France's coastal areas have been polluted by industry and tourism. The French government has recently introduced policies which aim to protect the country's environment. France's reliance on nuclear energy – 75% of its electricity is generated by nuclear power – means that it suffers less from the pollution caused by burning fossil fuels than many other countries in Europe.

ENVIRONMENTAL ISSUES
- Nuclear power station
- Sea pollution
- Polluted rivers
- Major industrial centre

EUROPE

CLIMATE

In winter, the coldest areas of France are the mountains of the Massif Central, and the Alps. Summers are hottest on the Mediterranean coast.

TEMPERATURE AND PRECIPITATION
- More than 20°C
- 15 to 20°C
- 10 to 15°C
- 5 to 10°C
- 0 to 5°C
- 0 to -5°C
- Less than -5°C
- 100 Precipitation (mm)

January

July

SCALE BAR
0 km 50 100
0 miles 50 100

LAND HEIGHT
- Above 4000 m
- 2000–4000 m
- 1000–2000 m
- 500–1000 m
- 250–500 m
- 100–250 m
- 0–100 m

SEA DEPTH
- 0–50 m
- 50–100 m
- 100–250 m
- 250–500 m
- 500–1000 m
- 1000–2000 m
- Below 2000 m

CITIES AND TOWNS
- Over 500,000 people
- 100,000–500,000
- 50,000–100,000
- Less than 50,000

SPAIN AND PORTUGAL

PORTUGAL, SPAIN

Spain and Portugal occupy the Iberian Peninsula, which is cut off from the rest of Europe by the Pyrenees. Over the centuries, Iberia has been invaded and settled by many different peoples. The Moors, who arrived from North Africa in the 8th century, ruled much of Spain for almost 800 years and their influence can still be seen in Spanish culture. Portugal is one of the poorest countries in western Europe, but Spain's economy is rapidly expanding.

FARMING AND LAND USE

Cereals, especially wheat and barley, are Iberia's chief crops. In the dry south of Spain, the land is irrigated to grow citrus fruits, especially oranges, and vegetables. In both countries, olive trees and vineyards occupy large areas of land; olive oil and wine are important exports. Cork oak trees from Iberia's forests supply 80% of the world's cork.

FARMING AND LAND USE

- 🐑 Sheep
- 🌾 Cereals
- 🍊 Citrus fruit
- 🫒 Olive oil
- 🍇 Vineyards
- 🌰 Cork
- ⬜ Pasture
- ▨ Cropland
- ▦ Forest
- ⬜ Mountain region
- ● Major conurbation

LAND USE

Other 10%
Cropland 39%
Forest 33%
Pasture 18%

INDUSTRY

Madrid, Barcelona and the northern ports are Spain's industrial centres. Here, iron ore from Spanish mines is used to make steel, and factories produce cars, machinery and chemicals. Portugal exports textiles, clothing and footwear, along with fish such as sardines and tuna, caught off the Atlantic coast. In both countries, tourism is very important to the economy.

STRUCTURE OF INDUSTRY

Primary 5%
Services 62%
Manufacturing 33%

INDUSTRY

- 🚗 Car manufacture
- 🧪 Chemicals
- ⚙ Engineering
- Fish processing
- Shipbuilding
- 👕 Textiles
- ● Mining
- 🛈 Tourism
- ▣ Major industrial centre / area
- — Major road

THE LANDSCAPE

Most of inland Spain is taken up by the Meseta, a dry, almost treeless plateau surrounded by steep mountain ranges. The only lowlands, apart from narrow strips along the Mediterranean coast, are the valleys of the Ebro, Tagus, Guadiana and Guadalquivir rivers. Portugal's coast is lined by wide plains. Inland, the River Tagus divides the country in two. To the north the land is hilly and wooded; to the south it is low-lying and drier.

Westward-flowing rivers
The Duero, Tagus and Guadalquivir rivers flow across the Meseta on their courses to the Atlantic Ocean.

River Ebro (E 2)
The River Ebro carries vital irrigation water to Spain's northeastern plains before flowing into the Mediterranean Sea.

Cordillera Cantábrica (C 1)
These rugged, forested mountains rise on Spain's Atlantic coast. They form the northern edge of the Meseta.

The Pyrenees (F 2)
These high mountains form a natural boundary with France.

River Duero (D 2)

River Tagus (B 4)

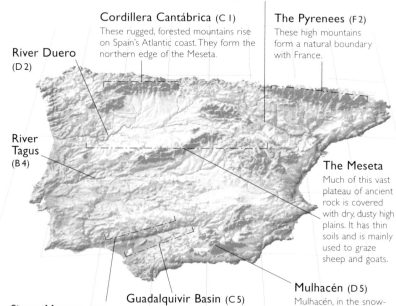

The Meseta
Much of this vast plateau of ancient rock is covered with dry, dusty high plains. It has thin soils and is mainly used to graze sheep and goats.

Mulhacén (D 5)
Mulhacén, in the snow-capped Sierra Nevada range in southern Spain, is 3,481 m high. It is Iberia's tallest mountain.

Sierra Morena (C 5)
The southern end of the Meseta is marked by this low range of mountains.

Guadalquivir Basin (C 5)
The River Guadalquivir has deposited layers of rich soil called alluvium on its flood plain, making this one of Spain's most fertile regions.

POPULATION

In the first half of the 20th century, most Spaniards lived in villages or small towns, scattered around the country. Today, tourism and industry have drawn most of the population to the cities and coastal areas. Most Portuguese still live in rural areas along the coast or in the river valleys, but the cities are growing fast.

URBAN/RURAL POPULATION DIVIDE

Madrid 7.8%
Barcelona 6.8%
Lisbon 3.4%
Other towns and cities 52%
Rural population 30%

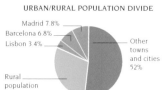

INHABITANTS PER SQ KM

- ▨ More than 200
- ▨ 100–200
- ▨ 50–100
- ⬜ Less than 50
- ■ Capital city
- ● Major city

ENVIRONMENTAL ISSUES

Soil erosion – where the top layer of soil has been worn away by wind and rain – has affected much of the Iberian Peninsula. This is caused by farming, combined with drought and deforestation. In Spain, a national tree-planting scheme has been started to combat this problem. Industrial and tourist development along the Mediterranean coast of Spain, and in the Balearic Islands, has damaged natural habitats on both land and sea.

ENVIRONMENTAL ISSUES

- Overbuilding
- Soil degradation
- Severe soil degradation
- Polluted rivers

CLIMATE

Northern Spain is wetter and cooler than the south. On the central plateau, summers are very hot and dry, and winters often freezing. The north of Portugal is cooled by winds blowing off the Atlantic Ocean. The south is warmer, with dry, mild winters.

TEMPERATURE AND PRECIPITATION

- More than 25°C
- 20 to 25°C
- 15 to 20°C
- 10 to 15°C
- 5 to 10°C
- 0 to 5°C
- 0 to -5°C
- -5 to -10°C
- Less than -10°C

100 — Precipitation (mm)

GERMANY AND THE ALPINE STATES

AUSTRIA, GERMANY, LIECHTENSTEIN, SLOVENIA, SWITZERLAND

Germany lies at the heart of Europe and is the biggest industrial power in the continent. In 1945, Germany was divided into two separate countries, East and West Germany, which were reunited in 1990. To the south, the snow-capped peaks of the Alps, Europe's highest mountains, tower over the Alpine states – Switzerland, Austria, Liechtenstein and the former Yugoslavian state of Slovenia.

INDUSTRY

Germany is a leading manufacturer of cars, chemicals, machinery and transport equipment. Switzerland and Liechtenstein, with few raw materials, make high-value products such as watches and pharmaceuticals, and provide services such as banking. The Alpine states are a popular tourist location all year round.

INDUSTRY

- 🚗 Car manufacture
- ⚗ Chemicals
- ⚙ Engineering
- ⚒ Iron & steel
- ⚓ Shipbuilding
- ⚗ Pharmaceuticals
- 💻 Hi-tech industry
- 🛏 Tourism

▪ Major industrial centre / area

— Major road

STRUCTURE OF INDUSTRY

Primary 1%   Services 62%

Manufacturing 37%

POPULATION

Western and central Germany are the most densely populated areas in this region – particularly in and around the Rhine and Ruhr valleys, where there are many industries. In the south, the steep slopes of the Alps and permanent snow cover on the higher peaks means that most large towns and cities are in scattered lowland areas.

INHABITANTS PER SQ KM

- More than 200
- 100–200
- 50–100
- Less than 50

- ▪ Capital city
- • Major city

URBAN/RURAL POPULATION DIVIDE

Vienna 1.4%   Berlin 3.6%
Munich 1%
Rural population 18%
Other towns and cities 76%

FARMING AND LAND USE

Germany produces three-quarters of its own food. Crop farming is widespread, with cereals and root crops grown in flat, fertile areas. Cattle and pig farming supplies meat and dairy products. Across the Alps, the mountains limit farming, although vines are grown on the warmer, south-facing slopes. The rich pastures of the lower slopes are used to graze beef and dairy cattle.

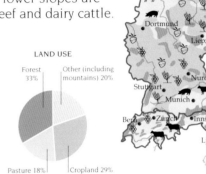

FARMING AND LAND USE

- 🐄 Cattle
- 🐖 Pigs
- 🌾 Cereals
- Root crops
- Vineyards

Pasture
Cropland
Forest
Mountain region
• Major conurbation

LAND USE

Forest 33%   Other (including mountains) 20%

Pasture 18%   Cropland 29%

THE LANDSCAPE

To the north, flat plains and heathlands surround the North Sea coast. Further south are Germany's central uplands, which are lower and older than the jagged peaks of the Alps, which began to form about 65 million years ago. From its source in the Black Forest, the River Danube flows eastward across Germany and Austria on its course to the Black Sea. The other major river, the Rhine, flows northward.

The Harz mountains (C 4)
These rugged, wooded mountains are much older than the Alps. They were formed over 300 million years ago.

The River Rhine (B 5)
The Rhine is Germany's main waterway. It is an important transport route to and from northern ports. It twists and turns across 1,320 km of Europe, from its source in southeast Switzerland, to the North Sea.

Karst region (E 8)
Most of the water in this limestone region of Slovenia flows underground, through huge caves and caverns.

The Danube (B 7)
The Danube is Europe's second longest river, flowing 2,840 km.

Lake Constance (B 7)
Lake Constance covers 540 sq km and is Germany's largest lake, although its waters are shared by Austria and Switzerland.

The Alps (C 8)
The Alps were formed when the African Plate collided with the Eurasian Plate, pushing up and crushing huge amounts of rock, to form mountains.

EUROPE

Germany and the Alpine States

SCALE BAR

0 km 50 100

0 miles 50 100

CITIES AND TOWNS
- ■ Over 500,000 people
- ● 100,000–500,000
- ○ 50,000–100,000
- ○ Less than 50,000

ENVIRONMENTAL ISSUES

The large number of industries in Germany, especially in the east of the country, has led to high levels of pollution in cities, and in rivers like the Rhine. Acid rain from car fumes and industrial pollution has poisoned many of Germany's forests. The popularity of the Alps as a year-round tourist destination puts great demands on the environment. The development of new resorts has destroyed the natural habitats of many plants and animals.

ENVIRONMENTAL ISSUES
- Urban air pollution
- Winter tourist resort
- Affected by acid rain
- Polluted rivers
- Major industrial centre

CLIMATE

Winter temperatures decrease eastwards, and the high Alpine region is coldest. Rainfall is higher in the summer. Climate variations in the Alps are common, due to turbulent air flows.

January

July

TEMPERATURE AND PRECIPITATION
- More than 20°C
- 15 to 20°C
- 10 to 15°C
- 5 to 10°C
- 0 to 5°C
- 0 to -5°C
- -5 to -10°C
- Less than -10°C

100 Precipitation (mm)

LAND HEIGHT
- Above 4000 m
- 2000–4000 m
- 1000–2000 m
- 500–1000 m
- 250–500 m
- 100–250 m
- 0–100 m

SEA DEPTH
- 0–10 m
- 10–25 m
- 25–50 m
- 50–100 m

59

ITALY

ITALY, SAN MARINO, VATICAN CITY

Italy has played an important role in Europe since the Romans based their mighty empire here over 2,000 years ago. The famous boot shape divides into two very different halves. Northern Italy has a varied range of industries and agriculture. Beautiful cities like Venice, Florence, and Rome draw tourists from all over the world. Southern Italy is poorer and less developed than the north, with a hotter, drier climate and less productive land.

THE LANDSCAPE

Italy is a peninsula jutting south from mainland Europe into the Mediterranean Sea. In northern and central Italy the land is mainly mountainous. Most of the flat land is in the Po Valley and along the eastern coast. Italy lies within an earthquake zone, which makes the land unstable, and there are also a number of active volcanoes.

Italian lakes
Great lakes like Garda (B3) and Como (B2) fill several south-facing valleys once occupied by glaciers.

The Dolomites (D 2)
These high mountains are part of the same range as the Alps. They were formed 65 million years ago.

Po Valley (C 2)
The basin of the River Po has the best soils in Italy. Rich alluvium is washed from the mountains by the river to form a wide plain.

The Apennines (C 4)
This mountain range forms the 'backbone' of Italy, dividing the rocky west coast from the flatter, sandy east coast.

Tyrrhenian Sea (C 6)
This sea, which divides the Italian mainland from Sardinia, is gradually filling with sediment from the rivers which flow into it.

Earthquakes
The southern Apennines, as well as coastal areas of southwestern Italy, often experience earthquakes and mudslides.

Sardinia
The island of Sardinia is made from very old rocks which were thrust up to form mountains.

Sicily
Sicily is the largest island in the Mediterranean. It has a famous active volcano called Mount Etna, and often experiences earthquakes

Gulf of Taranto (F 7)
During earthquakes, great blocks of land have broken away and sunk into the sea, forming the Gulf's square shape.

FARMING AND LAND USE

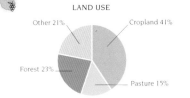

The Po Valley is a broad, flat plain in the north of Italy. It contains the most fertile land in the country, and wheat and rice are the main cereal crops grown here. Grapes for wine are grown everywhere in Italy. In much of the south, the land must be irrigated to support crops. Where there is enough water, citrus fruits, olives, and many kinds of tomatoes are grown.

LAND USE

Other 21%
Cropland 41%
Forest 23%
Pasture 15%

FARMING AND LAND USE

- Cattle
- Cereals
- Citrus fruits
- Olive oil
- Rice
- Vineyards
- Pasture
- Cropland
- Forest
- Mountain region
- Major conurbation

INDUSTRY

Italian industry is located mainly in the north. Design is extremely important to Italians and they are proud of the elegant designs of their furniture, clothes and shoes. Though many firms are small, they are very efficient. Italy has few mineral resources so it needs to import raw materials to make cars, engines and other hi-tech products.

INDUSTRY

- Car manufacture
- Chemicals
- Iron & steel
- Textiles
- Finance
- Hi-tech industry
- Tourism
- ● Major industrial centre / area
- — Major road

STRUCTURE OF INDUSTRY

Primary 3%
Services 66%
Manufacturing 31%

POPULATION

Most of Italy's population lives in the north, mainly in and around the Po Valley, which is home to over 25 million people. Most people here have a high standard of living. Southern Italy is much more rural; towns are smaller and life is often much harder.

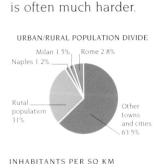

URBAN/RURAL POPULATION DIVIDE

Milan 1.5%
Rome 2.8%
Naples 1.2%
Rural population 31%
Other towns and cities 63.5%

INHABITANTS PER SQ KM

- More than 200
- 100–200
- 50–100
- 0–50
- ■ Capital city
- ● Major city

Map labels and place names

Grid references (top): A B C D E
Longitude (top): 6° 8° 10° 48° 12° 14° N E

Countries and regions
GERMANY
SWITZERLAND
LIECHTENSTEIN
AUSTRIA
SLOVENIA
CROATIA
FRANCE
MONACO
TUNISIA
MALTA

Water features
Lake Constance
Lake Geneva
Lake Maggiore
Lake Como
Lake Garda
Ligurian Sea
Gulf of Genoa
Gulf of Venice
Adriatic Sea
Tyrrhenian Sea
Ionian Sea
Mediterranean Sea
Strait of Bonifacio
Strait of Sicily
Strait of Messina
Strait of Otranto
Gulf of Gaeta
Gulf of Salerno
Gulf of Taranto
Malta Channel
Rhône
Rhine
Inn
Drava (Drau)
Mur
Arno
Adige
Istra

Mountains and passes
Mont Blanc 4807m
Great Saint Bernard Pass
le Saint Bernard Pass 2188m
Gran Paradiso 4061m
Monte Etna 3340m
Vesuvio 1277m
Punta La Marmora 1834m
Bremner Pass 1374m
Dolomites
Alps
Apennines

Cities and towns
Bolzano, Bressanone, Merano, Cortina d'Ampezzo, Tarvisio
Trento, Edolo, Arco, Gemona del Friuli
Bergamo, Monza, Como, Varese, Novara, Vercelli
Turin (Torino), Rivoli, Moncalieri, Susa, Asti
Milan (Milano), Brescia, Pavia, Casteggio
Vicenza, Verona, Padua (Padova), Mestre, Venice (Venezia)
Treviso, Udine, Pordenone, Bassano del Grappa, Monselice, Monfalcone, Portogruaro, Trieste
Piacenza, Parma, Cremona, Mantova, Ostiglia, Rovigo, Chioggia
Genoa (Genova), Reggio nell' Emilia, Modena, Bologna, Ferrara, Comacchio
Savona, Alessandria, Savigliano, Cuneo, Mondovi, Imperia, San Remo, Ventimiglia, Finale Ligure
La Spezia, Carrara, Massa, Viareggio, Pistoia, Prato, Lucca, Pisa, Livorno, Cecina
Faenza, Forlì, Ravenna, Rimini, Cesena, Imola
Florence (Firenze), Arezzo, Siena, Pesaro, Fano, San Marino
Piombino, Portoferraio, Grosseto, Orbetello, Perugia, Foligno, Viterbo
Falconara Marittima, Ancona, Civitanova Marche, Fermo, Ascoli Piceno, Giulianova
Terni, Teramo, L'Aquila, Chieti, Pescara, Ortona, Avezzano
Civitavecchia, Tivoli, ROME (ROMA), VATICAN CITY, Anzio, Latina, Terracina, Gaeta
Termoli, Isernia, Campobasso, San Severo, Manfredonia
Naples (Napoli), Torre del Greco, Caserta, Benevento, Avellino, Salerno, Battipaglia, Agropoli, Sala Consilina
Foggia, Cerignola, Barletta, Andria, Bitonto, Molfetta, Bari, Altamura, Potenza, Matera
Taranto, Brindisi, Lecce, Manduria, Maglie, Gallipoli
Cosenza, Amantea, Rossano, Ciro Marina, Crotone, Lamezia, Catanzaro, Castrovillari, Sapri, Lauria
Reggio di Calabria, Palmi, Siderno, Messina
Palermo, Trapani, Marsala, Alcamo, Cefalù, Castelvetrano, Agrigento, Caltanissetta, Gela, Vittoria, Ragusa, Modica, Catania, Siracusa, Pozzallo
Sassari, Alghero, Porto Torres, Tempio Pausania, Olbia, Ozieri, Nuoro, Macomer, Oristano, Villacidro Iglesias, Carbonia, Cagliari, Quartu Sant'Elena, Siniscola

Islands
Corsica (Corse) (part of France)
Sardinia (Sardegna)
Sicily (Sicilia)
Elba
Asinara
la Maddalena
Ponziane Is.
Capri
Ustica
Aeolian Islands, Stromboli, Lipari, Vulcano
Egadi Is.
Pantelleria
Pelagie
Archipelago Toscano
Lago Trasimeno

Regions
Piedmont (Piemonte)
Lombardy (Lombardia)
Tuscany (Toscana)
Campania
Apulia (Puglia)
Dalmatia

Seas labels (other)
Gulf of Venice

Locator maps (top right)
EUROPE
Italy
NORTH AMERICA, SOUTH AMERICA, AFRICA, ASIA, AUSTRALASIA AND OCEANIA, ANTARCTICA

ENVIRONMENTAL ISSUES

Sewage and chemical by-products from industry have polluted the Mediterranean and Adriatic seas. In many northern cities, severe air pollution is a health hazard. Southern Italy is subject to natural dangers like earthquakes and mudslides.

Earthquake locations: Turin, Milan, Genoa, Gemona del Friuli 1976, Ancona 1972, Tuscania 1971, L'Aquila 1980, Rome, Isernia 1984, Irpino 1980, Naples, Palermo, Belice 1968, Sicily, Siracusa 1990

ENVIRONMENTAL ISSUES (legend)
- ⊚ Catastrophic earthquakes
- Urban air pollution
- Acid rain
- Sea pollution
- • Major industrial centre

CLIMATE

The Alpine north has cold winters, often with snow. Further south, temperatures are higher. Sicily has Italy's highest temperatures, due to warm African winds.

January
July

TEMPERATURE AND PRECIPITATION
- More than 25°C
- 20 to 25°C
- 15 to 20°C
- 10 to 15°C
- 5 to 10°C
- 0 to 5°C
- 0 to -5°C
- -5 to -10°C
- Less than -10°C

Less than 50
100 Precipitation (mm)

SCALE BAR
0 km   40   80
0 miles   40   80

CITIES AND TOWNS
- ◼ Over 500,000 people
- ◉ 100,000–500,000
- ○ 50,000–100,000
- ∘ Less than 50,000

LAND HEIGHT
- Above 4000m
- 2000–4000 m
- 1000–2000 m
- 500–1000 m
- 250–500 m
- 100–250 m
- 0–100 m

SEA DEPTH
- 0–50 m
- 50–100 m
- 100–250 m
- 250–500 m
- 500–1000 m
- 1000–2000 m
- Below 2000 m

CENTRAL EUROPE

CZECH REPUBLIC, HUNGARY, POLAND, SLOVAKIA

Central Europe has been invaded many times throughout history. The countries have changed shape frequently as their borders have shifted backwards and forwards. From the end of the Second World War until 1989, they were ruled by communist governments, which were supported by the Soviet Union. In 1993, the state of Czechoslovakia voted to split into two separate nations, called the Czech Republic and Slovakia.

FARMING AND LAND USE

Central Europe's main crops are cereals such as maize, wheat and rye, along with sugar beet and potatoes. In Hungary, sweet peppers grow, helped by the warm summers and mild winters. They are used to make paprika. Grapes are also grown, to make wine. Large areas of the plains of Hungary and Poland are used for rearing pigs and cattle. Trees for timber grow in the mountains of Slovakia and the Czech Republic.

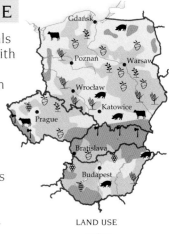

FARMING AND LAND USE

- 🐂 Cattle
- 🐖 Pigs
- 🌿 Cereals
- 🌱 Root crops
- 🌿 Potatoes
- 🌾 Timber
- ⬜ Pasture
- ⬜ Cropland
- ⬛ Forest
- • Major conurbation

LAND USE

Other 11%
Cropland 47%
Forest 29%
Pasture 13%

INDUSTRY

Brown coal, or lignite, is central Europe's main fuel, and one of Poland's major exports. A variety of minerals are mined in the mountains of the Czech Republic and Slovakia. Hungary has a wide range of industries producing vehicles, metals, and chemicals, as well as textiles and electrical goods. The Czech Republic is famous for its breweries and glass-making.

STRUCTURE OF INDUSTRY

Primary 6%
Services 56%
Manufacturing 38%

INDUSTRY

- 🍺 Brewing
- 🚗 Car manufacture
- ⚗ Chemicals
- ⚙ Engineering
- 🍴 Food processing
- Iron & steel
- ⛏ Coal mining
- ◉ Major industrial centre / area
- — Major road

THE LANDSCAPE

The high Carpathian Mountains sweep across northern Slovakia. The lower Sudeten Mountains lie on the border of the Czech Republic and Poland. Together, these mountains form a barrier which divides the Great Hungarian Plain and the River Danube basin in the south from Poland and the vast rolling lowlands of the North European Plain.

Pomerania (C 2)

This is a sandy coastal area with lakes formed by glaciers. It stretches west from the River Vistula to just beyond the German border.

River Vistula (F 4)

Poland's largest river is the Vistula. It flows northwards, passing through the capital, Warsaw, on its way to the Baltic Sea.

North European Plain

Hot springs

The Sudeten mountains (C5) are famous for their hot mineral springs. These occur where water heated deep within the Earth's crust finds its way to the surface along fractures in the rock.

ENVIRONMENTAL ISSUES

The growth of heavy industries that took place under communist rule has caused terrible environmental pollution in some places. Hungary's oil and Poland's brown coal have a high sulphur content. Burning these fuels to produce electricity causes air pollution, and the sulphur dioxide produced combines with moisture in the air, leading to acid rain.

ENVIRONMENTAL ISSUES

- 😷 Severe industrial pollution
- 😷 Urban air pollution
- ⬜ Affected by acid rain
- ～ Polluted rivers
- • Major industrial centre

River Danube (D 7)

The River Danube forms the border between Slovakia and Hungary for over 162 km. It then turns south to flow across the Great Hungarian Plain.

Great Hungarian Plain (E 8)

This huge plain covers almost half of Hungary's land area. It is a mixture of farmland and steppe.

Tatra Mountains (E 6)

The Tatra Mountains are a small range at the northern end of the Carpathian Mountains. They include Gerlachovský Stít, which is Central Europe's highest point at 2,655 m.

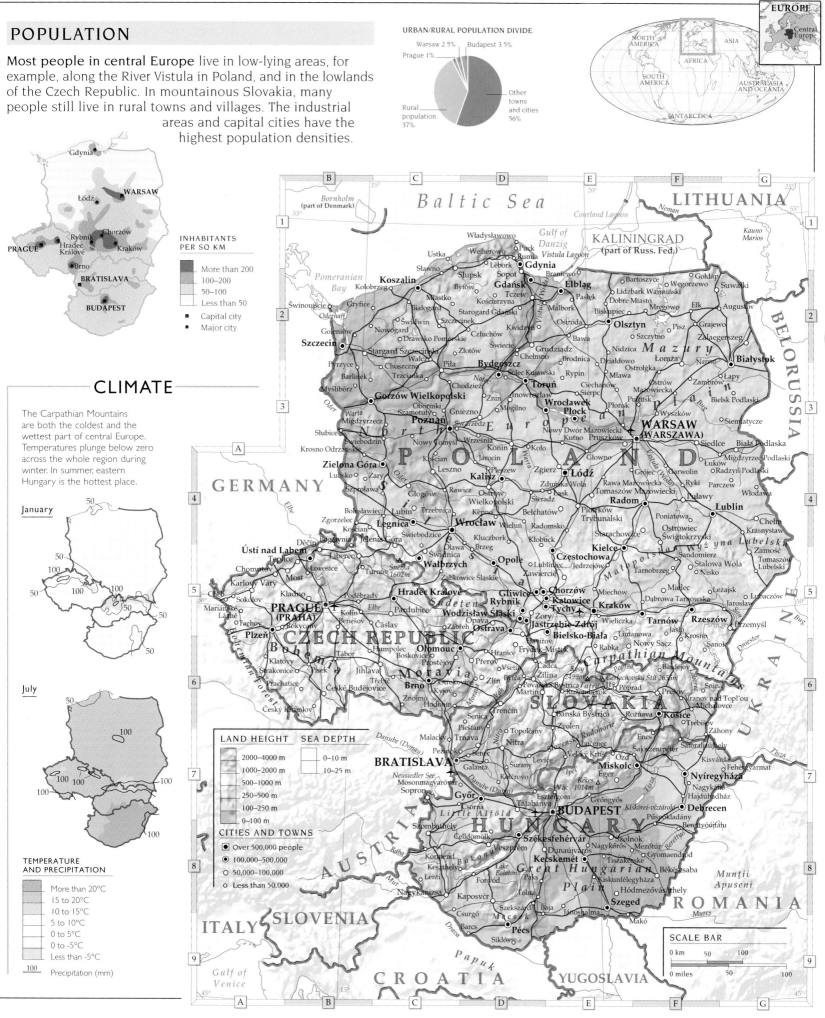

POPULATION

Most people in central Europe live in low-lying areas, for example, along the River Vistula in Poland, and in the lowlands of the Czech Republic. In mountainous Slovakia, many people still live in rural towns and villages. The industrial areas and capital cities have the highest population densities.

URBAN/RURAL POPULATION DIVIDE

Warsaw 2.5%
Budapest 3.5%
Prague 1%
Rural population 37%
Other towns and cities 56%

EUROPE
Central Europe

NORTH AMERICA
ASIA
AFRICA
SOUTH AMERICA
AUSTRALASIA AND OCEANIA
ANTARCTICA

INHABITANTS PER SQ KM

More than 200
100–200
50–100
Less than 50

■ Capital city
● Major city

Gdynia
ŁÓDŹ
WARSAW
Rybnik
Chorzów
PRAGUE
Hradec Králové
Kraków
Brno
BRATISLAVA
BUDAPEST

CLIMATE

The Carpathian Mountains are both the coldest and the wettest part of central Europe. Temperatures plunge below zero across the whole region during winter. In summer, eastern Hungary is the hottest place.

January

July

TEMPERATURE AND PRECIPITATION

More than 20°C
15 to 20°C
10 to 15°C
5 to 10°C
0 to 5°C
0 to -5°C
Less than -5°C

100 Precipitation (mm)

LAND HEIGHT

2000–4000 m
1000–2000 m
500–1000 m
250–500 m
100–250 m
0–100 m

SEA DEPTH

0–10 m
10–25 m

CITIES AND TOWNS

● Over 500,000 people
● 100,000–500,000
○ 50,000–100,000
○ Less than 50,000

SCALE BAR

0 km   50   100
0 miles   50   100

Map labels

Baltic Sea
Bornholm (part of Denmark)
LITHUANIA
Gulf of Danzig
Courland Lagoon
Neman
KALININGRAD (part of Russ. Fed.)
Kauno Marios
Vistula Lagoon
Władysławowo
Ustka
Wejherowo
Puck
Rumia
Gdynia
Sopot
Braniewo
Bartoszyce
Gołdap
Słupsk
Lębork
Gdańsk
Tczew
Elbląg
Lidzbark Warmiński
Wegorzewo
Suwałki
Koszalin
Bytów
Kościerzyna
Starogard Gdański
Malbork
Pasłek
Dobre Miasto
Mrągowo
Ełk
Augustów
Kołobrzeg
Miastko
Olsztyn
Biskupiec
Grajewo
Świnoujście
Gryfice
Białogard
Szczecinek
Kwidzyn
Ostróda
Nidzica
Szczytno
Pisz
Zalaegerszeg
Goleniów
Świdwin
Nowogard
Drawsko Pomorskie
Człuchów
Świecie
Grudziądz
Chełmno
Brodnica
Działdowo
Ostrołęka
Łomża
Zambrów
Białystok
Szczecin
Stargard Szczeciński
Wałcz
Piła
Bydgoszcz
Mława
Ostrów Mazowiecka
Bielsk Podlaski
Pyrzyce
Barlinek
Choszczno
Złotów
Chodzież
Noteć
Rypin
Sierpc
Ciechanów
Pułtusk
Bug
Siematycze
Myślibórz
Trzcianka
Toruń
Wrocławek
Płock
Wyszków
Odra
Oborniki
Gorzów Wielkopolski
Żnin
Mogilno
Płońsk
WARSAW (WARSZAWA)
Siedlce
Biała Podlaska
Warta
Międzyrzecz
Szamotuły
Poznań
Gniezno
Nowy Dwór Mazowiecki
Pruszków
Słubice
Swarzędz
Września
Konin
Koło
Głowno
Łuków
Międzyrzec Podlaski
Świebodzin
Nowy Tomyśl
Radzyń Podlaski
Krosno Odrzańskie
Kościan
Jarocin
Zgierz
Grójec
Garwolin
Ryki
Parczew
Zielona Góra
Leszno
Warta
Kalisz
Łódź
Rawa Mazowiecka
Puławy
Włodawa
Lubsko
Żary
Pleszew
Zduńska Wola
Tomaszów Mazowiecki
GERMANY
Szprotawa
Ostrów Wielkopolski
Sieradz
Łask
Piotrków Trybunalski
Radom
Poniatowa
Lublin
Głogów
Rawicz
Kępno
Bełchatów
Starachowice
Ostrowiec Świętokrzyski
Krasnystaw
Bolesławiec
Trzebnica
Wieluń
Radomsko
Zamość
Zgorzelec
Kłobuck
Świętokrzyski
Wyżyna Lubelska
Legnica
Lubin
Wrocław
Kielce
Sandomierz
Tomaszów Lubelski
Bogatynia
Jelenia Góra
Świdnica
Opole
Częstochowa
Jędrzejów
Tarnobrzeg
Lubelski
Děčín
Liberec
Oława
Lubliniec
Zawiercie
Stalowa Wola
Nisko
Ústí nad Labem
Teplice
Śnieżka 1602m
Wałbrzych
Ząbkowice Śląskie
Miechów
Mielec
Leżajsk
Chomutov
Lovosice
Turnov
Hradec Králové
Gliwice
Chorzów
Katowice
Dąbrowa Tarnowska
Lubaczów
Karlovy Vary
Kladno
Poděbrady
Rybnik
Kraków
Jarosław
Mariánské Lázně
Kolín
Pardubice
Świdnica
Wodzisław Śląski
Tychy
Wieliczka
Tarnów
Rzeszów
Przemyśl
Tachov
Rokycany
Benešov
Čáslav
Ostrava
Jastrzębie-Zdrój
Żory
Bug
PRAGUE (PRAHA)
Elbe
Bielsko-Biała
Nowy Sącz
Krosno
Sanok
Plzeň
CZECH REPUBLIC
Olomouc
Hranice
Frýdek-Místek
Rabka
Dniester
Klatovy
Humpolec
Boskovice
Přerov
Vsetín
Čadca
Žilina
UKRAINE
Strakonice
Písek
Jihlava
BOHEMIA
Tábor
Třebíč
Brno
Otrokovice
Zlín
Považská Bystrica
Tatra
Poprad
Bardejov
Prachatice
MORAVIA
Znojmo
Hodonín
Kyjov
Trenčín
Rosy
Popraď
Gerlachovský Štít 2655m
Snina
České Budějovice
Český Krumlov
Dunaj
Martin
Ružomberok
Prešov
Vranov nad Topľou
Michalovce
Malacky
Trnava
Senica
Piešťany
Topoľčany
SLOVAKIA
Banská Bystrica
Rožňava
Košice
Trebišov
Záhony
Danube (Dunaj)
Pezinok
Nitra
Levice
Zvolen
Lučenec
Encs
Sátoraljaújhely
BRATISLAVA
Galanta
Surany
Ipeľ
Veľký Krtíš
Ózd
Kisvárda
Neusiedler See
Mosonmagyaróvár
Győr
Vác
Kékes 1014m
Miskolc
Eger
Nyíregyháza
Fehérgyarmat
Sopron
Kisköre
Esztergom
Gyöngyös
Hajdúnánás
Szombathely
Tatabánya
BUDAPEST
Kiskörei-víztároló
Debrecen
Celldömölk
Székesfehérvár
Szolnok
Mezőkövesd
Püspökladány
Berettyóújfalu
Veszprém
Dunaújváros
Nagykőrös
Gyomaendrőd
Little Alföld
Kecskemét
Tiszakécske
Keszthely
Bakony
AUSTRIA
Lake Balaton
Great Hungarian Plain
Békéscsaba
Fonyód
Paks
Kiskunfélegyháza
Hódmezővásárhely
Nagykanizsa
Mur
HUNGARY
Tolna
Szeged
Muntii Apuseni
Kaposvár
Szekszárd
Baja
Jánoshalma
Makó
Mures
ITALY
SLOVENIA
Dráva
Csurgó
Barcs
Mecsek
Siklós
Pécs
ROMANIA
Gulf of Venice
Papuk
CROATIA
YUGOSLAVIA
Pomeranian Bay
Oderhaff
Stargard Szczeciński
North European Plain
POLAND
Małopolska
Carpathian Mountains
BELORUSSIA

SOUTHEAST EUROPE

ALBANIA, BOSNIA AND HERZEGOVINA, BULGARIA, CROATIA, GREECE, MACEDONIA, YUGOSLAVIA (SERBIA & MONTENEGRO)

Southeast Europe extends inland from the coasts of the Aegean, Adriatic and Black seas. Ancient Greece was the birthplace of European civilization. Albania and Bulgaria were ruled by communists for over 50 years, until the early 1990s. The rest of the region was part of a communist union of states called Yugoslavia. The collapse of this union in 1991 led to a civil war, after which five separate countries emerged.

THE LANDSCAPE

Southeast Europe is largely mountainous, with ranges running from northwest to southeast. The Dinaric Alps run parallel to the Dalmatian coast, and the Pindus Mountains continue this line into Greece. In the Aegean Sea, the drowned peaks of an old mountain chain form thousands of islands.

Earthquakes
Bulgaria, Greece, and Macedonia lie in earthquake zones. Major earthquakes have hit the Ionian Islands in 1953, and Macedonia in 1963.

Great Hungarian Plain (D 1)
The Vojvodina region of Yugoslavia is the southern part of the Great Hungarian Plain. The plain is flat and fertile soils allow grain crops like corn and wheat to be grown.

Dinaric Alps (C 2)

Balkan Mountains (F 3)
The mountains form a spur running east to west through Bulgaria and separate the two main rivers, the Danube and the Maritsa.

Dalmatian coast (B 2)
The Dalmatian coast has many long, narrow islands near the shore. These were formed as the Adriatic Sea flooded the river valleys which ran parallel to the coast.

Greek Islands

The Peloponnese (E 6)
The Peloponnese is a mountainous peninsula linked to the Greek mainland only by a narrow strip of land called an isthmus. Here, it is the Isthmus of Corinth.

Greek Islands
There are two groups of Greek Islands, the Ionian Islands to the west of mainland Greece, and the more numerous islands to the east in the Aegean Sea.

FARMING AND LAND USE

Cereals like wheat, and fruits, vegetables and grapes are grown in the fertile north of the region. The band of mountains across southeast Europe is used mainly for grazing sheep and goats. Further south, and in coastal areas, the warm Mediterranean climate is ideal for growing grapes, olives and tobacco.

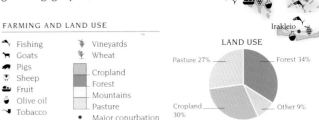

FARMING AND LAND USE

- Fishing
- Goats
- Pigs
- Sheep
- Fruit
- Olive oil
- Tobacco
- Vineyards
- Wheat
- Cropland
- Forest
- Mountains
- Pasture
- Major conurbation

LAND USE
- Forest 34%
- Pasture 27%
- Cropland 30%
- Other 9%

STRUCTURE OF INDUSTRY
- Primary 16%
- Services 52%
- Manufacturing 32%

INDUSTRY

Mainland Greece and the many islands in the Aegean Sea are centres of a thriving tourist trade, while tourism on the Black Sea coast continues to grow. The Dalmatian coast had a small, but growing tourist industry, until the civil war in former Yugoslavia disrupted that, and other industries. Heavy industries like chemicals, engineering and shipbuilding remain an important source of income in Bulgaria.

INDUSTRY
- Chemicals
- Engineering
- Food processing
- Metal refining
- Shipbuilding
- Textiles
- Mining
- Tourism
- Major industrial centre / area
- Major road

POPULATION

Greece's population is mostly urban; over 50% live in the capital, Athens and in Salonica. In Bulgaria, most people live in cities. About half of Albania's and Macedonia's people are still rural. Since the civil war, the different ethnic groups in Bosnia and Herzegovina, Yugoslavia and Croatia have lived apart from one another.

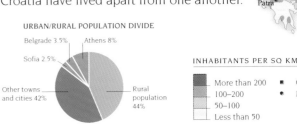

URBAN/RURAL POPULATION DIVIDE
- Belgrade 3.5%
- Athens 8%
- Sofia 2.5%
- Other towns and cities 42%
- Rural population 44%

INHABITANTS PER SQ KM
- More than 200
- 100–200
- 50–100
- Less than 50
- Capital city
- Major city

CLIMATE

Southeastern Europe's climate varies from north to south. Continental climates are found in the north; winters are cold and dry, while towards the south, winters are milder and summers much hotter. Europe's wettest place is found in the mountains in Bosnia and Herzegovina.

January

July

TEMPERATURE AND PRECIPITATION

More than 25°C
20 to 25°C
15 to 20°C
10 to 15°C
5 to 10°C
0 to 5°C
0 to -5°C
Less than -5°C

100 ____ Precipitation (mm)

EUROPE
Southeast Europe

NORTH AMERICA
SOUTH AMERICA
AFRICA
ASIA
AUSTRALASIA AND OCEANIA
ANTARCTICA

SCALE BAR
0 km 50 100
0 miles 50 100

CITIES AND TOWNS
■ Over 500,000 people
◉ 100,000–500,000
○ 50,000–100,000
∘ Less than 50,000

ENVIRONMENTAL ISSUES

Emissions from industry and traffic fumes have polluted the air in Athens and Zagreb. In Athens, smog caused by vehicle exhausts can become so severe on some days that the use of cars is banned. Earthquakes are common; Macedonia's capital city, Skopje, was badly hit in 1963, and Bulgaria's run-down Kozloduy nuclear power station lies within the earthquake zone.

Zagreb
Danube
Kozloduy
Skopje 1963
Salonica 1978
Athens

ENVIRONMENTAL ISSUES
◉ Catastrophic earthquake
☢ Unstable nuclear reactor
☣ Urban air pollution
Sea pollution
Polluted river
• Major town

LAND HEIGHT
2000–4000 m
1000–2000 m
500–1000 m
250–500 m
100–250 m
0–100 m

SEA DEPTH
0–50 m
50–100 m
100–250 m
250–500 m
500–1000 m
1000–2000 m
Below 2000 m

EASTERN EUROPE

BELORUSSIA, MOLDAVIA, ROMANIA, UKRAINE

Much of Eastern Europe, which extends north from the River Danube and the Black Sea, is covered by open grasslands called steppe. Ukraine's excellent farmland and large mineral reserves make it one of the strongest new countries to emerge from the former Soviet Union. Moldavia and Belorussia were also part of the USSR, until they became independent in 1991. Romania was a strict communist regime from 1945 until 1989.

INDUSTRY

In Ukraine, most industry is based around the country's mineral reserves. The Donbass region has Europe's largest coalfield and is an important centre for iron and steel production. Belorussia's main industries are chemicals, machine building and food-processing. Romania's manufacturing industries are growing, with the help of foreign investment.

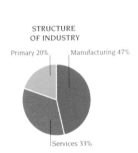

STRUCTURE OF INDUSTRY

Primary 20%
Manufacturing 47%
Services 33%

INDUSTRY

- 🚗 Car manufacture
- ♨ Chemicals
- ⚙ Engineering
- ▣ Food processing
- ⚒ Iron & steel
- ♈ Textiles
- ♔ Coal
- ♠ Mining
- ♦ Oil and gas
- ⬛ Tourism
- ▣ Major industrial centre / area
- — Major road

FARMING AND LAND USE

The black soils found across much of Ukraine are very fertile and the country is a big producer of cereals, sugar beet, and sunflowers, which are grown for their oil. In Moldavia and southern Romania, the warm summers are ideal for growing grapes for wine, along with sunflowers and a variety of vegetables. Cattle and pigs are farmed throughout Eastern Europe.

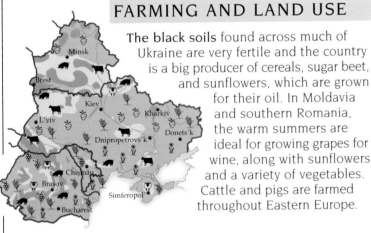

LAND USE

Other 11%
Forest 24%
Pasture 15%
Cropland 50%

FARMING AND LAND USE

- 🐄 Cattle
- 🐖 Pigs
- 🐑 Sheep
- Root crops
- 🌻 Sunflowers
- Vineyards
- Wheat

- Cropland
- Forest
- Pasture
- Wetland
- • Major conurbation

POPULATION

Most Romanians live in Bucharest, the capital, or in other cities and towns. In Ukraine, two-thirds of the population lives in cities in the Donbass industrial area. Most of Belorussia's people are city dwellers. Moldavia is the most rural country in Eastern Europe; half its people live in the countryside and make their living from farming.

URBAN/RURAL POPULATION DIVIDE

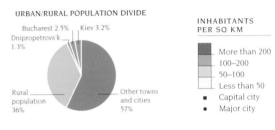

Bucharest 2.5%
Kiev 3.2%
Dnipropetrovs'k 1.3%
Rural population 36%
Other towns and cities 57%

INHABITANTS PER SQ KM

- More than 200
- 100–200
- 50–100
- Less than 50
- ■ Capital city
- • Major city

THE LANDSCAPE

Flat or rolling grasslands, marshes and river flood plains cover almost all of Ukraine and Belorussia. The Carpathian Mountains cross the southwestern corner of Ukraine and continue in a large arc-shaped chain of high peaks at the heart of Romania. Along the southern part of this chain, the Carpathians are called the Transylvanian Alps.

Pripet Marshes (C 3)
The Pripet Marshes in Belorussia and Ukraine form the largest area of marshland in Europe.

The steppes
The steppes are great, wide grasslands which are found across eastern Europe and central Asia. Over 70% of the Ukrainian landscape is steppe. Little rain falls throughout the steppes.

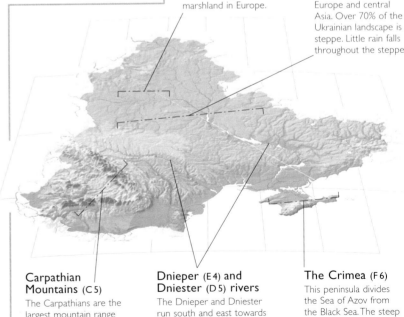

Carpathian Mountains (C 5)
The Carpathians are the largest mountain range in Eastern Europe. They are a rich source of timber and minerals.

Dnieper (E 4) and Dniester (D 5) rivers
The Dnieper and Dniester run south and east towards the Black Sea. They flow slowly across huge areas of low-lying land.

The Crimea (F 6)
This peninsula divides the Sea of Azov from the Black Sea. The steep mountains of Kryms'ki Hory run along the southeastern coast of the Crimea.

CLIMATE

January

July

The climate is continental, with warm, dry summers and very cold, dry winters. Temperatures are higher along the fringes of the Black Sea, while the Carpathian Mountains are colder and wetter all year round.

TEMPERATURE AND PRECIPITATION

- More than 20°C
- 15 to 20°C
- 10 to 15°C
- 5 to 10°C
- 0 to 5°C
- 0 to -5°C
- Less than -5°C

100 — Precipitation (mm)

EUROPE
NORTH AMERICA · ASIA · AFRICA · SOUTH AMERICA · AUSTRALASIA AND OCEANIA · ANTARCTICA
Eastern Europe

ENVIRONMENTAL ISSUES

The worst nuclear accident in history happened at Chornobyl' nuclear power station in northern Ukraine in 1986. Around 70% of the nuclear fallout was received by Belorussia, contaminating its farmland, forests and water supplies. Four million Ukrainians still live in dangerously radioactive areas.

ENVIRONMENTAL ISSUES
- Destroyed nuclear reactor
- Urban air pollution
- Levels of nuclear fallout
  - Very high
  - High
  - Moderate
- Polluted river
- Major industrial centre

LAND HEIGHT
- 2000–4000 m
- 1000–2000 m
- 500–1000 m
- 250–500 m
- 100–250 m
- 0–100 m

SEA DEPTH
- 0–50 m
- 50–100 m
- 100–250 m
- 250–500 m
- 500–1000 m
- 1000–2000 m
- Below 2000 m

CITIES AND TOWNS
- Over 500,000 people
- 100,000–500,000
- 50,000–100,000
- Less than 50,000

SCALE BAR
0 km 50 100
0 miles 50 100

EUROPEAN RUSSIA

RUSSIAN FEDERATION

European Russia is separated from the Asiatic part of the Russian Federation by the Ural Mountains. It is home to two-thirds of the country's population. Russia was the largest and most powerful republic of the communist Soviet Union, which collapsed in 1991. Though new businesses were set up when communism ended, many old state industries closed down, causing unemployment and further hardship for many people.

POPULATION

Three-quarters of European Russia's people live in towns and cities, most in a broad band stretching south from Saint Petersburg to Moscow, and eastwards to the Urals. The capital, Moscow, and Saint Petersburg are very crowded cities. Living conditions there are cramped, with two families often sharing one flat. The southeast is also heavily populated. Over 12 million people live in the cities and towns which line the banks of the River Volga.

INHABITANTS PER SQ KM

- More than 100
- 50–100
- 10–50
- Less than 10
- ■ Capital city
- ● Major city

INDUSTRY

European Russia is rich in natural resources. Minerals are mined on the Kola Peninsula, and in the Urals, while dense forests are felled and processed in many of the larger northern cities. The Volga basin is one of Europe's largest sources of oil and gas. Moscow, and the cities near the Volga are centres of skilled labour for a wide range of manufacturing industries like cars, chemicals and heavy engineering and steel production.

INDUSTRY

- 🚗 Car manufacture
- 🧪 Chemicals
- ⚙ Engineering
- Iron & steel
- Textiles
- Mining
- ◇ Oil & gas
- Timber processing
- ■ Major industrial centre/area
- — Major road

FARMING AND LAND USE

Russia's best farmland lies within this region. Big crops of wheat, barley and oats, potatoes and sunflowers are produced in the fertile black soil which forms a thick band across the country to the south of Moscow. The far north is cold and frozen, with bare mountains and tundra making cultivation impossible. Further south there are extensive forests, and rough pastures used for herding and hunting.

FARMING AND LAND USE

- Cattle
- Pigs
- Reindeer
- Sheep
- Cereals
- Root crops
- Sunflowers
- Timber
- Barren land
- Cropland
- Forest
- Mountain region
- Pasture
- Tundra
- Wetland
- ● Major conurbation

THE LANDSCAPE

European Russia lies on the North European Plain, a huge, rolling lowland with wide river basins. The northern half of the plain, which was once covered by glaciers, has many lakes and swamps. The River Volga drains much of the plain as it flows south to the Caspian Sea. The Caucasus and Ural mountains form natural boundaries in the south and east.

Northern European Russia (C 3)
Northern European Russia reaches into the Arctic Circle. It is a region of pine and birch forests, marshes and tundra. There are also tens of thousands of lakes, including the biggest in Europe, Ladoga, which covers about 17,700 sq km.

Ural Mountains (E 5)
The Ural Mountains run from north to south, stretching almost 4,020 km.

Lake Ladoga (B 4)

Valdai Hills (A 5)
The Valdai Hills are a high, swampy region of the North European Plain. Two of Europe's biggest rivers, the Volga and the Western Dvina, have their sources here.

Caucasus (A 9)
This massive barrier of mountains stretches from the Black Sea to the Caspian Sea. It includes El'brus, the highest peak in Europe, at 5,642 m.

Caspian Sea (C 9)

River Volga (C 7)
The River Volga flows for 3,688 km, making it Europe's longest river and Russia's most important inland waterway. It is used for transport and to generate hydro-electric power.

The North European Plain (C 4)
The North European Plain sweeps west from the Ural Mountains, all the way to the River Rhine in Germany. In European Russia it includes a number of hill ranges, such as the Volga Uplands and the Central Russian Upland.

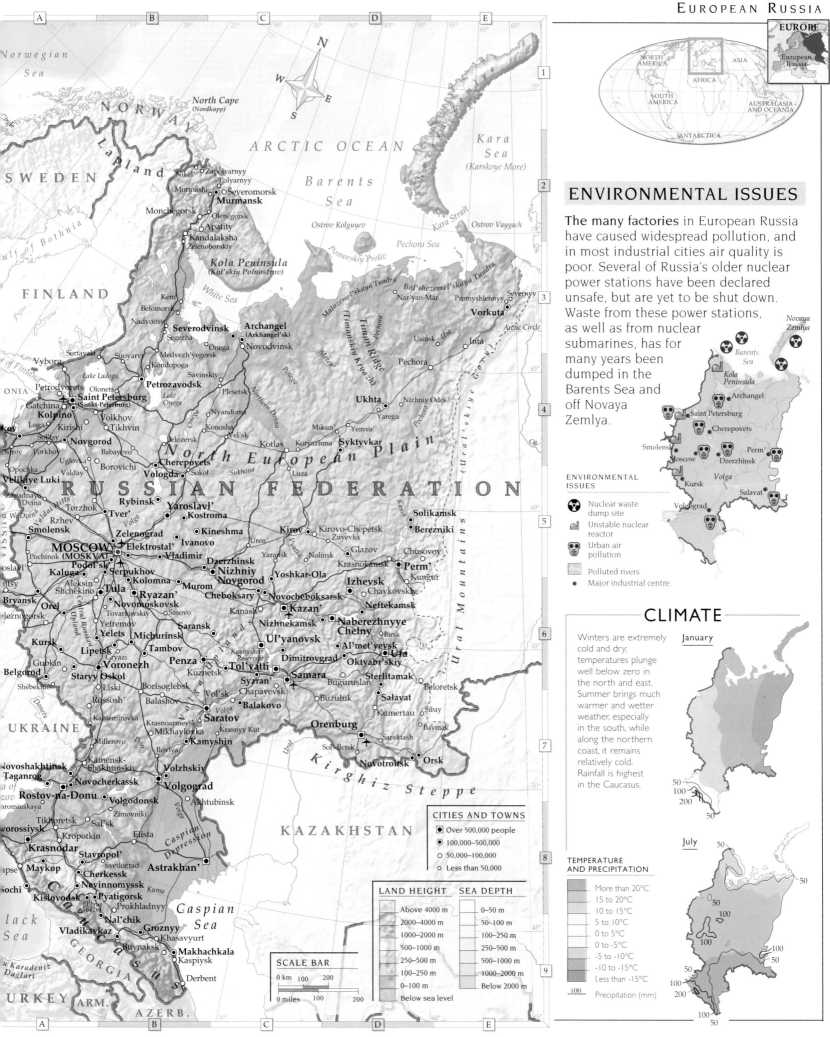

ENVIRONMENTAL ISSUES

The many factories in European Russia have caused widespread pollution, and in most industrial cities air quality is poor. Several of Russia's older nuclear power stations have been declared unsafe, but are yet to be shut down. Waste from these power stations, as well as from nuclear submarines, has for many years been dumped in the Barents Sea and off Novaya Zemlya.

ENVIRONMENTAL ISSUES

- ☢ Nuclear waste dump site
- ⚠ Unstable nuclear reactor
- ☻ Urban air pollution
- Polluted rivers
- • Major industrial centre

CLIMATE

Winters are extremely cold and dry; temperatures plunge well below zero in the north and east. Summer brings much warmer and wetter weather, especially in the south, while along the northern coast, it remains relatively cold. Rainfall is highest in the Caucasus.

January

July

TEMPERATURE AND PRECIPITATION

Temperature
More than 20°C
15 to 20°C
10 to 15°C
5 to 10°C
0 to 5°C
0 to -5°C
-5 to -10°C
-10 to -15°C
Less than -15°C

100 Precipitation (mm)

CITIES AND TOWNS

- ■ Over 500,000 people
- ◉ 100,000–500,000
- ○ 50,000–100,000
- ○ Less than 50,000

LAND HEIGHT

Above 4000 m
2000–4000 m
1000–2000 m
500–1000 m
250–500 m
100–250 m
0–100 m
Below sea level

SEA DEPTH

0–50 m
50–100 m
100–250 m
250–500 m
500–1000 m
1000–2000 m
Below 2000 m

SCALE BAR

0 km 100 200

0 miles 100 200

THE MEDITERRANEAN

The **Mediterranean Sea** separates Europe from Africa. It stretches more than 4,000 km from east to west and is almost completely enclosed by land. Many great civilizations, including the Greek and Roman empires grew up around the Mediterranean. It has been a crossroads of international trade routes for many centuries. More than 100 million people live in the 28 countries which border the sea and their numbers are increased by the large crowds of tourists who regularly visit the area.

ENVIRONMENTAL ISSUES

Sea pollution is widespread in the Mediterranean, especially near the large coastal resorts where raw sewage and industrial effluent is pumped out to sea and often ends up on the beaches. Oil refining and oil spills have also furthered pollution.

ENVIRONMENTAL ISSUES

- 🌀 Oil spill
- Mild sea pollution
- Severe sea pollution

LAND HEIGHT

- Above 4000 m
- 2000–4000 m
- 1000–2000 m
- 500–1000 m
- 250–500 m
- 100–250 m
- 0–100 m
- Below sea level

SEA DEPTH

- 0–250 m
- 250–500 m
- 500–1000 m
- 1000–2000 m
- 2000–3000 m
- 3000–4000 m
- Below 4000 m

CITIES AND TOWNS

- ■ Over 500,000 people
- ● 100,000–500,000
- ○ 50,000–100,000
- ○ Less than 50,000

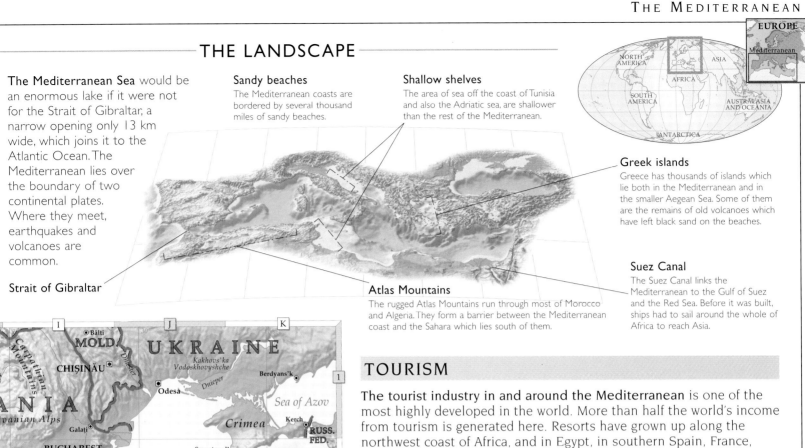

THE LANDSCAPE

The Mediterranean Sea would be an enormous lake if it were not for the Strait of Gibraltar, a narrow opening only 13 km wide, which joins it to the Atlantic Ocean. The Mediterranean lies over the boundary of two continental plates. Where they meet, earthquakes and volcanoes are common.

Strait of Gibraltar

Sandy beaches
The Mediterranean coasts are bordered by several thousand miles of sandy beaches.

Shallow shelves
The area of sea off the coast of Tunisia and also the Adriatic sea, are shallower than the rest of the Mediterranean.

Greek islands
Greece has thousands of islands which lie both in the Mediterranean and in the smaller Aegean Sea. Some of them are the remains of old volcanoes which have left black sand on the beaches.

Suez Canal
The Suez Canal links the Mediterranean to the Gulf of Suez and the Red Sea. Before it was built, ships had to sail around the whole of Africa to reach Asia.

Atlas Mountains
The rugged Atlas Mountains run through most of Morocco and Algeria. They form a barrier between the Mediterranean coast and the Sahara which lies south of them.

TOURISM

The tourist industry in and around the Mediterranean is one of the most highly developed in the world. More than half the world's income from tourism is generated here. Resorts have grown up along the northwest coast of Africa, and in Egypt, in southern Spain, France, Italy, Greece and Turkey. Tourism brings huge economic benefits, but the ever-increasing number of visitors has also damaged the environment.

TOURISM
- Major tourist destinations/resorts
- Tourist centre

INDUSTRY

The Mediterranean has a large fishing industry, although most of the fishing is small-scale. Tuna and sardines are caught throughout the region and mussels are farmed off the coast of Italy. Fish canning and packing takes place at most of the larger ports. Small oil and gas reserves are extracted off the coast of North Africa and near Greece, Spain and Italy.

INDUSTRY
- Fishing ports
- Oil and gas
- Major city

CONTINENTAL ASIA

Asia is the world's largest continent, and has the greatest range of physical extremes. Some of the highest, lowest, and coldest places on Earth are found in Asia: Mount Everest in the Himalayas is the highest, the Dead Sea in the west is the lowest, and the frozen wastes of northern Siberia are among the coldest. More people live in Asia than on any other continent – 1.2 billion of them in China, and 940 million in India.

6,500 km

9,700 km

CROSS-SECTION THROUGH ASIA

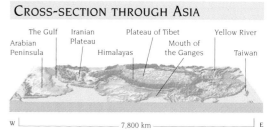

The Gulf
Arabian
Peninsula
Iranian
Plateau
Himalayas
Plateau of Tibet
Mouth of
the Ganges
Yellow River
Taiwan

W — 7,800 km — E

The Arabian Peninsula and the mountainous Iranian Plateau are divided by The Gulf, fed by the Tigris and Euphrates rivers. Further east, the land begins to rise, the mountains spreading north to the Plateau of Tibet, and south to the Himalayas. The plains to the south of the Himalayas are drained by the Indus and Ganges, and to the east of the Plateau of Tibet by the Yellow River.

PHYSICAL ASIA

Northern Asia is made up of old mountains and ancient, stable plateaus. The jagged Himalayan mountains dominate the central part of the continent, along with the Plateau of Tibet, which stretches north into China. In Southeast Asia, there are many islands. Volcanoes and earthquakes are common, and some of the islands are volcanically-formed.

TUNDRA AND PERMAFROST 1

In the far north of Asia, the land is permanently frozen – this is known as permafrost. During the summer, the surface thaws and lakes appear.

2 GREAT RIVERS

Asia is watered by many great rivers. India's Ganges has its source high in the Himalayas. The huge delta is a maze of inlets and marshes.

TROPICAL RAINFORESTS 3

Tropical forests blanket the landscape across much of Southeast Asia, especially in Burma, Thailand and the islands of Borneo, Celebes, Java and Sumatra.

4 DESERTS

The Takla Makan is one of several deserts in central Asia. Moist air is prevented from reaching them by the mountain chains to the south.

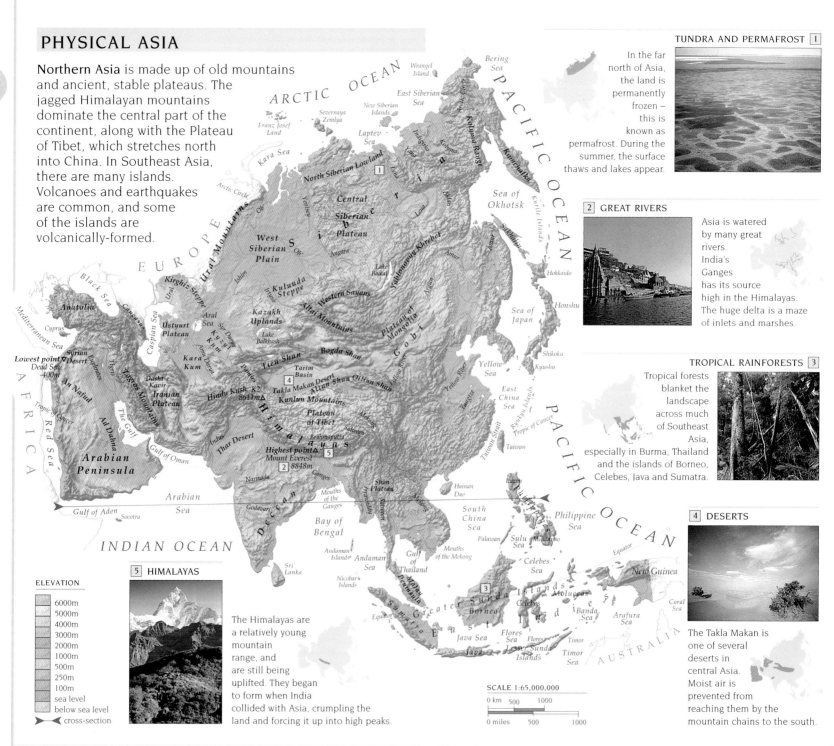

5 HIMALAYAS

ELEVATION

6000m
5000m
4000m
3000m
2000m
1000m
500m
250m
100m
sea level
below sea level
cross-section

The Himalayas are a relatively young mountain range, and are still being uplifted. They began to form when India collided with Asia, crumpling the land and forcing it up into high peaks.

SCALE 1:65,000,000

0 km 500 1000

0 miles 500 1000

POLITICAL ASIA

Asia is a continent of many contrasts: in its lands, its peoples and its traditions. The break up of the Soviet Union, which once stretched south from Russia to Iran, produced the new central Asian republics of Kazakhstan, Kyrgyzstan, Tajikistan, Turkmenistan and Uzbekistan. The countries in southwest Asia are mainly Muslim, but are divided by religious differences and conflicts. India is the world's largest democracy, while China is a communist power with restricted access to the rest of the world.

POPULATION

Capital cities
● Above 500,000
◉ 100,000 to 500,000
● 50,000 to 100,000
• Below 50,000

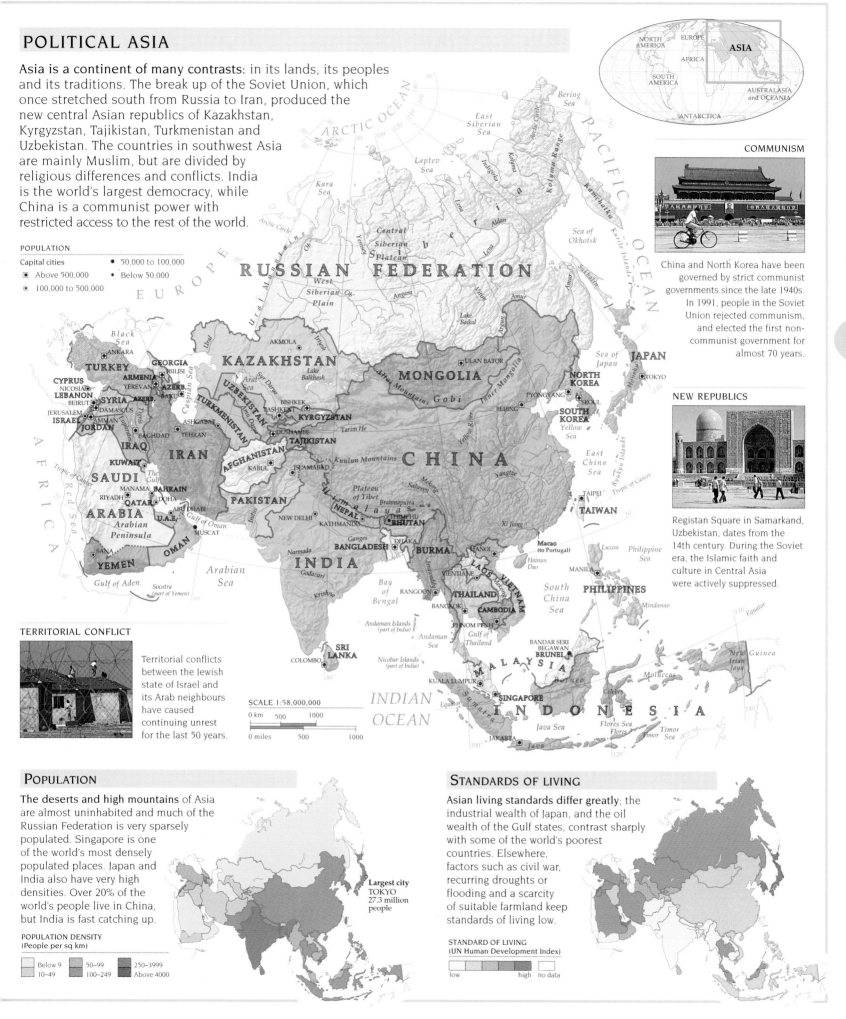

COMMUNISM

China and North Korea have been governed by strict communist governments since the late 1940s. In 1991, people in the Soviet Union rejected communism, and elected the first non-communist government for almost 70 years.

NEW REPUBLICS

Registan Square in Samarkand, Uzbekistan, dates from the 14th century. During the Soviet era, the Islamic faith and culture in Central Asia were actively suppressed.

TERRITORIAL CONFLICT

Territorial conflicts between the Jewish state of Israel and its Arab neighbours have caused continuing unrest for the last 50 years.

SCALE 1:58,000,000

0 km   500   1000

0 miles   500   1000

POPULATION

The deserts and high mountains of Asia are almost uninhabited and much of the Russian Federation is very sparsely populated. Singapore is one of the world's most densely populated places. Japan and India also have very high densities. Over 20% of the world's people live in China, but India is fast catching up.

Largest city
TOKYO
27.3 million
people

POPULATION DENSITY
(People per sq km)

Below 9
10-49
50-99
100-249
250-3999
Above 4000

STANDARDS OF LIVING

Asian living standards differ greatly; the industrial wealth of Japan, and the oil wealth of the Gulf states, contrast sharply with some of the world's poorest countries. Elsewhere, factors such as civil war, recurring droughts or flooding and a scarcity of suitable farmland keep standards of living low.

STANDARD OF LIVING
(UN Human Development Index)

low   high   no data

ASIAN GEOGRAPHY

Asia's forbidding mountain ranges, barren deserts and fertile plains have affected the way in which people settled the continent. Intensive agriculture is found in the more fertile areas, and the largest concentrations of people grew up near fertile land, and close to great rivers. Asia's mineral wealth has brought people to the more inhospitable parts of the continent; the deserts of southwest Asia for oil, and frozen Siberia for oil, gas, and minerals.

MINERAL RESOURCES

Over half of the world's oil and gas reserves are in Asia, most importantly around The Gulf, and in western Siberia. Coal in Siberia and China has provided power for steel industries. Metallic minerals are also abundant: tin in Southeast Asia, and platinum and nickel in Siberia.

MINERAL RESOURCES

- Chromium
- Tin
- Nickel
- Iron
- Platinum
- Gold
- Lead
- Oil/gas field
- Coal field

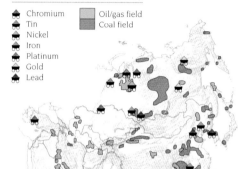

INDUSTRY

Many people in Asia still rely on agriculture as a source of income, and some countries have very few industries. Heavy industry dominates eastern China and Russia, but Japan is the most industrially productive country. In recent years, booming 'tiger' economies have developed in countries such as Taiwan, which border the Pacific Ocean.

OIL AND GAS

The discovery of oil in The Gulf has generated enormous wealth, and produced rapid industrial and social change in countries such as Saudi Arabia, U.A.E. and Kuwait which control the oil supplies.

HI-TECH INDUSTRIES

Japan is a world-leading producer of electronic and hi-tech goods like computers, cameras and hi-fi equipment. Taiwan, South Korea and Singapore also produce electronic goods.

INDUSTRY

- ✈ Aerospace
- ◊ Brewing
- 🚗 Car/vehicle manufacture
- ♨ Cement
- ⚗ Chemicals
- ⛏ Coal
- Electronics
- ⚙ Engineering
- $ Finance
- Food processing
- 💻 Hi-tech industry
- Iron & steel
- Mining
- ◊ Oil & gas
- Pharmaceuticals
- Printing & publishing
- Shipbuilding
- Textiles
- Timber processing

FINANCE

Bombay (Mumbai) is India's leading industrial city, and has a thriving stock market. Modern office blocks stand close to sprawling slums.

INDUSTRIAL COMPLEXES

Noril'sk is one of several Soviet-era industrial complexes built in Russia. It is a processing centre for the rich mineral reserves found nearby.

GNP per capita (US$)

- Below 1999
- 2000-4999
- 5000-9999
- 10,000-19,999
- 20,000-24,999
- Above 25,000
- • Industrial centre

TRADITIONAL INDUSTRIES

Traditional industries and methods of working are still important to less industrialized nations. Here in Vietnam, sea water has been evaporated by the sun, and the salt is collected for market.

CLIMATE

Most of Asia has a continental climate, apart from coastal areas. Without the moderating effects of the ocean, temperatures can soar during the day, and plummet at night; while rainfall is generally low – producing several large deserts. Temperatures as low as –68°C have been recorded in the frozen wastes of Siberia, while the islands in Southeast Asia have tropical climates. Southern and eastern Asia are also affected by a seasonal wind called the monsoon. This originates in the Indian Ocean and brings heavy rainfall and high winds, often devastating small coastal and low-lying villages and towns.

EXTREME WEATHER EVENTS

Symbols indicate climatic extremes

Coldest place
VERKHOYANSK (Russ. Fed.)
Temp -68°C

Hottest place
TIRAT TSVI (Israel)
Temp 54°C

Driest place
ADEN (Yemen)
Annual rainfall 4.6 cm

Wettest place
CHERRAPUNJI (India)
Annual rainfall 1143cm

CLIMATE
- Tundra
- Subarctic
- Cool continental
- Warm temperate
- Mediterranean
- Semi-arid
- Arid
- Humid equatorial
- Tropical
- Hot humid

RAINFORESTS

The tropical climate across the islands of Southeast Asia produces warm, humid conditions in which rainforests flourish. Each island provides a slightly different habitat, so the animals and plants that have evolved on one island may be very different to those on the next.

LAND USE AND AGRICULTURE

Large expanses of Asia are uncultivated, because the soil is too poor, or the climate is too cold or dry for crops to grow. The Plateau of Tibet, much of Siberia, and the Arabian Peninsula have limited agriculture. Some of the most fertile land is found in eastern China and India, where rice is a staple. Elsewhere, cash crops are grown for profit, such as dates in southwest Asia, rubber in Southeast Asia, tea in India, China and Sri Lanka, and coconuts throughout the island archipelago of Southeast Asia.

LAND USE AND AGRICULTURE
- Cattle
- Goats
- Pigs
- Sheep
- Cereals
- Coconuts
- Corn (maize)
- Cotton
- Dates
- Fishing
- Fruit
- Jute
- Peanuts
- Rice
- Root crops
- Rubber
- Shellfish
- Sugar cane
- Soya beans
- Tea
- Timber

- Mountains
- Cropland
- Desert
- Forest
- Pasture
- Wetland
- • Major conurbation

RICE

China is the world's largest producer of rice, which is grown in muddy fields called paddy fields. Water buffaloes are used to plough the ground before planting.

COTTON

Uzbekistan is the world's fourth largest producer of cotton. Water has been diverted from nearby rivers to water the crops, which has led to the drying-up of the Aral Sea.

DATES

Dates have been cultivated on the Arabian Peninsula since ancient times. They are an important cash crop, grown for export in dry sandy areas where few other crops can grow.

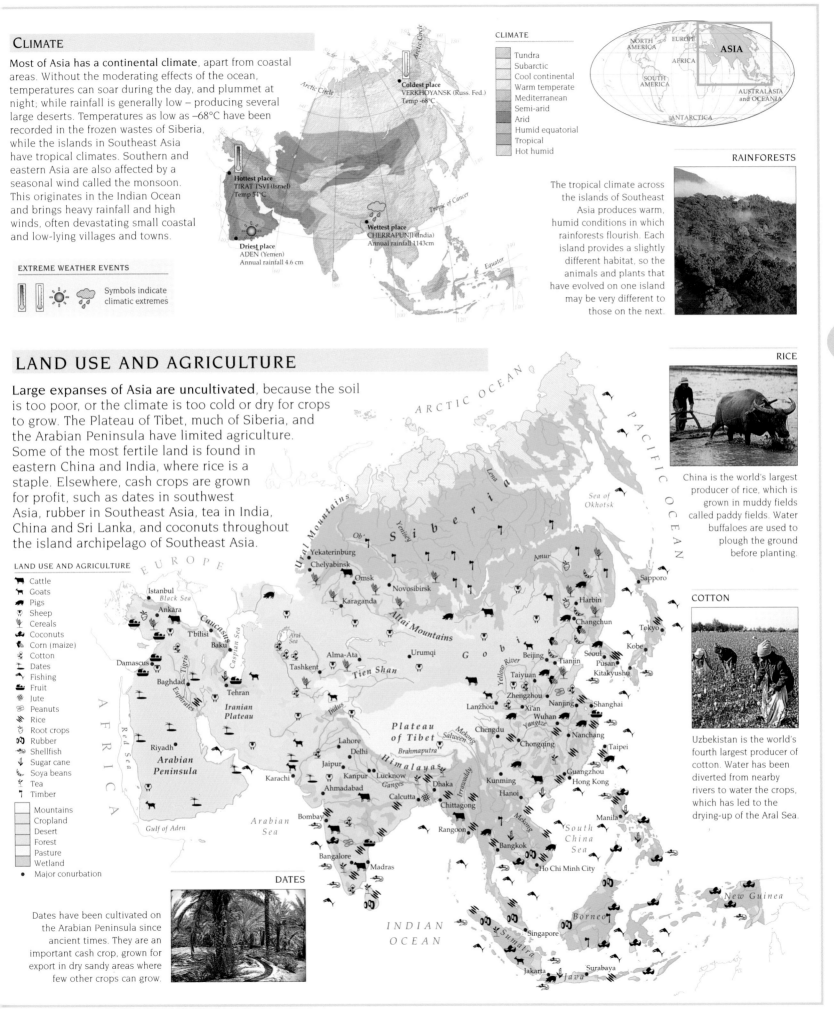

RUSSIA AND KAZAKHSTAN

Russia lies partly in Europe, but mostly in Asia. The land to the east of the Ural Mountains is called Siberia. This immense stretch of grasslands, thick, evergreen forest and tundra is crossed by giant rivers. Vast areas of Siberia are almost untouched by human activity, yet in the industrial regions set up under communism (1922–1991), air, water and soil are heavily polluted with harmful substances. Along with the former Soviet state of Kazakhstan, Siberia is rich in a huge variety of minerals.

INDUSTRY

The discovery of gold in the 19th century opened Siberia up to economic and industrial development. Later, vast reserves of oil, coal and gas were found, especially in the west, which is now the main centre for oil extraction. Gold and diamonds are mined in the east. In Kazakhstan, mining and other industries are growing, with the help of foreign investors.

STRUCTURE OF INDUSTRY

Primary 9%
Services 53%
Manufacturing 38%

INDUSTRY

- 🚗 Car manufacture
- 🛢 Chemicals
- ⚙ Engineering
- Iron & steel
- Textiles
- Mining
- Oil and gas
- Timber manufacturing
- ■ Major industrial centre / area
- — Major road

ASIA

Russia and Kazakhstan

THE LANDSCAPE

East of the Ural Mountains lies the West Siberian Plain – the world's biggest area of flat ground. The plain gradually rises to the Central Siberian Plateau, and then again to highlands in the southeast. Great coniferous forests called *taiga* stretch across most of this land. The far north of Siberia extends into the Arctic Circle. There, the landscape is made up of frozen plains called tundra. Much of Kazakhstan is covered by huge rolling grasslands, or steppe; in the south are arid sandy deserts.

Tundra and *taiga*

Stubby birch trees, dwarf bushes, moss and lichen huddle close to the ground in the frozen tundra wastes of northern Russia. They lie between the permanent ice and snow of the Arctic, and the thick *taiga* forests which cover an area greater than the Amazon rainforest.

The Caspian Sea (A 5)

The Caspian Sea covers 371,000 sq km and is the world's largest expanse of inland water. It is fed by the Volga and Ural rivers, which flow in from the plains of the north.

West Siberian Plain (D 4)

This vast, flat expanse is covered with a network of marshes and streams. The Ob' river, which winds its way north across the plains, is frozen for up to half the year.

Lake Baikal (F 5)

Lake Baikal is the deepest lake in the world, and the largest freshwater one – it is more than 1.6 km deep, and covers 32,500 sq km. It is fed by 336 rivers and contains around 20% of all the fresh water in the world.

CLIMATE

Russia and Kazakhstan have strongly continental climates, and their distance away from seas and oceans means that temperatures fluctuate wildly, both daily and seasonally. Temperatures in eastern Siberia have been known to reach -68°C.

January

July

TEMPERATURE AND PRECIPITATION

- More than 30°C
- 25 to 30°C
- 20 to 25°C
- 15 to 20°C
- 10 to 15°C
- 5 to 10°C
- 0 to 5°C
- 0 to -5°C
- -5 to -10°C
- -10 to -15°C
- Less than -15°C

100 — Precipitation (mm)

FARMING AND LAND USE

Siberia's harsh climate has restricted farming to the south, where there are a few areas warm enough to grow cereal crops, such as wheat and oats, and to raise cattle on the small pockets of pasture. The rest of the region is used for hunting, herding reindeer, and forestry – the *taiga* forests contain the world's biggest timber reserves. In Kazakhstan, big herds of cattle, goats and sheep are raised for wool and meat, and wheat is cultivated in the fertile north.

FARMING AND LAND USE

- Cattle
- Fishing
- Reindeer
- Sheep
- Root crops
- Timber
- Wheat

- Barren land
- Cropland
- Desert
- Forest
- Mountains
- Pasture
- Tundra
- Wetland
- ● Major conurbation

LAND USE

Cropland 9%
Forest 41%
Pasture 14%
Other (including mountains) 36%

POPULATION

Siberia has some of the world's largest areas of uninhabited land – the bitingly cold climate and harsh living conditions have kept the population small. The industrial cities in the west hold the most people. Despite its huge size, Kazakhstan has only 17 million people; most of whom live in urban areas.

INHABITANTS PER SQ KM

- More than 100
- 50–100
- 10–50
- Less than 10
- ■ Capital city
- ● Major city

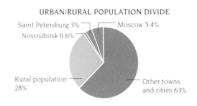

URBAN/RURAL POPULATION DIVIDE

Saint Petersburg 3%
Moscow 5.4%
Novosibirsk 0.6%
Rural population 28%
Other towns and cities 63%

ENVIRONMENTAL ISSUES

Decades of industrial development during the communist regime brought new industries to undeveloped parts of the region, like Siberia. This industrial development has led to environmental degradation on a massive scale and river, air and land pollution in Russia is among the worst in the world.

ENVIRONMENTAL ISSUES

- Urban air pollution
- Polluted rivers
- ● Major industrial centre

ALASKA (part of US)

Arctic Circle

Bering Strait

Gulf of Anadyr

Anadyr

Koryak Range

Bering Sea

Limit of winter pack ice

Ostrov Karaginskiy

Ossora

Shelekhov Gulf

Ust'-Kamchatsk

Vulkan Klyuchevskaya, Sopka 4750m

Atlasovo

Mil'kovo

Magadan

Kamchatka

Petropavlovsk-Kamchatskiy

Pervyy Kuril'skiy Proliv

Ostrov Paramushir

Kuril'sk

Sea of Okhotsk

Ostrov Urup

Ostrov Iturup

Kuril'skiye Ostrova

Sakhalin

Komsomol'sk-na-Amure

Yuzhno-Sakhalinsk

Khabarovsk

Kuril Islands (administered by Russian Federation, claimed by Japan)

La Perouse Strait

Lake Khanka

Ussuriysk

Nakhodka

Vladivostok

JAPAN

Sea of Japan

NORTH KOREA

Honshu

TURKEY AND THE CAUCASUS

ARMENIA, AZERBAIJAN, GEORGIA, TURKEY

Turkey and the Caucasus lie partly in Europe, partly in Asia. Turkey has a long Islamic tradition, and although the country is now a secular (non-religious) one, most Turks are Muslims. Turkey is becoming more industrialized, although half its workforce is still employed in agriculture. The ancient countries of the Caucasus were under Russian rule for 70 years, until 1991. They are home to more than 50 different ethnic groups.

INDUSTRY

Turkey has a wide range of industries and growing trade links with Europe. Azerbaijan has large oil reserves and is able to export oil. The other states use imported fuel and hydro-electric power generated by their rushing rivers. Georgia produces industrial machinery and chemicals. Armenia's economy is recovering from civil war and earthquake damage.

FARMING AND LAND USE

With its warm climate and good soils, Turkey is able to produce all of its own food. Cattle and goats are kept on the central plateau. Along the Mediterranean coast, farmers grow olives, figs, grapes and peaches. Hazelnuts are cultivated along the shores of the Black Sea. Across the Caucasus, the limited fertile land is used to grow wine grapes, tobacco and cotton.

FARMING AND LAND USE

- 🐂 Livestock
- 🐟 Fishing
- ✿ Cotton
- 🍓 Fruit
- 🌰 Hazelnuts
- 🌱 Root crops
- 🌿 Tobacco
- 🍇 Vineyards
- Pasture
- Cropland
- Forest
- • Major conurbation

LAND USE

Other 26%

Cropland 31%

Forest 25%

Pasture 18%

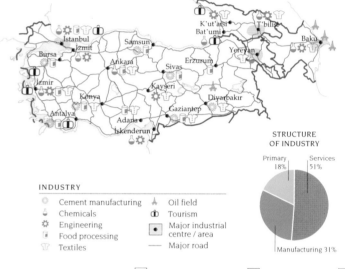

INDUSTRY

- ⚙ Cement manufacturing
- 🏭 Chemicals
- ⚙ Engineering
- 🏭 Food processing
- 👕 Textiles
- ⚓ Oil field
- 🏛 Tourism
- ▣ Major industrial centre / area
- — Major road

STRUCTURE OF INDUSTRY

Primary 18%

Services 51%

Manufacturing 31%

THE LANDSCAPE

A huge semi-arid plateau called Anatolia runs across the centre of Turkey. It is rimmed by several mountain ranges along the Black Sea coast, and the steep Taurus Mountains in the south. A narrow strip of lowland separates the Caucasus and the Lesser Caucasus mountains in the northeast.

Anatolia

Anatolia has large areas of soft limestone rock. Over a long period of time, layers of rock have been worn away by water to produce weird landscapes with caves, and tall, isolated rock pinnacles.

Caucasus Mountains (H1)

Lesser Caucasus (H2)

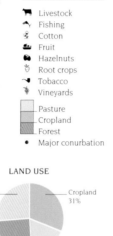

Earthquakes

In 1988, 25,000 people were killed in an earthquake in the west of Armenia.

Between two continents

The city of Istanbul (B2) in Turkey is divided in two by a narrow channel of water called the Bosporus. One part of the city is in Europe, the other in Asia. The two parts are linked by bridges.

Taurus Mountains (D5)

The Taurus Mountains were formed around 60 to 65 million years ago. Weathering has formed caves and deep gorges.

Lake Van (H4)

Lake Van is one of the shallow salt lakes found in Anatolia. Salt lakes develop in hot, dry areas where large quantities of water evaporate, leaving behind salty deposits.

POPULATION

Over 60% of Turks live in large towns or cities, mostly in the western half of the country. The eastern and southeastern parts of Anatolia are home to the Kurdish people. The Caucasian republics became more industrialized under Russian rule, and today, over half of their people live in urban places.

URBAN/RURAL
POPULATION DIVIDE

Istanbul 10.3%
Baku 2.4%
Ankara 2.3%
Other towns and cities 46%
Rural population 39%

INHABITANTS PER SQ KM

- More than 200
- 100–200
- 50–100
- Less than 50
- ■ Capital city
- • Major city

ENVIRONMENTAL ISSUES

Turkey has built many large dams to use water from rivers – especially the Euphrates – to irrigate its farmland. Syria and Iraq, which lie downstream, have opposed the dams, because they will have less water flowing into their countries. In Armenia, a nuclear power plant which was closed after being damaged in the 1988 earthquake has re-opened, although it is still unsafe.

ENVIRONMENTAL ISSUES

- ⚒ Major dam
- 🏭 Unstable nuclear power station
- 😷 Urban air pollution
- • Major industrial centre

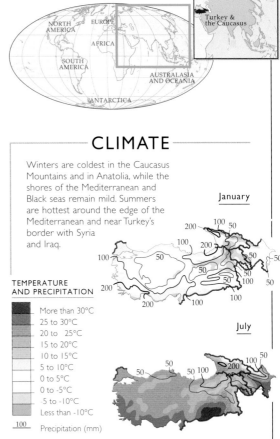

ASIA

Turkey & the Caucasus

CLIMATE

Winters are coldest in the Caucasus Mountains and in Anatolia, while the shores of the Mediterranean and Black seas remain mild. Summers are hottest around the edge of the Mediterranean and near Turkey's border with Syria and Iraq.

January

July

TEMPERATURE AND PRECIPITATION

- More than 30°C
- 25 to 30°C
- 20 to 25°C
- 15 to 20°C
- 10 to 15°C
- 5 to 10°C
- 0 to 5°C
- 0 to -5°C
- -5 to -10°C
- Less than -10°C

100 — Precipitation (mm)

SCALE BAR

0 km 75 150
0 miles 75 150

CITIES AND TOWNS
- ■ Over 500,000 people
- ◉ 100,000–500,000
- ◎ 50,000–100,000
- ○ Less than 50,000

LAND HEIGHT	SEA DEPTH
Above 4000 m	0–50 m
2000–4000 m	50–100 m
1000–2000 m	100–250 m
500–1000 m	250–500 m
250–500 m	500–1000 m
100–250 m	1000–2000 m
0–100 m	Below 2000 m
Below sea level	

SOUTHWEST ASIA

BAHRAIN, IRAN, IRAQ, ISRAEL, JORDAN, KUWAIT, LEBANON, OMAN, QATAR, SAUDI ARABIA, SYRIA, UNITED ARAB EMIRATES, YEMEN

Most of southwest Asia is barren desert, yet the world's first cities developed here, over 5,000 years ago. It was also the birthplace of three major religions: Islam, Judaism and Christianity. In recent years, the discovery of oil has brought great wealth to much of the region, but it has been torn by civil wars, and conflict between neighbouring countries. Most people here are Muslims, although Israel is the world's only Jewish state.

ENVIRONMENTAL ISSUES

Water shortages are common because of the hot, dry climate and the lack of rivers. Desalination plants convert sea water into fresh water, and are found along the Red Sea and Gulf coasts. Lack of water also makes the risk of desertification greater. Iran has had many catastrophic earthquakes; in 1978 an earthquake killed 25,000 people.

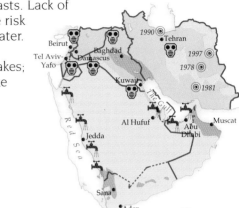

ENVIRONMENTAL ISSUES

- 🚰 Area with many desalination plants
- ◉ Catastrophic earthquake
- 💀 Urban air pollution
- ▢ Existing desert
- ▨ Risk of desertification
- • Major industrial centre

INDUSTRY

Oil has made the previously poor Arab states very wealthy. Oil and natural gas continue to be the main source of income for many of the countries here, although other industries are being developed to support their economies when these resources run out. Iran is famous for its carpets, which are woven from wool or silk.

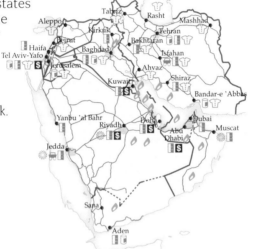

INDUSTRY

- ⚙ Cement manufacturing
- 🍴 Food processing
- ⚒ Iron and steel
- 🛢 Oil refining
- 🧵 Textiles
- 🛢 Oil and gas
- Ⓢ Finance
- •▣ Major industrial centre / area
- — Major road

STRUCTURE OF INDUSTRY

Primary 10%
Services 49%
Manufacturing 41%

FARMING AND LAND USE

The best farmland is found along the Mediterranean coast, and in the fertile valleys of the Tigris, Euphrates and Jordan rivers. Wheat is the main cereal crop, and cotton, dates, citrus and orchard fruits are grown for export. Elsewhere, modern irrigation techniques have created patches of fertile land in the desert. Dates, wheat and coffee are cultivated in the oases and along the Gulf coast.

LAND USE

Forest 5%
Pasture 36%
Cropland 7%
Other (including desert) 52%

FARMING AND LAND USE

- 🐐 Goats
- 🐟 Fishing
- 🐑 Sheep
- 🍊 Citrus fruits
- ☕ Coffee
- 🌿 Cotton
- 🌴 Dates
- 🍇 Fruit
- 🌾 Wheat
- ▢ Cropland
- ▢ Desert
- ▨ Forest
- ▢ Pasture
- ▢ Wetland
- • Major conurbation

THE LANDSCAPE

Great desert plateaus, both sandy and rocky, cover much of southwest Asia. On the enormous Arabian Peninsula, which covers an area almost the size of India, narrow, sandy plains along the Red Sea and south coast rise to dry mountains. In the centre is a vast, high plateau that slopes gently down to the flat shores of the Gulf. The mountainous areas of Iran experience frequent earthquakes.

Wadis
Valleys or riverbeds, called *wadis*, are found in the Saudi Arabian desert. Usually they are dry, but after heavy rains, they are briefly filled by fast flowing rivers.

Syrian Desert (B 2)
The Syrian Desert extends from the Jordan valley in the west, to the fertile plains of the Tigris and Euphrates rivers in the east. It is mainly a rocky desert, as the sand has been swept away by winds and occasional heavy rainstorms.

Oases
Oases are areas within a desert where water is available for plants, and human use. They are usually formed when a fault, or split, in the rock allows water to come to the surface. Oases can be no bigger than a few palm trees, or cover several hundred sq km.

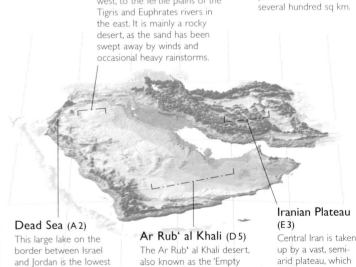

Dead Sea (A 2)
This large lake on the border between Israel and Jordan is the lowest point on the Earth's surface – its shores lie 392 m below sea level. It is also the world's saltiest body of water, and can support no life forms.

Ar Rub' al Khali (D 5)
The Ar Rub' al Khali desert, also known as the 'Empty Quarter', is the largest uninterrupted stretch of sand on Earth. It covers some 650,000 sq km and is one of the world's driest and most hostile deserts.

Iranian Plateau (E 3)
Central Iran is taken up by a vast, semi-arid plateau, which rises steeply from the coastal lowlands bordering the Gulf. It is ringed by the high Zagros and Elburz mountains.

POPULATION

Desert has kept much of the population clustered along the coastal areas and rivers, or around the oases. Most people live in the cities, some of which are the fastest growing in the world. Oman and Yemen have mainly rural populations, and in Saudi Arabia, small groups of Bedouin tribespeople roam the desert with their animals.

URBAN/RURAL POPULATION DIVIDE

Baghdad 3%
Tehran 5%
Riyadh 1%
Other towns and cities 52%
Rural population 39%

INHABITANTS PER SQ KM

- More than 200
- 100–200
- 50–100
- Less than 50
- ■ Capital city
- ● Major city

ASIA
Southwest Asia

NORTH AMERICA · EUROPE · AFRICA · SOUTH AMERICA · AUSTRALASIA AND OCEANIA · ANTARCTICA

CLIMATE

Most of the region receives very little rain, apart from a few isolated pockets. During July, temperatures soar, but in January temperatures are much cooler, especially in the north.

TEMPERATURE AND PRECIPITATION

- More than 30°C
- 25 to 30°C
- 20 to 25°C
- 15 to 20°C
- 10 to 15°C
- 5 to 10°C
- 0 to 5°C
- Less than 0°C
- 100 Precipitation (mm)

January

July

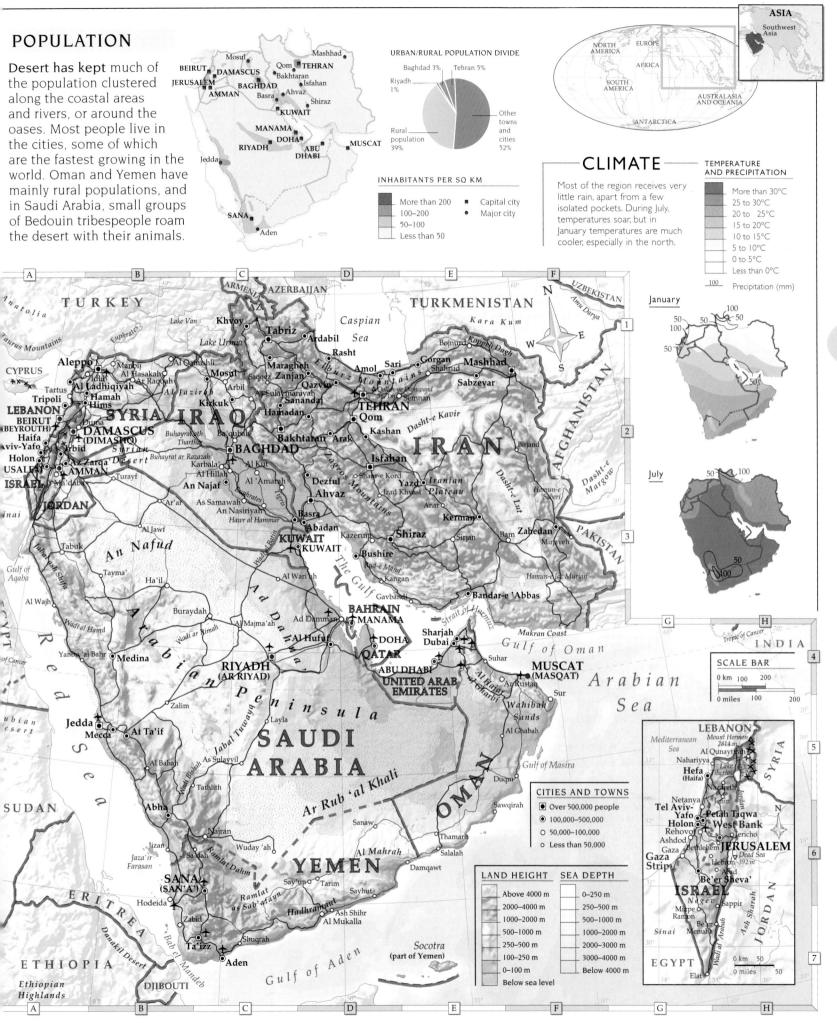

SCALE BAR
0 km 100 200
0 miles 100 200

CITIES AND TOWNS
- ■ Over 500,000 people
- ◉ 100,000–500,000
- ◎ 50,000–100,000
- ○ Less than 50,000

LAND HEIGHT
- Above 4000 m
- 2000–4000 m
- 1000–2000 m
- 500–1000 m
- 250–500 m
- 100–250 m
- 0–100 m
- Below sea level

SEA DEPTH
- 0–250 m
- 250–500 m
- 500–1000 m
- 1000–2000 m
- 2000–3000 m
- 3000–4000 m
- Below 4000 m

CENTRAL ASIA

AFGHANISTAN, KYRGYZSTAN, TAJIKISTAN, TURKMENISTAN, UZBEKISTAN

Central Asia is a land of hot, dry deserts and high, rugged mountains. It lies on the ancient Silk Road, an important trade route between China and Europe for over 400 years, until the 15th century. All of the countries here, apart from Afghanistan, were part of the Soviet Union from the 1920s, until 1991, when they gained independence. Since then, their people have re-established their local languages and Islamic faith, all of which were restricted under Russian rule.

INDUSTRY

Fossil fuels, especially coal, natural gas and oil, are extracted and processed throughout Central Asia. Agriculture supplies the raw materials for many industries, including food and textile processing, and the manufacture of leather goods and clothing. The region is famous for its colourful traditional carpets, hand-woven from the wool of the Karakul sheep. The Fergana Valley, southeast of Tashkent, is the main industrial area.

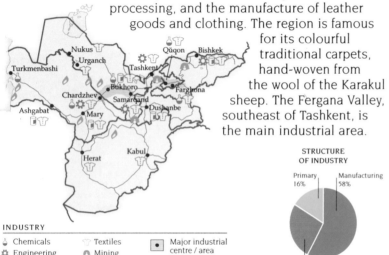

INDUSTRY

⚗ Chemicals	⏚ Textiles	● Major industrial centre / area
✿ Engineering	⛏ Mining	
▣ Food processing	⬦ Oil and gas	— Major road

STRUCTURE OF INDUSTRY

Primary 16%
Manufacturing 58%
Services 26%

POPULATION

The peoples of Central Asia are mostly rural farmers, living in the river valleys and in oases. There are few large cities. A few still lead a traditional nomadic lifestyle, moving from place to place with their animals, in search of new pastures. Large areas of Afghanistan, the western deserts and the mountain regions in the east, are virtually uninhabited.

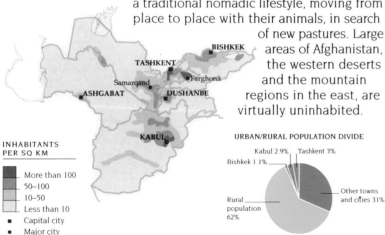

INHABITANTS PER SQ KM

- More than 100
- 50–100
- 10–50
- Less than 10
- ● Capital city
- ● Major city

URBAN/RURAL POPULATION DIVIDE

Kabul 2.9%
Tashkent 3%
Bishkek 1.1%
Rural population 62%
Other towns and cities 31%

FARMING AND LAND USE

Farming is concentrated around the fertile river valleys in the east, like the Fergana Valley. A variety of cereals, and fruits, including peaches, melons and apricots, are grown. In drier areas, animal breeding is important, with goats, sheep and cattle supplying wool, meat and hides. Big crops of cotton, which is a major export, are produced on land irrigated by the Amu Darya river.

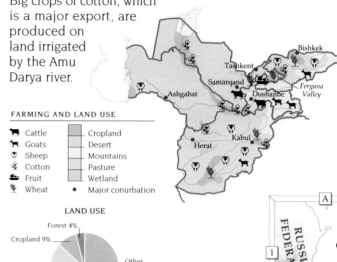

FARMING AND LAND USE

🐂 Cattle		Cropland
🐐 Goats		Desert
🐑 Sheep		Mountains
❀ Cotton		Pasture
🍇 Fruit		Wetland
🌾 Wheat	● Major conurbation

LAND USE

Forest 4%
Cropland 9%
Other (including mountains and deserts) 45%
Pasture 41%

THE LANDSCAPE

Two of the world's great deserts, the Kara Kum and the Kyzyl Kum, cover much of the western portion of Central Asia. In the east, a belt of high mountain ranges – the Hindu Kush, the Tien Shan and the Pamirs – tower above the land. Few rivers cross the deserts, apart from the Amu Darya, which flows from the Pamirs to the shrinking Aral Sea.

The Aral Sea (D 1)
The Aral Sea was once the fourth largest lake in the world, but it has shrunk by 40% since 1960. Diversion of its water for irrigation has made the lake shallower, so its waters evaporate faster.

Kara Kum (D 3)
The sandy desert of the Kara Kum occupies over 70% of Turkmenistan. Its surface consists of wind-sculpted dunes and depressions. Human settlement is limited to the desert's fringes.

Tien Shan (H 2)

Fergana Valley (G 3)
Stresses and strains in the Earth created the Fergana Valley, a deep depression encircled by high mountains. The valley's fertile soils are irrigated by water from the Syr Darya river, and underground sources.

Amu Darya river (E 3)

Hindu Kush (G 4)

Pamirs (G 4)
The Pamirs lie mainly in Tajikistan. Their highest point, at 7,495 m, is Communism Peak, so named because it was the highest peak in the former Soviet Union.

ENVIRONMENTAL ISSUES

The Aral Sea is rapidly drying up, as the rivers feeding it are being diverted to irrigate fields of cotton. Central Asia is a very dry area, and desertification is a constant threat, especially in Afghanistan. Severe urban and industrial air pollution is a legacy from the communist era, when heavy industries were established in the countries here.

ENVIRONMENTAL ISSUES

- Urban air pollution
- Existing desert
- Risk of desertification
- Severe risk of desertification
- Polluted river
- Major industrial centre

CLIMATE

Central Asia's climate is strongly inflenced by its position deep within Asia, far from the moderating effects of the oceans. Winters are cold, summers are very hot everywhere. Rainfall is virtually non-existent all year round.

ASIA

Central Asia

January

Less than 50mm precipitation

July

Less than 50mm precipitation

TEMPERATURE AND PRECIPITATION

- More than 30°C
- 25 to 30°C
- 5 to 10°C
- 0 to 5°C
- Less than 0°C

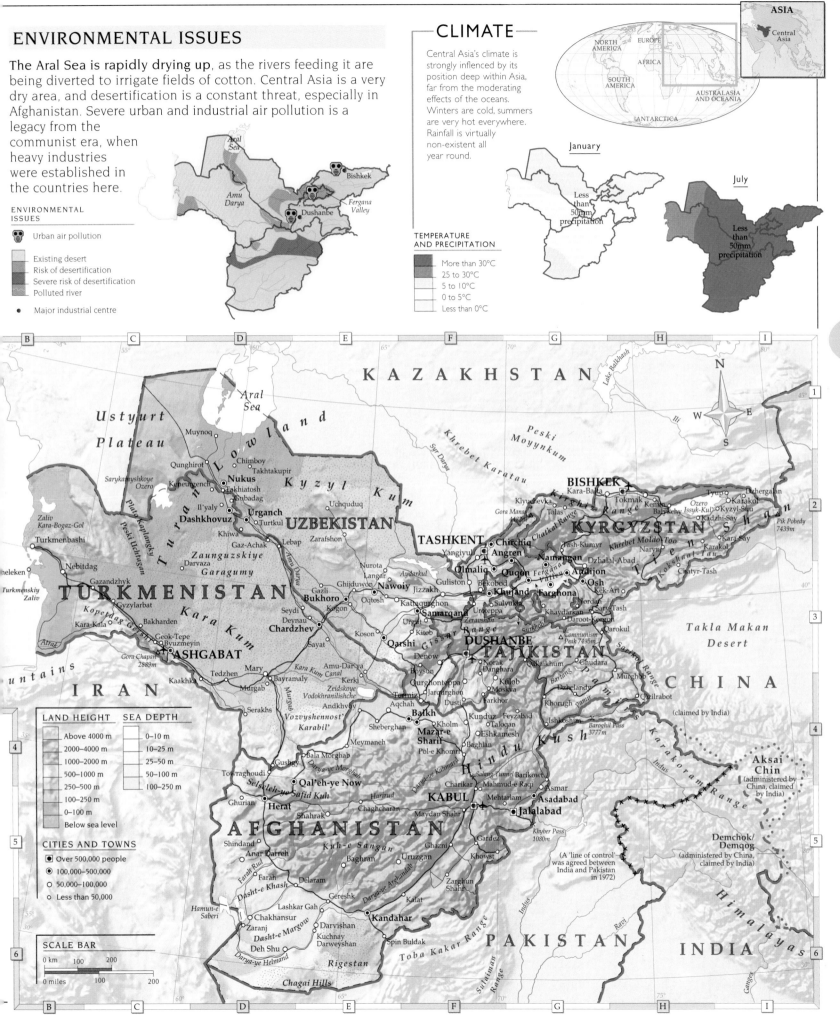

LAND HEIGHT
- Above 4000 m
- 2000–4000 m
- 1000–2000 m
- 500–1000 m
- 250–500 m
- 100–250 m
- 0–100 m
- Below sea level

SEA DEPTH
- 0–10 m
- 10–25 m
- 25–50 m
- 50–100 m
- 100–250 m

CITIES AND TOWNS
- Over 500,000 people
- 100,000–500,000
- 50,000–100,000
- Less than 50,000

SCALE BAR

0 km 100 200

0 miles 100 200

JAPAN AND KOREA

JAPAN, NORTH KOREA, SOUTH KOREA

Japan is a curved chain of over 4,000 islands in the Pacific Ocean. To the west, Korea juts out from northern China. Japan has few natural resources but it has become one of the world's most successful industrial nations due to investment in new technology and a highly efficient workforce. North Korea is a communist state with limited contact with the outside world, while South Korea is a democracy with major international trade links.

FARMING AND LAND USE

Modern farming methods allow Japan to grow much of its own food, despite a shortage of farmland. Rice is the main crop grown throughout the region. Japan has a large fishing fleet; the Japanese eat more fish than any other nation. In North Korea, farming is controlled by the government.

FARMING AND LAND USE

- 🐂 Cattle
- 🐟 Fishing
- 🐗 Pigs
- 🍎 Fruit
- 🌾 Rice
- 🫘 Soya beans
- 🌱 Tea
- Cropland
- Forest
- Pasture
- • Major conurbation

LAND USE

Pasture 1%
Cropland 14%
Other (including mountains) 30%
Forest 55%

POPULATION

Most of Japan's 125 million people live in crowded cities on the coasts of the four main islands. The Kanto Plain around Tokyo is Japan's biggest area of flat land, and the most populous part of the country. In South Korea, a quarter of the population lives in the capital, Seoul. Most North Koreans live on the coastal plains.

URBAN/RURAL POPULATION DIVIDE

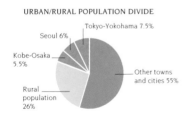

- Tokyo-Yokohama 7.5%
- Seoul 6%
- Kobe-Osaka 5.5%
- Rural population 26%
- Other towns and cities 55%

INHABITANTS PER SQ KM

- More than 200
- 100–200
- 50–100
- Less than 50
- ■ Capital city
- • Major city

THE LANDSCAPE

Most of Japan is covered by forested mountains and hills, among which are many short, fast-flowing rivers and small lakes. Only about a quarter of the land is suitable for building and farming and new land has been created by cutting back hillsides and reclaiming land from the sea. North and South Korea are mostly mountainous, with some coastal plains.

Hokkaido, Honshu, Shikoku and Kyushu

Japan's four main islands were formed when two giant plates making up the Earth's crust collided, making their edges buckle upwards.

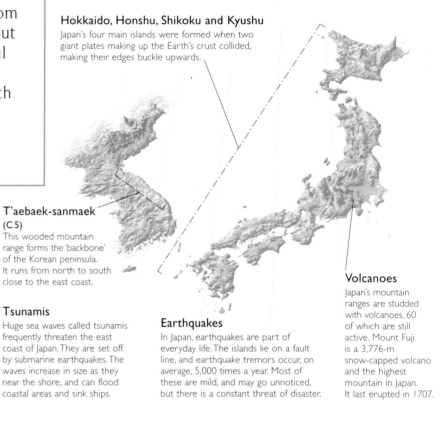

T'aebaek-sanmaek (C 5)

This wooded mountain range forms the 'backbone' of the Korean peninsula. It runs from north to south close to the east coast.

Tsunamis

Huge sea waves called tsunamis frequently threaten the east coast of Japan. They are set off by submarine earthquakes. The waves increase in size as they near the shore, and can flood coastal areas and sink ships.

Earthquakes

In Japan, earthquakes are part of everyday life. The islands lie on a fault line, and earthquake tremors occur, on average, 5,000 times a year. Most of these are mild, and may go unnoticed, but there is a constant threat of disaster.

Volcanoes

Japan's mountain ranges are studded with volcanoes, 60 of which are still active. Mount Fuji is a 3,776-m snow-capped volcano and the highest mountain in Japan. It last erupted in 1707.

INDUSTRY

Japan is a world leader in hi-tech electronic goods like computers, televisions and cameras, as well as cars. South Korea also has a thriving economy. It produces ships, cars, hi-tech goods, shoes and clothes for worldwide export. Both countries have to import most of their raw materials and energy. North Korea has little trade with other countries, but it is rich in minerals such as coal and silver.

STRUCTURE OF INDUSTRY

Primary 3%
Services 57%
Manufacturing 40%

INDUSTRY

- 🚗 Car manufacture
- ⚗ Chemicals
- ⚙ Engineering
- Food processing
- Iron & steel
- Shipbuilding
- 👕 Textiles
- $ Finance
- 💻 Hi-tech
- ☢ Research & Development
- ▪ Major industrial centre / area
- — Major road

ENVIRONMENTAL ISSUES

Industrial pollution from Korea and China has produced acid rain, and pollution in Japanese cities has led to people wearing masks to filter the air. Russia regularly dumps nuclear waste into the Sea of Japan. In 1995, an earthquake caused great destruction to the city of Kobe.

ENVIRONMENTAL ISSUES

- ⊚ Catastrophic earthquake
- ☢ Nuclear waste dump site
- ☻ Urban air pollution
- ░ Affected by acid rain
- • Major industrial area

CLIMATE

Korea has hot summers and dry, very cold winters, especially in the north, where snow is common. In Japan, winters are less cold than on the Asian mainland; summers are hot, wet and humid.

January

July

TEMPERATURE AND PRECIPITATION

- More than 20°C
- 15 to 20°C
- 10 to 15°C
- 5 to 10°C
- 0 to 5°C
- 0 to -5°C
- Less than -5°C
- 100 Precipitation (mm)

ASIA
Japan and Korea

(North and South Korea have been divided by a ceasefire agreement since 1953)

Liancourt Rocks (claimed by Japan and South Korea)

Kurile Islands (administered by Russian Federation, claimed by Japan)

SCALE BAR

LAND HEIGHT / SEA DEPTH

LAND HEIGHT	SEA DEPTH
2000–4000 m	0–250 m
1000–2000 m	250–500 m
500–1000 m	500–1000 m
250–500 m	1000–2000 m
100–250 m	2000–3000 m
0–100 m	3000–4000 m
	Below 4000 m

CITIES AND TOWNS
- ■ Over 500,000 people
- ◉ 100,000–500,000
- ○ 50,000–100,000
- ○ Less than 50,000

EAST ASIA

CHINA, MONGOLIA, TAIWAN

China is the world's third largest country and its most populous – over one billion people live there. Under its communist government, which came to power in 1949, China has become a major industrial nation, but most of its people still live and work on the land, as they have for thousands of years. Taiwan also has a booming economy and exports its products around the world. Mongolia is a vast, remote country with a small population, many of whom are nomads.

INDUSTRY

Chemicals, iron and steel, engineering and textiles are the main industries in China's east coast cities, and in industrial centres like Shenyang. Shanghai, Hong Kong and Beijing are also important financial centres. In the interior, large deposits of coal support the heavy industries in major cities such as Chengdu and Wuhan. Taiwan specializes in textiles and shoe manufacture, along with electronic goods. Mongolia's economy is mainly agricultural.

INDUSTRY

🚗 Car manufacture	⊽ Textiles
⚗ Chemicals	🜚 Coal
⚡ Electronics	S Finance
⚙ Engineering	
🍴 Food processing	◉ Major industrial centre / area
⚓ Iron & steel	— Major road
⚒ Shipbuiding	

STRUCTURE OF INDUSTRY

Services 21%
Manufacturing 47%
Primary 32%

POPULATION

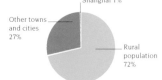

Most of China's people live in the eastern part of the country, where the climate, landscape and soils are most favourable. Urban areas there house over 250 million people, but almost 75% of the population lives in villages and farm the land. Taiwan's lowlands are very densely populated. In Mongolia, about 50% of the people live in the countryside.

URBAN/RURAL POPULATION DIVIDE

Shanghai 1%
Other towns and cities 27%
Rural population 72%

INHABITANTS PER SQ KM

■ More than 200	■ Capital city
100–200	• Major city
50–100	
Less than 50	

FARMING AND LAND USE

Despite its size, about 90% of China is unsuitable for farming. Either the soils and climate are poor, or the landscape is too mountainous. In the north and west, most farmers make their living by herding animals. On the fertile eastern plains, soya beans, wheat, corn and cotton are grown. Further south, rice becomes the main crop, and pigs are raised in large numbers.

FARMING AND LAND USE

⤙ Fishing	🌾 Wheat
🐖 Pigs	▨ Cropland
🐑 Sheep	▨ Desert
🌽 Corn (maize)	▨ Forest
❀ Cotton	Mountain region
🍎 Fruit	Pasture
⚘ Rice	
🫘 Soya beans	• Major conurbation
⤓ Sugar cane	

LAND USE

Cropland 7%
Pasture 42%
Other (including mountains) 24%
Forest 27%

THE LANDSCAPE

China's landscape divides into three areas. The vast Plateau of Tibet in the southwest is the highest and largest plateau on Earth. It contains both dry deserts and pockets of pasture surrounded by high mountains. Northwest China has dry highlands. The great plains of eastern China were formed from soils deposited by rivers like the Yellow River over thousands of years. Most of Mongolia is dry, grassland steppe and cold, arid desert.

Tien Shan mountains (B 2)
The Tien Shan, or 'Heavenly Mountains' reach heights of 7,435 m. They surround fields of permanent ice and spectacular glaciers.

Gobi (E 2) and Takla Makan (B 3) deserts
The arid landscapes of the Gobi and Takla Makan deserts are made up of bare rock surfaces and huge areas of shifting sand dunes. They are hot in summer, but unlike most other deserts, are extremely cold in winter.

Takla Makan Desert

'The Roof of the World'
The cold, remote Plateau of Tibet (C4) averages 4,000 m in height. Many of China's great rivers have their sources here. The world's highest human settlement, a town called Wenquan, is found in the east of the plateau. It lies 5,099 m above sea level.

The Yellow River (E 3)
The Yellow River (Huang He) is the world's muddiest river, carrying hundreds of lorry loads of sediment to the sea every minute. The river has burst its banks many times throughout history, causing enormous damage and claiming millions of human lives.

A handmade landscape
In the farming areas of eastern and southern China, terraces have been carved into the hillsides to make them flat enough to grow rice and other crops. This method of farming has been used for over 7,000 years.

ENVIRONMENTAL ISSUES

The Three Gorges hydro-electric scheme on the Yangtze River will be the world's largest. Nearly 563 km of canyon will be flooded, and 1.3 million people forced to move. Earthquakes are common in the area and 100 million people downstream will be threatened if the dam breaks. In eastern China, many cities are affected by industrial pollution.

ENVIRONMENTAL ISSUES

- Major dam
- Urban air pollution
- Industrial city

CLIMATE

Two air masses control climate; one cold and dry from Siberia, and one moist and warm from the Pacific. Winters are long and cold away from the coast – especially on the Plateau of Tibet.

TEMPERATURE AND PRECIPITATION

- More than 30°C
- 20 to 30°C
- 10 to 20°C
- 0 to 10°C
- 0° to -10°C
- -10°C to -20°C
- Less than -20°C

100 — Precipitation (mm)

January

July

LAND HEIGHT
- Above 4000 m
- 2000–4000 m
- 1000–2000 m
- 500–1000 m
- 250–500 m
- 100–250 m
- 0–100 m

SEA DEPTH
- 0–250 m
- 250–500 m
- 500–1000 m
- 1000–2000 m
- 2000–3000 m
- 3000–4000 m

CITIES AND TOWNS
- Over 500,000 people
- 100,000–500,000
- 50,000–100,000
- Less than 50,000

SOUTH ASIA

BANGLADESH, BHUTAN, INDIA, NEPAL, PAKISTAN, SRI LANKA

South Asia is a land of many contrasts. Its landscape ranges from the mighty peaks of the Himalayas in the north, through vast plains and arid desert, to tropical forests and palm-fringed beaches in the south. More than one-fifth of the world's people live here, and a long history of foreign invasions has left a mosaic of hugely different cultures, religions and traditions, and thousands of languages and dialects.

FARMING AND LAND USE

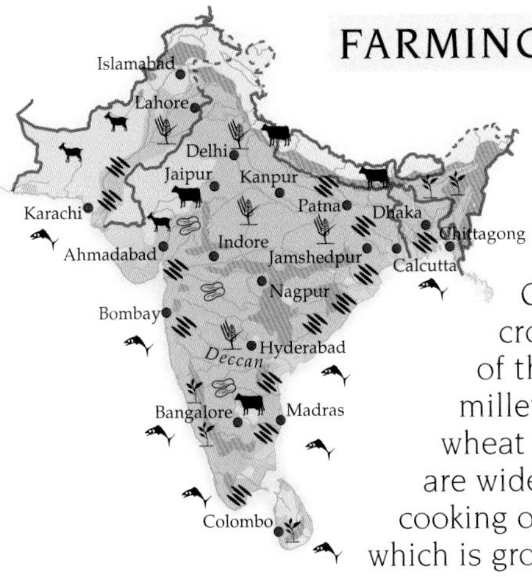

Over 60% of the population is involved in agriculture, but most farms are small, and produce only enough food to feed one family. Grains are the staple food crops – rice in the wetter parts of the east and west, corn and millet on the Deccan plateau, and wheat in the north. Groundnuts are widely grown as a source of cooking oil. Cash crops include tea, which is grown on plantations, and jute.

FARMING AND LAND USE

- Cattle
- Fishing
- Goats
- Cereals
- Groundnuts
- Rice
- Tea
- Cropland
- Desert
- Forest
- Pasture
- Wetland
- Major conurbation

LAND USE

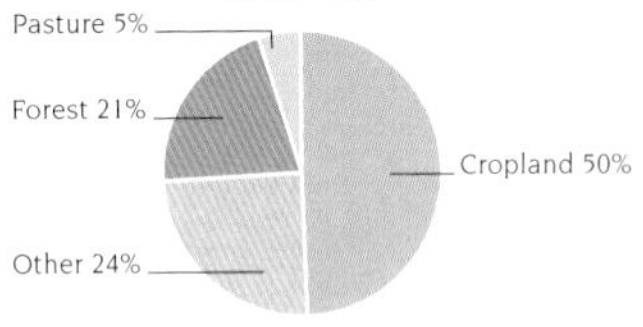

INDUSTRY

Industry has expanded in India in recent years, and in the cities a variety of goods are produced and processed, including cars, aeroplanes, chemicals, food and drink. Service industries such as tourism and banking are also growing. Elsewhere, small-scale cottage industries serve the needs of local people, but many products, mainly silk and cotton textiles, clothing, leather and jewellery, are also exported.

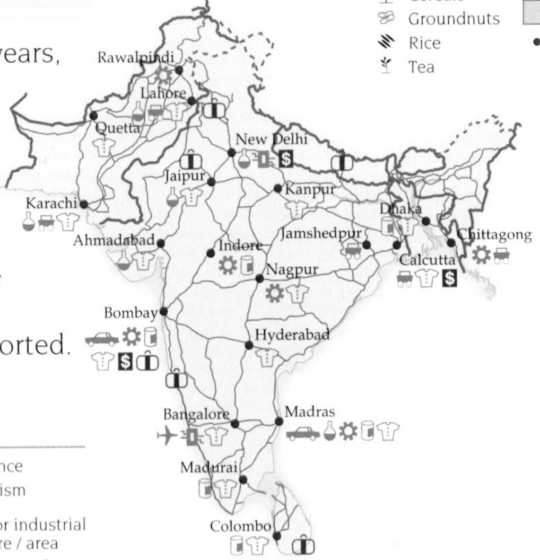

STRUCTURE OF INDUSTRY

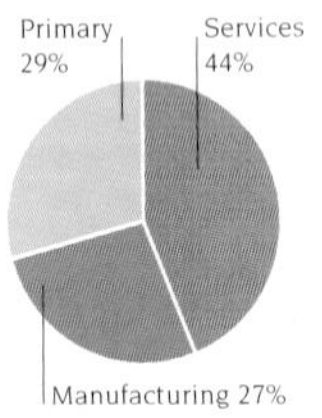

INDUSTRY

- Aerospace
- Car manufacture
- Chemicals
- Electronics
- Engineering
- Food processing
- Iron and steel
- Textiles
- Finance
- Tourism
- Major industrial centre / area
- Major road

POPULATION

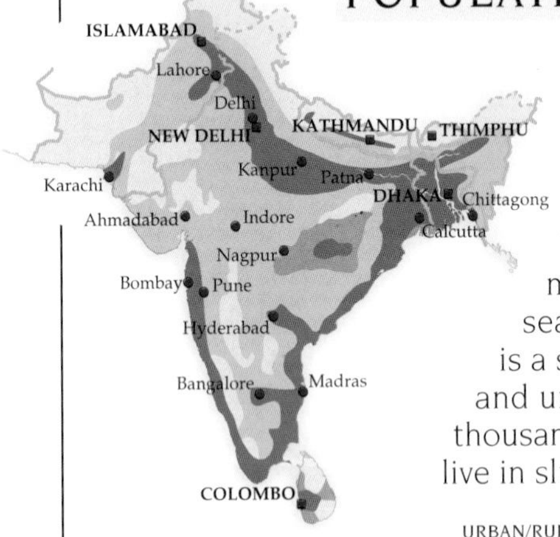

Most of South Asia's people live in villages scattered across the fertile river floodplains, in mountain valleys or along the coasts, but increasing numbers are migrating to the cities in search of work. Overcrowding is a serious problem in both rural and urban areas; in many cities, thousands of people are forced to live in slums, or on the streets.

INHABITANTS PER SQ KM

- More than 200
- 100–200
- 50–100
- Less than 50
- Capital city
- Major city

URBAN/RURAL POPULATION DIVIDE

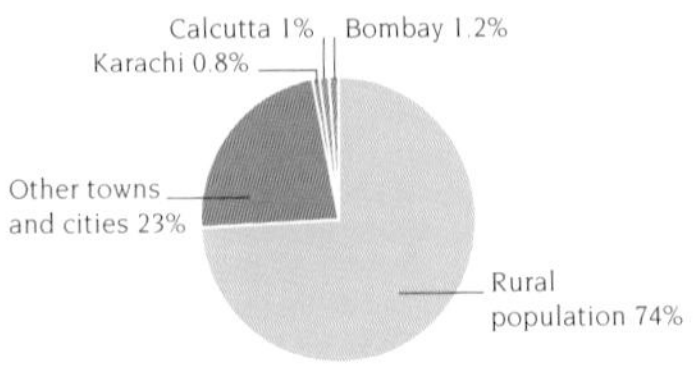

THE LANDSCAPE

A massive, towering wall of snow-capped mountains stretches in an arc across the north, isolating South Asia from the rest of the continent. The huge floodplains and deltas of the Indus, Ganges and Brahmaputra rivers separate the mountains from the rest of the peninsula: a great rolling plateau, bordered on either side by coastal hills called the Eastern and Western Ghats.

Himalayas (E 2)
The Himalayas are the highest mountain system in the world. They were formed about 40 million years ago when two of the Earth's plates collided, thrusting up huge masses of land.

Mount Everest (F 3)
The northern ranges of the Himalayas average 7,000 m in height. They include the highest point on Earth, Mount Everest on the Nepal–China border, which soars to 8,848 m.

Thar Desert (C 3)
The border between India and Pakistan runs through the arid, sandy Thar Desert.

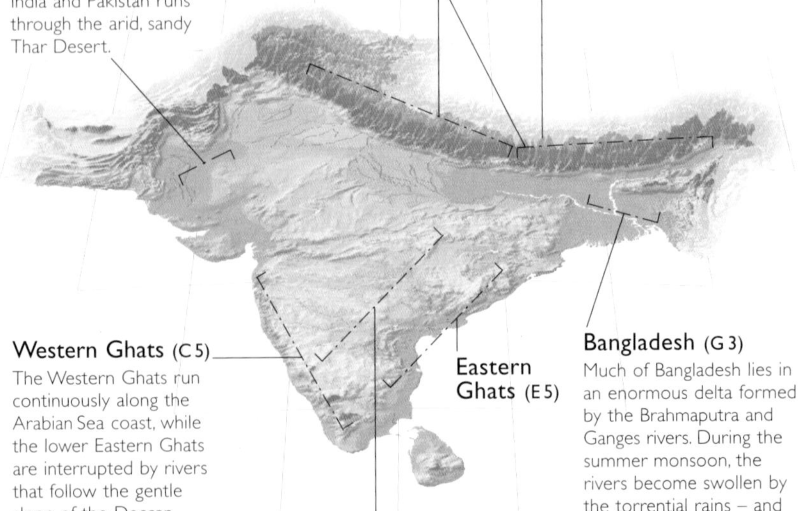

Western Ghats (C 5)
The Western Ghats run continuously along the Arabian Sea coast, while the lower Eastern Ghats are interrupted by rivers that follow the gentle slope of the Deccan plateau and flow across broad lowlands into the Bay of Bengal. This is one of the wettest regions in the world.

Eastern Ghats (E 5)

Deccan plateau (D 5)
This giant plateau makes up most of central and southern India. Its volcanic rock has been deeply cut by rivers such as the Krishna, creating stepped valleys called *traps*.

Bangladesh (G 3)
Much of Bangladesh lies in an enormous delta formed by the Brahmaputra and Ganges rivers. During the summer monsoon, the rivers become swollen by the torrential rains – and meltwater from the Himalayas – and the delta floods. Over the years, millions of people have drowned or been made homeless by heavy flooding.

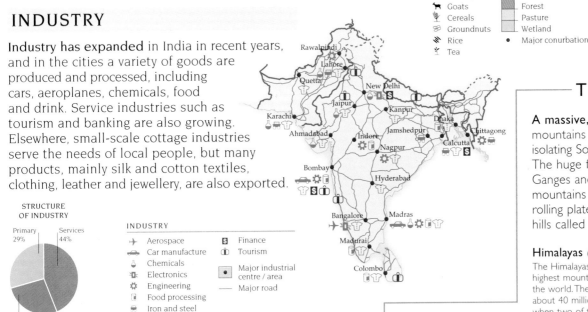

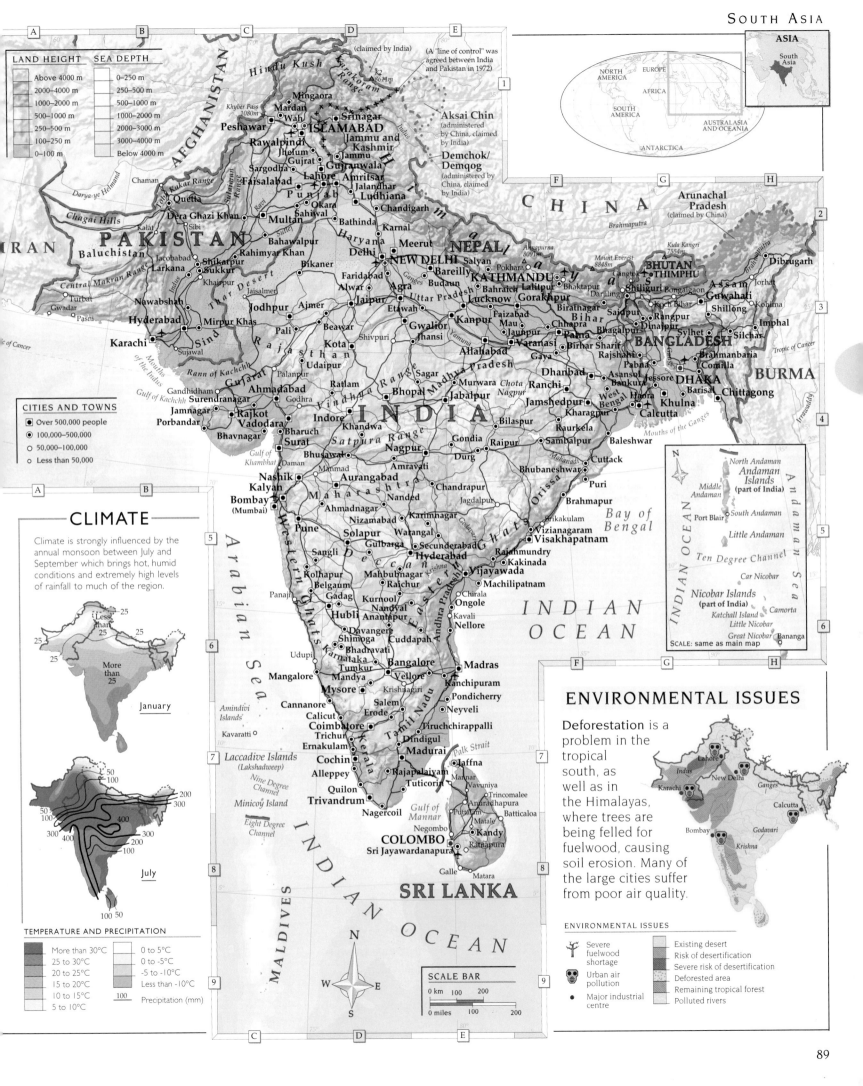

ASIA
South Asia

LAND HEIGHT
- Above 4000 m
- 2000–4000 m
- 1000–2000 m
- 500–1000 m
- 250–500 m
- 100–250 m
- 0–100 m

SEA DEPTH
- 0–250 m
- 250–500 m
- 500–1000 m
- 1000–2000 m
- 2000–3000 m
- 3000–4000 m
- Below 4000 m

(claimed by India)

(A "line of control" was agreed between India and Pakistan in 1972)

Aksai Chin (administered by China, claimed by India)

Demchok/Demqog (administered by China, claimed by India)

Arunachal Pradesh (claimed by China)

CITIES AND TOWNS
- ● Over 500,000 people
- ◉ 100,000–500,000
- ○ 50,000–100,000
- ○ Less than 50,000

CLIMATE

Climate is strongly influenced by the annual monsoon between July and September which brings hot, humid conditions and extremely high levels of rainfall to much of the region.

January

July

TEMPERATURE AND PRECIPITATION
- More than 30°C
- 25 to 30°C
- 20 to 25°C
- 15 to 20°C
- 10 to 15°C
- 5 to 10°C
- 0 to 5°C
- 0 to -5°C
- -5 to -10°C
- Less than -10°C

Precipitation (mm)

ENVIRONMENTAL ISSUES

Deforestation is a problem in the tropical south, as well as in the Himalayas, where trees are being felled for fuelwood, causing soil erosion. Many of the large cities suffer from poor air quality.

ENVIRONMENTAL ISSUES
- Severe fuelwood shortage
- Urban air pollution
- Major industrial centre
- Existing desert
- Risk of desertification
- Severe risk of desertification
- Deforested area
- Remaining tropical forest
- Polluted rivers

SCALE BAR
0 km 100 200
0 miles 100 200

SCALE: same as main map

SOUTHEAST ASIA

BRUNEI, BURMA, CAMBODIA, INDONESIA, LAOS, MALAYSIA, PHILIPPINES, SINGAPORE, THAILAND, VIETNAM

Southeast Asia is made up of a mainland area and many thousands of tropical islands. The region has great natural wealth – from precious stones to oil – and has recently experienced fast industrial growth. Some countries here, especially Singapore and Malaysia, have become prosperous, but Laos and Cambodia remain poor, and are still recovering from years of terrible warfare.

ENVIRONMENTAL ISSUES

In Burma, Malaysia and across Indonesia, ancient rainforests are being cut down faster than they can grow back. The fantastic biodiversity of the forests, with their thousands of unique species of plants and animals, is severely threatened. Forest burning has recently caused terrible smog in Indonesia.

ENVIRONMENTAL ISSUES
- Urban air pollution
- Deforested area
- Remaining tropical forest
- Major industrial centre

POPULATION

On the mainland, the population is concentrated in the river valleys, plateaus or plains. Upland areas are inhabited by small groups of hill peoples. Most people still live in rural areas, but the cities are growing fast. In Indonesia and the Philippines, the population is unevenly distributed. Some islands, such as Java, are densely settled; others are barely occupied.

- More than 200
- 100–200
- 50–100
- Less than 50
- ■ Capital city
- ● Major city

URBAN/RURAL POPULATION DIVIDE

Bangkok 1.8%
Rural population 28.2%
Other towns and cities 70%

INDUSTRY

Industries based on the processing of raw materials, like metallic minerals, timber, oil and gas and agricultural produce, are important here, but manufacturing has grown dramatically in recent years. Many foreign firms, attracted by low labour costs, have invested in the region. Malaysia and Singapore are major producers of electronic goods like disk drives for computers.

STRUCTURE OF INDUSTRY

Primary 19%
Services 45%
Manufacturing 36%

INDUSTRY
- Chemicals
- Engineering
- Food processing
- Textiles
- Mining
- Oil and gas
- Timber
- Hi-tech
- Tourism
- ■ Major industrial centre / area
- — Major road

THE LANDSCAPE

On the mainland, a belt of mountain ranges, cloaked in thick forest, runs north–south. The mountains are cut through by the wide valleys of five great rivers. On their route to the sea, these rivers have deposited sediment, forming immense, fertile flood plains and deltas. To the southeast of the mainland lies a huge arc of over 20,000 mountainous, volcanic islands.

Borneo (D 7)
Borneo is the world's third-largest island, with a total area of 757,050 sq km. Lying on the Equator and in the path of two monsoons, the island is hot, and one of the wettest places on Earth. The landscape contains thickly-forested central highlands and swampy lowlands.

Mekong river (C 4)
The mighty Mekong river flows through southern China and Burma and forms much of the border between Laos and Thailand. It then travels through Cambodia before ending in a vast delta on the southern coast of Vietnam, that is one of the world's most productive rice-growing areas.

Volcanoes
Indonesia is the most active volcanic region in the world; Java alone has over 50 active volcanoes out of the country's total of more than 220.

Philippines (E 4)
The Philippines' 7,000 islands are mountainous and volcanic with narrow coastal plains.

Irian Jaya (I 7)
Irian Jaya is a province of Indonesia. Its dense rainforests are some of the last unexplored areas on Earth and are inhabited by many rare plant and animal species.

Indonesia (C 7)
Indonesia is an archipelago of 13,677 islands, scattered over almost 5,000 km. The islands lie on the boundary between two of the Earth's tectonic plates and frequently experience earthquakes.

SCALE BAR
0 km   200   400
0 miles   200

FARMING AND LAND USE

The staple crop here is rice, which grows in low-lying flooded fields called paddies, or on terraces cut into the hillsides. Sugar cane, coconuts, bananas and pineapples are widely grown as cash crops, and Malaysia produces 25% of the world's rubber. Freshwater and marine fish are caught in large quantities; fish is one of the main foods in this region.

FARMING AND LAND USE

- Cattle
- Fishing
- Shellfish
- Coconuts
- Fruit
- Rice
- Rubber
- Sugar cane
- Timber
- Cropland
- Forest
- Pasture
- Wetland
- Major conurbation

LAND USE

- Pasture 4%
- Cropland 21%
- Forest 51%
- Other 24%

ASIA
Southeast Asia

NORTH AMERICA · EUROPE · AFRICA · SOUTH AMERICA · ANTARCTICA · AUSTRALASIA AND OCEANIA

CLIMATE

Southeast Asia's climate is strongly affected by the monsoon, which brings warm, humid air and high rainfall to mainland southeast Asia during July, and to maritime southeast Asia during January.

January

July

TEMPERATURE AND PRECIPITATION

- More than 30°C
- 20 to 30°C
- 10 to 20°C
- Less than 10°C
- 100 Precipitation (mm)

LAND HEIGHT
- Above 4000 m
- 2000–4000 m
- 1000–2000 m
- 500–1000 m
- 250–500 m
- 100–250 m
- 0–100 m

SEA DEPTH
- 0–250 m
- 250–500 m
- 500–1000 m
- 1000–2000 m
- 2000–3000 m
- 3000–4000 m
- Below 4000 m

CITIES AND TOWNS
- Over 500,000 people
- 100,000–500,000
- 50,000–100,000
- Less than 50,000

91

CONTINENTAL NORTH AMERICA

North America is the world's third largest continent, stretching from icy Greenland to the tropical Caribbean. The first people came from Asia more than 20,000 years ago. Their descendants spread across the continent, ate fish, meat, and wild and cultivated plants, and developed a wide variety of cultures and languages. About 500 years ago, immigrants from Europe, Africa, and Asia began to arrive in North America, bringing their own languages and cultures.

CROSS-SECTION THROUGH NORTH AMERICA

Rocky Mountains — Great Plains — Great Lakes — Appalachian Mountains

W — 5,200 km — E

The land immediately rises from the Pacific Ocean to the Rocky Mountains. Further east, the continent flattens into the Great Plains and the freshwater Great Lakes – gouged out by glaciers at the end of the last Ice Age. The Appalachian Mountains are older than the Rockies, and very worn down.

PHYSICAL NORTH AMERICA

The high peaks of the Rocky Mountains of Canada and the USA tower above the lower mountains of the western coasts. These ranges stretch from the icy north of Alaska, south to Mexico and Central America. The heart of the continent is flatter, and much of it is drained by the mighty Mississippi-Missouri river system.

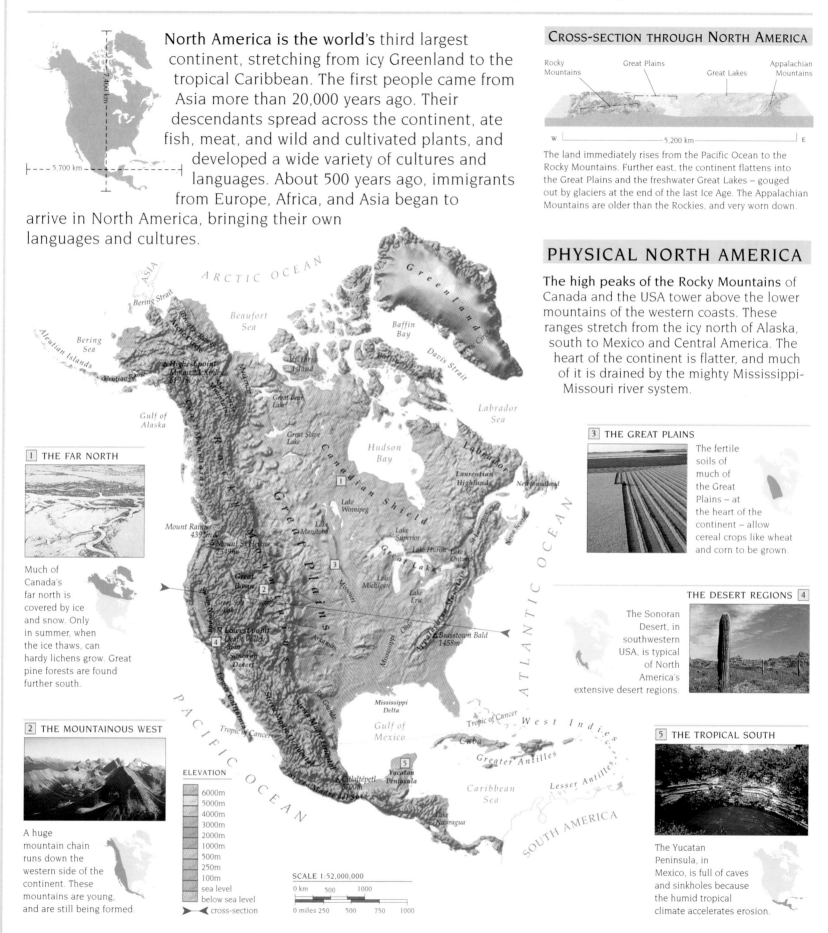

1 THE FAR NORTH

Much of Canada's far north is covered by ice and snow. Only in summer, when the ice thaws, can hardy lichens grow. Great pine forests are found further south.

2 THE MOUNTAINOUS WEST

A huge mountain chain runs down the western side of the continent. These mountains are young, and are still being formed.

3 THE GREAT PLAINS

The fertile soils of much of the Great Plains – at the heart of the continent – allow cereal crops like wheat and corn to be grown.

THE DESERT REGIONS 4

The Sonoran Desert, in southwestern USA, is typical of North America's extensive desert regions.

5 THE TROPICAL SOUTH

The Yucatan Peninsula, in Mexico, is full of caves and sinkholes because the humid tropical climate accelerates erosion.

ELEVATION

6000m
5000m
4000m
3000m
2000m
1000m
500m
250m
100m
sea level
below sea level
cross-section

SCALE 1:52,000,000

0 km   500   1000
0 miles 250   500   750   1000

POLITICAL NORTH AMERICA

The USA, Canada and Mexico are all federal countries. This means that political power is shared between the national government and the state government. Canada and the USA are democracies with a long history of freedom and equal rights. Governments in the countries south of the USA have been less stable, often ruled by dictators or harsh regimes. Many people have suffered for their political beliefs. Until about 20 years ago many of the Caribbean islands were ruled by European countries as colonies.

THE SPACE RACE

The USA has pioneered some of the great achievements of 20th century technology, including mass production of the motor car and the development of space craft.

POPULATION

The most densely populated parts of North America are the east and west coasts of the USA, central Mexico, the countries of Central America and the Caribbean islands. The far north of Canada, covered by ice, lakes and forests, has a very small and scattered population.

Largest city
MEXICO CITY
13.6 million people

POPULATION DENSITY
(People per sq km)

Below 9	50–99	250–499
10–49	100–249	Above 500

STANDARDS OF LIVING

The USA and Canada are two of the world's wealthiest countries, although pockets of poverty remain. In Central America and the Caribbean, people are less well off. Many in Mexico City live in overcrowded and inadequate housing.

STANDARD OF LIVING
(UN Human Development Index)

low   high

STATE ABBREVIATIONS

AL Alabama
CT Connecticut
IN Indiana
MA Massachusetts
MS Mississippi
NH New Hampshire
PA Pennsylvania
RI Rhode Island
VT Vermont
WV West Virginia

GREAT DISTANCES

Most people in the USA rely on automobiles to transport them from place to place. Since the 1930s, great highway systems have been built to link all parts of the continent.

POPULATION

◉ Above 500,000
◎ 100,000 to 500,000
● 50,000 to 100,000
• Below 50,000

SCALE 1:47,500,000

0 km   500   1000

0 miles 250   500   750   1000

NORTH AMERICAN GEOGRAPHY

Canada and the USA are among the world's wealthiest countries. They have rich natural resources, good farmland and thriving, varied industries. The range of different industries in Mexico is growing, but other Central American countries and the Caribbean islands rely on one or two important cash crops and tourism for most of their incomes. They have a lower standard of living than Canada and the USA.

MINERAL RESOURCES

North America still has large amounts of mineral resources. Canada has important nickel reserves, Mexico is renowned for its silver, and bauxite – used to make aluminium – is found in Jamaica. Oil and gas are plentiful, particularly in the arctic northwest by the Beaufort Sea, and further south by the Gulf of Mexico.

INDUSTRY

The USA and Canada have an extremely wide range of industries, from mining and the processing of farm produce, to heavy and light manufacturing and service industries like banking. A variety of goods are produced, including aeroplanes, cars and computers. Oil exports and machine assembly are Mexico's main industries. In Central America and the Caribbean nations, most industry is based on agricultural produce.

MINERAL RESOURCES

- Bauxite
- Copper
- Iron
- Nickel
- Phosphates
- Uranium
- Silver

Oil/gas field
Coal field

TIMBER PROCESSING

Huge tracts of forest are found across the north of the continent; over 40% of Canada is covered by forest. Timber is processed to make paper in cities such as Portland and Vancouver.

HI-TECH INDUSTRY

The Santa Clara Valley, just south of San Francisco is also known as Silicon Valley, because of the number of firms producing computer hardware and software and micro-electronics which have set up in the area.

FOOD PROCESSING

Jamaica has been famous for its rum since the 16th century. Syrup is extracted from sugar cane which is then fermented to make rum.

INDUSTRY

- ✈ Aerospace
- Brewing
- Car/vehicle manufacture
- Chemicals
- Coal
- Defence
- Engineering
- Film industry
- Finance
- Food processing
- Hi-tech industry
- Iron & steel
- Oil & gas
- Pharmaceuticals
- Printing & publishing
- Research & development
- Shipbuilding
- Textiles
- Timber processing

GNP per capita (US$)

- Below 1999
- 2000-4999
- 5000-9999
- 10,000-19,999
- 20,000-24,999
- Above 25,000
- Industrial centre

MANUFACTURING

Mexico has many car assembly plants, like this Volkswagen plant. Labour costs in Mexico are low, making it cheap to assemble cars here.

ARCTIC OCEAN
ASIA
Bering Sea
Beaufort Sea
Baffin Bay
Greenland (to Denmark)
US
Gulf of Alaska
Labrador Sea
Hudson Bay
C A N A D A
Vancouver
Calgary
Seattle
Winnipeg
Portland
Montréal
Minneapolis
Toronto
Boston
UNITED STATES
Detroit
Buffalo
New York
Chicago
Cleveland
Pittsburgh
Philadelphia
San Francisco
Denver
Kansas City
Baltimore
OF AMERICA
Saint Louis
Los Angeles
Tulsa
Birmingham
Atlanta
Phoenix
San Diego
Dallas
El Paso
Houston
Ciudad Juárez
New Orleans
Tampa
Monterrey
Miami
Gulf of Mexico
DOMINICAN REPUBLIC
BAHAMAS
West Indies
Puerto Rico (to US)
San Juan
Guadalajara
Havana
CUBA
HAITI
Santo Domingo
MEXICO
Port-au-Prince
Mexico City
Puebla
JAMAICA
Caribbean Sea
TRINIDAD & TOBAGO
Port-of-Spain
GUATEMALA
BELIZE
HONDURAS
Guatemala City
San Salvador
NICARAGUA
EL SALVADOR
Managua
Panama City
COSTA RICA
San José
PANAMA
PACIFIC OCEAN
ATLANTIC OCEAN
SOUTH AMERICA

CLIMATE

Much of northern Canada lies within the Arctic Circle and is permanently covered by ice or the sparse vegetation known as tundra. Southern Canada and much of central USA have a continental climate, with hot summers and cold winters. The southern parts of the USA, Central America and the Caribbean have a hot, humid tropical climate. The islands and the eastern and central states of the USA often experience hurricane-force winds, waterspouts and tornadoes.

EXTREME WEATHER EVENTS

Symbols indicate climatic extremes

CLIMATE

Ice cap
Tundra
Sub-arctic
Cool continental
Warm temperate
Mediterranean
Semi-arid
Arid
Humid equatorial
Tropical
Hot Humid

Coldest place
NORTHICE (Greenland)
Temp. -66°C

Wettest place
HENDERSON LAKE (BC, Canada)
Annual rainfall 6650mm

Hottest place
DEATH VALLEY (CA, USA)
Temp. 57°C

Driest place
BATAQUES (Mexico)
Annual rainfall 30mm

NORTH AMERICA

NORTH AMERICA'S HOTTEST PLACE

Death Valley in California is the hottest and driest place in the USA. Strong, dry winds sweep through the valley, constantly reshaping the sand and salt deposits which cover its floor.

LAND USE AND AGRICULTURE

On the Great Plains of Canada and the USA, vast quantities of cereal crops, including corn and wheat, grow in the fertile soils. Cattle are also raised on great ranches throughout these regions and on the foothills of the Rocky Mountains. In California, vegetables and fruits are grown with the aid of irrigation. Bananas, coffee and sugar cane are grown for export in Central America and the Caribbean, while sorghum and maize are grown as subsistence crops.

BANANA PLANTATION

Banana plantations are common in the Caribbean and Central America. The fruit is grown for local consumption and for export to the USA and Europe, where they are valued for their flavour and nutritional qualities.

FISHING

The Grand Banks off the eastern coast of Canada were once home to almost limitless fish stocks. Overfishing has reduced the number of fish to very low levels. Quotas limiting the numbers of fish caught are helping numbers to rise.

LAND USE AND AGRICULTURE

Cattle
Poultry
Pigs
Reindeer
Sheep
Bananas
Cereals
Citrus fruits
Coffee
Corn (maize)
Cotton
Fishing
Fruit
Peanuts
Rice
Shellfish
Soya beans
Sugar cane
Timber
Tobacco
Vineyards

Cropland
Desert
Forest
Ice cap
Mountain region
Pasture
Tundra
Wetland
Major conurbation

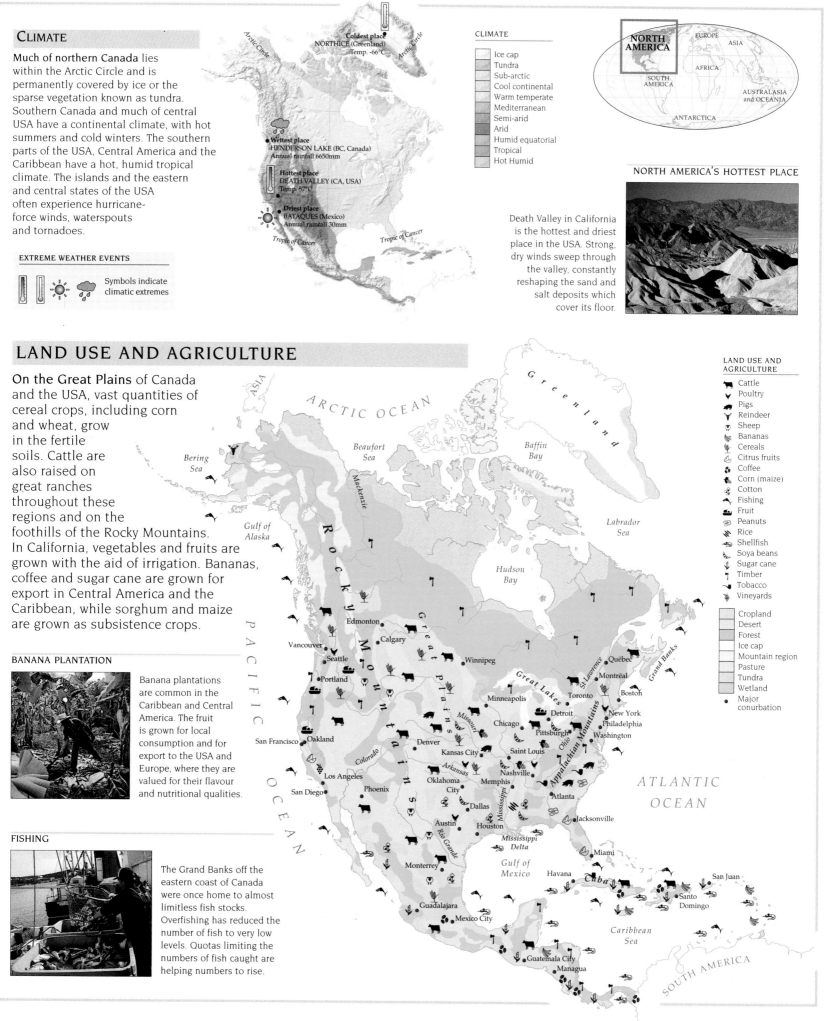

WESTERN CANADA & ALASKA

ALBERTA, BRITISH COLUMBIA, MANITOBA, NORTHWEST
TERRITORIES, SASKATCHEWAN, YUKON TERRITORY, ALASKA

The first inhabitants of Canada's western provinces
were native Americans. By the late 1800s, the
Canadian Pacific Railroad was completed and
European settlers moved west, turning most of the
prairie into huge grain farms. North of the prairies
lie the vast, empty territories. Alaska is part of the
USA. It has immense oil reserves amidst some of
the world's greatest wilderness areas.

POPULATION

Most of western Canada's people live near the Canada/US
border, taking advantage of the warmer climate and convenient
transport routes. In Alaska, most people live in the city of
Anchorage and in southern regions. Further north, the
population is sparse, with only a few people per 100 sq km –
many of them native Americans such as the
Inuit and Inupiaq.

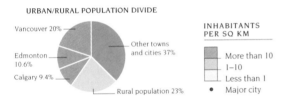

URBAN/RURAL POPULATION DIVIDE

Vancouver 20%
Other towns
and cities 37%
Edmonton
10.6%
Calgary 9.4%
Rural population 23%

INHABITANTS
PER SQ KM

More than 10
1–10
Less than 1
● Major city

ENVIRONMENTAL ISSUES

Across the north of the region, the ground
is permanently frozen. This is called
permafrost. Building on this frozen surface
is very difficult, because the heat from
houses or roads can cause the ground to
melt, and subside. The Trans-Alaskan
Pipeline, which brings oil from Prudhoe
Bay to Valdez, was built above
ground to prevent the
permafrost melting.

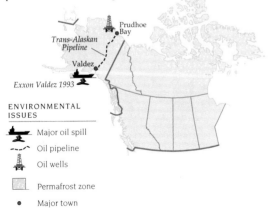

Prudhoe
Bay
Trans-Alaskan
Pipeline
Valdez
Exxon Valdez 1993

ENVIRONMENTAL
ISSUES

Major oil spill
Oil pipeline
Oil wells
Permafrost zone
● Major town

FARMING AND LAND USE

More than 20% of the world's wheat is grown in
Canada's prairie provinces: Manitoba, Alberta
and Saskatchewan. Beef cattle
graze on the ranches of Alberta
and British Columbia. Fruits,
especially apples, flourish
in the sheltered southern
valleys of British Columbia,
and Pacific salmon and herring are
caught off the west coast. Much of
the region is heavily forested.

Anchorage
Edmonton
Vancouver Calgary Winnipeg

LAND USE

Pasture 5%
Cropland 4%
Forest 38%
Other
(including
mountains)
53%

FARMING AND LAND USE

Cattle
Fishing
Cereals
Fruit
Timber
● Major conurbation

Pasture
Cropland
Forest
Mountain region
Barren
Tundra

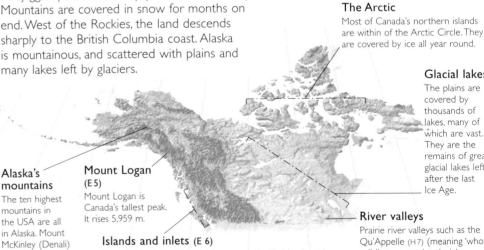

Near
Islands
Attu Island

B e r i n g

S e a

Limit o Winter pack ice

Rat
Islands

Amchitka
Island

Nunivak Is

Andreanof
Islands

Aleutian Islands

Pribilof
Islands

Atka

Umnak Island
Unalaska Island

Dutch Harbor

Unimak Island
Belkofski

Anchorage

Edmonton Saskatoon
Vancouver Calgary Winnipeg
Regina

THE LANDSCAPE

The prairie provinces are mostly flat. Occasionally,
the level plains are broken up by river valleys such
as the Qu'Appelle in Saskatchewan. In the west,
the jagged peaks and steep passes of the Rocky
Mountains are covered in snow for months on
end. West of the Rockies, the land descends
sharply to the British Columbia coast. Alaska
is mountainous, and scattered with plains and
many lakes left by glaciers.

The Arctic
Most of Canada's northern islands
are within of the Arctic Circle. They
are covered by ice all year round.

Glacial lakes
The plains are
covered by
thousands of
lakes, many of
which are vast.
They are the
remains of great
glacial lakes left
after the last
Ice Age.

River valleys
Prairie river valleys such as the
Qu'Appelle (H7) (meaning 'who
calls') were cut by glacial
meltwater thousands of years ago.

Alaska's
mountains
The ten highest
mountains in
the USA are all
in Alaska. Mount
McKinley (Denali)
(D4) is the highest
at 6,194 m.

Mount Logan
(E 5)
Mount Logan is
Canada's tallest peak.
It rises 5,959 m.

Islands and inlets (E 6)
The British Columbia coast is peppered with islands and
fjord-like inlets, created by the force of the Pacific Ocean.

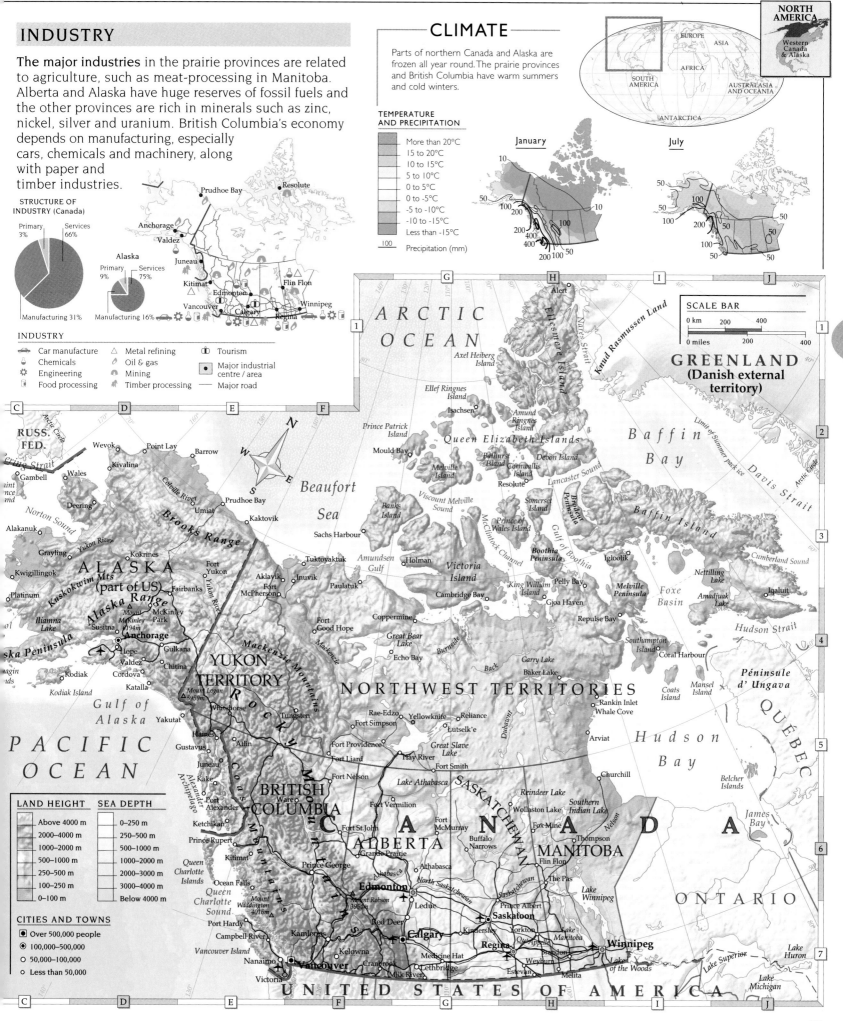

INDUSTRY

The major industries in the prairie provinces are related to agriculture, such as meat-processing in Manitoba. Alberta and Alaska have huge reserves of fossil fuels and the other provinces are rich in minerals such as zinc, nickel, silver and uranium. British Columbia's economy depends on manufacturing, especially cars, chemicals and machinery, along with paper and timber industries.

STRUCTURE OF INDUSTRY (Canada)

Primary 3%
Services 66%
Manufacturing 31%

Alaska

Primary 9%
Services 75%
Manufacturing 16%

INDUSTRY

- Car manufacture
- Chemicals
- Engineering
- Food processing
- Metal refining
- Oil & gas
- Mining
- Timber processing
- Tourism
- Major industrial centre / area
- Major road

CLIMATE

Parts of northern Canada and Alaska are frozen all year round. The prairie provinces and British Columbia have warm summers and cold winters.

TEMPERATURE AND PRECIPITATION

- More than 20°C
- 15 to 20°C
- 10 to 15°C
- 5 to 10°C
- 0 to 5°C
- 0 to -5°C
- -5 to -10°C
- -10 to -15°C
- Less than -15°C
- —— Precipitation (mm)

January

July

NORTH AMERICA
Western Canada & Alaska

EUROPE
ASIA
AFRICA
SOUTH AMERICA
AUSTRALASIA AND OCEANIA
ANTARCTICA

SCALE BAR
0 km 200 400
0 miles 200 400

LAND HEIGHT

- Above 4000 m
- 2000–4000 m
- 1000–2000 m
- 500–1000 m
- 250–500 m
- 100–250 m
- 0–100 m

SEA DEPTH

- 0–250 m
- 250–500 m
- 500–1000 m
- 1000–2000 m
- 2000–3000 m
- 3000–4000 m
- Below 4000 m

CITIES AND TOWNS

- Over 500,000 people
- 100,000–500,000
- 50,000–100,000
- Less than 50,000

EASTERN CANADA

NEW BRUNSWICK, NEWFOUNDLAND AND LABRADOR,
NOVA SCOTIA, ONTARIO, PRINCE EDWARD ISLAND, QUÉBEC

The first towns built by European settlers grew up in the maritime provinces, close to the rich fishing grounds of the Atlantic Ocean. In recent years, people have migrated to cities along the St. Lawrence River and near to the Great Lakes. Although most Canadians speak English, people in Québec speak mainly French and have sought independence from the rest of Canada.

INDUSTRY

In the maritime provinces the traditional fishing industry has declined, causing unemployment. However, Newfoundland has a thriving food processing industry. Ontario and Québec have a wide range of industries, including the generation of hydro-electricity, mining, and chemicals, car manufacture and fruit canning in the great cities. Large amounts of wood pulp and paper are also produced.

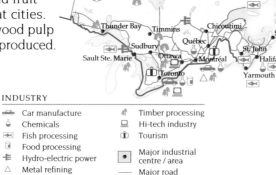

STRUCTURE
OF INDUSTRY

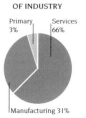

Primary 3%
Services 66%
Manufacturing 31%

INDUSTRY

Car manufacture	Timber processing
Chemicals	Hi-tech industry
Fish processing	Tourism
Food processing	
Hydro-electric power	Major industrial centre / area
Metal refining	Major road
Mining	

FARMING AND LAND USE

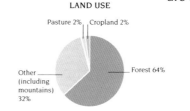

The best farmland lies on the flat, fertile plains close to the St. Lawrence River and on the strip of land between lakes Erie and Ontario. It is used to grow fruits such as grapes, cherries and peaches, and to raise cattle. Nova Scotia has fruit farms, and the rich red soils of Prince Edward Island produce a big crop of potatoes. The vast forests that grow across the north are a major source of timber.

LAND USE

Pasture 2%   Cropland 2%

Other (including mountains) 32%

Forest 64%

FARMING AND LAND USE

Cattle		Pasture	
Fishing		Cropland	
Fruit		Forest	
Potatoes		Tundra	
Timber		Major conurbation	

ENVIRONMENTAL ISSUES

Acid rain caused by emissions from factories in the USA and along the St. Lawrence River destroys forests and kills marine life. Several huge new hydro-electric power schemes are planned for James Bay on Hudson Bay, which will flood huge areas of land. Overfishing in the Atlantic has led to limits being set on the number of fish that can be caught.

ENVIRONMENTAL ISSUES

Depleted fish stocks	
Major dam	
Urban air pollution	
Affected by acid rain	
Major industrial centre	

THE LANDSCAPE

A huge, ancient mass of rock called the Canadian Shield lies beneath much of eastern Canada. It is covered by low hills, rocky outcrops, thousands of lakes and huge areas of forest. Much of the Canadian Shield is permanently frozen. The St. Lawrence River flows out of Lake Ontario and on into the Atlantic Ocean. It is surrounded by rolling hills and flat areas of very fertile farmland.

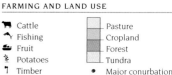

Scoured by ice
About 20,000 years ago, Labrador and northern Québec were completely covered by ice. The glaciers scraped hollows in the rock beneath. When the ice melted, lakes were left in the hollows that remained.

Lake Superior (B 5)
Lake Superior is the largest freshwater lake in the world. It covers an area of 83,270 sq km and lies between Canada and the USA.

St. Lawrence River (E 5)
The St. Lawrence River is 1,197 km long. Parts of it have become silted up, causing it to be 'braided' into many different channels. Between December and mid-April the river freezes over.

Highlands
The highlands of New Brunswick, Nova Scotia and Newfoundland are the most northerly part of the Appalachian mountain chain.

The Bay of Fundy (F 5)
This bay has the world's highest tides. It is shaped like a funnel, and as the Atlantic flows into it, the ever narrowing shores cause the water level to rise 6–15 m at every high tide.

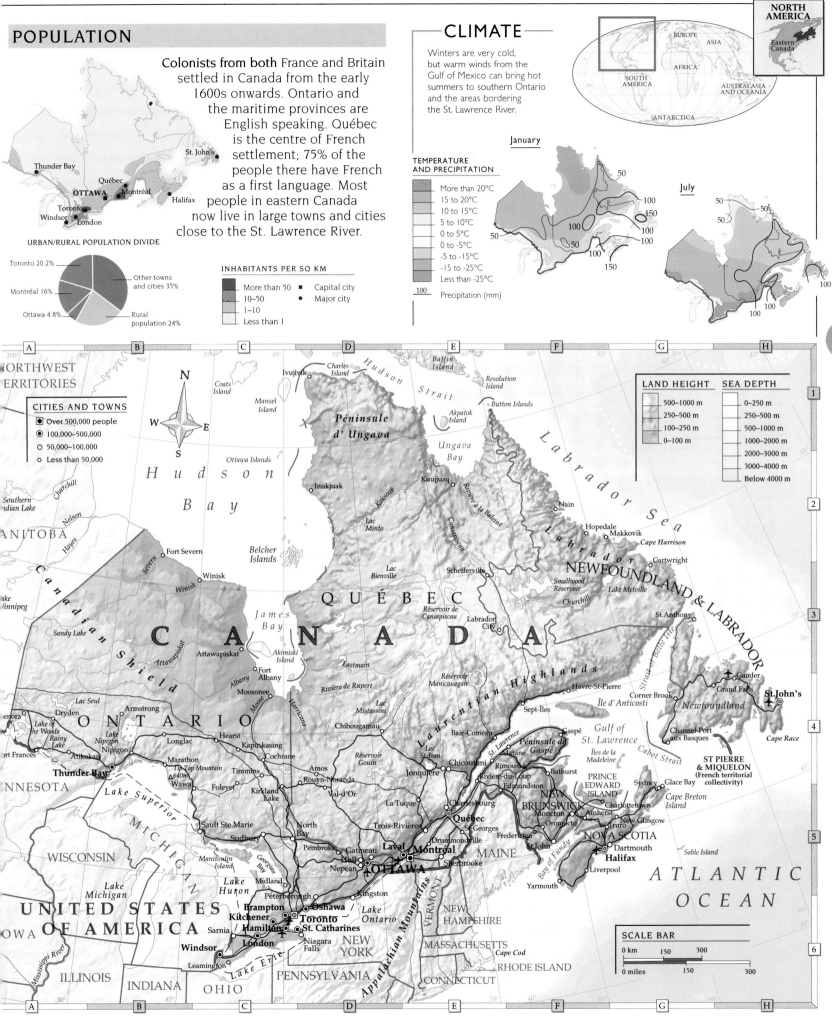

POPULATION

Colonists from both France and Britain settled in Canada from the early 1600s onwards. Ontario and the maritime provinces are English speaking. Québec is the centre of French settlement; 75% of the people there have French as a first language. Most people in eastern Canada now live in large towns and cities close to the St. Lawrence River.

URBAN/RURAL POPULATION DIVIDE

Toronto 20.2%

Montréal 16%

Ottawa 4.8%

Other towns and cities 35%

Rural population 24%

INHABITANTS PER SQ KM

More than 50
10–50
1–10
Less than 1

■ Capital city
● Major city

CLIMATE

Winters are very cold, but warm winds from the Gulf of Mexico can bring hot summers to southern Ontario and the areas bordering the St. Lawrence River.

January

TEMPERATURE
AND PRECIPITATION

More than 20°C
15 to 20°C
10 to 15°C
5 to 10°C
0 to 5°C
0 to -5°C
-5 to -15°C
-15 to -25°C
Less than -25°C

100 Precipitation (mm)

July

LAND HEIGHT
500–1000 m
250–500 m
100–250 m
0–100 m

SEA DEPTH
0–250 m
250–500 m
500–1000 m
1000–2000 m
2000–3000 m
3000–4000 m
Below 4000 m

CITIES AND TOWNS
■ Over 500,000 people
◉ 100,000–500,000
○ 50,000–100,000
○ Less than 50,000

SCALE BAR

0 km 150 300

0 miles 150 300

EASTERN USA

The east coast of the USA was settled by European colonists from the 17th century onwards. When the USA became independent in 1776, people gradually spread westwards towards the Mississippi River, and down towards the southern states. In the late 19th and early 20th centuries, thousands of immigrants from all over the world passed through New York on their way to new lives elsewhere in the USA. Today, the eastern USA contains some of the world's most developed and powerful cities.

POPULATION

The northeastern and Great Lakes states are the most populous parts of North America, with people taking advantage of the good transport routes and the availability of jobs. Some of the USA's biggest cities, like New York, are found here, yet in New England many towns have less than 30,000 people. In recent years, many have migrated to the 'Sunbelt' states of the south – especially to Florida.

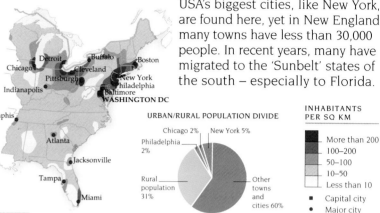

URBAN/RURAL POPULATION DIVIDE

Chicago 2% | New York 5%
Philadelphia 2%
Rural population 31%
Other towns and cities 60%

INHABITANTS PER SQ KM
- More than 200
- 100–200
- 50–100
- 10–50
- Less than 10
- ■ Capital city
- ● Major city

INDUSTRY

The northeast is the USA's industrial heartland. The Great Lakes states are the centre of car manufacturing, but service industries are also developing. Hi-tech industries such as computers and electronics are found around Boston and in New Jersey. New York is the USA's financial capital. Further south, states like North Carolina are centres for research and development and Florida has a successful tourist industry.

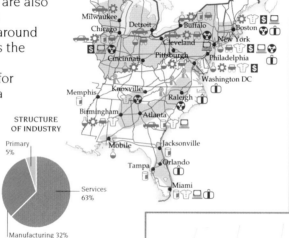

STRUCTURE OF INDUSTRY

Primary 5%
Services 63%
Manufacturing 32%

INDUSTRY
- 🚗 Car manufacture
- ⚗ Chemicals
- ⚙ Engineering
- Food processing
- Iron & steel
- Textiles
- Coal
- $ Finance
- Hi-tech industry
- Research & Development
- Tourism
- ▪ Major industrial centre / area
- — Major road

THE LANDSCAPE

The Atlantic and Gulf coasts are bordered in the south by a wide and mainly low-lying plain, with many swampy areas. Towards the north, the plain gradually falls away, forming salt marshes, lagoons and offshore sandbars. Inland, the plain is overlooked by the rounded peaks of the Appalachian Mountains. West of the mountains is the vast Mississippi Basin.

Great Lakes
The five Great Lakes were formed during the last Ice Age and contain 20% of the world's fresh water. The area around the lakes is rich in natural resources, including coal, iron, copper and timber.

Appalachian Mountains (E4)
The forest-covered Appalachians are one of the oldest mountain chains in the world. Over a period of about 400 million years they have been lowered and rounded by erosion. Their eastern side has been worn down to a plain called a piedmont, or 'mountain foot'.

FARMING AND LAND USE

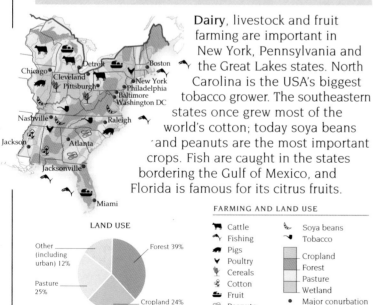

Dairy, livestock and fruit farming are important in New York, Pennsylvania and the Great Lakes states. North Carolina is the USA's biggest tobacco grower. The southeastern states once grew most of the world's cotton; today soya beans and peanuts are the most important crops. Fish are caught in the states bordering the Gulf of Mexico, and Florida is famous for its citrus fruits.

LAND USE
Other (including urban) 12%
Forest 39%
Pasture 25%
Cropland 24%

FARMING AND LAND USE
- Cattle
- Fishing
- Pigs
- Poultry
- Cereals
- Cotton
- Fruit
- Peanuts
- Soya beans
- Tobacco
- Cropland
- Forest
- Pasture
- Wetland
- ● Major conurbation

Flooded valleys (F4)
Along the Atlantic coast the lower reaches of many river valleys have been flooded by the sea. This has created large bays and inlets such as Long Island Sound and Chesapeake Bay.

Mississippi River (C4)
The Mississippi is the world's third longest river, and one of its busiest waterways. Goods from the agricultural and industrial regions around the Great Lakes are transported by barge down to the Gulf of Mexico.

The Everglades (E7)
One-fifth of Florida is covered by swampy tropical wetlands. Part of this area includes the Everglades National Park, which is home to many wild animals and plants, including some endangered species.

NORTH AMERICA
Eastern USA

ENVIRONMENTAL ISSUES

Air pollution, caused by emissions from industry and power stations, and car fumes, is a problem in the cities and sprawling built-up areas close to the Great Lakes and along the Atlantic coast. Acid rain affects most of the area, and many of the larger rivers have been polluted by industrial effluent.

ENVIRONMENTAL ISSUES

☠ Urban air pollution

　 Affected by acid rain
　 Built-up areas
　 Polluted rivers
• Major industrial centre

CLIMATE

The northeast has warm summers and cold winters, often with heavy snow. The Great Lakes often freeze over in winter. The southern states have hot humid summers and mild winters.

January

July

TEMPERATURE AND PRECIPITATION

More than 25¡C
20 to 25¡C
15 to 20¡C
10 to 15¡C
5 to 10¡C
0 to 5¡C

0 to -5¡C
-5 to -10¡C
Less than -10¡C

—100— Precipitation (mm)

LAND HEIGHT

2000–4000 m
1000–2000 m
500–1000 m
250–500 m
100–250 m
0–100 m

SEA DEPTH

0–250 m
250–500 m
500–1000 m
1000–2000 m
2000–3000 m
3000–4000 m
Below 4000 m

SCALE BAR

0 km   100   200

0 miles 100   200

CITIES AND TOWNS

▪ Over 500,000 people
● 100,000–500,000
○ 50,000–100,000
∘ Less than 50,000

101

WESTERN USA

Western USA stretches from the Mississippi Basin across the Great Plains to the mighty Rocky Mountains and the Pacific Ocean. Its dramatic scenery varies from vast evergreen forests and lush valleys in the north, to the huge farming and cattle-ranching prairies of the Midwest and the deserts of the southwest, where temperatures soar over 40°C in summer. The western states have a very racially mixed population. Many people have ancestors from Europe, Africa and Asia, and the southwest is home to communities of native Americans such as the Navajo.

INDUSTRY

Western USA is a major agricultural producer, although its cities have a variety of manufacturing and service industries. Washington has an important aerospace industry, and its forests, along with those in Oregon, supply most of the USA's timber. Oklahoma and Texas have big oil and gas fields, and minerals are mined in Montana and Wyoming. 'Silicon Valley' in California is a world centre for micro-electronics.

INDUSTRY

- ✈ Aerospace industry
- 🚗 Car manufacture
- 🝪 Chemicals
- ⚙ Engineering
- 🍲 Food processing
- 👕 Textiles
- ⛏ Mining
- ⬭ Oil & gas
- 🪚 Timber processing
- 💻 Hi-tech industry
- ⚙ Research & development
- ⓘ Tourism
- ▪ Major industrial centre / area
- — Major road

STRUCTURE OF INDUSTRY

Primary 7%
Services 65%
Manufacturing 28%

POPULATION

California has more people than any other US state. Immigrants from Asia and Latin America, especially Mexico, make up a large, and growing, part of its population. Outside the big cities, most of the other western states are sparsely populated, and people depend on cars to cover the huge distances between places.

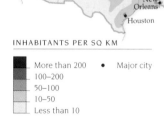

INHABITANTS PER SQ KM

- ■ More than 200
- ■ 100–200
- ■ 50–100
- ■ 10–50
- □ Less than 10
- ● Major city

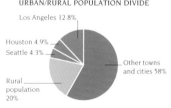

URBAN/RURAL POPULATION DIVIDE

Los Angeles 12.8%
Houston 4.9%
Seattle 4.3%
Other towns and cities 58%
Rural population 20%

FARMING AND LAND USE

Huge cereal farms and cattle ranches take up most of the Great Plains. More maize and wheat is produced here than anywhere else in the world. Fruit is grown in the sheltered valleys of Oregon and Washington, and in California, where the fertile but dry land is irrigated almost all year round to produce the country's biggest crop of citrus and other fruits.

LAND USE

Other 11%
Pasture 45%
Forest 15%
Cropland 29%

FARMING AND LAND USE

- 🐄 Cattle
- 🐟 Fishing
- 🐖 Pigs
- 🦃 Poultry
- 🦐 Shellfish
- 🌾 Cereals
- 🌱 Cotton
- 🍎 Fruit
- 🫘 Soya beans
- 🌲 Timber
- ■ Cropland
- ■ Desert
- ■ Forest
- ■ Pasture
- □ Wetland
- ● Major conurbation

THE LANDSCAPE

The Great Plains sweep west from the Mississippi River flood plain. At the western edge of the plains the land rises, becoming the Rocky Mountains. Within this chain there are many high plateaus and basins. Further west are the Sierra Nevada, the Cascade Range, and finally the Coast Ranges, which run along the Pacific seaboard.

Cascade Range (B 2)

These mountains run from Washington through Oregon and south into California. They include a chain of volcanoes, one of which, Mount Saint Helens, last erupted in 1980.

Death Valley (C 3)

Death Valley in California lies 86 m below sea level. It is the lowest point in the western hemisphere, and one of the hottest places on Earth.

Rocky Mountains (D 3)

The Rockies stretch in an almost unbroken chain from Alaska to New Mexico. Some of North America's highest peaks are found here, as well as many active volcanoes.

Badlands (E 2)

About 5,200 sq km of South Dakota is covered by 'badlands'. These are created in dry areas with little or no vegetation; occasional heavy rainstorms wear away the exposed rock to create deep gullies and sharp pinnacles.

Earthquakes

The San Andreas Fault is a break in the Earth's crust that runs for 1,050 km through California. A sudden movement of land along the fault causes earthquakes, such as the one in 1994 which caused much damage in Los Angeles.

Grand Canyon (C 4)

The Grand Canyon in Arizona is a spectacular gorge cut by the Colorado River. The canyon is about 446 km long, between 8–29 km wide and up to 1,829 m deep.

Great Plains (E 3)

The landscape of the Great Plains is largely treeless farmland. The region was once natural grassland or prairie, grazed by huge herds of buffalo. Being far from any oceans, summers here are very hot and winters freezing.

ENVIRONMENTAL ISSUES

Water shortages have led to the building of many dams and reservoirs in the mountains, and the transport of water over ever greater distances. The Ogallala Aquifer is a vast source of underground water, but it is being rapidly reduced by extraction for irrigation. The USA was the first country to create national parks; beginning with Yellowstone in 1872; it now has 350 others.

ENVIRONMENTAL ISSUES

- Major dam
- National park
- Aquifer
- Polluted river

CLIMATE

In winter, moist air from the Pacific brings heavy rainfall to the coastal mountains in the west, while temperatures plunge below zero on the Great Plains. Summers are dry and hot, especially in the south, where drought and water shortages are common.

TEMPERATURE AND PRECIPITATION

- More than 30°C
- 25 to 30°C
- 20 to 25°C
- 15 to 20°C
- 10 to 15°C
- 5 to 10°C
- 0 to 5°C
- 0 to -5°C
- -5 to -10°C
- Less than -10°C

100 — Precipitation (mm)

NORTH AMERICA

January   July

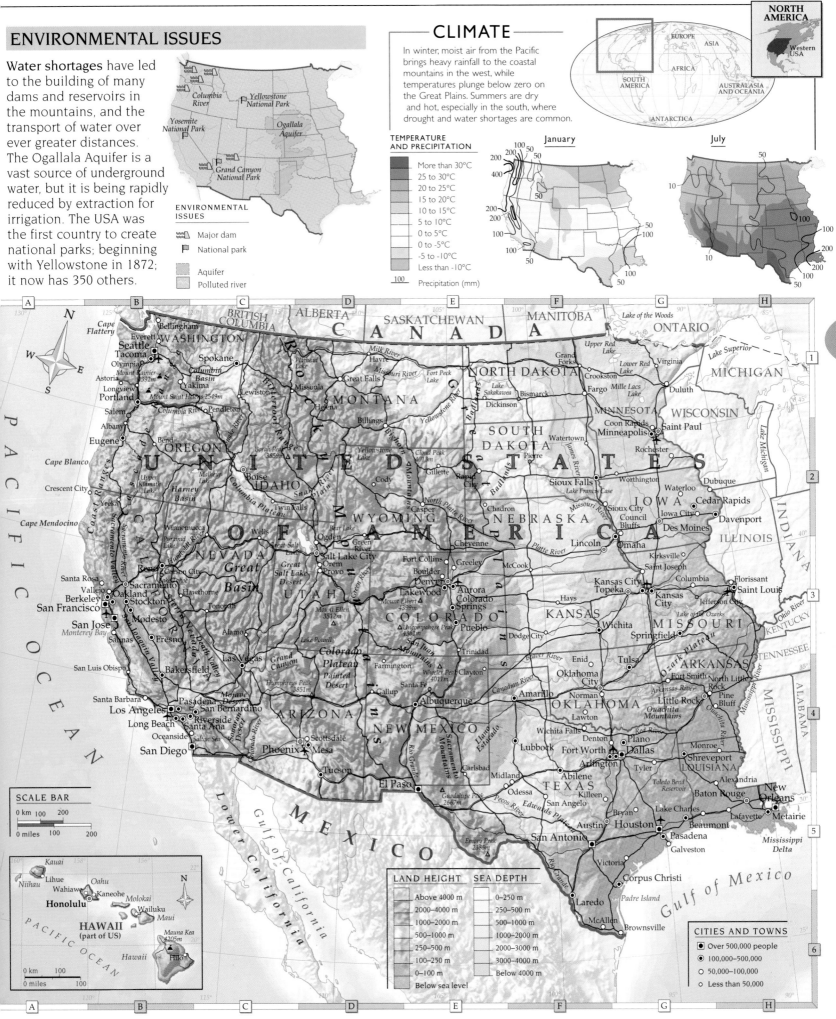

LAND HEIGHT
- Above 4000 m
- 2000–4000 m
- 1000–2000 m
- 500–1000 m
- 250–500 m
- 100–250 m
- 0–100 m
- Below sea level

SEA DEPTH
- 0–250 m
- 250–500 m
- 500–1000 m
- 1000–2000 m
- 2000–3000 m
- 3000–4000 m
- Below 4000 m

CITIES AND TOWNS
- Over 500,000 people
- 100,000–500,000
- 50,000–100,000
- Less than 50,000

SCALE BAR
0 km 100 200
0 miles 100 200

HAWAII (part of US)

MEXICO

Mexico is a large country with a rich mixture of traditions and cultures. The ancient civilization of the Aztecs which flourished here was crushed by Spanish invaders in the 16th century. Spain ruled Mexico until its independence in 1836 and today, the country has the world's largest and fastest growing Spanish-speaking population. Mexico is mostly dry and mountainous, and farm land is limited, so the country has to import most of the basic foods it needs to feed its people.

FARMING AND LAND USE

Most of the land suitable for farming is planted with corn – a big part of the Mexican diet. Along the Gulf coast coffee, sugar cane and cotton are grown on plantations for export. Parts of the dry north are irrigated to grow cotton, but most of the land is taken up by large cattle ranches. Fishing, especially for shellfish such as lobster and shrimp is important in coastal areas.

FARMING AND LAND USE

- 🐂 Cattle
- ⚓ Fishing
- ☕ Coffee
- 🌽 Corn (maize)
- 🧵 Cotton
- 🦐 Shellfish
- ⚡ Sugar cane
- 🌲 Timber

- Cropland
- Desert
- Forest
- Pasture
- Wetland
- ● Major conurbation

LAND USE

- Cropland 13%
- Other 22%
- Forest 26%
- Pasture 39%

THE LANDSCAPE

Much of Mexico is made up of a high plateau. The climate there is very dry and varies between true desert in the north, and semi-desert further south. The plateau is separated from the coastal plains by two long, rugged mountain chains: the Eastern Sierra Madre and the Western Sierra Madre. Towards the south, the mountain ranges join, meeting in the region of high volcanic peaks that surround Mexico City.

The Rio Grande (D 2)
This river flows from Colorado in the USA and forms much of Mexico's northern border. It crosses a vast arid area on its way to the Gulf of Mexico.

Earthquakes and volcanoes
Volcanic activity is common in Mexico. Popocatépetl (F 5) and Volcán El Chichónal (G 5) have erupted recently, and Mexico City was hit by a devastating earthquake in 1985

Eastern Sierra Madre (D 5).

Yucatan Peninsula (H 4)
The Yucatan Peninsula is a low, wide tableland, formed by layers of limestone. Limestone absorbs water, so there are few rivers on the peninsula, and the tropical rainforests found there are fed mainly by streams and underground water.

Lower California (B 3)
This long and very dry peninsula, separates the Gulf of California from the Pacific Ocean. The Gulf was formed after the last Ice Age, when the sea rose to flood a major rift valley.

Western Sierra Madre (C 3).

POPULATION

Most of the north is sparsely populated due to the hot, dry climate and lack of cultivable farm land. As people have migrated from the countryside in search of work, the cities have grown dramatically; almost 75% of Mexicans now live in urban areas. Mexico City is home to almost a quarter of the population and is one of the world's largest cities.

INHABITANTS PER SQ KM

- More than 200
- 100–200
- 50–100
- Less than 50
- ■ Capital city
- ● Major city

URBAN/RURAL POPULATION DIVIDE

- Mexico City 21.6%
- Guadalajara 2.4%
- Monterrey 2%
- Rural population 26%
- Other towns and cities 48%

ENVIRONMENTAL ISSUES

Fast, unplanned growth has led to poor sanitation and water supplies in Mexico City, while the wall of mountains which surround the city traps pollution from cars and factories, giving it some of the world's worst air pollution. Much of Mexico's tropical rainforest has been felled, leading to increased soil erosion. Land clearance further north is also causing desertification.

ENVIRONMENTAL ISSUES

- 🌋 Volcanic eruption
- ☠ Urban air pollution
- Risk of desertification
- Deforested areas
- Remaining tropical forests
- ● Major industrial city

CALIFORNIA

Tijuana Mexicali

Rosarito
Ensenada

Sierra San Pedro Mártir

Isla Cedros Sebastián Vizcaíno
Guerrero Neg

Tropic of Cancer

Isla Clarión

NORTH AMERICA

Mexico

INDUSTRY

Oil and gas on the Gulf coast are the biggest source of income. Mexico is also rich in other minerals; it is the world's top silver producer. Manufacturing is centred around Mexico City and along the US border, where mainly foreign owned factories assemble products for export.

Tourism is increasing throughout Mexico.

STRUCTURE OF INDUSTRY

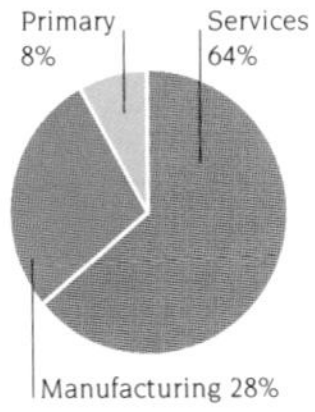

Primary 8%
Services 64%
Manufacturing 28%

INDUSTRY

- 🚗 Car manufacture
- Electronics
- ⚙ Engineering
- Food processing
- Iron & steel
- Oil refining
- Textiles
- Mining
- Oil and gas
- Tourism
- ◉ Major industrial centre / area
- — Major road

Industry map labels: Mexicali, Tijuana, Ciudad Juárez, Chihuahua, Piedras Negras, Nuevo Laredo, Reynosa, Torreón, Monterrey, San Luis Potosí, Tampico, Mérida, Guadalajara, Veracruz, Mexico City, Puebla, Minatitlán, Manzanillo, Oaxaca, Salina Cruz

CLIMATE

Northern Mexico and the peninsula of Lower California are dry, hot and largely desert. Towards the south, rainfall increases, especially in July. Moist, warm conditions allow rainforests to grow.

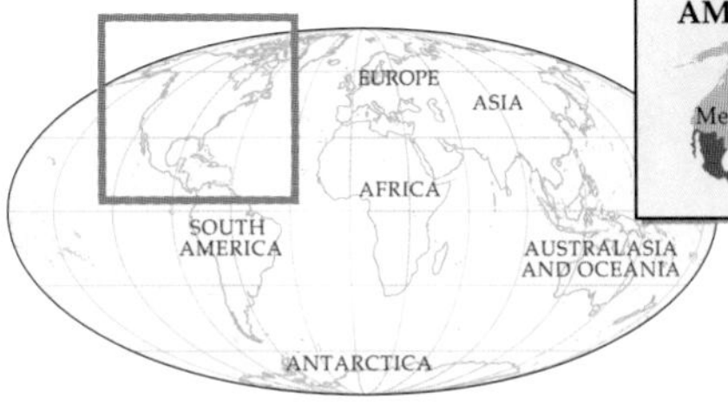

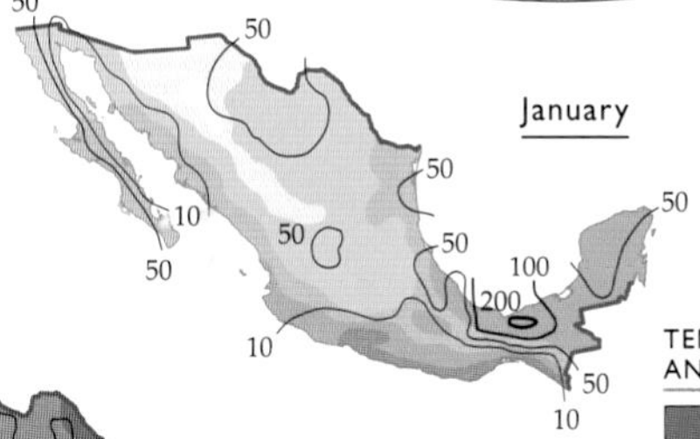

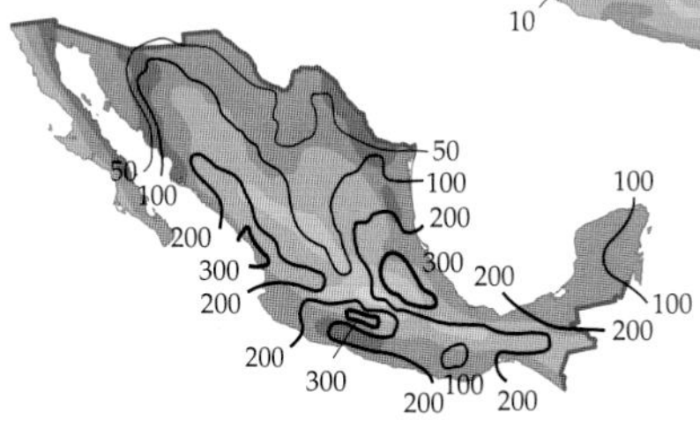

January

July

TEMPERATURE AND PRECIPITATION

- More than 30°C
- 25 to 30°C
- 20 to 25°C
- 15 to 20°C
- 10 to 15°C
- 5 to 10°C
- Less than 5°C

— 100 Precipitation (mm)

Globe labels: EUROPE, ASIA, AFRICA, SOUTH AMERICA, AUSTRALASIA AND OCEANIA, ANTARCTICA

LAND HEIGHT
- Above 4000 m
- 2000–4000 m
- 1000–2000 m
- 500–1000 m
- 250–500 m
- 100–250 m
- 0–100 m

SEA DEPTH
- 0–250 m
- 250–500 m
- 500–1000 m
- 1000–2000 m
- 2000–3000 m
- 3000–4000 m
- Below 4000 m

CITIES AND TOWNS
- Over 500,000 people
- 100,000–500,000
- 50,000–100,000
- Less than 50,000

Main map labels:

ARIZONA, NEW MEXICO, TEXAS, UNITED STATES OF AMERICA, LOUISIANA, ALABAMA, GEORGIA, FLORIDA, MISSISSIPPI

Red River, Sabine River, Brazos River, Colorado River, Pecos River, Mississippi River, Mississippi Delta

Ciudad Juárez, Nogales, Agua Prieta, Cananea, Magdalena, Cumpas, San Pedro de la Cueva, Samalayuca, Nuevo Casas Grandes, El Sueco, Ojinaga, Acuña, Boquillas, Piedras Negras, San Miguel, Nueva Rosita, Sabinas, Nuevo Laredo, Padre Island

Hermosillo, Isla Tiburón, Guaymas, Empalme, Esperanza, Chihuahua, Cuauhtémoc, Delicias, Camargo, Jiménez, San Francisco del Oro, Hidalgo del Parral, Santa Barbara, Monclova, Sabinas Hidalgo, Ciudad Miguel Alemán

Ciudad Obregón, Navojoa, Huatabampo, San Blas, Los Mochis, Guasave, Guamúchil, Navolato, Culiacán, Gómez Palacio, Ciudad Lerdo, San Pedro, Parras, Torreón, Saltillo, Monterrey, Montemorelos, Linares, Reynosa, Río Bravo, Matamoros, Laguna Madre

Loreto, La Paz, Isla Santa Margarita, Santa Genoveva 2406m, Miraflores, San Lucas Cape, Bahía de La Paz

MEXICO, Sierra Madre Occidental, Western Sierra Madre, Eastern Sierra Madre

Miguel Asua, Juan Aldama, Ciudad Victoria, Gulf of Mexico, Laguna Madre

Durango, Fresnillo, Mazatlán, Escuinapa, Río Grande, El Dorado, Zacatecas, Guadalupe, Villanueva, San Luis Potosí, Ciudad Mante, Ciudad Madero, Tampico, Pánuco, Ciudad Valles, Laguna de Tamiahua

Aguascalientes, Jalpa, Acaponeta, Tuxpan, Río Verde, Tamazunchale, Dolores, Tuxpán, Papantla, Poza Rica

Tepic, Lagos de Moreno, León, Guanajuato, Islas Tres Marías, Isla San Juanito, Isla María Madre, Isla María Magdalena, Isla María Cleofas

Tequila, Guadalajara, Lago de Chapala, Irapuato, Querétaro, Tulancingo, Teziutlán, Xalapa, Veracruz, Bay of Campeche

Puerto Vallarta, Tlaquepaque, Zamora de Hidalgo, Morelia, Pachuca, Perote, Córdoba, Alvarado

Ciudad Guzmán, Toluca, MEXICO CITY, Cuernavaca, Puebla, Tlaxcala, Tehuacán, San Andrés, Coatzacoalcos

Colima, Tuxpan, Uruapan, Zacatepec, Popocatépetl 5452m, Cuautla, Taxco, Iguala, Tehuantepec, Tuxtepec, Minatitlán, Volcán El Chichonal 1360m

Manzanillo, Tecomán, Aguililla, Presa del Infiernillo, Huajuapan, Oaxaca, Matías Romero, Tuxtla, San Cristóbal de Las Casas, Comitán, Cerro

Lázaro Cárdenas, Río Balsas, Chilpancingo, Ixtapa, Tecpan, Sierra Madre del Sur, Ixtepec, Juchitán, Arriaga, Presa de la Angostura

Acapulco, Pinotepa Nacional, Mahuatlán, Tehuantepec, Salina Cruz, Pijijiapan, GUATEMALA, HONDURAS

Puerto Escondido, Puerto Angel, Gulf of Tehuantepec, Escuintla, Huixtla, Tapachula, Ciudad Hidalgo, EL SALVADOR

Rio Lagartos, Tizimín, Cancún, Isla Cozumel, Progreso, Motul, Mérida, Umán, Ticul, Oxkutzcab, Peto, Valladolid, Yucatan Channel

Campeche, Champotón, Yucatan Peninsula, Felipe Carrillo Puerto, Chetumal, Laguna de Términos, Frontera, Carmen, Comalcalco, Villahermosa, Macuspana, Teapa, BELIZE, Fransisco Escárcega, Gulf of Honduras

Río Usumacinta, PACIFIC OCEAN, Isla San Benedicto, Roca Partida, Isla Socorro, Islas Revillagigedo (part of Mexico), Tropic of Cancer

SCALE BAR
0 km 200
0 miles 200

105

CENTRAL AMERICA

BELIZE, COSTA RICA, EL SALVADOR, GUATEMALA, HONDURAS, NICARAGUA, PANAMA

Central America lies on a narrow bridge of land which links North and South America. All the countries here, except Belize, were once governed by Spain. Today, most of their people are *mestizos* – a mix of the original Maya Indian inhabitants and Spanish settlers. The hot, steamy climate is ideal for growing tropical crops, such as coffee and bananas, which are exported worldwide.

FARMING AND LAND USE

About half of all the agricultural products grown here are exported. The Pacific coast has fertile, well-watered land suitable for growing cotton and sugar cane. In the central highlands are big coffee plantations, and ranches where beef cattle are raised. Bananas grow well along the humid Caribbean coastal plain, and shrimp and lobster are caught offshore.

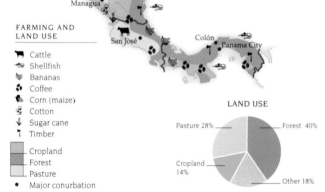

FARMING AND LAND USE

- 🐄 Cattle
- 🦐 Shellfish
- 🍌 Bananas
- ☕ Coffee
- 🌽 Corn (maize)
- 🌿 Cotton
- ⚘ Sugar cane
- 🌲 Timber

- Cropland
- Forest
- Pasture
- Major conurbation

LAND USE

Pasture 28%
Forest 40%
Cropland 14%
Other 18%

ENVIRONMENTAL ISSUES

Central America's rainforests are rapidly being cut down for timber and to make way for farmland and land for building. Over half of Guatemala's forests have been felled, mostly in the last 30 years. The situation is also bleak in Honduras, Costa Rica and Nicaragua. Central America lies in a volcanically active zone, and the line of volcanoes running through the region have erupted many times this century.

Volcán Tacaná 1986
Volcán de Fuego 1974
Volcán de Izalco 1958
Volcán Cerro Negro 1995
Volcán Concepcion 1986
Volcán Arenal 1995

ENVIRONMENTAL ISSUES

- 🌋 Volcanic eruption
- Deforested areas
- Remaining forests

POPULATION

Central America's people live mainly in the valleys of the central highlands or along the Pacific coastal plains. Despite the threat of volcanic eruptions and earthquakes, towns and cities developed in these areas because of the fertile volcanic soils found there. Just over half the population still live in rural areas, mostly in small villages or remote settlements, but the cities have expanded rapidly and overcrowding has become a serious problem.

BELMOPAN
GUATEMALA CITY
TEGUCIGALPA
SAN SALVADOR
MANAGUA
SAN JOSÉ
PANAMA CITY

INHABITANTS PER SQ KM

- More than 50
- 25–50
- Less than 25
- ■ Capital city

URBAN/RURAL POPULATION DIVIDE

San Salvador 3.3%
Tegucigalpa 3.2%
Managua 3.5%
Other towns and cities 37%
Rural population 53%

THE LANDSCAPE

The Sierra Madre in the north and the Cordillera Central to the south form a mountainous ridge that stretches down most of Central America. Along the Pacific coast north of Panama is a belt of more than 40 active volcanoes. The mountains are broken by valleys and basins with large, fertile areas of rich, volcanic soil.

Sierra Madre (A 3)

Coral reef (C 2)
Off the coast of Belize is a 290-km-long coral reef – the second longest in the world. Its waters contain spectacular marine life. In places, the reef has become built up into dozens of small sandy islands called cayes.

The Mosquito Coast (E 4)
The Mosquito Coast is a remote area of tropical rainforests, lagoons, and rivers lined with mangroves. Most of it is uninhabited by humans, but there is a huge variety of animal species, including monkeys and alligators.

Lake Nicaragua (E 5)
This large freshwater lake contains about 400 islands, some of which are active volcanoes like Volcán Concepcion. The lake is also home to the world's only freshwater sharks.

Cordillera Central (G 6)

The Panama Canal (H 6)
The Panama Canal links the Atlantic and Pacific oceans along a distance of 82 km. Half of its route passes through Lake Gatún, a freshwater lake which acts as a reservoir for the canal, providing water to operate the locks.

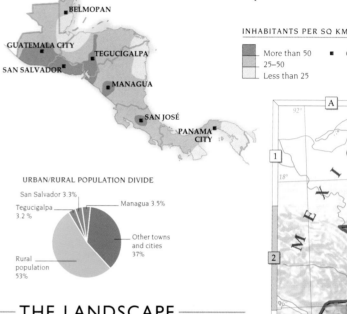

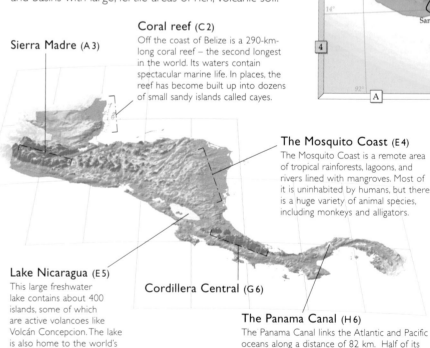

CLIMATE

Temperatures are high all year round, although in January the Caribbean side of Central America is is cooler and wetter than the Pacific side. Summers are generally much wetter, especially in the Sierra Madre in Guatemala and on the Pacific coasts of Costa Rica and Panama.

TEMPERATURE AND PRECIPITATION

More than 25°C
20 to 25°C
Less than 20°C
100   Precipitation (mm)

January

July

INDUSTRY

Coffee, fish, and timber processing, fruit exporting and textile-weaving are typical of the small-scale industries found in Central America. Most industries are based in the capital cities and larger towns. In Panama, many people work at the Panama Canal, which is one of the world's busiest shipping routes. The country is also a major financial centre, with many banking and insurance companies.

INDUSTRY
⚗ Chemicals
☕ Coffee processing
🐟 Fish processing
🍴 Food processing
👕 Textiles
🍌 Banana exporting
🌲 Timber processing
$ Finance
■ Major industrial centre / area
— Major road

STRUCTURE OF INDUSTRY
Primary 18%
Services 60%
Manufacturing 22%

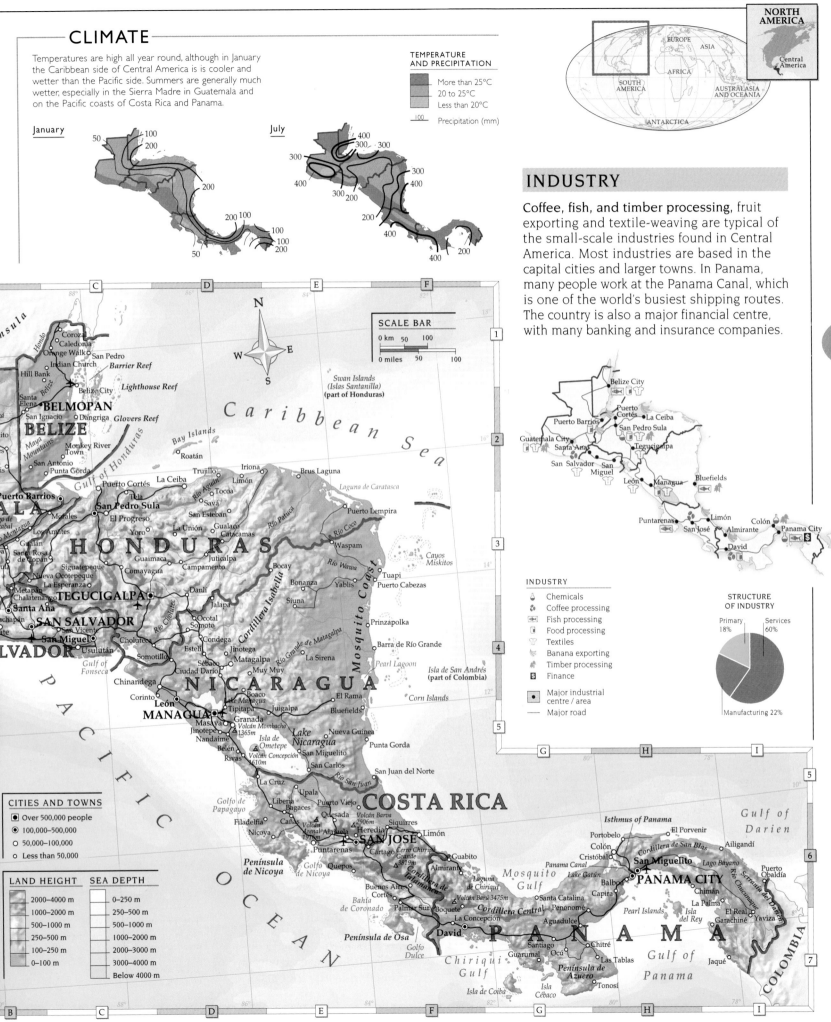

SCALE BAR
0 km   50   100
0 miles   50   100

CITIES AND TOWNS
● Over 500,000 people
◉ 100,000–500,000
○ 50,000–100,000
○ Less than 50,000

LAND HEIGHT
2000–4000 m
1000–2000 m
500–1000 m
250–500 m
100–250 m
0–100 m

SEA DEPTH
0–250 m
250–500 m
500–1000 m
1000–2000 m
2000–3000 m
3000–4000 m
Below 4000 m

THE CARIBBEAN

The Caribbean Sea is enclosed by an arc of many hundreds of islands, islets and offshore reefs which reach from Florida in the USA round to Venezuela in South America. From 1492, Spain, France, Britain and the Netherlands claimed the islands as colonies. Most of the islands' original inhabitants were wiped out by disease and a wide mixture of peoples – of African, Asian and European descent – now make up the population. The islands are prone to earthquakes, hurricanes and volcanic eruptions.

THE LANDSCAPE

The Bahamas
The Bahamas are low-lying, islands formed from limestone rock. Their coastlines are fringed by coral reefs, lagoons and mangrove swamps. Some of the bigger islands are covered by forests.

The islands are formed from two main mountain chains: the Greater Antilles, which are part of a chain running from west to east, and the Lesser Antilles, which run from north to south. The mountains are now almost submerged under the Atlantic Ocean and Caribbean Sea. Only the higher peaks reach above sea level to form islands.

Hispaniola (F 4)
Two countries, Haiti and the Dominican Republic occupy the island of Hispaniola. The land is mostly mountainous, broken by fertile valleys.

Cuba (C3)
Cuba is the largest island in the Antilles. Its landscape is made up of wide, fertile plains with rugged hills and mountains in the southeast.

The Lesser Antilles
Most of these small volcanic islands have mountainous interiors. Barbados and Antigua and Barbuda are flatter, with some higher volcanic areas. Monserrat was evacuated in 1997, following volcanic eruptions on the island.

FARMING AND LAND USE

Agriculture is an important source of income, with over half of all produce exported. Many islands have fertile, well-watered land and large areas are set aside for commercial crops such as sugar cane, tobacco and coffee. Some islands rely heavily on a single crop; in Dominica, bananas provide over half the country's income. Cuba is one of the world's biggest sugar producers.

Havana
San Juan
Kingston
Port-au-Prince

FARMING AND LAND USE
- 🐄 Cattle
- 🐟 Fishing
- 🍌 Bananas
- ☕ Coffee
- 🦐 Shellfish
- Sugar cane
- Tobacco
- Cropland
- Forest
- Pasture
- • Major conurbation

ENVIRONMENTAL ISSUES

The islands of the Caribbean are often under threat from hurricane storm systems which sweep in from the Atlantic Ocean between May and October. The winds can reach speeds of up to 250 km per hour, devastating everything that lies in their path and causing severe flooding. The storms themselves are enormous; a hurricane can extend outwards for 650 km from its calm centre, which is known as the 'eye'.

Grand Bahama Island
Freeport
UNITED STATES OF AMERICA
Bimini Islands
Berry Islands
Nicholls Town
Andros Town
Andros Island
Gulf of Mexico
The Everglades
Florida Keys
Straits of Florida
Anguilla Cays
Tropic of Cancer
Cay Sal
HAVANA (LA HABANA) Guanabacoa
Cárdenas
Matanzas
Sagua la Grande
Archipiélago de
Pinar del Río Artemisa
Consolación del Sur
Santa Clara
Placetas
Motón
Cienfuegos
Sancti Spíritus
Ciego de Á
Nueva Gerona
Bay of Pigs
Camagüey
Archipiélago de los Canarreos
Cayo Largo
Archipiélago de los Jardines de la Reina
Manz
G
Little Cayman
Cayman Brac
r
GEORGE TOWN Grand Cayman
CAYMAN ISLANDS (UK dependent territory)
e
Montego Bay
Spanish
JAMAICA

N W E S

SCALE BAR
0 km 100 200
0 miles 100 200

TOURISM

Tourism is thriving in the Caribbean, often bringing more income to the region than other, traditional industries. Long sandy beaches, clear, warm waters and the climate are the main attractions. In Cuba and the Dominican Republic, tourism is expanding at some of the fastest rates in North America. As hotel complexes and new roads and airports are developed, the environment is often damaged. Local people who work in the industry often receive little of the extra cash brought in by the tourists.

TOURISM
🏖 Major tourist destinations

Bahamas
Cuba
Puerto Rico
Virgin Islands
Antigua & Barbuda
Jamaica
Dominican Republic
Guadeloupe
St Lucia
Barbados
Aruba
Grenada
Trinidad & Tobago

NORTH AMERICA

The Caribbean

EUROPE
ASIA
AFRICA
SOUTH AMERICA
AUSTRALASIA AND OCEANIA
ANTARCTICA

ENVIRONMENTAL ISSUES

Path of recent, devastating hurricane

Hurricane Flora – over 7,000 dead
Hurricane David – 2,000 dead
Hurricane Gordon – 1,100 dead
Hurricane Gilbert – over 300 dead
Hurricane Hugo – 50 dead
Hurricane Andrew – 25 dead

Andrew 1992
Hugo 1989
Gilbert 1988
David 1979
Gordon 1994
Flora 1963

INDUSTRY

Food processing – such as sugar cane refining and fruit exporting – and textiles, are typical of traditional Caribbean industry, which mainly supplies foreign markets. Cuba's economy has suffered from years of neglect and a trade ban imposed by the US government. Minerals and oil are also important. Jamaica has some of the world's largest reserves of bauxite – used to make aluminium – and oil is extracted and refined in Trinidad and Tobago and the Bahamas.

INDUSTRY

Chemicals
Engineering
Oil refining
Textiles
Mining
Sugar processing
Tobacco processing
Major industrial centre / area
Major road

Freeport
Havana
Santa Clara
Camagüey
Santiago de Cuba
Santiago
Port-au-Prince
San Juan
St Croix
Kingston
Santo Domingo
Ponce
Willemstad
Port-of-Spain

ATLANTIC OCEAN

Eleuthera Island
Rock Sound
Cat Island
San Salvador
Rum Cay
Tropic of Cancer
Exuma Island
Long Island
Clarence Town
Crooked Island
Acklins Island
Mayaguana
Caicos Passage
Little Inagua
COCKBURN TOWN
Lake Rosa
TURKS & CAICOS ISLANDS
(UK dependent territory)
Matthew Town
Great Inagua

Crooked Island Passage
Mayaguana Passage

BAHAMAS
sh Harbour
at Abaco
SAU
ge Town
ed Island Range

Tunas
Holguín
yamo
alma
ciano
tiago de Cuba
INGSTON

Guantánamo

Windward Passage

Hispaniola

Cap-Haïtien
Monte Cristi
Puerto Plata
Santiago
San Francisco de Macorís
La Vega
Gonaïves
Cordillera Central
HAITI
Pico Duarte 3175m
SANTO DOMINGO
PORT-AU-PRINCE
La Romana
Jérémie
Cayes
Jacmel
DOMINICAN REPUBLIC
Isla Saona
Isla Beata

NAVASSA ISLAND
(US unincorporated territory)
Île de la Gonâve

Jamaica Channel

Caribbean Sea

Lesser Antilles

Mona Passage
Isla Mona

SAN JUAN
Mayagüez
Caguas
Ponce
PUERTO RICO
(US commonwealth territory)
St Croix

VIRGIN ISLANDS
(US unincorporated territory)
BRITISH VIRGIN ISLANDS
(UK dependent territory)
Sombrero (part of Anguilla)
ROAD TOWN
CHARLOTTE AMALIE
ANGUILLA (UK dependent territory)
THE VALLEY
St-Martin (part of Guadeloupe)
St-Barthélemy (part of Guadeloupe)
NETH. ANTILLES (autonomous part of Neth.)
ANTIGUA & BARBUDA
Barbuda
ST JOHN'S
Antigua
BASSETERRE
SAINT KITTS & NEVIS
MONTSERRAT (UK dependent territory)
Grande Terre
Pointe-à-Pitre
GUADELOUPE (French overseas department)
Basse-Terre
BASSE-TERRE
Marie-Galante
DOMINICA
ROSEAU
Martinique Passage
MARTINIQUE (French overseas department)
FORT-DE-FRANCE
St Lucia Channel
CASTRIES
ST LUCIA
Vieux Fort
BARBADOS
Saint Vincent
Saint Vincent Passage
KINGSTOWN
BRIDGETOWN
SAINT VINCENT & THE GRENADINES
The Grenadines
GRENADA
ST GEORGE'S
Tobago
Scarborough
TRINIDAD & TOBAGO
PORT-OF-SPAIN
Trinidad
San Fernando
Gulf of Paria

Leeward Islands
Windward Islands

ARUBA (autonomous part of Netherlands)
ORANJESTAD
NETHERLANDS ANTILLES (autonomous part of Netherlands)
WILLEMSTAD
Curaçao
Bonaire
Isla La Orchila
Isla Blanquilla
Los Testigos
Isla de Margarita

COLOMBIA
Gulf of Venezuela
Isla La Tortuga
Islas Los Roques

VENEZUELA

LAND HEIGHT

2000–4000 m
1000–2000 m
500–1000 m
250–500 m
100–250 m
0–100 m

SEA DEPTH

0–250 m
250–500 m
500–1000 m
1000–2000 m
2000–3000 m
3000–4000 m
Below 4000 m

CITIES AND TOWNS

Over 500,000 people
100,000–500,000
50,000–100,000
Less than 50,000

CONTINENTAL SOUTH AMERICA

The towering peaks of the Andes stand high above the western side of the South America. They act as a barrier to the sparsely inhabited interior of the continent which includes the dense rainforest of the Amazon Basin – one of the Earth's last great wildernesses. Most people live on South America's coastal fringes. Brazil is both the largest country, and the most populous. Over half the continent's land area and half its people are found there.

← 4,990 km →
↕ 7,640 km

CROSS-SECTION ACROSS SOUTH AMERICA

Andes · Amazon River · Guiana Highlands · Mouths of the Amazon · Brazilian Highlands

W — 5,400 km — E

The high peaks of the Andes rise up from a narrow strip of land bordering the Pacific Ocean. East of the Andes, the land flattens into a broad, shallow basin into which the Amazon River flows. To the north are the older Guiana Highlands where rock has been eroded to form flat-topped 'table' mountains.

ELEVATION

6000m
5000m
4000m
3000m
2000m
1000m
500m
250m
100m
sea level
below sea level
cross-section

SCALE 1:40,000,000

0 km   400   800
0 miles   400   800

PHYSICAL SOUTH AMERICA

Ancient masses of rocks, like the Guiana and Brazilian highlands, which are known as shields, form the core of South America. The Andes are the solid backbone of the continent. They are relatively young, formed by collisions between different plates of the Earth's crust. The major rivers; the Paraná and the mighty Amazon flow in deep depressions to the east of the mountains.

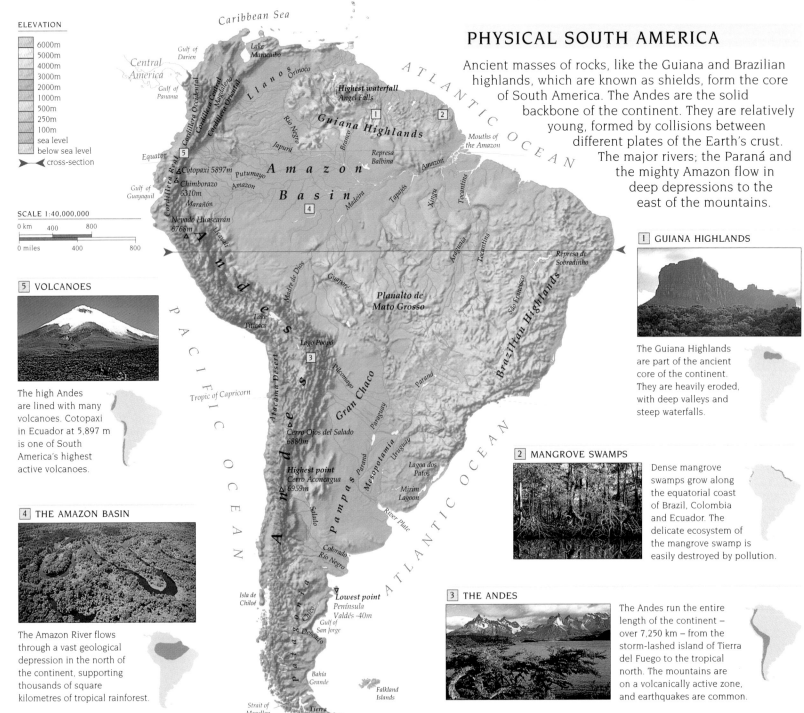

5 VOLCANOES

The high Andes are lined with many volcanoes. Cotopaxi in Ecuador at 5,897 m is one of South America's highest active volcanoes.

4 THE AMAZON BASIN

The Amazon River flows through a vast geological depression in the north of the continent, supporting thousands of square kilometres of tropical rainforest.

1 GUIANA HIGHLANDS

The Guiana Highlands are part of the ancient core of the continent. They are heavily eroded, with deep valleys and steep waterfalls.

2 MANGROVE SWAMPS

Dense mangrove swamps grow along the equatorial coast of Brazil, Colombia and Ecuador. The delicate ecosystem of the mangrove swamp is easily destroyed by pollution.

3 THE ANDES

The Andes run the entire length of the continent – over 7,250 km – from the storm-lashed island of Tierra del Fuego to the tropical north. The mountains are on a volcanically active zone, and earthquakes are common.

POLITICAL SOUTH AMERICA

In the 17th century, explorers from Spain and Portugal claimed most of South America for their rulers in Europe. Their influences are still strong today: Brazilians speak Portuguese, while much of the rest of the continent is Spanish-speaking. The small nations of the north, Surinam and Guyana, were Dutch and British colonies and French Guiana is a French overseas department. The mix of peoples is mainly European, native American and African. Some native peoples still live in the dense Amazon rainforest.

TRANSPORT LINKS

The Pan American Highway is a vital transport link, running from the far south of the continent, northwards along the Pacific coast. Its route takes it through sparsely populated areas like the Atacama Desert.

POPULATION

Many South American countries have a similar pattern of population distribution. The largest numbers of people are found near the coasts. Migration to the coastal cities has led to rocketing population figures, and growing social problems. São Paulo is now the world's third largest city after Mexico City and Tokyo; its outskirts are fringed with sprawling, shantytown suburbs – known as *favelas*.

Largest city
SÃO PAULO
15 million people

POPULATION DENSITY
(People per sq km)

Below 5	10–14	20–29
5–9	15–19	Above 29

BORDER DISPUTES

Many of South America's borders have been, or remain, disputed. Bolivia is landlocked as a result of a dispute with Chile in 1883, when it lost its lands bordering the Pacific Ocean.

URBAN GROWTH

Urban growth has transformed São Paulo into a major population and industrial centre. Its rapid growth has created many problems, like traffic congestion, overcrowding, and inadequate sewerage.

STANDARDS OF LIVING

There are many inequalities in living standards across South America. Argentina's wealth and strong economy means its living standards are well above those of Guyana and Bolivia, which have weak economies, and are heavily reliant upon trade in raw materials. The booming black market drug trade increases crime and corruption.

STANDARD OF LIVING
(UN Human Development Index)

low   high   no data

SCALE 1:35,000,000
0 km   400   800
0 miles   400   800

Map labels

Caribbean Sea

CARACAS
Lake Maracaibo
Orinoco
(Venezuelan territorial claim)
GEORGETOWN
VENEZUELA
GUYANA
PARAMARIBO
Central America
Magdalena
Río Negro
Branco
CAYENNE
SURINAM
French Guiana (to France)
BOGOTÁ
COLOMBIA
(Surinamese territorial claims)
Japurá
Represa Balbina
Amazon
ATLANTIC OCEAN
Equator
QUITO
ECUADOR
(Ecuadorean territorial claim)
Putumayo
Marañón
(Ecuadorean territorial claims)
Amazon
Madeira
Tapajós
Xingu
Tocantins
Araguaia
Tocantins
Represa de Sobradinho
Utayali
PERU
B R A Z I L
LIMA
Madre de Dios
São Francisco
BOLIVIA
BRASÍLIA
La Paz
Lake Titicaca
Lago Poopó
SUCRE
Pilcomayo
PARAGUAY
São Paulo
Tropic of Capricorn
Paraná
Paraguay
ASUNCIÓN
Uruguay
Paraguay
ATLANTIC OCEAN
URUGUAY
Sabato
C H I L E
A R G E N T I N A
SANTIAGO
BUENOS AIRES
MONTEVIDEO
River Plate
Chaco
Colorado
Río Negro
Desado
PACIFIC OCEAN
Falkland Islands (to UK)

POPULATION

Capital cities
- Above 500,000
- 100,000 to 500,000
- 50,000 to 100,000
- Below 50,000

Other cities
- Above 500,000
- 50,000 to 100,000

SOUTH AMERICAN GEOGRAPHY

Agriculture is still the most common form of employment in South America. Cattle and cash crops of coffee, cocoa and, in some places, coca for cocaine, provide the main sources of income. Brazil has the greatest range of industries, followed by Argentina, Venezuela and Chile. The large coastal cities such as Rio de Janeiro, Lima and Buenos Aires are where most of the jobs are found. This encourages people to migrate from the country to the city, in search of employment.

INDUSTRY

Brazil is the continent's leading industrial producer and São Paulo the major industrial city. Manufactured products include iron and steel, automobiles, chemicals, textiles, and meat and leather products from the continent's vast cattle herds. In the mountains of Bolivia and Colombia, coca plants are grown to make cocaine, which has created a black market for this illegal drug.

OIL AND GAS

Under the waters of Lake Maracaibo, Venezuela, lie some of South America's biggest oil reserves. Oil exploitation has brought great wealth to Venezuela. The money has helped the country to build new roads and develop other industries.

INDUSTRIAL CENTRE

São Paulo, Brazil, is the largest city in South America and a leading industrial centre. A wide range of goods is manufactured here, including automobiles, chemicals, textiles and electronic products. São Paulo is also a leading financial centre Hundreds of people flock to the city daily in search of work.

TRADE AND EXPORTS

The Chilean port of Valparaíso ships many different products out of South America. Trade is growing with Japan and other countries around the Pacific Ocean.

MINERAL RESOURCES

South America's mineral resources are highly localized. Few countries have both fossil fuels and metallic ores. The richest oilfields are in the north, especially in Venezuela. Coal, however, is scarce. When the Andes formed, heat helped create the many metallic minerals which are mined today.

MINERAL RESOURCES

- 🪨 Bauxite
- 🪨 Copper
- 🪨 Iron
- 🪨 Lead
- 🪨 Silver
- 🪨 Tin
- Oil/Gas field
- Coal field

COPPER MINES

Metallic mineral reserves are abundant in the Andes. Chuquicamata, northern Chile, is one of the world's largest copper mines.

Map labels: Caribbean Sea, Central America, Barranquilla, Cartagena, Maracaibo, Barquisimeto, Caracas, Valencia, Ciudad Guayana, VENEZUELA, Georgetown, GUYANA, Paramaribo, SURINAM, French Guiana (to France), Medellín, Bogotá, COLOMBIA, Cali, Quito, ECUADOR, Guayaquil, Amazon Basin, Manaus, Belém, ATLANTIC OCEAN, Fortaleza, Natal, BRAZIL, Recife, Chiclayo, Chimbote, Maceió, Lima, PERU, Cusco, Salvador, Arequipa, La Paz, Santa Cruz, BOLIVIA, Brasília, Arica, Sucre, Iquique, Chuquicamata, Belo Horizonte, PARAGUAY, Antofagasta, Asunción, São Paulo, Rio de Janeiro, San Miguel de Tucumán, Corrientes, Curitiba, Córdoba, Santa Fe, Rosario, URUGUAY, Porto Alegre, Valparaíso, Mendoza, Santiago, Buenos Aires, Rio Grande, Montevideo, CHILE, Talca, ARGENTINA, Concepción, Neuquén, Bahía Blanca, Valdivia, PACIFIC OCEAN, ATLANTIC OCEAN, Comodoro Rivadavia, Falkland Islands (to UK), Punta Arenas, Cape Horn

GNP per capita (US$)

- Below 499
- 500-999
- 1000-1499
- 1500-2999
- 3000-5999
- Above 6000
- • Industrial centre

ECONOMIC ACTIVITY

- ✈ Aerospace
- 🍺 Brewing
- 🚗 Car/vehicle manufacture
- ⚗ Chemicals
- Coal
- 📺 Electronics
- ⚙ Engineering
- 💲 Finance
- 🐟 Fish processing
- Food processing
- 🖥 Hi-tech industry
- Iron & steel
- △ Metal refining
- Narcotics
- ◊ Oil and gas
- Pharmaceuticals
- 📖 Printing & publishing
- Shipbuilding
- 👕 Textiles
- 🌲 Timber processing
- Tobacco processing

CLIMATE

South America has four main climatic regions; tropical, arid, temperate, and the cold climate of the far south. The Amazon Basin, covered by massive rain forests, and the Guiana Highlands have a humid, tropical climate which allows vegetation to flourish. West of the Andes the climate tends to be very dry. Moist air flowing west from the Atlantic Ocean is prevented from reaching the shores of the Pacific Ocean by the Andes and rain falls before it can pass over the mountains. This creates arid deserts like the Atacama.

EXTREME WEATHER EVENTS

Symbols indicate climatic extremes

Wettest place
QUIBDO (Colombia)
Annual rainfall 899cm

Equator

Driest place
ARICA (Chile)
Annual rainfall 0.08cm

Hottest place
RIVADAVIA (Argentina)
Temp 49°C

Tropic of Capricorn

Coldest place
SARMIENTO (Argentina)
Temp -33°C

CLIMATE

- Subarctic
- Cool continental
- Warm temperate
- Semi-arid
- Arid
- Temperate
- Tropical
- Humid equatorial

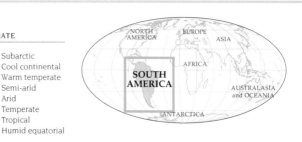

NORTH AMERICA   EUROPE   ASIA

AFRICA

SOUTH AMERICA

AUSTRALASIA and OCEANIA

ANTARCTICA

PATAGONIAN ICEFIELDS

Towards the south of the continent, the climate becomes very cold. Large expanses of ice, forming glaciers are found in southern Patagonia and on islands such as Tierra del Fuego at the tip of South America.

LAND USE AND AGRICULTURE

Many plants now found throughout the world originated in South America, like the tomato, potato and cassava. Today, coffee, cocoa, rubber, soya beans, corn (maize), and sugar cane are widely cultivated, and grapes are grown in sheltered valleys in the Andes. Much of the Amazon Basin is covered by dense rainforest and is unsuitable for cultivation, although some farmers practise 'slash and burn' techniques to make land for crops and cattle farming, which destroy ancient forest.

LAND USE AND AGRICULTURE

- Cattle
- Pigs
- Sheep
- Bananas
- Corn (Maize)
- Citrus fruits
- Coca
- Cocoa
- Cotton
- Coffee
- Fishing
- Oil palms
- Peanuts
- Rubber
- Shellfish
- Soya beans
- Sugar cane
- Vineyards
- Wheat

- Barren land
- Cropland
- Desert
- Forest
- Mountain region
- Pasture
- Wetland
- Major conurbation

COFFEE

South America, and Brazil in particular, is a major producer of coffee. The plants thrive in the rich red soils of southern Brazil and are grown on huge plantations on the mountain slopes.

LOCAL MARKETS

At traditional markets such as this one in Ecuador, high in the Andes, local people trade fruit, vegetables and goods such as clothing, rugs and blankets. Some goods produced by Ecuadorean Indians are now exported world wide.

Caribbean Sea
Barranquilla
Maracaibo
Caracas
Central America
Llanos
Orinoco
Medellín
Bogotá
Cali
Guiana Highlands
Rio Negro
Amazon Basin
Putumayo
Amazon
Manaus
Amazon
Belém
Marañón
Tapajós
Fortaleza
Purus
Madeira
Xingu
Tocantins
Araguaia
Recife
Lima
São Francisco
Salvador
Brasília
Brazilian Highlands
Belo Horizonte
Pilcomayo
Gran Chaco
Paraguay
Paraná
Rio de Janeiro
São Paulo
Curitiba
Córdoba
Uruguay
Porto Alegre
Rosario
Santiago
Pampas
Montevideo
Buenos Aires
Colorado
Rio Negro
Patagonia
Gulf of San Jorge
Falkland Islands
Cape Horn

ATLANTIC OCEAN

PACIFIC OCEAN

ATLANTIC OCEAN

CATTLE

The vast plains of the Pampas, to the west of Buenos Aires, support large herds of cattle. Meat processing and canning is a major industry in Argentina, Paraguay and Uruguay.

NARCOTICS

Coca, grown in forest clearings in remote mountain areas, is used to make the drug cocaine. Government troops burn any coca plants they discover to discourage production.

NORTHERN SOUTH AMERICA

BRAZIL, COLOMBIA, ECUADOR, GUYANA, PERU,
SURINAM, VENEZUELA

High mountains, steamy rainforests and hot, grassy
plains cover much of northern South America. From
the 16th century, after the conquest of the Incas, the
western countries were ruled by Spain, while Brazil was
governed by Portugal, Guyana by Britain and Surinam
by the Dutch. The more recent history of some of these
countries has included periods of civil war and military
rule. Most are still troubled by widespread poverty.

INDUSTRY

Important oil reserves are found in
Venezuela and parts of the Amazon
Basin; Venezuela is one of the world's
top oil producers. Brazil's cities have
a wide range of industries including
chemicals, clothes and shoes,
and textiles. Metallic minerals,
particularly iron ore, are mined
throughout the area and specially-built
industrial centres like Ciudad Guayana
have been developed to refine them.

STRUCTURE OF INDUSTRY

Primary 11%
Services 50%
Manufacturing 39%

INDUSTRY

Chemicals	Oil
Food processing	Timber processing
Iron & steel	Tourism
Metal refining	
Textiles	Major industrial centre / area
Mining	Major road

POPULATION

Most of the population lives in urban
areas. Many cities are extremely
overcrowded, with poor housing.
São Paulo in Brazil is one of
the world's fastest-growing
cities. The rainforests of
the interior and high Andes
are sparsely populated. The
few native American peoples
live in remote areas.

INHABITANTS PER SQ KM

- More than 200
- 100–200
- 50–100
- 10–50
- Less than 10
- Capital city
- Major city

URBAN/RURAL POPULATION DIVIDE

Rio de Janeiro 4.6%
São Paulo 8.4%
Lima 3%
Rural population 24%
Other towns and cities 60%

FARMING AND LAND USE

The variety of climates means a wide
range of crops including sugar cane,
cocoa and bananas can be grown
for export. Coffee is the most
important cash crop; Brazil is the
world's leading coffee grower.
Cattle are farmed on the plains
of Colombia, Venezuela and
southern Brazil. Much of the good
farmland is owned by a few rich
landowners and many peasant farmers
do not have enough land to make a living.

FARMING AND LAND USE

Cattle		Sugar cane	
Fishing		Timber	
Goats			
Sheep		Cropland	
Bananas		Forest	
Cocoa		Mountain region	
Coffee		Pasture	
Rubber		Wetland	
		Major conurbation	

LAND USE

Cropland 6%
Other (including mountains) 15%
Pasture 23%
Forest 56%

THE LANDSCAPE

The Andes run down the western side of South
America. There are many volcanoes among their peaks
and earthquakes are common. The tropical rainforests
surrounding the River Amazon take up most of western
Brazil. Huge, dry, flat grasslands called *llanos* cover
central Venezuela and part of eastern Colombia.

Angel Falls (D 2)
Venezuela's Angel Falls is the
world's highest waterfall. Twenty
times as high as Niagara Falls, it
drops 980 m from a spectacular
plateau deep in the Guiana Highlands.

River Amazon (D 4)
The Amazon is the longest
river in South America, and
the second longest in the
world. It flows over 6,439 km
from the Peruvian Andes to
the coast of Brazil. One-fifth
of the world's fresh water is
carried by the river.

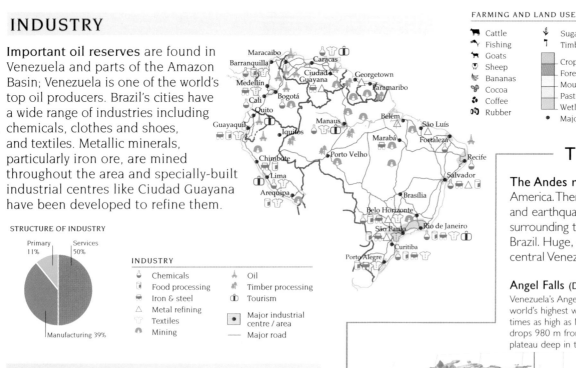

Andes (B 5)
The snow-capped
Andes are the
longest mountain
range on Earth.
They stretch
7,250 km down
the whole length
of South America.

Lake Titicaca (C 6)
South America's
largest lake is the
highest navigable
lake in the world
at 3,810 m above
sea level. It lies
across the border
between Peru
and Bolivia.

Pantanal (E 6)
This is the largest area of
wetlands in the world. It spreads
across 130,000 sq km of Brazil.
Many hundreds of plant and
animal species are found here.

Amazon rainforest (D 4)
The enormous rainforest
surrounding the Amazon
River and its tributaries
covers 6,500,000 sq km,
an area almost as big as
Australia. It is estimated
that at least half of all
known living species
are found in the forest.

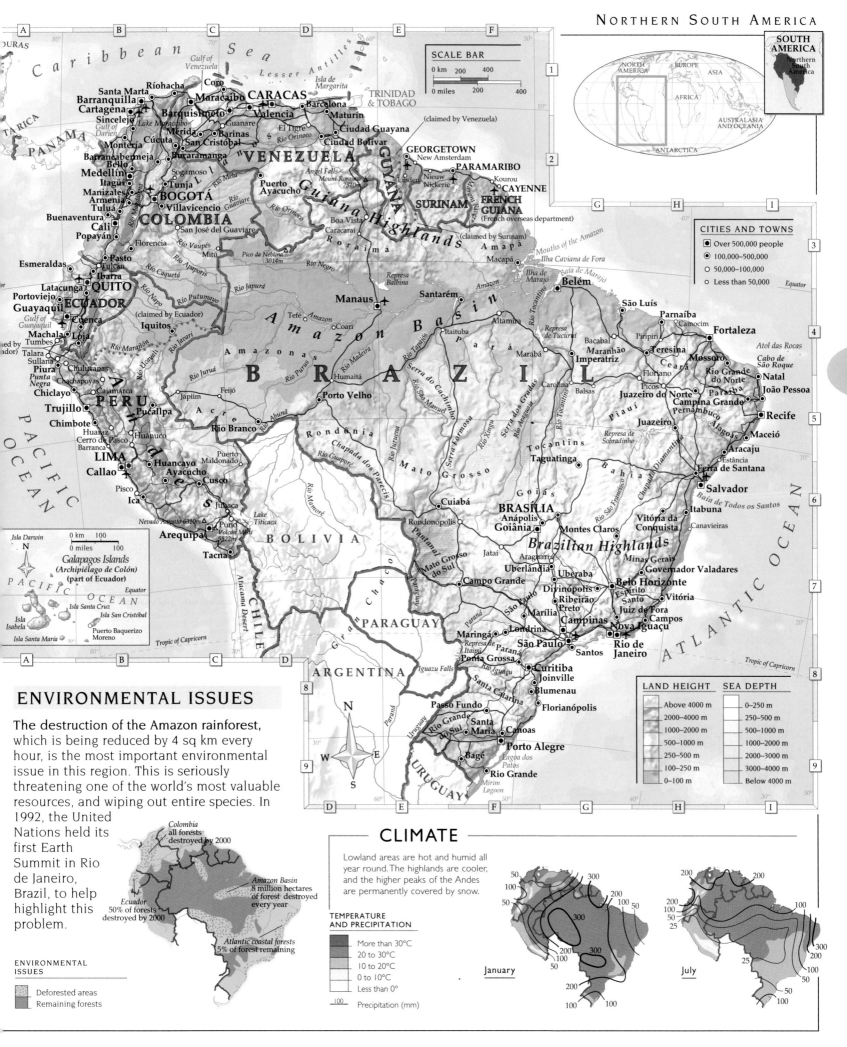

SOUTH AMERICA
Northern South America

SCALE BAR

0 km   200   400

0 miles   200   400

CITIES AND TOWNS
- ■ Over 500,000 people
- ◉ 100,000–500,000
- ○ 50,000–100,000
- ○ Less than 50,000

Galapagos Islands
(Archipiélago de Colón)
(part of Ecuador)

0 km   100

0 miles   100

Isla Darwin

Isla Isabela
Isla Santa María
Isla Santa Cruz
Isla San Cristóbal
Puerto Baquerizo Moreno

PACIFIC OCEAN

Equator
Tropic of Capricorn

LAND HEIGHT
- Above 4000 m
- 2000–4000 m
- 1000–2000 m
- 500–1000 m
- 250–500 m
- 100–250 m
- 0–100 m

SEA DEPTH
- 0–250 m
- 250–500 m
- 500–1000 m
- 1000–2000 m
- 2000–3000 m
- 3000–4000 m
- Below 4000 m

ENVIRONMENTAL ISSUES

The destruction of the Amazon rainforest, which is being reduced by 4 sq km every hour, is the most important environmental issue in this region. This is seriously threatening one of the world's most valuable resources, and wiping out entire species. In 1992, the United Nations held its first Earth Summit in Rio de Janeiro, Brazil, to help highlight this problem.

Colombia all forests destroyed by 2000

Amazon Basin 8 million hectares of forest destroyed every year

Ecuador 50% of forests destroyed by 2000

Atlantic coastal forests 5% of forest remaining

ENVIRONMENTAL ISSUES
- Deforested areas
- Remaining forests

CLIMATE

Lowland areas are hot and humid all year round. The highlands are cooler, and the higher peaks of the Andes are permanently covered by snow.

TEMPERATURE AND PRECIPITATION
- More than 30°C
- 20 to 30°C
- 10 to 20°C
- 0 to 10°C
- Less than 0°

100 Precipitation (mm)

January

July

115

SOUTHERN SOUTH AMERICA

ARGENTINA, BOLIVIA, CHILE, PARAGUAY, URUGUAY

The southern half of South America forms a long, narrow cone, with landscapes ranging from barren desert in the west, to frozen glaciers in the far south. The whole area was governed by Spain until the early 19th century, and Spanish is still the main language spoken, although the few remaining native American groups use their own languages. Most people now live in vast cities such as Buenos Aires and Santiago.

INDUSTRY

Rich deposits of minerals – especially copper – in the Andes have led to the development of large metal refining industries in Chile. The capital cities, Buenos Aires and Santiago, are home to the widest range of industries and Argentina is an important producer of processed foods like canned beef. There are fewer industries in the south, although oil and gas are extracted in southern Argentina and Chile.

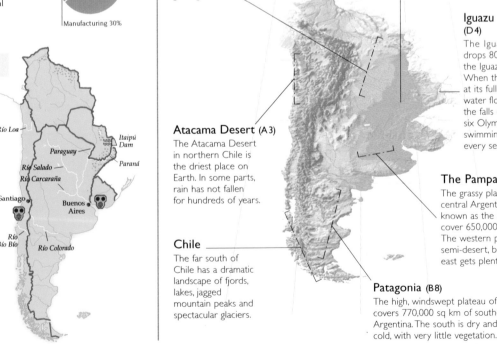

INDUSTRY

- 🚗 Car manufacture
- Chemicals
- Food processing
- △ Metal refining
- ⊺ Textiles
- Oil and gas
- Timber processing
- ⊡ Major industrial centre / area
- — Major road

STRUCTURE OF INDUSTRY

Primary 6%
Services 64%
Manufacturing 30%

ENVIRONMENTAL ISSUES

Many of southern South America's rivers are polluted, particularly close to Buenos Aires. The Itaipú Dam on the Paraná River is the world's largest hydro-electric power project. Deforestation is a persistent problem. In Bolivia, forests are being cut down at a record rate of 200,000 hectares a year. Air quality in Buenos Aires and Santiago is poor, especially in Santiago which is surrounded by mountains, making it difficult for pollution to escape.

ENVIRONMENTAL ISSUES

- 〰 Major dam
- ☠ Urban air pollution
- Deforested areas
- Polluted river
- • Major industrial centre

POPULATION

Since the 1950s, there has been a tremendous move from the countryside to the cities, and in Argentina, Chile and Uruguay more than 80% of the people are now city dwellers. The capital cities of all these countries have grown hugely – Buenos Aires now holds a third of Argentina's population, and more than half of Uruguay's people live in the capital, Montevideo.

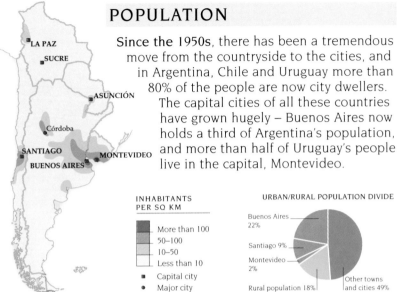

INHABITANTS PER SQ KM

- More than 100
- 50–100
- 10–50
- Less than 10
- ▪ Capital city
- • Major city

URBAN/RURAL POPULATION DIVIDE

Buenos Aires 22%
Santiago 9%
Montevideo 2%
Rural population 18%
Other towns and cities 49%

THE LANDSCAPE

Southern South America's landscape varies from tropical forest and dry desert in the north, to sub-Arctic conditions in the south. The towering Andes divide Chile from Argentina. East of the Andes lie forests and rolling grasslands. To the west is a thin coastal strip. The wet, windswept, freezing southern tip of the continent has volcanoes alongside glaciers and fjords.

Gran Chaco (C3)
This huge stretch of forest and grassland runs from Bolivia, through Paraguay and into Argentina. The south and east provide grazing for cattle.

The Paraná River (C4)
South America's second longest river is the Paraná. It stretches 4,200 km from the Brazilian Highlands, finally flowing into the River Plate near Buenos Aires in Argentina.

Iguazu Falls (D4)
The Iguazu River drops 80 m over the Iguazu Falls. When the river is at its fullest, the water flowing over the falls could fill six Olympic swimming pools every second.

Atacama Desert (A3)
The Atacama Desert in northern Chile is the driest place on Earth. In some parts, rain has not fallen for hundreds of years.

Chile
The far south of Chile has a dramatic landscape of fjords, lakes, jagged mountain peaks and spectacular glaciers.

The Pampas (B5)
The grassy plains in central Argentina – known as the Pampas – cover 650,000 sq km. The western part is semi-desert, but the east gets plenty of rain.

Patagonia (B8)
The high, windswept plateau of Patagonia covers 770,000 sq km of southern Argentina. The south is dry and freezing cold, with very little vegetation.

SOUTH AMERICA
Southern South America

LAND HEIGHT
- Above 4000 m
- 2000–4000 m
- 1000–2000 m
- 500–1000 m
- 250–500 m
- 100–250 m
- 0–100 m

SEA DEPTH
- 0–250 m
- 250–500 m
- 500–1000 m
- 1000–2000 m
- 2000–3000 m
- 3000–4000 m
- Below 4000 m

CITIES AND TOWNS
- Over 500,000 people
- 100,000–500,000
- 50,000–100,000
- Less than 50,000

BOLIVIA'S TWO CAPITALS
LA PAZ – legislative and administrative capital
SUCRE – legal capital

CLIMATE

Temperature patterns are similar in January and July; warmer to the north and east, colder to the south and west, although January is much warmer than July. Temperatures are always low high in the Andes.

January   July

TEMPERATURE AND PRECIPITATION
- More than 20°C
- 10 to 20°C
- 0 to 10°C
- Less than 0°C
- 100 Precipitation (mm)

SCALE BAR
0 km 200 400
0 miles 200 400

FARMING AND LAND USE

The enormous grasslands to the east of the Andes provide good grazing for cattle and sheep, and Argentina is one of the world's leading suppliers of meat, milk and hides. The country is also an important grower of wheat and fruit. Chile is the world's top producer of fishmeal, and grows grapes for its successful wine industry, and for eating. The illegal growing of coca, used to make the drug cocaine, is a major source of income in Bolivia.

LAND USE
- Cropland 7%
- Pasture 43%
- Other (including mountains) 23%
- Forest 27%

FARMING AND LAND USE
- Cattle
- Fishing
- Sheep
- Fruit
- Sugar cane
- Timber
- Vineyards
- Wheat
- Barren land
- Cropland
- Desert
- Forest
- Mountain region
- Pasture
- Wetland
- Major conurbation

FALKLAND ISLANDS
(UK dependent territory)

CONTINENTAL AFRICA

Africa is the second largest continent in the world. Its dramatic landscapes include arid deserts, humid rainforests, and the valleys of the east African rift – the place where humans first evolved. Today, there are 53 separate countries in Africa, and its people speak a rich variety of languages. The world's highest temperatures have been recorded in Africa's deserts.

7,260 km
7,623 km

CROSS-SECTION THROUGH AFRICA

Niger Delta
Congo Basin
Great Rift Valley
Ethiopian Highlands
Lake Victoria
Horn of Africa

W — 5,200 km — E

In the west, the Niger River flows into the Atlantic Ocean through the swampy Niger Delta. Further east is the immense Congo Basin, where the Congo River winds its way through thick rainforests. In the east is the Great Rift Valley, and the Ethiopian Highlands. The Horn of Africa is Africa's most easterly point.

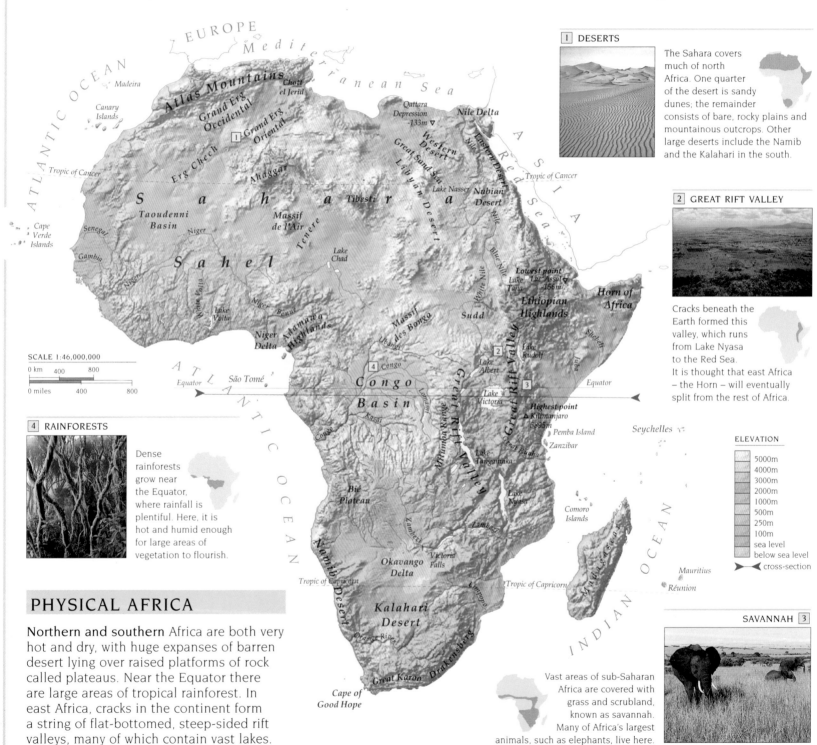

1 DESERTS

The Sahara covers much of north Africa. One quarter of the desert is sandy dunes; the remainder consists of bare, rocky plains and mountainous outcrops. Other large deserts include the Namib and the Kalahari in the south.

2 GREAT RIFT VALLEY

Cracks beneath the Earth formed this valley, which runs from Lake Nyasa to the Red Sea. It is thought that east Africa – the Horn – will eventually split from the rest of Africa.

4 RAINFORESTS

Dense rainforests grow near the Equator, where rainfall is plentiful. Here, it is hot and humid enough for large areas of vegetation to flourish.

SAVANNAH 3

Vast areas of sub-Saharan Africa are covered with grass and scrubland, known as savannah. Many of Africa's largest animals, such as elephants, live here.

SCALE 1:46,000,000
0 km 400 800
0 miles 400 800

ELEVATION

5000m
4000m
3000m
2000m
1000m
500m
250m
100m
sea level
below sea level
cross-section

PHYSICAL AFRICA

Northern and southern Africa are both very hot and dry, with huge expanses of barren desert lying over raised platforms of rock called plateaus. Near the Equator there are large areas of tropical rainforest. In east Africa, cracks in the continent form a string of flat-bottomed, steep-sided rift valleys, many of which contain vast lakes.

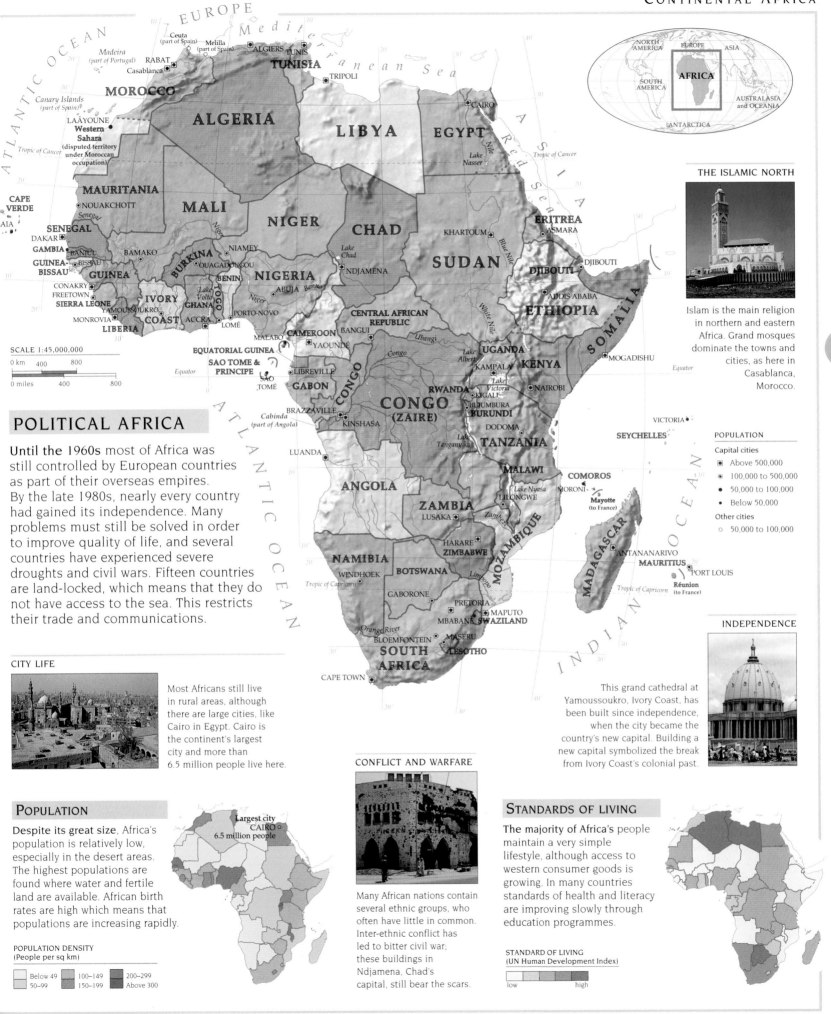

Islam is the main religion in northern and eastern Africa. Grand mosques dominate the towns and cities, as here in Casablanca, Morocco.

THE ISLAMIC NORTH

POLITICAL AFRICA

Until the 1960s most of Africa was still controlled by European countries as part of their overseas empires. By the late 1980s, nearly every country had gained its independence. Many problems must still be solved in order to improve quality of life, and several countries have experienced severe droughts and civil wars. Fifteen countries are land-locked, which means that they do not have access to the sea. This restricts their trade and communications.

POPULATION

Capital cities
- ◉ Above 500,000
- ◉ 100,000 to 500,000
- ● 50,000 to 100,000
- ● Below 50,000

Other cities
- ○ 50,000 to 100,000

CITY LIFE

Most Africans still live in rural areas, although there are large cities, like Cairo in Egypt. Cairo is the continent's largest city and more than 6.5 million people live here.

INDEPENDENCE

This grand cathedral at Yamoussoukro, Ivory Coast, has been built since independence, when the city became the country's new capital. Building a new capital symbolized the break from Ivory Coast's colonial past.

POPULATION

Despite its great size, Africa's population is relatively low, especially in the desert areas. The highest populations are found where water and fertile land are available. African birth rates are high which means that populations are increasing rapidly.

Largest city
CAIRO
6.5 million people

POPULATION DENSITY
(People per sq km)
- Below 49
- 50–99
- 100–149
- 150–199
- 200–299
- Above 300

CONFLICT AND WARFARE

Many African nations contain several ethnic groups, who often have little in common. Inter-ethnic conflict has led to bitter civil war; these buildings in Ndjamena, Chad's capital, still bear the scars.

STANDARDS OF LIVING

The majority of Africa's people maintain a very simple lifestyle, although access to western consumer goods is growing. In many countries standards of health and literacy are improving slowly through education programmes.

STANDARD OF LIVING
(UN Human Development Index)
low ——— high

SCALE 1:45,000,000

AFRICAN GEOGRAPHY

Africa's massive reserves of minerals, including oil, gold, copper and diamonds, are amongst the largest in the world. Mining is a very important industry for many countries, and has provided money for growth and development. Africa's wide range of environments means that many different types of crops can be grown. Rubber, bananas and oil palms are grown for export in the tropics, and east Africa is especially famous for its tea and coffee.

INDUSTRY

Most African industries are based on processing raw materials such as food crops or mineral ores. Some African countries depend on one product or crop for most of their income, but in many larger cities different industries are developing. Northern Africa, Nigeria, and South Africa have the widest range of industries.

MINERAL RESOURCES

The southern countries, in particular South Africa, have large reserves of diamonds, gold, uranium and copper. The large copper deposits in Congo (Zaire) and Zambia are known as the 'copper belt'. Oil and gas are extracted in Algeria, Angola, Egypt, Libya, and Nigeria.

MINING

The world's largest uranium mine is in Namibia. Uranium is used to fuel nuclear power stations, and is also mined in Niger and South Africa,

MINERAL RESOURCES

	Bauxite			Oil/gas field
	Copper			Coal field
	Diamonds			
	Iron			
	Phosphates			
	Gold			
	Uranium			

OIL AND GAS

In the desert wastes of Algeria, a drilling rig searches for new sources of oil in the rich north African oilfields. There are several large oil fields in the Niger delta, and north Africa.

INDUSTRY

- Brewing
- Car/vehicle manufacture
- Cement
- Chemicals
- Coal
- Engineering
- Fish processing
- Finance
- Food processing
- Iron & steel
- Mining
- Oil and gas
- Pharmaceuticals
- Shipbuilding
- Textiles
- Timber processing

GNP per capita (US$)

- Below 1999
- 2000-4999
- 5000-9999
- 10,000-19,999
- 20,000-24,999
- Above 25,000
- • Industrial centre

EUROPE

Mediterranean Sea

ATLANTIC OCEAN

Madeira (part of Portugal)
Ceuta (part of Spain)
Melilla (part of Spain)
Casablanca
Algiers
Tunis
Oran
MOROCCO
TUNISIA
Tripoli
Benghazi
Alexandria
Port Said
Cairo
Canary Islands (part of Spain)
ALGERIA
LIBYA
Western Sahara (disputed territory under Moroccan occupation)
EGYPT
Red Sea
ASIA
MAURITANIA
Khartoum
ERITREA
CAPE VERDE
MALI
NIGER
CHAD
SUDAN
DJIBOUTI
Dakar
SENEGAL
Kano
Addis Ababa
GAMBIA
GUINEA-BISSAU
GUINEA
BURKINA
BENIN
Kaduna
NIGERIA
CENTRAL AFRICAN REPUBLIC
ETHIOPIA
SIERRA LEONE
IVORY COAST
GHANA
TOGO
Lagos
Monrovia
LIBERIA
Accra
Abidjan
CAMEROON
Douala
Bangui
UGANDA
KENYA
Mogadishu
SOMALIA
EQUATORIAL GUINEA
Libreville
Kisangani
Kampala
SAO TOME & PRINCIPE
GABON
Port-Gentil
CONGO
Nairobi
CONGO (ZAIRE)
RWANDA
BURUNDI
Mombasa
Pointe-Noire
Kinshasa
Dodoma
Dar es Salaam
SEYCHELLES
Luanda
TANZANIA
ATLANTIC OCEAN
Lubumbashi
MALAWI
COMOROS
Mayotte (to France)
ANGOLA
ZAMBIA
Lusaka
Blantyre
MOZAMBIQUE
MADAGASCAR
Harare
Antananarivo
MAURITIUS
Réunion (to France)
NAMIBIA
ZIMBABWE
Bulawayo
Beira
Walvis Bay
Windhoek
BOTSWANA
Johannesburg
Pretoria
Maputo
SWAZILAND
SOUTH AFRICA
LESOTHO
Durban
Cape Town
East London
Port Elizabeth
INDIAN OCEAN

CHEMICALS

In Abidjan, Ivory Coast, petrochemicals are manufactured from oil. The chemical industry has expanded with the growth of Africa's oil and gas industry.

FOOD PROCESSING

Fruit and vegetables are sold in Africa's numerous local markets, as here in Dakar, Senegal. Many crops are grown specially for canning and export overseas and are known as 'cash crops.'

FINANCE AND TRADE

Johannesburg, in South Africa, is home to many international banks. Wealth has been generated from the country's large mineral resources, such as diamonds.

CLIMATE

Africa is the world's hottest continent: temperatures of more than 50°C have been recorded in the Sahara. The northern coast has a hot, dry climate with little rainfall. Further inland, the Sahara is extremely arid, with strong, dry winds. South of the Sahara is the Sahel, where cutting down trees for fuel has turned farmland into desert. Close to the Equator there is more rainfall, and huge rainforests can grow in western and central Africa. In the south, the climate is much drier, and drought is a problem.

EXTREME WEATHER EVENTS

Symbols indicate climatic extremes

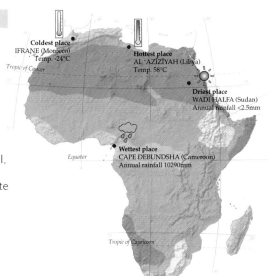

Coldest place
IFRANE (Morocco)
Temp. -24°C

Hottest place
AL 'AZĪZĪYAH (Libya)
Temp. 58°C

Driest place
WADI HALFA (Sudan)
Annual rainfall <2.5mm

Wettest place
CAPE DEBUNDSHA (Cameroon)
Annual rainfall 10290mm

Tropic of Cancer

Equator

Tropic of Capricorn

CLIMATE

- Warm temparate
- Mediterranean
- Semi-arid
- Arid
- Humid equatorial
- Tropical

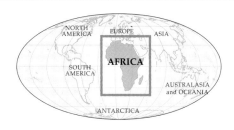

NORTH AMERICA · EUROPE · ASIA · SOUTH AMERICA · **AFRICA** · AUSTRALASIA and OCEANIA · ANTARCTICA

THE ENCROACHING DESERT

Africa has three main desert areas: the Sahara in the north and the Namib and Kalahari deserts in the south. They are a mixture of sandy dunes and bare, rocky plateaus. At the desert's edges, low rainfall and land clearance is causing the deserts to expand into areas that were once grassland.

LAND USE AND AGRICULTURE

The quality of land and the amount of rainfall has a great impact on the type of farming. In the mountain regions of countries such as Rwanda, Uganda, and Kenya, tea and coffee are grown. In the north, there is not enough water to produce staple crops such as wheat for all the population, but 'cash crops' such as citrus fruits, dates and olives are grown for export. Sub-tropical west Africa grows peanuts, cocoa and coffee. In the southern part of the continent, South Africa grows many different crops: citrus fruits are grown for export, as well as grapes, which are used to make wine.

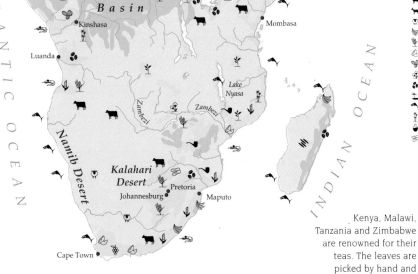

EUROPE
Mediterranean Sea
Algiers
Casablanca
Alexandria
Cairo
Libyan Desert
Nile
Red Sea
ASIA
ATLANTIC OCEAN
Sahara
Niger
Sahel
Dakar
Nile
Lake Volta
Addis Ababa
Lagos
Accra
Abidjan
ATLANTIC OCEAN
Congo
Congo Basin
Lake Victoria
Nairobi
Kinshasa
Mombasa
Mogadishu
Luanda
Lake Nyasa
Zambezi
Zambezi
INDIAN OCEAN
Namib Desert
Kalahari Desert
Pretoria
Johannesburg
Maputo
Cape Town

LAND USE AND AGRICULTURE

- Cattle
- Goats
- Sheep
- Bananas
- Cereals
- Citrus fruits
- Cocoa
- Cotton
- Coffee
- Dates
- Fishing
- Oil palms
- Olives
- Peanuts
- Rice
- Rubber
- Shellfish
- Sugar cane
- Tea
- Tobacco
- Vineyards
- Cropland
- Desert
- Forest
- Pasture
- Wetland
- Major conurbation

PASTORALISM

At the southern edge of the Sahara is a fragile region known as the Sahel. In this area shifting cultivation and nomadic herding are widely practised.

SUBSISTENCE AGRICULTURE

Although African countries produce a wide range of crops, in many cases people rely on a few basic crops, like cassava and yams, as a staple. The yam is a starchy root which is ground to make flour.

CASH CROPS

Kenya, Malawi, Tanzania and Zimbabwe are renowned for their teas. The leaves are picked by hand and dried. When mixed with boiling water, tea is enjoyed by over half the world's population.

NORTH AFRICA

ALGERIA, EGYPT, LIBYA, MOROCCO, TUNISIA.

Sandwiched between the Mediterranean and the Sahara, North Africa has a history dating back to the dawn of civilization. 6,000 years ago, settlements were established along the banks of the River Nile, and since that time, waves of settlers, including Romans, Arabs and Turks have brought a mix of different cultures to the area. In the 19th century, Spain, France and Britain claimed colonies in the region, but today North Africa is independent, although Western Sahara is occupied by Morocco.

FARMING AND LAND USE

Most farming in North Africa is restricted to the fertile Mediterranean coastal strip, and the banks of the Nile where it relies heavily on irrigation. In spite of these seemingly inhospitable conditions, the region is a major producer of dates, which grow in desert oases, and of cork, made from the bark of the cork oak tree. A wide variety of other crops is also grown, including grapes, olives and cotton.

FARMING AND LAND USE

- Fishing
- Goats
- Sheep
- Cork
- Cotton
- Dates
- Olives
- Vineyards
- Cropland
- Desert
- Forest
- Pasture
- Major conurbation

CLIMATE

Most of north Africa is desert, and the climate is harsh. Rainfall is scarce, and drought is common. Temperatures are freezing at night, scorching by day and have been known to climb to over 50°C.

January

July

whole area has below 25mm rainfall

LAND USE

Forest 3%
Pasture 9%
Cropland 12%
Other (including desert) 76%

TEMPERATURE AND PRECIPITATION

- More than 35°C
- 30 to 35°C
- 25 to 30°C
- 20 to 25°C
- 15 to 20°C
- 10 to 15°C
- 5 to 10°C
- Less than 5°C

100 Precipitation (mm)

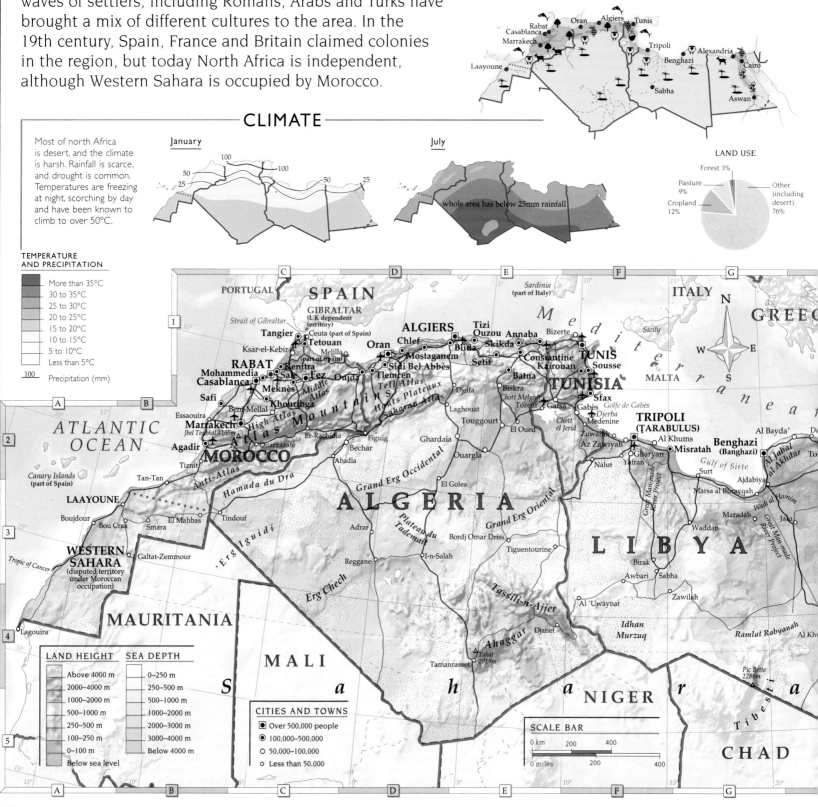

LAND HEIGHT
- Above 4000 m
- 2000–4000 m
- 1000–2000 m
- 500–1000 m
- 250–500 m
- 100–250 m
- 0–100 m
- Below sea level

SEA DEPTH
- 0–250 m
- 250–500 m
- 500–1000 m
- 1000–2000 m
- 2000–3000 m
- 3000–4000 m
- Below 4000 m

CITIES AND TOWNS
- Over 500,000 people
- 100,000–500,000
- 50,000–100,000
- Less than 50,000

SCALE BAR

0 km 200 400

0 miles 200 400

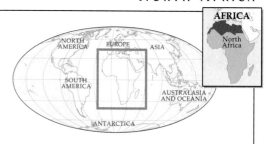

POPULATION

The majority of the population, and all of the big towns and cities, are found on the coastal plains, or along the banks of the Nile – about 99% of Egyptians live along the river. Egypt's capital, Cairo, is Africa's largest city, with over six million people. Western Sahara, and the southern portions of Egypt, Algeria and Libya are sparsely populated by Taureg nomads who roam the Sahara.

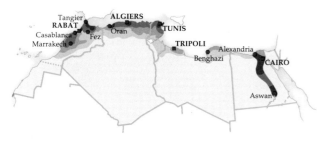

INHABITANTS PER SQ KM

- More than 200
- 100–200
- 50–100
- 10–50
- Less than 10
- ■ Capital city
- ● Major city

URBAN/RURAL POPULATION DIVIDE

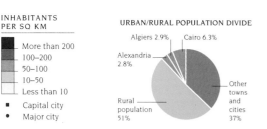

Algiers 2.9%
Cairo 6.3%
Alexandria 2.8%
Other towns and cities 37%
Rural population 51%

THE LANDSCAPE

The parched rocks and endless sandy expanses of the Sahara occupy much of North Africa. The only major river here is the Nile, with a delta that extends into the Mediterranean Sea. The old, eroded Atlas Mountains are the highest mountain range.

Sand dunes
Winds blowing across the Sahara cause the sand to build up into dunes which can reach heights of up to 430 m.

Nile Delta (I 2)
As the River Nile nears the Mediterranean, it separates into many small streams, which flow over a fertile triangle of land. Mud and rock carried by the river and deposited in the delta have formed new land.

Red Sea (J 3)
The Red Sea gets its name from red algae that live on the sea floor and make the water appear red.

Atlas Mountains (C2)
The Atlas Mountains are made up of a number of different ranges – the Anti-Atlas, High Atlas, Middle Atlas, Tell Atlas and Saharan Atlas. They stretch some 2,250 km from the north of Tunisia to the Atlantic coast of Morocco.

Qattara Depression (I3)
In the northwest of Egypt is a huge desert depression 320 km long and 120 km wide. Its floor, part of which is 134 m below sea level, is covered with sand, brackish ponds and salt marshes.

The River Nile (I3)
The world's longest river flows 6,695 km to the Mediterranean Sea. The system of rivers and lakes that flow into the Nile drain some 2,850,000 sq km – about 10% of the entire African continent.

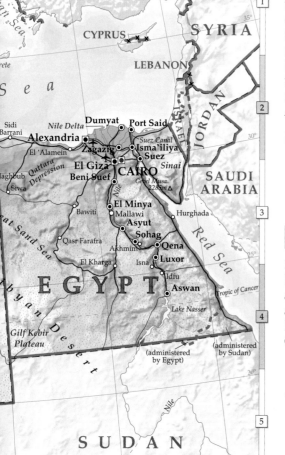

INDUSTRY

Oil and natural gas have brought wealth to the area, particularly to Libya, which has enough oil reserves to last well into the next century. Textile manufacture is widespread – North Africa is famous for its exotic cloths and rugs. Several large chemical refineries and steel plants have been established along the coast, especially in the major industrial cities like Alexandria and Cairo in Egypt.

STRUCTURE OF INDUSTRY
Primary 16%
Services 49%
Manufacturing 35%

INDUSTRY
- ⚗ Chemicals
- 🍴 Food processing
- ⚙ Iron and steel
- 👕 Textiles
- 🛢 Oil and gas
- 🏛 Tourism
- ▣ Major industrial centre / area
- — Major road

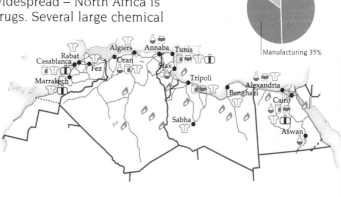

ENVIRONMENTAL ISSUES

Droughts, overgrazing and the stripping of vegetation for fuelwood and animal fodder have caused the Sahara to expand northwards. This has reduced the already limited amount of land available for farming. The risk of desertification is acute in many coastal areas. North Africa is very dry, and there are severe droughts periodically. Many of the larger cities like Alexandria and Cairo have very poor air quality.

ENVIRONMENTAL ISSUES
- 🐟 Drought
- 😷 Urban air pollution
- Existing desert
- Risk of desertification
- Severe risk of desertification
- Non-affected area
- ● Major industrial centre

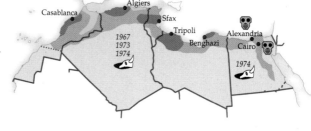

WEST AFRICA

BENIN, BURKINA, CAMEROON, CENTRAL AFRICAN REPUBLIC, CHAD, EQUATORIAL GUINEA, GAMBIA, GHANA, GUINEA, GUINEA-BISSAU, IVORY COAST, LIBERIA, MALI, MAURITANIA, NIGER, NIGERIA, SAO TOME & PRINCIPE, SENEGAL, SIERRA LEONE, TOGO

West Africa's varied climate and agricultural and mineral wealth have provided the foundation for some of Africa's greatest civilizations, like those of the Malinke and Asante people. The area remains ethnically and culturally diverse today, as well as densely populated; Nigeria is by far the most populous country in Africa. Since independence from European colonial powers in the 1960s, political instability has been a feature of many countries here.

INDUSTRY

Agricultural products still form the basis of most economies in West Africa. Food processing is widespread – oil palms and groundnuts are processed for their valuable vegetable oils. Oil and gas are found off the coast of Ivory Coast and around the Niger delta, where a large chemical industry has developed.

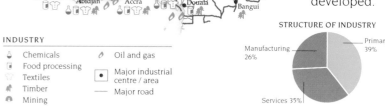

INDUSTRY

🜹	Chemicals	◊	Oil and gas
🗍	Food processing	■	Major industrial centre / area
👕	Textiles		Major road
🌲	Timber		
⛏	Mining		

STRUCTURE OF INDUSTRY

Manufacturing 26%
Primary 39%
Services 35%

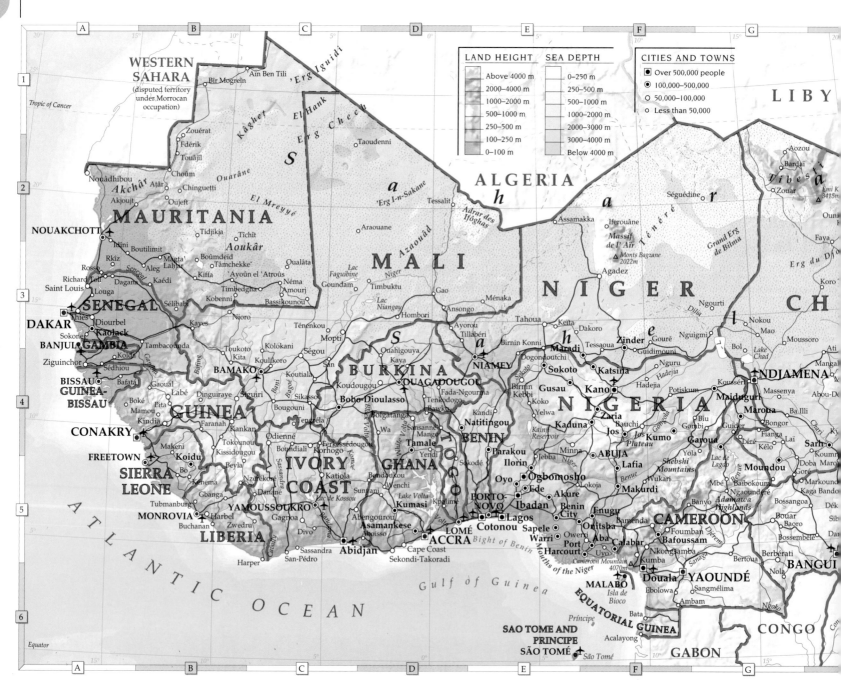

LAND HEIGHT
- Above 4000 m
- 2000–4000 m
- 1000–2000 m
- 500–1000 m
- 250–500 m
- 100–250 m
- 0–100 m

SEA DEPTH
- 0–250 m
- 250–500 m
- 500–1000 m
- 1000–2000 m
- 2000–3000 m
- 3000–4000 m
- Below 4000 m

CITIES AND TOWNS
- ■ Over 500,000 people
- ● 100,000–500,000
- ○ 50,000–100,000
- ○ Less than 50,000

FARMING AND LAND USE

Well-watered land along the coast allows a wide variety of crops to be grown, including cocoa and oil palms, both of which provide important cash crops. In the drier north, goats and sheep are grazed, and subsistence crops such as yams, millet and cassava are grown.

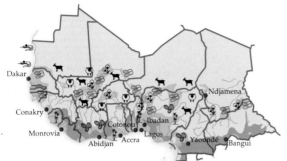
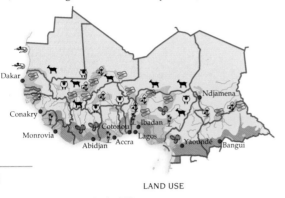
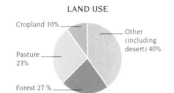

FARMING AND LAND USE

🐐 Goats		▨ Cropland
🐑 Sheep		▨ Desert
🦐 Shellfish		▨ Forest
🍫 Cocoa		▨ Pasture
🌿 Cotton		▨ Wetland
🌴 Oil palms		● Major conurbation
🥜 Peanuts		

LAND USE

Cropland 10%
Other (including desert) 40%
Pasture 23%
Forest 27 %

CLIMATE

The climate differs immensely from the hot desert north, through to the tropical rainforest south. July is the wet season, and rainfall is heavy in the south, while the desert areas remain dry throughout the year.

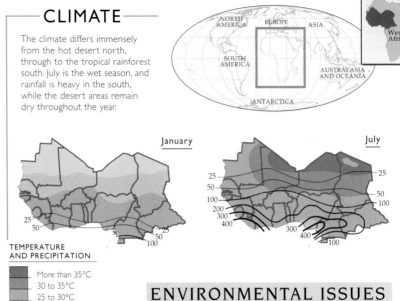

January

July

TEMPERATURE AND PRECIPITATION

▨	More than 35°C
▨	30 to 35°C
▨	25 to 30°C
▨	20 to 25°C
▨	Less than 20°C
—100—	Precipitation (mm)

ENVIRONMENTAL ISSUES

Persistent droughts are the main concerns in the north of the region. The problem is made worse by a shortage of wood needed for fuel, which leads to the cutting down of any available trees for fuelwood. In the tropical south, the timber industry is destroying much of the ancient forest.

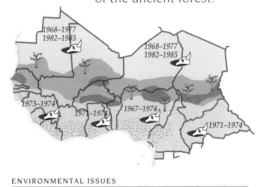

1968–1977 1982–1985
1968–1977 1982–1985
1973–1974
1971–1974
1967–1974
1971–1974

ENVIRONMENTAL ISSUES

🐟	Drought	▨	Existing desert
🌲	Severe fuelwood shortage	▨	Risk of desertification
		▨	Severe risk of desertification
		▨	Deforested area

POPULATION

Most of the population lives in the southern coastal regions. In the drier north, settlement becomes more sporadic, and nomadic tribespeople are best suited to live in the desert north. Nigeria is the most populated country in Africa and Lagos is one of the continent's larger cities, although West Africa's population remains mainly rural.

INHABITANTS PER SQ KM

▨	More than 200
▨	100–200
▨	50–100
▨	10–50
▨	Less than 10
■	Capital city
●	Major city

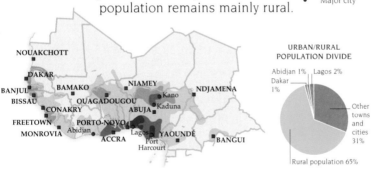

NOUAKCHOTT
DAKAR
BANJUL
BAMAKO
NIAMEY
BISSAU
OUAGADOUGOU
Kano
NDJAMENA
CONAKRY
ABUJA
Kaduna
FREETOWN
PORTO-NOVO
MONROVIA
Abidjan
Lagos
YAOUNDÉ
ACCRA
Port Harcourt
BANGUI

URBAN/RURAL POPULATION DIVIDE

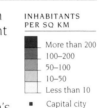

Abidjan 1%   Lagos 2%
Dakar 1%
Other towns and cities 31%
Rural population 65%

THE LANDSCAPE

Large differences in rainfall from north to south have led to a varied landscape. The wet coastal regions contain tropical rainforest. To the north, savannah grasslands, arid Sahel scrubland and barren desert lie in successive bands. The Niger is one of the larger rivers and is unusual because it has two deltas; one at the sea, and one inland.

River Niger (D 3)

The River Niger is West Africa's longest river. When it reaches the sea, it flows through a vast delta of mud flats and mangrove swamps. Great oil deposits have been found here.

Sahel (E 3)

The band of semi-desert stretching from Senegal to Sudan along the southern boundary of the Sahara is called the Sahel. Frequent droughts in recent years, and excessive cutting of trees have meant that much of the Sahel is turning to desert.

Tibesti mountains (G 2)

These mountains in north-western Chad are a chain of extinct volcanoes which now form solitary peaks in the midst of the Sahara.

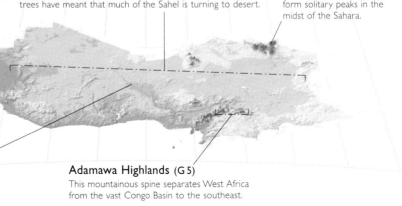

Adamawa Highlands (G 5)

This mountainous spine separates West Africa from the vast Congo Basin to the southeast.

Left map panel

I
EGYPT
Tropic of Cancer
25°
30°
25°
1
Erdi
20°
N
W E
S
2
Ennedi
15°
SUDAN
3
...tine
...éché
Beïda
...nal Azoum
10°
4
...man ○Birao
○Ouanda Djallé
Massif des Bongo
Kotto
...NTRAL AFRICAN
Ippy ○Bria Djéma
...la REPUBLIC
5°
5
...ari Bambari Dembia
Bangassou Obo
...Alindao Bomu
...ui Mobaye
CONGO (ZAIRE)

SCALE BAR

0 km   200   400
0 miles   200   400
6
Equator
I

EAST AFRICA

BURUNDI, DJIBOUTI, ERITREA, ETHIOPIA, KENYA, RWANDA, SOMALIA, SUDAN, TANZANIA, UGANDA

Much of East Africa is covered by long grass, scrub and scattered trees, called savannah. This land is grazed by both domestic animals and a great variety of wild animals including lions, giraffes and elephants. The east of the region is known as the Horn of Africa, because it is shaped like an animal horn. Along with Sudan, the countries there have recently been devastated by civil wars, and periods of drought and famine. In contrast, Kenya in the south is one of Africa's more stable and wealthy countries.

INDUSTRY

East Africa has few mineral resources, and industry is mainly based on processing raw materials. Coffee, tea, sugar cane and sisal, are harvested and processed before being exported. Textile production is widespread, but is only on a small scale. Tourism is increasingly important in Kenya and Tanzania; each year, many thousands of people visit the wildlife reserves there.

Port Sudan
Khartoum
Asmara
Addis Ababa
Dire Dawa
Mogadishu
Kampala
Kigali
Bujumbura
Arusha
Nairobi
Mombasa
Dodoma
Dar es Salaam

INDUSTRY

- Cement manufacturing
- Chemicals
- Food processing
- Textiles
- Tourism

◉ Major industrial centre / area
— Major road

STRUCTURE OF INDUSTRY

Primary 15%
Services 46%
Manufacturing 39%

ENVIRONMENTAL ISSUES

Rapid population growth has created a need for increasing amounts of land for farming. This, as well as the need for fuelwood, has led to tree cover being stripped, allowing the soil to be washed or blown away. Over the past 25 years, eastern Africa has been stricken by many catastrophic droughts which have made desertification worse, and brought much human suffering.

1973
1980
1985–1986
1989

1973–1975
1980
1985
1989

1973–1975
1980
1985
1989
1986–1987
1989

1986

1973–1975
1980
1985
1987
1989

1972–1974

1973–1974

ENVIRONMENTAL ISSUES

🦴 Drought

🌳 Severe fuelwood shortage

Existing desert
Risk of desertification
Severe risk of desertification

FARMING AND LAND USE

Much of the north and east is too dry for farming, but in Sudan, cotton is grown on land irrigated by the River Nile. The Lake Victoria basin and rich volcanic soils of the highlands in Kenya, Uganda and Tanzania support staple food crops, and those grown for export, such as tea and coffee. Kenya also grows high-quality vegetables, like mangetout, and exports them by air to supermarkets abroad. Sheep, goats and cattle are herded on the savannah.

Khartoum
Addis Ababa
Mogadishu
Kampala
Nairobi
Mombasa
Dar es Salaam

FARMING AND LAND USE

- Cattle
- Goats
- Sheep
- Coffee
- Cotton
- Dates
- Market gardening
- Sugar cane
- Sisal
- Tea

Cropland
Desert
Forest
Pasture
Wetland
● Major conurbation

LAND USE

Cropland 9%
Pasture 40%
Other 26%
Forest 25%

THE LANDSCAPE

The south of East Africa is savannah grassland, broken by the rugged mountains – some of them active volcanoes – and large fresh and saltwater lakes that make up part of the Great Rift Valley. The River Nile has its source here, flowing through lakes Victoria, Kyoga and Albert as it takes much-needed water to the arid desert areas in the north.

Great Rift Valley (D 6) (D 4)
The Great Rift Valley is like a deep scar running 7,000 km from north to south through East Africa. It has been formed by the movements of two of the Earth's plates over millions of years. If these movements continue, East Africa may eventually become an island, separated by the ocean from the rest of the continent.

Sudd (B 4)
The north of Sudan is rocky desert, but in the south, the waters of the White Nile run into a swampy area called the Sudd where much of its water disperses and evaporates.

River Juba (E 5)
This river rises in the highlands of Ethiopia and flows some 1,200 km southwards to the Indian Ocean. It, and the River Shebeli, which joins it about 30 km from the coast, are the only permanent rivers in Somalia.

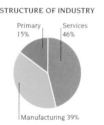

Lake Victoria (C 5)
Lake Victoria is Africa's largest lake and the second largest freshwater lake in the world. It lies on the Equator, between Kenya, Tanzania and Uganda, and covers 69,500 sq km. Its only outlet is the River Nile in the north.

Kilimanjaro (D 6)
This old volcano, made up of alternating layers of lava and ash, is Africa's highest mountain, rising to 5,895 m. Although it lies only three degrees from the Equator, its peak is permanently covered with snow.

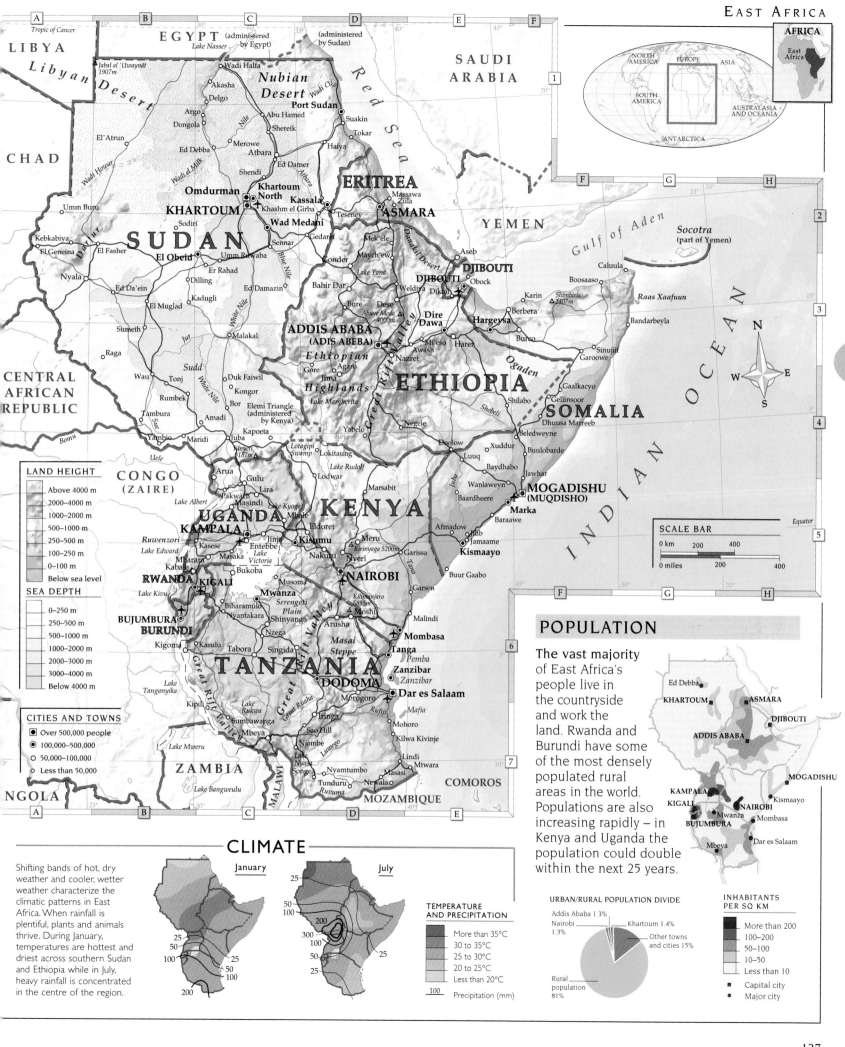

LAND HEIGHT

- Above 4000 m
- 2000–4000 m
- 1000–2000 m
- 500–1000 m
- 250–500 m
- 100–250 m
- 0–100 m
- Below sea level

SEA DEPTH

- 0–250 m
- 250–500 m
- 500–1000 m
- 1000–2000 m
- 2000–3000 m
- 3000–4000 m
- Below 4000 m

CITIES AND TOWNS

- ■ Over 500,000 people
- ● 100,000–500,000
- ○ 50,000–100,000
- ○ Less than 50,000

SCALE BAR

0 km   200   400
0 miles   200   400

POPULATION

The vast majority of East Africa's people live in the countryside and work the land. Rwanda and Burundi have some of the most densely populated rural areas in the world. Populations are also increasing rapidly – in Kenya and Uganda the population could double within the next 25 years.

URBAN/RURAL POPULATION DIVIDE

Addis Ababa 1.3%
Nairobi 1.3%
Khartoum 1.4%
Other towns and cities 15%
Rural population 81%

INHABITANTS PER SQ KM

- More than 200
- 100–200
- 50–100
- 10–50
- Less than 10

■ Capital city
● Major city

CLIMATE

Shifting bands of hot, dry weather and cooler, wetter weather characterize the climatic patterns in East Africa. When rainfall is plentiful, plants and animals thrive. During January, temperatures are hottest and driest across southern Sudan and Ethiopia while in July, heavy rainfall is concentrated in the centre of the region.

January   July

TEMPERATURE AND PRECIPITATION

- More than 35°C
- 30 to 35°C
- 25 to 30°C
- 20 to 25°C
- Less than 20°C
- 100 Precipitation (mm)

SOUTHERN AFRICA

ANGOLA, BOTSWANA, COMOROS, CONGO, CONGO (ZAIRE), GABON, LESOTHO, MADAGASCAR, MALAWI, MOZAMBIQUE, NAMIBIA, SOUTH AFRICA, SWAZILAND, ZAMBIA, ZIMBABWE

Southern Africa contains the richest deposits of valuable minerals on the continent. South Africa is the wealthiest and most industrialized country in the region and most of the countries that surround it rely on it for trade and work. Racial segregation under apartheid operated from 1948 until 1994, when South Africa held its first multiracial elections.

FARMING AND LAND USE

Most of southern Africa's farmers grow just enough to feed their families, though much of the farmland is in the hands of a few wealthy landowners. In the tropical north, oil palms and rubber are grown on large commercial plantations. Fruits are cultivated in the south, and tea and coffee are important in the east. Cattle farming is widespread across the dry grasslands.

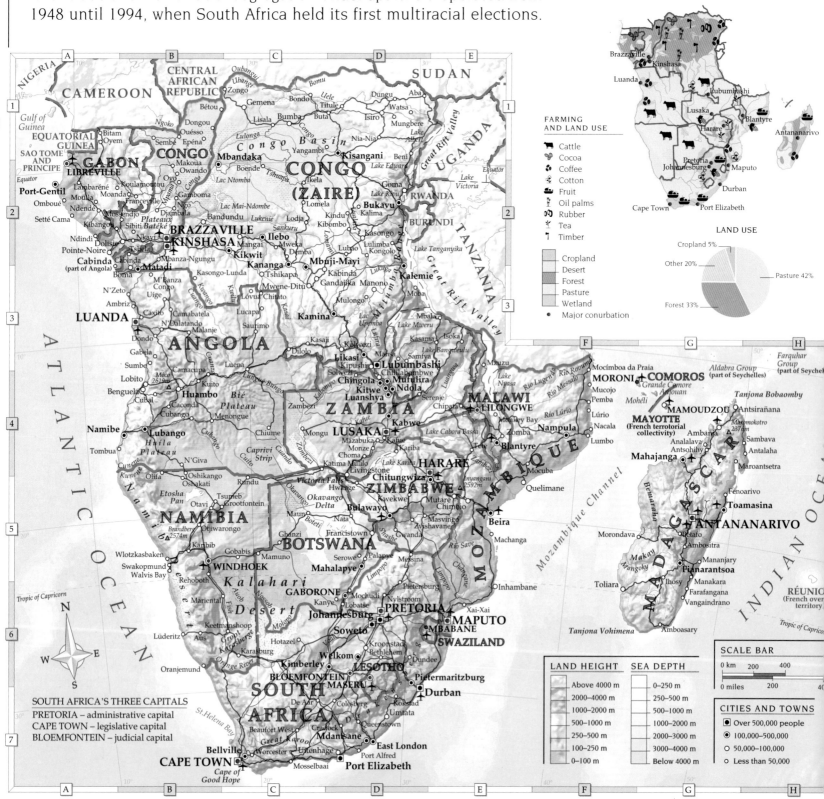

FARMING AND LAND USE

- 🐂 Cattle
- 🌰 Cocoa
- ☕ Coffee
- 🌱 Cotton
- 🍌 Fruit
- 🌴 Oil palms
- Rubber
- 🌿 Tea
- 🌲 Timber

Cropland
Desert
Forest
Pasture
Wetland
• Major conurbation

LAND USE

Cropland 5%
Other 20%
Pasture 42%
Forest 33%

SOUTH AFRICA'S THREE CAPITALS
PRETORIA – administrative capital
CAPE TOWN – legislative capital
BLOEMFONTEIN – judicial capital

SCALE BAR

0 km   200   400

0 miles   200

LAND HEIGHT

Above 4000 m
2000–4000 m
1000–2000 m
500–1000 m
250–500 m
100–250 m
0–100 m

SEA DEPTH

0–250 m
250–500 m
500–1000 m
1000–2000 m
2000–3000 m
3000–4000 m
Below 4000 m

CITIES AND TOWNS

- ▣ Over 500,000 people
- ◉ 100,000–500,000
- ○ 50,000–100,000
- ∘ Less than 50,000

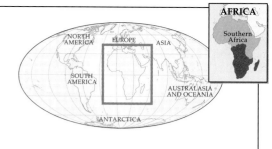

CLIMATE

During January, temperatures are highest in the Kalahari Desert and rainfall is plentiful in the centre of southern Africa. July is cooler and drier; rainfall is concentrated in the north of Congo (Zaire). The Atlantic coast of Namibia receives little rain all year round.

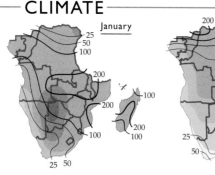

January

July

TEMPERATURE AND PRECIPITATION

- More than 35°C
- 30 to 35°C
- 25 to 30°C
- 20 to 25°C
- 15 to 20°C
- Less than 15°C
- 100 Precipitation (mm)

ENVIRONMENTAL ISSUES

The immense rainforests of the Congo Basin in the north remain relatively untouched, but deforestation is beginning to occur at its edges, and much more forest is due to be cleared in the future. Large parts of Madagascar have also been deforested. Further south, occasional drought and the clearing of bushlands for fuelwood can cause soil loss.

Congo Basin

1971–1974
1979–1985
1982–1984
1983–1985
1983 1985

ENVIRONMENTAL ISSUES

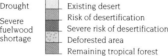

- Drought
- Severe fuelwood shortage
- Existing desert
- Risk of desertification
- Severe risk of desertification
- Deforested area
- Remaining tropical forest

INDUSTRY

Southern Africa has extraordinary mineral resources. Angola has large deposits of oil, and diamonds are found in Angola, Botswana, Namibia and South Africa. Copper is mined in the region known as the 'copper belt', which runs from Congo (Zaire) into Zambia, and South Africa produces 40% of the world's gold. Manufacturing, such as fruit canning and steel production, is most developed in South Africa.

Libreville
Kisangani
Brazzaville
Bukavu
Kinshasa
Luanda
Kolwezi
Lubumbashi
Ndola
Lusaka
Blantyre
Harare
Antananarivo
Bulawayo
Beira
Pretoria
Johannesburg
Maputo
Durban
Cape Town
Port Elizabeth

INDUSTRY

- Car manufacture
- Chemicals
- Engineering
- Food processing
- Iron & steel
- Metal refining
- Textiles
- Oil and gas
- Mining
- Timber processing
- Tourism
- Major industrial centre / area
- Major road

STRUCTURE OF INDUSTRY

Primary 10%
Services 59%
Manufacturing 31%

THE LANDSCAPE

Southern Africa stretches from just north of the Equator down to the southern tip of the continent and has extremely varied climate and geography. In the north are the tropical rainforests of the Congo Basin, while arid desert covers much of the southwest. The eastern regions are mostly grasslands, with lush vegetation found on the tropical coast of Mozambique.

Congo Basin (C 1)
The River Congo is Africa's second longest river, flowing in an arc through the dense tropical forests of the Congo Basin, before emptying into the Atlantic Ocean.

Namib Desert (B 5)
The Namib is one of the world's driest deserts. The only water it receives is from mists that roll in from the sea. Where the desert meets the coast is known as the Skeleton Coast, because of sailors who were shipwrecked and died there.

Victoria Falls (D 5)
On its way to the Indian Ocean, the River Zambezi plunges over a 128-m cliff, into a narrow chasm. The resultant spray rises up to 500 m, and the thunder of the water can be heard up to 40 km away.

Madagascar (G 5)
The world's fourth largest island lies in isolation 250 km off the east coast of southern Africa. It became separated from the African continent 135 million years ago, and its plant and animal life are unique. The rich biodiversity of the rainforests is being threatened by felling for fuelwood and timber.

Okavango Delta (C 5)
The Okavango River terminates in the Kalahari Desert, forming a vast, swampy inland delta.

Drakensberg (D 4)
The Drakensberg are a chain of mountains which lie at the edge of a broad plateau that has tilted because of the movement of the Earth's plates. Rivers have carved through the high mountains, creating dramatic gorges and waterfalls.

POPULATION

Although the population is still mostly rural, southern Africa has some of the continent's most urbanized nations. Dense tropical rainforest in the north, and arid desert in the southwest have kept habitation to a bare minimum. Malawi is the most densely populated country in the region.

LIBREVILLE
Kisangani
BRAZZAVILLE
Bukavu
KINSHASA
LUANDA
Lobito
Lubumbashi
LILONGWE
LUSAKA
Blantyre
HARARE
Bulawayo
WINDHOEK
ANTANANARIVO
GABORONE
PRETORIA
MAPUTO
Johannesburg
MBANE
BLOEMFONTEIN
MASERU
Durban
CAPE TOWN
Port Elizabeth

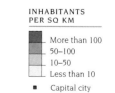

Cape Town 2%
Kinshasa 2.5%
Maputo 1.5%
Other towns and cities 28%
Rural population 66%

INHABITANTS PER SQ KM

- More than 100
- 50–100
- 10–50
- Less than 10
- Capital city
- Major city

AUSTRALASIA & OCEANIA

Australasia and Oceania encompasses the ancient land mass of Australia, the islands of New Zealand, and the scattering of thousands of small islands that stretch out into the Pacific Ocean. Indigenous peoples of the South Pacific, such as the Aborigines, Maoris, Polynesians, Micronesians and Melanesians, inhabit the region. In Australia and New Zealand, they live alongside people of European origin who settled in the 18th century, and more recent arrivals from East and Southeast Asia.

PACIFIC ISLANDS

Micronesia is one of the Pacific's island nations, consisting of a group of volcanic islands, low-lying coral reefs and lagoons. Many of the smaller Pacific islands are only a few metres above sea level.

LAND USE AND AGRICULTURE

Much of the centre of Australia is a dry, barren desert and unsuitable for agriculture. At its fringes, sheep farming is practised, and Australia and New Zealand alike are massive producers of wool and lamb. The Pacific islands export many exotic fruits and crops – especially oil palms and coconut palms. Oil from the palms is processed and sold, as well as the fruits themselves. Small-scale fishing is common, but larger scale operations are run by foreign fishing fleets, especially the Japanese, who fish tuna from the deeper waters of the Pacific.

SHEEP FARMING

New Zealand and Australia are the world's biggest producers of wool. In New Zealand, sheep outnumber people by 20 – 1.

POPULATION

Capital cities
- ◉ Above 500,000
- ◉ 100,000 to 500,000
- ◉ 50,000 to 100,000
- ● Below 50,000

State capitals
- ◉ Above 500,000
- ◉ 100,000 to 500,000
- ○ 50,000 to 100,000

BORDERS

- full international border
- indication of maritime country extent
- indication of maritime dependent territory extent
- state border

SCALE 1:37,250,000

0 km — 300 — 600

0 miles — 300 — 600

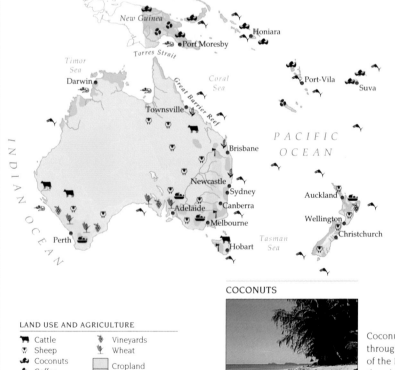

COCONUTS

Coconuts are grown throughout the islands of the Pacific, and the white flesh is dried in the sun to produce copra. Copra is a valuable export crop for many islands.

LAND USE AND AGRICULTURE

- 🐂 Cattle
- 🐑 Sheep
- 🥥 Coconuts
- ☕ Coffee
- 🎣 Fishing
- 🍎 Fruit
- 🦐 Shellfish
- 🌾 Sugar cane
- 🌲 Timber
- 🍇 Vineyards
- 🌾 Wheat

  Cropland
  Desert
  Forest
  Mountain region
  Pasture
- ● Major conurbation

MINERAL RESOURCES

Mineral resources are not widespread, but where they are found, it is in great abundance. Most of the small Pacific islands have no mineral resources, but Australia has enormous reserves of bauxite and iron ore, and also sizeable reserves of gold and zinc. Copper is found in Papua New Guinea, and New Caledonia has large nickel reserves. There are ample supplies of fossil fuels and although coal is plentiful in eastern Australia, oil and gas are found only in isolated pockets around Australia's coast.

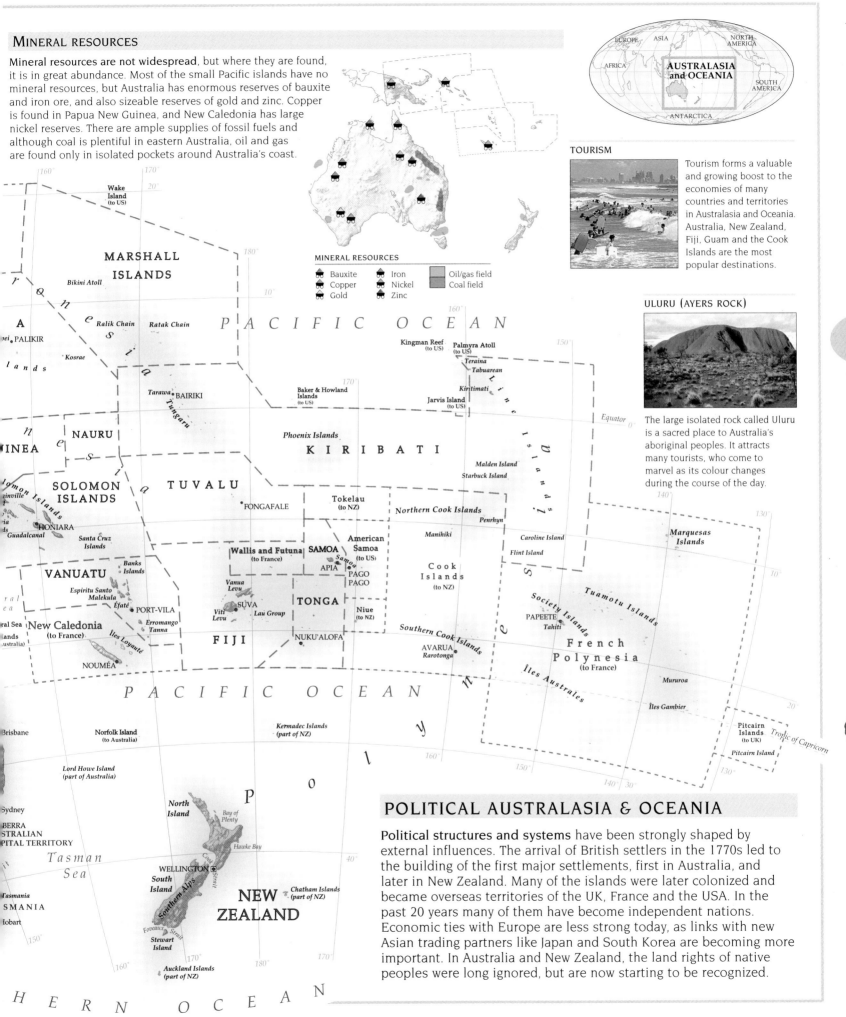

AUSTRALASIA and OCEANIA

MINERAL RESOURCES

- Bauxite
- Copper
- Gold
- Iron
- Nickel
- Zinc
- Oil/gas field
- Coal field

TOURISM

Tourism forms a valuable and growing boost to the economies of many countries and territories in Australasia and Oceania. Australia, New Zealand, Fiji, Guam and the Cook Islands are the most popular destinations.

ULURU (AYERS ROCK)

The large isolated rock called Uluru is a sacred place to Australia's aboriginal peoples. It attracts many tourists, who come to marvel as its colour changes during the course of the day.

Wake Island (to US)

MARSHALL ISLANDS

Bikini Atoll

PALIKIR

Ralik Chain   Ratak Chain

Kosrae

PACIFIC OCEAN

Kingman Reef (to US)   Palmyra Atoll (to US)

Teraina
Tabuarean

Kiritimati

Jarvis Island (to US)

Tarawa • BAIRIKI

Baker & Howland Islands (to US)

NAURU

Phoenix Islands

KIRIBATI

Malden Island
Starbuck Island

Equator

SOLOMON ISLANDS

TUVALU

FONGAFALE

Tokelau (to NZ)

Northern Cook Islands

Penrhyn

Manihiki

Caroline Island

Flint Island

Marquesas Islands

HONIARA

Guadalcanal

Santa Cruz Islands

Wallis and Futuna (to France)   SAMOA

American Samoa (to US)

APIA

Cook Islands (to NZ)

Society Islands

Tuamotu Islands

VANUATU

Banks Islands

Espiritu Santo
Malekula

Vanua Levu

PAGO PAGO

TONGA

PAPEETE
Tahiti

Éfaté • PORT-VILA

Viti Levu • SUVA   Lau Group

Niue (to NZ)

French Polynesia (to France)

New Caledonia (to France)

Erromango
Tanna

Îles Loyauté

FIJI

NUKU'ALOFA

Southern Cook Islands

AVARUA
Rarotonga

Îles Australes

Mururoa

NOUMÉA

Îles Gambier

PACIFIC OCEAN

Pitcairn Islands (to UK)   Tropic of Capricorn

Pitcairn Island

Brisbane

Norfolk Island (to Australia)

Kermadec Islands (part of NZ)

Lord Howe Island (part of Australia)

Sydney

BERRA
STRALIAN
PITAL TERRITORY

North Island

Bay of Plenty

Tasman Sea

Hawke Bay

Tasmania

SMANIA

WELLINGTON

South Island

Chatham Islands (part of NZ)

Hobart

NEW ZEALAND

Foveaux Strait

Stewart Island

Auckland Islands (part of NZ)

HERN OCEAN

POLITICAL AUSTRALASIA & OCEANIA

Political structures and systems have been strongly shaped by external influences. The arrival of British settlers in the 1770s led to the building of the first major settlements, first in Australia, and later in New Zealand. Many of the islands were later colonized and became overseas territories of the UK, France and the USA. In the past 20 years many of them have become independent nations. Economic ties with Europe are less strong today, as links with new Asian trading partners like Japan and South Korea are becoming more important. In Australia and New Zealand, the land rights of native peoples were long ignored, but are now starting to be recognized.

AUSTRALIA

Australia is the world's sixth-largest country, and also the smallest, flattest continent, with the lowest rainfall. Most Australians are of European, mainly British, origin but in the past 50 years almost five million settlers from more than 200 countries have made Australia their home. The Aboriginal peoples, now only a tiny minority, were the first inhabitants. Recently, there have been several moves to restore their ancient lands.

FARMING AND LAND USE

Away from the coasts, much of the land is too dry for agriculture. Fields of sugar cane grow close the east coast, and grapes for the thriving wine industry are cultivated in the south and west, along with wheat. Vast numbers of cattle and sheep are raised for their meat and wool – both of which are major exports. They are grazed in the desert, on huge farms called 'stations', and in more fertile areas.

FARMING AND LAND USE

- 🐂 Cattle
- 🐑 Sheep
- 🌾 Wheat
- Sugar cane
- Timber
- Vineyards

- Cropland
- Desert
- Forest
- Pasture
- • Major conurbation

LAND USE

Cropland 6%
Other (including desert) 21%
Forest 19%
Pasture 54%

INDUSTRY

Australia has one of the world's biggest mining industries. Bauxite, coal, copper, gold and iron ore are mined and exported, especially to Japan. In the cities, service industries, particularly tourism, are growing fast; Australia's sunshine and dramatic scenery are attracting an increasing number of overseas visitors.

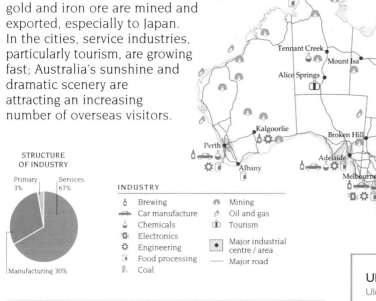

STRUCTURE OF INDUSTRY

Primary 3%
Services 67%
Manufacturing 30%

INDUSTRY

- 🍺 Brewing
- 🚗 Car manufacture
- Chemicals
- Electronics
- ⚙ Engineering
- Food processing
- Coal
- Mining
- Oil and gas
- Tourism
- Major industrial centre / area
- — Major road

THE LANDSCAPE

Most of Australia is dry, flat and barren; all of the wetter, fertile land is found along its coastline. Huge sun-baked deserts, fringed by semi-arid plains of scrub and grassland cover most of the west and centre of the country. In the east, the land rises to the highlands of the Great Dividing Range, which run the whole length of the east coast. The tropical north coast has rainforests and mangrove swamps.

Blue Mountains (G 6)

The Blue Mountains lie towards the southern end of the Great Dividing Range. They get their name from the blue haze of oil droplets given off by the eucalyptus trees covering their slopes.

Great Barrier Reef (G 2)

This spectacular coral reef, which stretches for over 2,000 km off the coast of Queensland, is the largest living structure on Earth. The reef has built up over millions of years and its waters are home to thousands of different species of coral and marine animals.

Uluru (Ayers Rock) (D 4)

Uluru is an enormous block of red sandstone, standing almost in the middle of Australia. It is the world's biggest free-standing rock – 9.4 km around the base, and 867 m high. It is the summit of a sandstone hill that is buried beneath the sands of the desert.

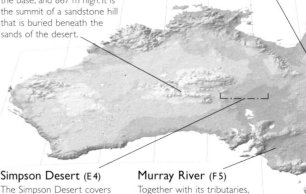

POPULATION

Despite its vast size, Australia is sparsely populated. The desert 'outback', which covers most of the interior, is too dry and barren to support many people. About 70% of the population live in the cities and towns on the east and southeast coasts, and around Perth in the west.

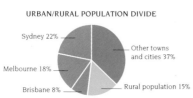

INHABITANTS PER SQ KM

- More than 50
- 10–50
- 1–10
- Less than 1
- ■ Capital city
- • Major city

URBAN/RURAL POPULATION DIVIDE

Sydney 22%
Melbourne 18%
Brisbane 8%
Other towns and cities 37%
Rural population 15%

Simpson Desert (E 4)

The Simpson Desert covers around 130,000 sq km. It contains long, parallel lines of sand dunes and is scattered with large salt pans and salt lakes, which were created when old rivers evaporated. They are now fed by the seasonal rains.

Murray River (F 5)

Together with its tributaries, the Murray River is Australia's main river system. It winds slowly westwards for more than 2,500 km from the Great Dividing Range to the Indian Ocean. It is fed by snow from mountains in the far southeast.

Great Dividing Range (H 5)

These highlands separate the desert regions from the fertile eastern plains. Rivers and streams have eroded them, creating deep valleys and gorges.

ENVIRONMENTAL ISSUES

Australia's dry climate and low rainfall make it susceptible to desertification. Around the fringes of the large deserts – especially in the north and southeast – cattle grazing and the removal of natural vegetation are destroying the natural habitat, allowing the desert areas to spread. During the dry season, vegetation becomes tinder-dry, and bush fires are common, burning huge tracts of land.

**ENVIRONMENTAL
ISSUES**

✗ Area at risk from bushfires

Existing desert
Risk of desertification
Severe risk of desertification

CLIMATE

Much of Australia's climate is continental, and temperatures soar during the day and fall rapidly at night. The climate is also arid and very little rain falls, apart from in the summer months when the north is affected by tropical storms.

EUROPE ASIA NORTH AMERICA
SOUTH AMERICA
ANTARCTICA

January

200
100
50
25
200
100

July

25
50
100
25
50
100
100

**TEMPERATURE
AND PRECIPITATION**

More than 35°C
30 to 35°C
25 to 30°C
20 to 25°C
15 to 20°C
10 to 15°C
5 to 10°C
Less than 5°C
100 Precipitation (mm)

Map labels

Timor Sea
Timor (part of Indonesia)
Arafura Sea
Badu Island Moa Island
Prince of Wales Island Strait
Endeavour Cape York
PAPUA NEW GUINEA
Melville Island
Croker Island
South Goulburn Island
Wessel Islands
Nhulunbuy
Cape York
Cape Londonderry
Bathurst Island
Van Diemen Gulf
Darwin
Arnhem Land
Gulf of Carpentaria
Princess Charlotte Bay
Coral Sea
Bonaparte Archipelago
Wyndham
Kununurra
Pine Creek
Katherine
Groote Eylandt
Sir Edward Pellew Group
Cape York Peninsula
Mitchell River
King Sound
Kimberley Plateau
Lake Argyle
NORTHERN TERRITORY
Daly Waters
Barkly Tableland
Wellesley Islands
Cooktown
Port Douglas
Cairns
Mareeba Atherton
CORAL SEA ISLANDS (Australian external territory)
Derby
Fitzroy Crossing
Ord River
Kalkarindji
Barkly Tableland
Burketown
Normanton
Innisfail
Tully
Hinchinbrook Island
Broome
Fitzroy River
Halls Creek
Tanami Desert
Tennant Creek
Flinders River
Gregory Range
Townsville
Bowen
Whitsunday Group
Eighty Mile Beach
Great Sandy Desert
Cloncurry
Charters Towers
Mackay
Port Hedland
Percival Lakes
Mount Isa
Hughenden
Bloomsbury
Dampier
Barrow Island
Marble Bar
Lake Mackay
AUSTRALIA
Winton
Longreach
Clermont
Emerald
Exmouth Gulf
Onslow
Fortescue River
Hamersley Range
Newman
WESTERN
Lake Disappointment
Gibson Desert
Little Sandy Desert
Alice Springs
Macdonnell Ranges
Lake Amadeus
QUEENSLAND
Barcaldine
Blackall
Springsure
Yeppoon
Rockhampton
Curtis Island
Gladstone
Exmouth
Ashburton River
Tropic of Capricorn
Barlee Range
Gascoyne River
AUSTRALIA
Uluru (Ayers Rock) 867m
Simpson Desert
Great Artesian Basin
Windorah
Charleville
Augathella
Biloela
Bundaberg
Fraser Island
Bernier Island
Lake Macleod
Carnavon
Lake Carnegie
Lake Wells
Musgrave Ranges
Lake Eyre Basin
Cooper Creek
Mitchell
Roma
Miles
Murgon
Maryborough
Gympie
Dorre Island
Shark Bay
Dirk Hartog Island
Denham
Meekatharra
SOUTH AUSTRALIA
Coober Pedy
Lake Eyre North
Charleville
Cunnamulla
Bollon
Moonie
Dalby
Caloundra
Mount Magnet
Great Victoria Desert
Lake Eyre South
Marree
Lake Blanche
Grey Range
Saint George
Goondiwindi
Toowoomba
Ipswich
Brisbane
Surfers Paradise
Kalbarri
Lake Carey
Lake Barlee
Lake Rebecca
Reid
Nullarbor plain
Lake Everard
Lake Torrens
Lake Callabonna
Warrego River
Bourke
Walgett
Stanthorpe
Warwick Gold Coast
Murwillumbah
Geraldton
Lake Moore
Lake Cowan
Rawlinna
Eucla
Tarcoola
Lake Frome
Wilcannia
NEW SOUTH
Cobar
Nyngan
Moree
Grafton
Mora
Southern Cross
Kalgoorlie
Coolgardie
Great Australian Bight
Ceduna
Penong
Lake Gairdner
Eyre
Port Augusta
Broken Hill
Barrier Range
Darling River
Nyngan
Narrabri
Armidale
Coffs Harbour
Gingin
Merredin
Norseman
Balladonia
Elliston
Lake Eyre
Peterborough
WALES
Tamworth
Port Macquarie
Perth
Northam
Brookton
Lake King
Esperance
Eyre Peninsula
Whyalla
Port Pirie
Ivanhoe
Lachlan River
Dubbo
Muswellbrook
Orange
Taree
Fremantle
Mandurah
Narrogin
Wagin
Spencer Gulf
Port Lincoln
Elizabeth
Cawler
Murray River
Mildura
Hay
Parkes
Bathurst
Lithgow
Blue Mts.
Newcastle
Bunbury
Collie
Katanning
Port Lincoln
Adelaide
Investigator Strait
Tailem Bend
Ouyen
Deniliquin
Murrumbidgee River
Wagga Wagga
Goulburn
Parramatta
Sydney
Wollongong
Busselton
Manjimup
Augusta
Albany
Kangaroo Island
Keith
Naracoorte
VICTORIA
Horsham
Bendigo
Shepparton
Wangaratta
Albury
Wodonga
Cooma
Mount Kosciusko 2228m
CANBERRA
AUSTRALIAN CAPITAL TERRITORY
Botany Bay
Mount Gambier
Ballarat
Portland
Geelong
Melbourne
Moe
Sale
Bega
Bairnsdale
Australian Alps
Warrnambool
Traralgon
South East Point
King Island
Bass Strait
Flinders Island
Tasman Sea
Hunter Island
Cape Barren Island
Marrawah
Burnie
Devonport
Launceston
TASMANIA
Hobart
Maria Island
South Bruny Island
INDIAN OCEAN
Coral Sea
Great Barrier Reef
Great Dividing Range
Botany Bay

LAND HEIGHT

2000–4000 m
1000–2000 m
500–1000 m
250–500 m
100–250 m
0–100 m
Below sea level

SEA DEPTH

0–250 m
250–500 m
500–1000 m
1000–2000 m
2000–3000 m
3000–4000 m
Below 4000 m

CITIES AND TOWNS

■ Over 500,000 people
◉ 100,000–500,000
◯ 50,000–100,000
○ Less than 50,000

SCALE BAR

0 km 100 200
0 miles 100 200

NEW ZEALAND

New Zealand is one of the most remote populated places in the world. The first people to settle on the islands were the Maori, a Polynesian people. When European settlers arrived during the 19th century, the Maori became a minority, and now only make up about 9% of the population. With a small population and rich natural resources, New Zealand's people have high living standards. The country's magnificent rugged scenery is popular with tourists.

INDUSTRY

Hi-tech industries such as electronics and computing are growing in the major cities of Auckland and Wellington, although agricultural products such as meat, wool and milk are still among New Zealand's major exports, and large pine forests supply wood for paper pulp and timber. The exciting scenery and varied climate draw tourists from all over the world, especially for walking and adventure holidays.

STRUCTURE
OF INDUSTRY

Primary 5%
Services 68%
Manufacturing 27%

INDUSTRY

🝕 Chemicals
🝕 Electronics
✿ Engineering
🖘 Fish processing
🝙 Food processing
🝙 Iron and steel
🝙 Textiles
🌲 Timber
🏛 Tourism

▪ Major industrial centre / area
— Major road

POPULATION

Most of the population is descended from European settlers, although immigrants from Asia and from the Pacific islands are increasing. More than one-third of New Zealand's 3.5 million people live in Auckland on North Island, which also has the largest Polynesian population of any city in the Pacific. Elsewhere, the population is clustered along the coasts, where the land is lower.

URBAN/RURAL POPULATION DIVIDE

Auckland 27.2%
Other towns and cities 38%
Wellington 9.5%
Christchurch 9.3%
Rural population 16%

INHABITANTS PER SQ KM

▪ More than 50
▪ 10–50
▪ 1–10
□ Less than 1

● Capital city
● Major city

ENVIRONMENTAL ISSUES

New Zealand is one of the world's least polluted countries – largely due to its low population and lack of heavy industries, although air quality is occasionally poor in Auckland and Christchurch. Environment-friendly geothermal energy is tapped to make electricity in the volcanic region of North Island. Recently, logging companies have begun to exploit the rich forest reserves, although this has been widely opposed.

ENVIRONMENTAL ISSUES

🝙 Geothermal power generation
⊛ Logging activity
☻ Urban air pollution
● Major industrial centre

THE LANDSCAPE

Two large, mountainous islands form New Zealand's main land areas. A large crack or fault – the Alpine Fault, in the west of South Island – is the boundary between two plates in the Earth's crust. Land either side of the fault tends to move, causing earthquakes. Volcanoes, many of them still active, are also found, on both islands. South Island has many high peaks, several more than 3,000 m high.

Geysers and boiling mud

Geysers occur when hot volcanic rocks come into contact with underground water. The water boils and turns to steam forcing the water above it to burst through the Earth's surface into the air. There are many geysers and boiling mud pools in the areas around Rotorua and Taupo.

Northland (C1)

This is a tropical region in the far northwest. Many of the inlets are fringed by mangrove swamps.

Mount Taranaki (C4)

The dormant volcano of Mount Taranaki lies on New Zealand's North Island. It rises to a height of 2,518 m.

Probable location of Alpine Fault

Lake Taupo (D3)

New Zealand's largest lake, Lake Taupo, covers 606 sq km of North Island. It lies in the crater of an extinct volcano

Southern Alps

New Zealand's Southern Alps stretch more than 483 km down the backbone of South Island. They were formed by the collision of the Indo-Australian and Pacific plates. Heavy snowfalls here, brought by westerly winds, feed the Fox Glacier which moves at a speed of 0.5–4.5 m a day.

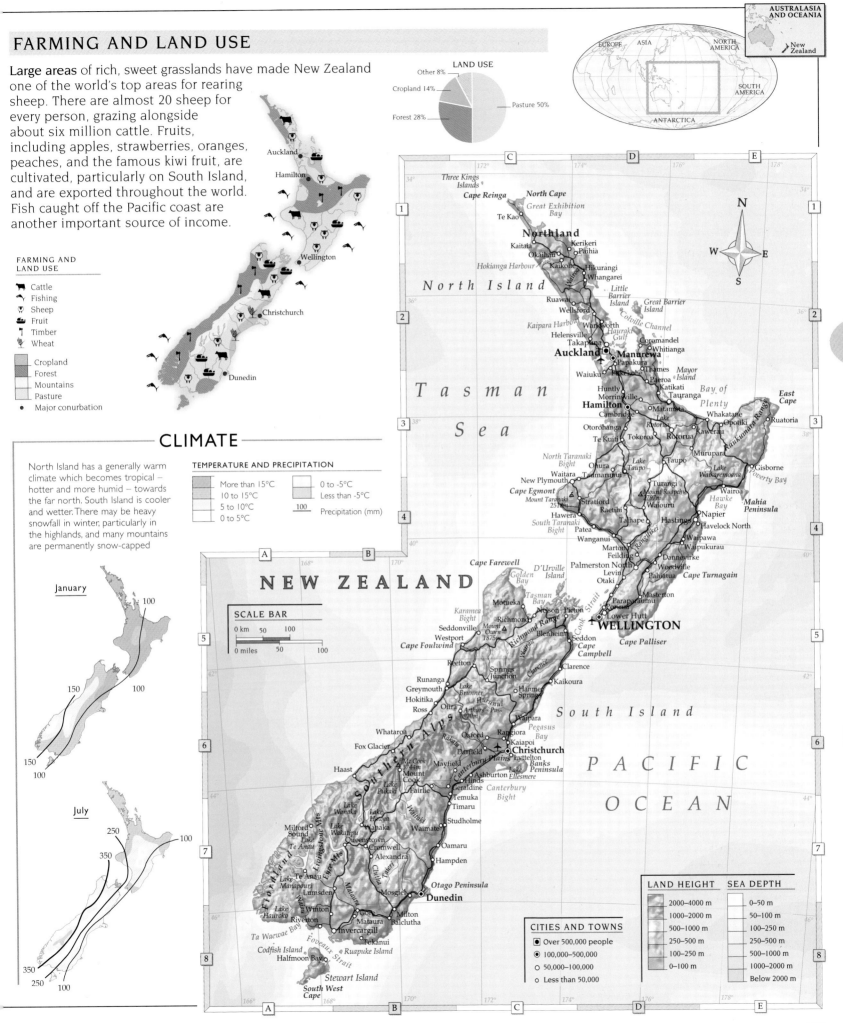

FARMING AND LAND USE

Large areas of rich, sweet grasslands have made New Zealand one of the world's top areas for rearing sheep. There are almost 20 sheep for every person, grazing alongside about six million cattle. Fruits, including apples, strawberries, oranges, peaches, and the famous kiwi fruit, are cultivated, particularly on South Island, and are exported throughout the world. Fish caught off the Pacific coast are another important source of income.

LAND USE

Other 8%
Cropland 14%
Forest 28%
Pasture 50%

FARMING AND LAND USE

- Cattle
- Fishing
- Sheep
- Fruit
- Timber
- Wheat

Cropland
Forest
Mountains
Pasture
• Major conurbation

Auckland
Hamilton
Wellington
Christchurch
Dunedin

CLIMATE

North Island has a generally warm climate which becomes tropical – hotter and more humid – towards the far north. South Island is cooler and wetter. There may be heavy snowfall in winter, particularly in the highlands, and many mountains are permanently snow-capped

TEMPERATURE AND PRECIPITATION

More than 15°C
10 to 15°C
5 to 10°C
0 to 5°C
0 to -5°C
Less than -5°C
100 Precipitation (mm)

January
100
150
100
150
100

July
250
350
100
350
250
100

NEW ZEALAND

SCALE BAR
0 km 50 100
0 miles 50 100

North Island

Three Kings Islands
Cape Reinga
North Cape
Great Exhibition Bay
Te Kao
Northland
Kaitaia
Okaihau Kerikeri Paihia
Hokianga Harbour Kaikohe
Hikurangi
Whangarei
Ruawai
Little Barrier Island
Wellsford
Great Barrier Island
Kaipara Harbour
Warkworth
Helensville Hauraki Gulf
Coromandel
Takapuna Whitianga
Auckland Manurewa
Papakura Thames
Waiuku Paeroa Mayor Island
Huntly Morrinsville Katikati Bay of Plenty
Hamilton Tauranga East Cape
Cambridge Matamata
Otorohanga Lake Rotorua Whakatane Opotiki Ruatoria
Te Kuiti Tokoroa Rotorua Kawerau Murupara
North Taranaki Bight Ohura Lake Taupo Taupo Lake Waikaremoana
New Plymouth Taumarunui Gisborne
Cape Egmont Waitara Turangi Poverty Bay
Mount Taranaki 2518m Mount Ruapehu 2797m Wairoa
Stratford Waiouru Hawke Bay
Hawera Raetihi Taihape Hastings Mahia Peninsula
South Taranaki Bight Patea Napier
Wanganui Marton Havelock North
Feilding Waipawa
Palmerston North Woodville Waipukurau
Levin Dannevirke
Otaki Pahiatua Cape Turnagain
Paraparaumu Masterton
Porirua
WELLINGTON Lower Hutt Cape Palliser

South Island

Cape Farewell
D'Urville Island
Golden Bay
Tasman Bay
Karamea Bight
Motueka
Nelson Picton
Richmond Mount Owen 1875m
Seddonville
Westport Blenheim
Cape Foulwind Seddon Cape Campbell
Reefton
Springs Junction Clarence
Runanga Kaikoura
Greymouth Lake Brunner Hanmer Springs
Hokitika Hurunui
Ross Arthur's Pass 920m Waipara Pegasus Bay
Whataroa Oxford Rangiora
Fox Glacier Darfield Kaiapoi
Haast **Christchurch** Lyttelton
Mt Cook 3744m Mayfield Banks Peninsula
Mount Cook Ashburton Lake Ellesmere
Lake Pukaki Hinds Canterbury Bight
Fairlie Geraldine
Lake Wanaka Temuka
Lake Hawea Timaru
Wanaka Waitaki Waimate
Milford Sound Queenstown Studholme
Lake Te Anau Cromwell Oamaru
Lake Wakatipu Alexandra Hampden
Te Anau
Lake Manapouri Lumsden
Winton Mosgiel
Lake Hauroko Gore **Dunedin**
Riverton Mataura Milton Otago Peninsula
Invercargill Balclutha
Ta Waewae Bay Tokanui
Foveaux Strait Ruapuke Island
Codfish Island Halfmoon Bay
South West Cape Stewart Island

Southern Alps
Fiordland
Livingstone Mts
Eyre Mts
Richmond Range
Raukumara Range
Ruahine Range
Tararua Range
Rangitikei
Rangitaiki

Tasman Sea
South Island
Pegasus Bay
PACIFIC OCEAN

CITIES AND TOWNS
■ Over 500,000 people
◉ 100,000–500,000
○ 50,000–100,000
○ Less than 50,000

LAND HEIGHT
2000–4000 m
1000–2000 m
500–1000 m
250–500 m
100–250 m
0–100 m

SEA DEPTH
0–50 m
50–100 m
100–250 m
250–500 m
500–1000 m
1000–2000 m
Below 2000 m

AUSTRALASIA AND OCEANIA
EUROPE ASIA NORTH AMERICA
SOUTH AMERICA
ANTARCTICA
New Zealand

SOUTHWEST PACIFIC

The many thousands of islands in the Pacific Ocean are scattered across an enormous area. The original inhabitants, the Polynesians, Melanesians and Micronesians, settled the islands following the last Ice Age. In the 1700s Europeans arrived. They colonized all of the Pacific islands, introducing their culture, languages and religion. Today, many, though not all, of the islands have become independent. Their economies are simple, based largely on fishing and agriculture. Many are increasingly relying on their beautiful scenery and tropical climates to attract tourists and give a valuable boost to their economies.

LANDSCAPE

Most of the Pacific islands are extremely small, the largest land mass is the half of the island of New Guinea occupied by Papua New Guinea. The edges of the Indo-Australian and Pacific plates meet on the western edge of the area, leading to much volcanic and earthquake activity. Many of the islands are coral atolls, originally formed by volcanic activity, and some are no more than a few metres above sea level.

New Guinea (A 2)
A mountainous spine runs through the centre of the island, separating the northern coast from the dense forests and mangroves found in the south.

Pacific Ocean
The Pacific Ocean is the Earth's oldest and deepest ocean. Its name means peaceful, though it is far from being so; the highest wave ever recorded on open ocean – 34 m – occurred during a hurricane in the Pacific.

Kavachi
Kavachi is a submarine volcano lying off the coast of New Georgia, in the Solomon Islands. It still erupts every few years.

Ring of Fire
The 'Ring of Fire' is the term used to describe the string of volcanoes which surround the entire Pacific Ocean and erupt frequently because of intense stress and movement from within the Earth. The ring crosses the south Pacific, running between Vanuatu and New Caledonia, along the edge of the Solomon Islands, and between New Britain and New Guinea.

Sea trenches
Deep trenches mark the sea floor boundary where the Indo-Australian plate 'dives' under the Pacific plate.

Coral atolls
Volcanic activity in the Pacific has led to the creation of many islands. These islands become fringed with a ring of coral. When the islands subside beneath the sea once again, only the circle of coral is left, forming an atoll.

INDUSTRY

Today, the main industry for many of the Pacific islands is tourism. Food processing and small-scale textile industries are also common on many islands.

INDUSTRY
- 🍺 Brewing
- Food processing
- Textiles
- Timber processing
- Mining
- Tourism
- ▪ Major industrial centre
- — Major road

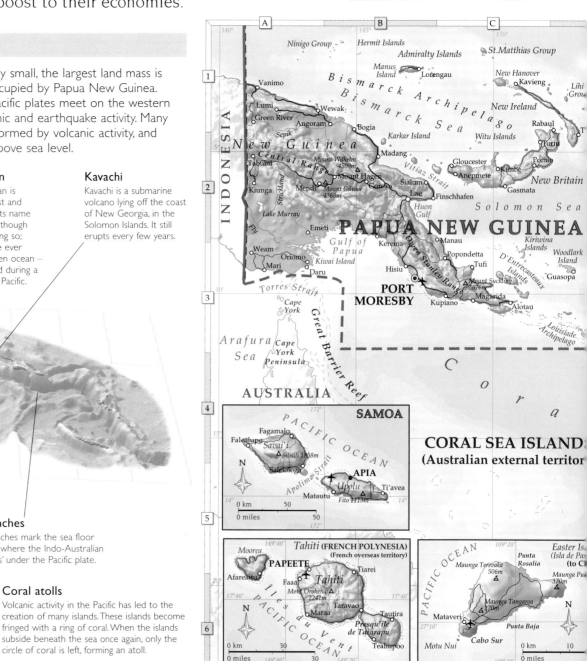

FARMING AND LAND USE

Most farming that takes place on the Pacific islands is at a subsistence level, and many people keep pigs and chickens. A few crops are grown for export, especially oil palms, and coconuts, which are dried in the sun to produce copra. Many islanders make their living from the rich fishing grounds of the Pacific. The thick forests of Papua New Guinea are increasingly cut down for timber.

AUSTRALASIA AND OCEANIA

EUROPE ASIA NORTH AMERICA
SOUTH AMERICA
ANTARCTICA
Southwest Pacific

LAND USE

- Fishing
- Bananas
- Cocoa
- Coconuts
- Oil palms
- Rubber
- Timber

Cropland
Forest
Wetland
● Major conurbation

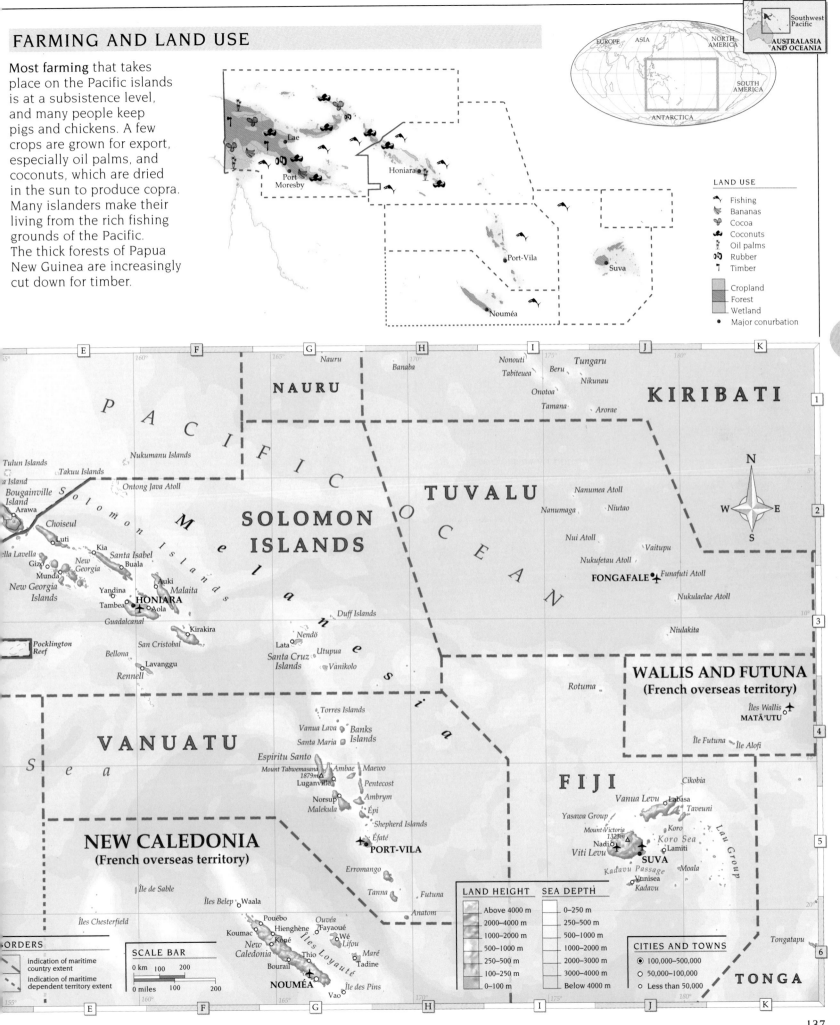

Lae
Port Moresby
Honiara
Port-Vila
Suva
Nouméa

PACIFIC OCEAN

NAURU
Nauru
Banaba

KIRIBATI
Nonouti
Tabiteuea
Beru
Nikunau
Onotoa
Tamana
Arorae

Tungaru

TUVALU
Nanumea Atoll
Nanumaga
Niutao
Nui Atoll
Vaitupu
Nukufetau Atoll
FONGAFALE Funafuti Atoll
Nukulaelae Atoll
Niulakita

Tulun Islands
Nukumanu Islands
Takuu Islands
Ontong Java Atoll

Bougainville Island
Arawa
Choiseul
Luti
Kia
Santa Isabel
New Georgia
Buala
Munda
Yandina
Malaita
Tambea
HONIARA
Aola
Guadalcanal
Kirakira
San Cristobal
Bellona
Lavanggu
Rennell

SOLOMON ISLANDS
Duff Islands
Nendö
Lata
Santa Cruz Islands
Utupua
Vanikolo

Vella Lavella
Gizo

Pocklington Reef

WALLIS AND FUTUNA
(French overseas territory)
Rotuma
Îles Wallis
MATĀ'UTU
Île Futuna Île Alofi

VANUATU
Torres Islands
Vanua Lava
Santa Maria
Banks Islands
Espiritu Santo
Mount Tabwemasana 1879m
Luganville
Ambae
Maewo
Norsup
Pentecost
Malekula
Ambrym
Épi
Shepherd Islands
Éfaté
PORT-VILA
Erromango
Tanna
Futuna
Anatom

FIJI
Cikobia
Vanua Levu
Labasa
Taveuni
Yasawa Group
Koro
Mount Victoria 1323m
Nadi
Lamiti
Viti Levu
SUVA
Koro Sea
Moala
Kadavu Passage
Vunisea
Kadavu

Lau Group

NEW CALEDONIA
(French overseas territory)
Île de Sable
Îles Belep
Waala
Îles Chesterfield
Pouébo
Koumac
Hienghène
Koné
New Caledonia
Thio
Bourail
NOUMÉA
Ouvéa
Fayaoué
Wé
Lifou
Maré
Tadine
Îles Loyauté
Île des Pins
Vao

Tongatapu
TONGA

BORDERS
indication of maritime country extent
indication of maritime dependent territory extent

SCALE BAR
0 km 100 200
0 miles 100 200

LAND HEIGHT
Above 4000 m
2000–4000 m
1000–2000 m
500–1000 m
250–500 m
100–250 m
0–100 m

SEA DEPTH
0–250 m
250–500 m
500–1000 m
1000–2000 m
2000–3000 m
3000–4000 m
Below 4000 m

CITIES AND TOWNS
◉ 100,000–500,000
◉ 50,000–100,000
○ Less than 50,000

ANTARCTICA

The continent of Antarctica has no permanent human population and very few animals can survive on the frozen land, although the surrounding seas teem with fish and mammals. Even in the summer the temperature is rarely above freezing and the sea-ice only partly melts; in winter, temperatures plummet to –80°C. The only people who live in Antarctica are teams of scientists who study the wildlife and monitor the ice for changes in the Earth's atmosphere.

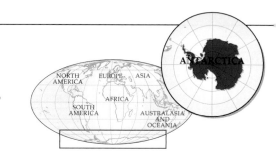

THE LANDSCAPE

Frozen seas
During the cold winter months, the seas surrounding Antarctica freeze, almost doubling the size of the continent.

Antarctica is the world's most southerly continent. It is also the world's coldest continent and its highest, mainly due to the great ice sheet – up to 2 km thick in parts – which lies over the mountains of the Antarctic Peninsula and the plateau of Greater Antarctica.

Lambert Glacier (E4)
The Lambert Glacier is the world's largest series of glaciers. It is 80 km wide at the coast and reaches more than 300 km inland.

Transantarctic Mountains (C5)
The Transantarctic Mountains run across the continent, splitting it into Greater and Lesser Antarctica.

Ice sheet
A massive sheet of ice, about 4,800 m thick at its deepest point, covers almost the entire area of Antarctica. It contains most of the fresh water on Earth. The weight of the ice pushes the land down below sea level.

The Ross Ice Shelf (C5)
The Ross Sea is part of the Pacific Ocean. This deep bay is covered by a thick sheet of ice which floats on the ocean.

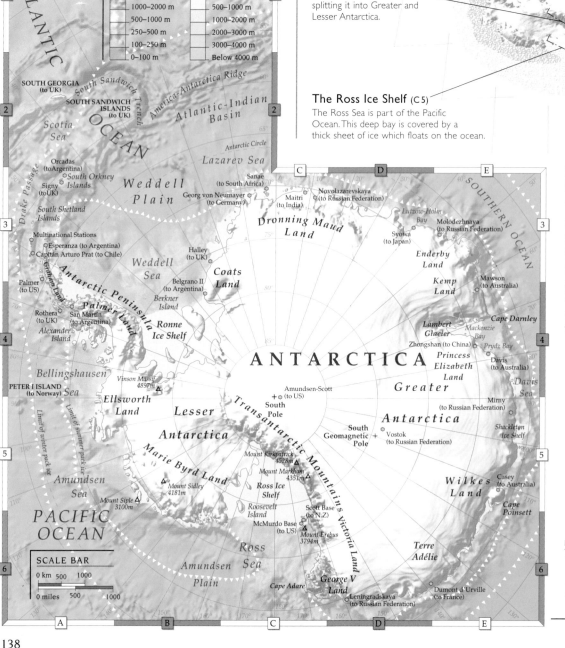

RESOURCES

The mountains of Antarctica have rich mineral reserves. Gold, iron and coal are found, and there is natural gas in the surrounding seas. The unique and abundant marine wildlife is Antarctica's greatest resource. Colonies of penguins breed on the ice sheet, and whales, seals and many bird and fish species thrive in the icy waters.

RESOURCES (including wildlife)

⤙	Fish	🐾	Coal
⌂	Penguins	⬤	Minerals
⬥	Seals	◊	Gas
Y	Whales		

THE ARCTIC

The ice-covered Arctic Ocean is encircled by the most northerly parts of Europe, North America and Asia. Very few people live in the often freezing conditions. Those who do, including the Sami of northern Scandinavia, the Siberian Yugyt and Nenet people and the Canadian Inuit, were nomads who lived by hunting and herding. Some live like this today, but many have now settled in small towns.

THE LANDSCAPE

The Arctic Ocean is the smallest ocean in the world, covering a total area of 15,100,000 sq km. The ocean is divided into two large basins, divided by three great underwater mountain ranges including the Lomonosov Ridge which is more than 3,000 m high on average.

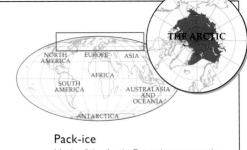

Lomonosov Ridge (C4)

Arctic islands (A4)
In the far north of Canada, there are many thousands of islands including Baffin Island and Victoria Island. Many of them are almost entirely surrounded by pack-ice.

Pack-ice
Much of the Arctic Ocean is permanently covered by pack-ice. When the ice breaks up, it forms enormous floating ice-masses called icebergs.

Greenland (A3)
Greenland is the world's largest island. It is covered by a huge ice sheet, more than 1,683,400 sq km across. The weight of the ice has pushed most of the land below sea level.

Sastrugi
Snow, blown by strong winds can scratch deep patterns in the snow. These patterns are known as sastrugi and line up with the direction of the wind.

RESOURCES

Coal, oil and gas are found beneath the Arctic Ocean and in Canada, Alaska and Russia. Fears about damage to the environment and the cost of extracting these resources have restricted the quantities removed. Overfishing has reduced fish stocks to very low levels. Quotas have been put in place to allow them to revive.

RESOURCES
- ⌐ Fish
- 🛠 Coal
- ◖ Minerals
- ◗ Oil and gas
- ● Major town/city

SCALE BAR
| 0 km | 250 | 500 |
| 0 miles | 250 | 500 |

CITIES AND TOWNS
- ● 100,000–500,000
- ○ Less than 50,000

SEA DEPTH
- 0–250 m
- 250–500 m
- 500–1000 m
- 1000–2000 m
- 2000–3000 m
- 3000–4000 m
- Below 4000 m

Glossary

This glossary defines certain geographical and technical terms used in this Atlas.

Acid rain Rain, sleet, snow or mist which has absorbed waste gases from fossil-fuelled power stations and vehicle exhausts, becoming acidic and poisonous.

Alluvium Material deposited by a river, such as silt, sand and mud.

Archipelago A group, or chain, of islands.

Atoll A circular or horseshoe-shaped coral reef enclosing a shallow area of water (lagoon).

Aquifer A body of rock that can absorb water. It may be a source of water for wells or springs.

Bar, coastal An offshore strip of sand or shingle, either above or below the water.

Biodiversity The quantity of different animal or plant species in a given area.

Birth rate The number of live births per 1000 individuals annually within a population.

Cash crop Agricultural produce grown for sale, often for foreign export, rather than to be consumed by the country or area where it was grown.

Climate The long term trends in weather conditions for an area.

Coniferous forest A type of forest containing trees or shrubs, like pines and firs, which have needles instead of leaves. They are found in temperate zones.

Continental plates The huge interlocking plates which make up the Earth's surface. A plate boundary is an area where two plates meet, and is the point at which earthquakes occur most frequently.

Conurbation A large urban area created by the merging of several towns.

Coral reef An underwater barrier created by colonies of coral polyps. The polyps secrete a protective skeleton of calcium carbonate, and reefs develop as live polyps build on the skeletons of dead generations.

Core The layers of liquid rock and solid iron at the centre of the Earth.

Crust The hard, thin outer shell of the Earth. The crust floats on the mantle, which is softer, but more dense.

Deciduous forest A type of broadleaf forest found in temperate regions.

Deforestation Cutting down trees or forest for timber or farmland. It can lead to soil erosion, flooding and landslides.

Delta A low-lying, fan-shaped area at a river mouth, formed by the deposition of successive layers of sediment. Slowing as it enters the sea, a river deposits sediment and may, as a result, split into many smaller channels called distributaries.

Deposition The laying down of material broken down by erosion or weathering and transported by the wind, water or gravity.

Desertification The spread of desert conditions into a region which was not previously a desert.

Drainage basin The land drained by a river and its tributaries.

Drought A long period of continuously low rainfall.

Earthquake A trembling or shaking of the ground caused by the sudden movement of rocks in the Earth's crust – and sometimes deeper than the crust. Earthquakes occur most frequently along continental plate boundaries.

Economy The organization of a country's finances, exports, imports, industry, agriculture and services.

Ecosytem A community of species dependent on each other and on the habitat in which they live.

Equator The 0° line of latitude. Equatorial climates are hot and there is plenty of rain.

Erosion The wearing down of the land surface by running water, waves, moving ice, wind and weather.

Estuary The mouth of a river, where the salt water from the sea meets the fresh water of the river.

Fault A crack or fracture in the Earth along which there has been movement of the rock masses relative to one another.

Fjord A coastal valley which was sculpted by glacial action.

Flood plain The broad, flat part of a river valley, next to the river itself, formed by sediment deposited during flooding.

Geyser A fountain of hot water or steam that erupts periodically as a result of underground streams coming into contact with hot rocks.

GDP Gross Domestic Product. The total value of goods and services produced by a country, excluding income from foreign countries.

GIS Geographical Information System. A computerized system for the collection, storage and retrieval of geographical data.

Glacier A huge mass of ice made up of compacted and frozen snow which moves slowly, eroding and depositing rock.

Glaciation The moulding of the land by a glacier or ice sheet.

GNP Gross National Product. The total value of goods and services produced by a country.

Groundwater Water that has seeped into the pores, cavities and cracks of rocks or into soil and water held in an aquifer or permeable rock.

Gully A deep, narrow chasm eroded in the landscape by a fast-flowing stream.

Heavy industry Industry that uses large amounts of energy and raw materials to produce heavy goods, such as machinery, ships, or locomotives.

Humidity The moisture content of the air.

Hurricane Violent tropical storms, also known as cyclones in the Indian Ocean and typhoons in the Pacific Ocean.

Hydroelectric power Energy produced by harnessing the rapid movement of water down steep mountain slopes to drive turbines to generate electricity.

Ice Age Periods of time in the past when much of the Earth's surface was covered by massive ice sheets. The most recent Ice Age began two million years ago and ended 10,000 years ago.

Iceberg A floating mass of ice that has broken off from a glacier or ice sheet.

Ice sheet A massive area of ice, thousands of metres thick.

Irrigation The artificial supply of water to dry areas – mainly for agricultural use. Water is carried or pumped to the area through pipes or ditches.

Lagoon A shallow stretch of coastal saltwater behind a partial barrier such as a sandbank or coral reef.

Latitude The distance north or south of the Equator, measured in degrees, and shown on a globe as imaginary circles running around the Earth parallel to the Equator.

Lava The molten rock, magma, which erupts onto the Earth's surface through a volcano, or through a fault or crack in the Earth's crust. Lava refers to the rock both in its liquid and its later, solidified form.

Load The material that is carried by a river or stream.

Longitude The distance, measured in degrees, east or west of the Prime Meridian.

Limestone A type of rock, formed by sediment, through which water can pass.

Magma Underground, molten rock, which is very hot and highly charged with gas. It originates in the Earth's lower crust or mantle.

Mantle The layer of the Earth's interior between the crust and the core. It is about 2,900 km thick.

Map projection A mathematical formula that is used to show the curved surface of the Earth on a flat map.

Market gardening The intensive growing of fruit and vegetables close to large local markets.

Meander A loop-like bend in a river. As a river nears the sea, it tends to wind more and more. The bigger the river and the shallower its slope, the more likely it is that meanders will form.

Mediterranean climate A temperate climate of hot, dry summers and warm, damp winters.

Meltwater Water which has melted from glaciers or ice sheets.

Mestizo A person of mixed native American and European origin.

Mineral A chemical compound that occurs naturally in the Earth.

Monsoon Winds that change direction according to the seasons. They are most common in South and East Asia, where they blow from the southwest in summer, bringing heavy rainfall, and the northeast in winter.

Moraine Sand and gravel that have been deposited by a glacier or ice sheet.

Nomads (nomadic) Wandering communities who move around in search of suitable pasture for their herds of animals.

Oasis A fertile area in a desert, usually watered by an underground aquifer.

Pack ice Ice masses more than three metres thick which form on the sea surface and are not attached to a landmass.

Pacific Rim The name given to the economically dynamic countries bordering the Pacific Ocean.

Peat Decomposed vegetation found in bogs. It can be dried and used as fuel.

Per capita A latin term meaning 'for each person'.

Plantation A large farm on which only one crop is usually grown, e.g. bananas or coffee.

Plain A flat, level region of land, often relatively low-lying.

Plateau A large area of high, flat land. When surrounded by steep slopes it is called a tableland.

Peninsula A thin strip of land surrounded on three of its sides by water. Large examples include Italy, Florida and Korea.

Permafrost Permanently frozen ground, in which temperatures have remained below 0°C for more than two years.

Precipitation The fall of moisture from the atmosphere onto the surface of the Earth, as dew, hail, rain, sleet or snow.

Prairie A Spanish-American term for grassy plains, with few or no trees.

Prime Meridian 0° longitude. Also known as the Greenwich Meridian because it runs through Greenwich in England.

Rainforest Dense forests in tropical zones with high rainfall, temperature and humidity.

Rainshadow An area downwind from high terrain which has little or no rainfall because it has fallen upon the high relief.

Remote-sensing A way of obtaining information about the environment by using unmanned equipment, such as a satellite, which relays the information to a point where it is collected.

Ria A flooded V-shaped river valley or estuary flooded by a rise in sea level or sinking land.

Rift valley A long, narrow depression in the Earth's crust, formed by the sinking of rocks between two faults.

Savannah Open grassland, where an annual dry season prevents the growth of most trees. They lie between the tropical rainforest and hot desert regions.

Scale The relationship between distance on a map and on the Earth's surface.

Sediment Grains of rock transported and deposited by rivers, sea, ice or wind.

Semi-arid Areas between deserts and better-watered areas, where there is sufficient moisture to support a little more vegetation than in a true desert.

Service industry An industry that supplies services, such as banking, rather than producing manufactured goods.

Shanty town An area in or around a city where people live in temporary shacks, usually without basic facilities such as running water.

Silt Small particles, finer than sand, often carried by water and deposited on riverbanks, at river mouths and harbours.

Soil A thin layer of rock particles mixed with the remains of dead plants and animals. Soil occurs naturally on the surface of the Earth and provides a medium for plants to grow.

Soil erosion The wearing away of soil more quickly than it is replaced by natural processes. Over-grazing and the clearing of land for farming speeds up the process.

Sorghum A type of grass found in South America, similar to sugar cane.

Spit A narrow bank of shingle or sand extending out from the sea shore. Spits are made out of material transported along the coast by currents, wind and waves.

Staple crop The main food crop grown in a region, for example rice in Southeast Asia.

Steppe Large areas of dry grassland in the northern hemisphere – particularly found in southeast Europe and central Asia.

Subsistence farming A method of farming where enough food is produced to feed farmers and their families but not providing any extra to generate an income.

Taiga A Russian name given to the belt of coniferous forest found in Russia, which borders tundra in the north and mixed forests and grasslands in the south.

Temperate The mild, variable climate found in areas between the tropics and cold polar regions.

Terrace Steps cut into steep slopes to create flat surfaces for cultivating crops.

Tropics An area between the Equator and the Tropic of Cancer and Tropic of Capricorn that has heavy rainfall, high temperatures, and lacks any clear seasonal variation.

Tundra The land area lying in the very cold northern regions of Europe, Asia and Canada, where winters are long and cold and the ground beneath the surface is permanently frozen.

U-shaped valley A river valley that has been deepened and widened by a glacier. They are flat-bottomed and steep-sided, and usually much deeper than river valleys.

V-shaped valley A typical valley eroded by a river in its upper course.

Volcano An opening or vent in the Earth's crust where magma erupts. Volcanos are caused by the movement of the Earth's plates. When the plates collide or spread apart, magma is forced to the surface, at or near the place where the plates meet.

Watershed The dividing line between one drainage basin and another.

INDEX

◊ Administrative region   ◆ Country   ● Country capital   ◊ Dependent territory   ⊙ Dependent territory capital   ▲ Mountain range   ▲ Mountain   ☈ Volcano   ☞ River   ⊚ Lake   ☒ Reservoir

141

◆ Administrative region   ◆ Country   ● Country capital   ◇ Dependent territory   ○ Dependent territory capital   ▲ Mountain range   ▲ Mountain   ☒ Volcano   ⚉ River   ● Lake   ☒ Reservoir

CALBAYOG

Bergeyk 50 D6 S Netherlands
Bergse Maas 50 D5 ~ S Netherlands
Beringen 50 D6 NE Belgium
Bering Sea 97 A2 *Sea,* N Pacific Ocean
Bering Strait 97 C2 *Strait,* Bering Sea/Chukchi Sea
Berja 57 E6 S Spain
Berkeley 103 B3 California, USA
Berkhamsted 37 F3 SE England, UK
Berkner Island 138 B4 *Island,* Antarctica
Berlin 59 D3 ● NE Germany
Berlin 101 G2 New Hampshire, USA
Bermejo, Río 117 B3 ~ N Argentina
Bermeo 57 E1 N Spain
Bermuda 40 *UK* ◇ NW Atlantic Ocean
Bern 59 A8 ● W Switzerland
Bernau 59 D3 NE Germany
Bernburg 59 D4 C Germany
Berner Alpen 59 A8 ⛰ SW Switzerland
Berneray 33 A4 *Island,* NW Scotland, UK
Bernier Island 133 A4 *Island,* Western Australia
Berry 55 D3 *Cultural region,* C France
Berry Islands 109 C1 *Island group,* N Bahamas
Bertoua 124 G5 E Cameroon
Berwick-upon-Tweed 35 D1 N England, UK
Besançon 55 E4 E France
Bessbrook 31 E3 S Northern Ireland, UK
Betafo 128 G5 C Madagascar
Betanzos 57 B1 NW Spain
Bethel 40 E Montserrat
Bethesda 39 C2 NW Wales, UK
Bethlehem 128 D6 C South Africa
Bethlehem 81 H6 C West Bank
Béticos, Sistemas 57 D5 ⛰ S Spain
Bétou 128 C1 N Congo
Bette, Pic 122 G4 ▲ S Libya
Betws-y-Coed 39 D2 N Wales, UK
Beulah 39 D5 C Wales, UK
Beveren 50 C6 N Belgium
Beverley 35 F4 E England, UK
Bexhill 37 G4 SE England, UK
Bexley 29 ◐ *London borough,* SE England, UK
Beyla 124 C4 SE Guinea
Beyrouth *see* Beirut
Beyşehir Gölü 79 B4 ◎ C Turkey
Béziers 55 D6 S France
Bhadravati 89 D6 SW India
Bhagalpur 89 F3 NE India
Bhaktapur 89 F3 C Nepal
Bharuch 89 C4 W India
Bhavnagar 89 C4 W India
Bhopal 89 D4 C India
Bhubaneshwar 89 F4 E India
Bhusawal 89 D4 C India
Bhutan 89 G3 ◆ *Monarchy,* S Asia
Biak, Pulau 91 H6 *Island,* E Indonesia
Biała Podlaska 63 G3 E Poland
Białogard 63 C2 NW Poland
Białystok 63 G2 E Poland
Biarritz 55 B6 SW France
Bicester 37 E3 C England, UK
Bideford 37 B4 SW England, UK
Biel 59 A8 W Switzerland
Bielefeld 59 B4 NW Germany
Bielsko-Biała 63 E5 S Poland
Bielsk Podlaski 63 G3 E Poland
Biên Hoa 91 C4 S Vietnam
Bienville, Lac 99 D3 ◎ Québec, C Canada
Bié Plateau 128 C4 *Plateau,* C Angola
Bigbury Bay 37 B6 *Bay,* SW England, UK
Big Cypress Swamp 101 E7 *Wetland,* SE USA
Biggleswade 37 F2 C England, UK
Big Point 40 *Headland,* N Tristan da Cunha
Bihać 65 B2 NW Bosnia and Herzegovina
Bihar 89 F3 *Cultural region,* N India
Biharamulo 127 C6 NW Tanzania
Bihosava 67 C1 NW Belorussia
Bijelo Polje 65 D3 SW Yugoslavia
Bikaner 89 D3 NW India
Bikin 76 H5 SE Russ. Fed.
Bilaspur 89 E4 C India
Biläsuvar 79 I3 SE Azerbaijan
Bila Tserkva 67 D4 N Ukraine
Bilauktaung Range 91 B4 ⛰ Burma/Thailand
Bilbao 57 E1 N Spain
Bilecik 79 B3 NW Turkey
Billingham 35 E3 N England, UK
Billings 103 D2 Montana, USA
Bilma, Grand Erg de 124 G2 *Desert,* NE Niger
Biloela 133 H4 Queensland, E Australia
Biltine 124 H3 E Chad
Bilzen 50 D6 NE Belgium
Bimini Islands 109 C1 *Island group,* W Bahamas
Binche 50 C7 S Belgium
Binghamton 101 G3 New York, USA
Bingöl 79 F3 E Turkey
Bintulu 91 D6 East Malaysia
Binzhou 87 G3 E China
Bío Bío, Río 117 A6 ~ C Chile
Bioco, Isla de 124 F6 *Island,* NW Equatorial Guinea
Birak 122 F3 C Libya
Birao 124 I4 NE CAR
Biratnagar 89 F3 SE Nepal
Birdhill 31 C5 S Ireland
Birhar Sharif 89 F3 N India
Birjand 81 F2 E Iran
Birkenfeld 59 A6 SW Germany
Birkenhead 35 C5 NW England, UK
Birmingham 35 D6 C England, UK
Birmingham 101 D5 Alabama, USA
Birmingham 29 ◐ *Unitary auth.,* C England, UK
Bîr Mogreïn 124 B1 N Mauritania
Birnin Kebbi 124 E4 NW Nigeria
Birnin Konni 124 E3 SW Niger
Birobidzhan 76 H5 SE Russ. Fed.
Birr 31 D4 C Ireland
Birsk 69 D6 W Russ. Fed.
Birżebbuġa 70 B6 SE Malta
Biscay, Bay of 55 B4 *Bay,* France/Spain
Bishah, Wadi 81 B5 *Dry watercourse,* C Saudi Arabia
Bishkek 83 H2 ● N Kyrgyzstan
Bishop Auckland 35 D3 N England, UK
Biskra 122 E1 NE Algeria
Biskupiec 63 F2 N Poland
Bislig 91 G5 S Philippines
Bismarck 103 F1 North Dakota, USA
Bismarck Archipelago 137 B1 *Island group,* NE PNG
Bismarck Sea 137 B1 *Sea,* W Pacific Ocean
Bissau 124 A4 ● W Guinea-Bissau
Bistrița 67 B6 N Romania
Bitam 128 A1 N Gabon
Bitburg 59 A5 SW Germany
Bitlis 79 G4 SE Turkey
Bitola 65 D4 S FYR Macedonia
Bitonto 61 E6 SE Italy
Bitterfeld 59 D4 E Germany
Bitterroot Range 103 C1 ⛰ NW USA
Biu 124 G4 E Nigeria
Biwa-ko 85 E6 ◎ Honshu, SW Japan
Bizerte 122 F1 N Tunisia
Bjørnøya 139 D5 *Island,* N Norway
Blackall 133 G4 Queensland, E Australia
Blackburn 35 C4 NW England, UK
Blackburn 29 ◐ *Unitary auth.,* NW England, UK
Black Drin 65 D3 ~ Albania/FYR Macedonia
Black Forest 59 B7 ⛰ SW Germany
Black Mountains 39 E5 ⛰ SE Wales, UK
Blackpool 35 C4 NW England, UK
Blackpool 29 ◐ *Unitary auth.,* NW England, UK
Black River 91 B2 ~ China/Vietnam
Black Sea 44 *Sea,* Asia/Europe
Black Sea Lowland 67 E6 *Depression,* SE Europe
Blacksod Bay 31 A3 *Inlet,* W Ireland
Black Volta 124 D4 ~ W Africa
Blackwater 31 E6 SE Ireland
Blackwater 31 D6 ~ S Ireland
Blackwater 31 E2 ~ Ireland/Northern Ireland, UK
Blaenau Ffestiniog 39 D2 NW Wales, UK
Blaenau Gwent 29 ◐ *Unitary auth.,* SE Wales, UK
Blaenavon 39 E6 SE Wales, UK
Blagoevgrad 65 E3 W Bulgaria
Blagoveshchensk 76 H5 SE Russ. Fed.
Blairgowrie 33 E5 C Scotland, UK
Blakeney Point 37 G1 *Headland,* E England, UK
Blanca, Bahía 117 B6 *Bay,* E Argentina
Blanca, Costa 57 F5 *Physical region,* SE Spain
Blanche, Lake 133 F4 ◎ S Australia
Blanc, Mont 55 F5 ▲ France/Italy
Blanco, Cape 103 A2 *Headland,* Oregon, USA
Blandford Forum 37 D5 S England, UK
Blanes 57 H2 NE Spain
Blankenberge 50 B5 NW Belgium
Blankenheim 59 A5 W Germany
Blanquilla, Isla 109 I7 *Island,* N Venezuela
Blantyre 128 E4 S Malawi
Blaricum 50 D4 C Netherlands
Bleaker Island 40 *Island,* SE Falkland Islands
Blenheim 135 C5 South Island, NZ
Blenheim Reef 40 *Reef,* N British Indian Ocean Territory
Blida 122 D1 N Algeria
Bloemfontein 128 D6 ● C South Africa
Blois 55 C3 C France
Bloody Foreland 31 C1 *Headland,* NW Ireland
Bloomington 101 D4 Indiana, USA
Bloomsbury 133 G3 Queensland, NE Australia
Bluefields 107 E4 SE Nicaragua
Blue Hills 40 NW Turks and Caicos Islands
Blue Mountains 133 G6 ⛰ NSW, SE Australia
Blue Nile 127 C3 ~ Ethiopia/Sudan
Bluff Cove 40 Falkland Islands
Blumenau 115 F8 S Brazil
Blyth 35 D2 N England, UK
Bo 124 B5 S Sierra Leone
Boaco 107 D4 S Nicaragua
Boa Vista 115 E3 NW Brazil
Bobaomby, Tanjona 128 G4 *Headland,* N Madagascar
Bobo-Dioulasso 124 C4 SW Burkina
Bocay 107 D3 N Nicaragua
Bocholt 59 A4 W Germany
Bochum 59 A4 W Germany
Bodaybo 76 F4 E Russ. Fed.
Boddam Island 40 *Island,* N British Indian Ocean Territory
Bodden Town 40 SW Cayman Islands
Boden 49 D3 N Sweden
Bodmin 37 B5 SW England, UK
Bodmin Moor 37 B5 *Moorland,* SW England, UK
Bodø 49 C2 C Norway
Bodrum 79 A4 SW Turkey
Boende 128 C2 C Congo (Zaire)
Bofin, Lough 31 D3 ◎ N Ireland
Bogatynia 63 B4 SW Poland
Boğazlıyan 79 D3 C Turkey
Boggeragh Mountains 31 C6 ⛰ S Ireland
Bogia 137 B1 N PNG
Bognor Regis 37 F5 SE England, UK
Bogor 91 C8 Java, C Indonesia
Bogotá 115 B2 ● C Colombia
Bo Hai 87 G3 *Gulf,* NE China
Bohemia 63 B6 *Cultural region,* W Czech Republic
Bohemian Forest 59 D6 ⛰ C Europe
Bohol Sea 91 F5 *Sea,* S Philippines
Bohoro Shan 87 B2 ⛰ NW China
Boise 103 C2 Idaho, USA
Boizenburg 59 C3 N Germany
Bojnūrd 81 E1 N Iran
Boké 124 A4 W Guinea
Boknafjorden 49 A5 *Fjord,* S Norway
Bol 124 G3 W Chad
Bolesławiec 63 C4 SW Poland
Bolgatanga 124 D4 N Ghana
Bolivia 117 A2 ◆ *Republic,* W South America
Bollene 55 E6 SE France
Bollnäs 49 C5 C Sweden
Bollon 133 G4 Queensland, C Australia
Bologna 61 C3 N Italy
Bol'shevik, Ostrov 76 F2 *Island,* Severnaya Zemlya, N Russ. Fed.
Bol'shezemel'skaya Tundra 69 E3 *Physical region,* NW Russ. Fed.
Bol'shoy Lyakhovskiy, Ostrov 76 G2 *Island,* NE Russ. Fed.
Bolton 35 C4 NW England, UK
Bolton 28 ◐ *Unitary auth.,* NW England, UK
Bolu 79 C2 NW Turkey
Bolungarvík 49 A1 NW Iceland
Bolus Head 31 A6 *Headland,* SW Ireland
Bolzano 61 C1 N Italy
Boma 128 B3 W Congo (Zaire)
Bombay 89 C5 W India
Bomu 128 C1 ~ CAR/Congo (Zaire)
Bonaire 109 H7 *Island,* E Netherlands Antilles
Bonanza 107 E3 NE Nicaragua
Bonaparte Archipelago 133 B2 *Island group,* Western Australia
Bon, Cap 70 E4 *Headland,* N Tunisia
Bondo 128 C1 N Congo (Zaire)
Bondoukou 124 D5 E Ivory Coast
Bone, Teluk 91 F7 *Bay,* Celebes, C Indonesia
Bongaigaon 89 G3 NE India
Bongo, Massif des 124 H4 ⛰ NE CAR
Bongor 124 G4 SW Chad
Bonifacio 55 G6 Corsica, France
Bonifacio, Strait of 61 A5 *Strait,* C Mediterranean Sea
Bonin Trench 15 *Undersea feature,* NW Pacific Ocean
Bonn 59 A5 W Germany
Bonvilston 39 E7 S Wales, UK
Booby Point 40 *Headland,* W Cayman Islands
Boosaaso 127 F3 N Somalia
Boothia, Gulf of 97 H3 *Gulf,* NW Terr., NE Canada
Boothia Peninsula 97 H3 *Peninsula,* NW Terr., NE Canada
Boppard 59 B5 W Germany
Boquete 107 F6 W Panama
Boquillas 105 D2 NE Mexico
Bor 127 C4 S Sudan
Bor 65 D2 E Yugoslavia
Borah Peak 103 C2 ▲ Idaho, USA
Borås 49 C6 S Sweden
Bordeaux 55 B5 SW France
Bordj Omar Driss 122 E3 E Algeria
Bordon 37 F4 S England, UK
Børgefjellet 49 C3 ⛰ C Norway
Borger 50 F2 NE Netherlands
Borgholm 49 C6 S Sweden
Borisoglebsk 69 B6 W Russ. Fed.
Borlänge 49 C5 C Sweden
Borne 50 F4 E Netherlands
Borneo 91 D7 *Island,* Brunei/Indonesia/Malaysia
Bornholm 49 C7 *Island,* E Denmark
Borovichi 69 A4 W Russ. Fed.
Borrisokane 31 C5 S Ireland
Borth 39 C4 W Wales, UK
Bosanski Novi 65 B1 NW Bosnia and Herzegovina
Boskovice 63 C6 SE Czech Republic
Bosna 65 C2 ~ N Bosnia and Herzegovina
Bosnia and Herzegovina 65 C2 ◆ *Republic,* SE Europe
Boso-hanto 85 G6 *Peninsula,* Honshu, S Japan
Bosporus 78 B2 *Strait,* NW Turkey
Bossangoa 124 H5 C CAR
Bossembélé 124 H5 C CAR
Bosten Hu 87 C3 ◎ NW China
Boston 35 F5 E England, UK
Boston 101 H3 Massachusetts, USA
Botany Bay 133 H6 *Inlet,* NSW, SE Australia
Boteti 128 C5 ~ N Botswana
Bothnia, Gulf of 49 D4 *Gulf,* N Baltic Sea
Botoşani 67 C5 NE Romania
Botrange 50 E7 ▲ E Belgium
Botswana 128 C5 ◆ *Republic,* S Africa
Bottle Creek 40 N Turks and Caicos Islands
Bouar 124 G5 W CAR
Bou Craa 122 B3 NW Western Sahara
Bougainville Island 137 D2 *Island,* NE PNG
Bougaroun, Cap 70 D4 *Headland,* NE Algeria
Bougouni 124 C4 SW Mali
Boujdour 122 A3 W Western Sahara
Boulder 103 E3 Colorado, USA
Boulogne-sur-Mer 55 D1 N France
Boûmdeïd 124 B3 S Mauritania
Boundiali 124 C4 N Ivory Coast
Bourail 137 G6 C New Caledonia
Bourbonnais 55 D4 *Cultural region,* C France
Bourg-en-Bresse 55 E4 E France
Bourges 55 D4 C France
Bourgogne *see* Burgundy
Bourke 133 G5 NSW, SE Australia
Bournemouth 37 E5 S England, UK
Bournemouth 29 ◐ *Unitary auth.,* S England, UK
Boutilimit 124 A3 SW Mauritania
Bowen 133 G3 Queensland, NE Australia
Bowland, Forest of 35 C4 *Forest,* N England, UK
Boxmeer 50 E5 SE Netherlands
Boyle 31 C3 C Ireland
Boyne 31 E4 ~ E Ireland
Boysun 83 F3 S Uzbekistan
Bozüyük 79 B3 NW Turkey
Brač 65 B3 *Island,* S Croatia
Bracknell Forest 29 ◐ *Unitary auth.,* SE England, UK
Bradford 35 D4 N England, UK
Bradford 29 ◐ *Unitary auth.,* N England, UK
Brae 33 A6 NE Scotland, UK
Braemar 33 E4 NE Scotland, UK
Braga 57 B2 NW Portugal
Bragança 57 C2 NE Portugal
Brahmanbaria 89 G3 E Bangladesh
Brahmapur 89 F5 E India
Brahmaputra 89 H3 ~ S Asia
Braich y Pwll 39 B3 *Headland,* NW Wales, UK
Brăila 67 D7 E Romania
Braine-le-Comte 50 C7 SW Belgium
Braintree 37 G3 SE England, UK
Brampton 99 D6 Ontario, S Canada
Brampton 35 C2 NW England, UK
Brandberg 128 B5 ▲ NW Namibia
Brandenburg 59 D3 NE Germany
Brandon 97 H7 Manitoba, S Canada
Brandon 31 A6 SW Ireland
Brandon Bay 31 A6 *Bay,* SW Ireland
Brandon Mountain 31 A6 ▲ SW Ireland
Braniewo 63 E2 N Poland
Brasília 115 G6 ● C Brazil
Braşov 67 C6 C Romania
Brasstown Bald 101 E5 ▲ Georgia, USA
Bratislava 63 D7 ● SW Slovakia
Bratsk 76 F5 C Russ. Fed.
Braunschweig 59 C4 N Germany
Brava, Costa 57 H2 *Coastal region,* NE Spain
Bravo, Río 105 D2 ~ Mexico/USA
Bray 31 E4 E Ireland
Brazil 115 C4 ◆ *Federal Republic,* South America
Brazil Basin 14 *Undersea feature,* W Atlantic Ocean
Brazilian Highlands 115 G6 ⛰ E Brazil
Brazzaville 128 B2 ● S Congo
Brechin 33 E4 E Scotland, UK
Brecht 50 C5 N Belgium
Brecon 39 E5 E Wales, UK
Brecon Beacons 39 D6 ⛰ S Wales, UK
Breda 50 D5 S Netherlands
Bree 50 D6 NE Belgium
Bregalnica 65 E3 ~ E FYR Macedonia
Bremen 59 B3 NW Germany
Bremerhaven 59 B3 NW Germany
Brenig, Llyn 39 D2 ◎ N Wales, UK
Brenner Pass 59 C8 *Pass,* Austria/Italy
Brent 29 ◐ *London borough,* SE England, UK
Brentwood 37 G3 E England, UK
Brescia 61 C2 N Italy
Bressanone 61 C1 N Italy
Bressay 33 B6 *Island,* NE Scotland, UK
Brest 67 B3 SW Belorussia
Brest 55 A2 NW France
Bretagne *see* Brittany
Bria 124 H5 C CAR
Briançon 55 F5 SE France
Bride 35 A3 N Isle of Man
Bridgend 39 D7 S Wales, UK
Bridgend 29 ◐ *Unitary auth.,* S Wales, UK
Bridgeport 101 G3 Connecticut, USA
Bridgetown 109 K6 ● SW Barbados
Bridgetown 31 D6 S Ireland
Bridgwater 37 D4 SW England, UK
Bridgwater Bay 37 C4 *Bay,* SW England, UK
Bridlington 35 F4 E England, UK
Bridlington Bay 35 F4 *Bay,* E England, UK
Bridport 37 D5 S England, UK
Brig 59 B8 SW Switzerland
Brigg 35 F5 N England, UK
Brighton 37 F5 SE England, UK
Brighton and Hove 29 ◐ *Unitary auth.,* SE England, UK
Brindisi 61 F6 SE Italy
Brisbane 133 H4 Queensland, E Australia
Bristol 37 D4 SW England, UK
Bristol 29 ◐ *Unitary auth.,* SW England, UK
Bristol Bay 97 C4 *Bay,* Alaska, USA
Bristol Channel 37 C4 *Inlet,* England/Wales, UK
Britain 27 *Island,* UK
British Columbia 97 E5 ◐ *Province,* SW Canada
British Indian Ocean Territory 40 *UK* ◇ C Indian Ocean
British Isles 44 *Island group,* Ireland/United Kingdom
British Virgin Islands 40 *UK* ◇ E West Indies
Briton Ferry 39 D6 S Wales, UK
Brittany 55 B2 *Cultural region,* NW France
Brive-la-Gaillarde 55 C5 C France
Brixham 37 C5 SW England, UK
Brno 63 C6 SE Czech Republic
Broad Bay 33 C2 *Bay,* NW Scotland, UK
Broadford 33 C4 N Scotland, UK
Broad Haven 31 B2 *Inlet,* NW Ireland
Broad Law 33 E6 ▲ S Scotland, UK
Broad Sound 39 A6 *Sound,* SW Wales, UK
Broadstairs 37 H4 SE England, UK
Broads, The 37 H2 *Wetland,* E England, UK
Brodeur Peninsula 97 H3 *Peninsula,* Baffin Island, NW Terr., NE Canada
Brodick 33 C6 W Scotland, UK
Brodnica 63 E2 N Poland
Broek-in-Waterland 50 D3 C Netherlands
Broken Hill 133 F5 NSW, SE Australia
Bromley 37 F4 SE England, UK
Bromley 29 ◐ *London borough,* SE England, UK
Bromsgrove 35 D7 W England, UK
Brooks Range 97 D3 ⛰ Alaska, USA
Brookton 133 B5 Western Australia
Broome 133 C2 Western Australia
Brora 33 D3 N Scotland, UK
Brora 33 D2 ~ N Scotland, UK
Brough 35 D3 NW England, UK
Brownsville 103 G6 Texas, USA
Bruges 50 B6 NW Belgium
Brugge *see* Bruges
Brummen 50 E4 E Netherlands
Brunei 91 D5 ◆ *Monarchy,* SE Asia
Brunner, Lake 135 C6 ◎ South Island, NZ
Brus Laguna 107 E2 E Honduras
Brussel *see* Brussels
Brussels 50 C6 ● C Belgium
Bruxelles *see* Brussels
Bryan 103 G5 Texas, USA
Bryansk 69 A6 W Russ. Fed.
Brynamman 39 D6 S Wales, UK
Bryn Du 39 D5 *Hill,* E Wales, UK
Brynmawr 39 E6 SE Wales, UK
Brzeg 63 D4 SW Poland
Buala 137 E2 E Solomon Islands
Bucaramanga 115 C2 N Colombia
Buchanan 124 B5 SW Liberia
Buchan Ness 33 F3 *Headland,* NE Scotland, UK
Bucharest 67 C7 ● S Romania
Buckie 33 E3 NE Scotland, UK
Buckinghamshire 29 ◐ *County,* SE England, UK
Buckley 39 E2 N Wales, UK
București *see* Bucharest
Budapest 63 E7 ● N Hungary
Budaun 89 E3 N India
Bude 37 B5 SW England, UK
Bude Bay 37 B5 *Bay,* SW England, UK
Buenaventura 115 B3 W Colombia
Buena Vista 117 B2 C Bolivia
Buena Vista 40 S Gibraltar
Buenos Aires 117 C5 ● E Argentina
Buenos Aires 107 F6 SE Costa Rica
Buenos Aires, Lago 117 A8 ◎ Argentina/Chile
Buffalo 101 F3 New York, USA
Buffalo Narrows 97 G6 Saskatchewan, C Canada
Bug 67 B3 ~ E Europe
Buguruslan 69 D6 W Russ. Fed.
Builth Wells 39 E5 E Wales, UK
Bujalance 57 D5 S Spain
Bujanovac 65 D3 SE Yugoslavia
Bujumbura 127 B6 ● W Burundi
Buka Island 137 D2 *Island,* NE PNG
Bukavu 128 D2 E Congo (Zaire)
Bukhoro 83 E3 C Uzbekistan
Bukoba 127 C5 NW Tanzania
Bülach 59 B7 NW Switzerland
Bulawayo 128 D5 SW Zimbabwe
Bulgaria 65 E3 ◆ *Republic,* SE Europe
Bulukumba 91 E7 Celebes, C Indonesia
Bumba 128 C1 N Congo (Zaire)
Bunbury 133 B6 Western Australia
Bunclody 31 E5 SE Ireland
Buncrana 31 D1 NW Ireland
Bundaberg 133 H4 Queensland, E Australia
Bungo-suido 85 D7 *Strait,* SW Japan
Bunmahon 31 D6 S Ireland
Bunratty 31 C5 W Ireland
Bünyan 79 D3 C Turkey
Buon Ma Thuot 91 C4 S Vietnam
Buraydah 81 C4 N Saudi Arabia
Burco 127 F3 NW Somalia
Burdur 79 B4 SW Turkey
Burdur Gölü 79 B4 *Salt lake,* SW Turkey
Bure 127 D3 NW Ethiopia
Bure 37 H1 ~ E England, UK
Burgas 65 G3 E Bulgaria
Burgaski Zaliv 79 A1 *Gulf,* E Bulgaria
Burgess Hill 37 F4 SE England, UK
Burgos 57 D2 N Spain
Burgundy 55 E4 *Cultural region,* E France
Burhan Budai Shan 87 D4 ⛰ C China
Burjassot 57 F4 E Spain
Burketown 133 F2 Queensland, NE Australia
Burkina 124 C4 ◆ *Republic,* W Africa
Burkina Faso *see* Burkina
Burma 91 A2 ◆ *military dictatorship,* SE Asia
Burnham-on-Crouch 37 G3 SE England, UK
Burnham-on-Sea 37 D4 SW England, UK
Burnie 133 F7 Tasmania, SE Australia
Burnley 35 D4 NW England, UK
Burnside 97 G4 ~ NW Terr., NW Canada
Burren 31 B5 *Physical region,* W Ireland
Burriana 57 F3 E Spain
Burry Port 39 C6 S Wales, UK
Bursa 79 B3 NW Turkey
Burton upon Trent 35 D6 C England, UK
Burundi 127 B6 ◆ *Republic,* C Africa
Buru, Pulau 91 F7 *Island,* E Indonesia
Bury 35 D4 NW England, UK
Bury 28 ◐ *Unitary auth.,* NW England, UK
Bury St Edmunds 37 G2 E England, UK
Bushire 81 D3 S Iran
Bushmills 31 E1 N Northern Ireland, UK
Busselton 133 B6 Western Australia
Buta 128 D1 N Congo (Zaire)
Bute, Island of 33 C6 *Island,* SW Scotland, UK
Buton, Pulau 91 F7 *Island,* C Indonesia
Buttevant 31 C6 S Ireland
Button Islands 99 E1 *Island group,* NW Terr., NE Canada
Butuan 91 F5 S Philippines
Buulobarde 127 F4 C Somalia
Buur Gaabo 127 E5 S Somalia
Buxton 35 D5 C England, UK
Buynaksk 69 B9 SW Russ. Fed.
Büyükmenderes Nehri 79 A4 ~ SW Turkey
Buzău 67 C7 SE Romania
Buzuluk 69 C6 W Russ. Fed.
Bydgoszcz 63 D3 W Poland
Byelaruskaya Hrada 67 C3 *Ridge,* N Belorussia
Byerezino 67 D2 ~ C Belorussia
Bylchau 39 D2 N Wales, UK
Bytča 63 D6 NW Slovakia
Bytów 63 D2 NW Poland
Byuzmeyin 83 C3 C Turkmenistan

C

Caazapá 117 C4 S Paraguay
Cabañaquinta 57 C1 N Spain
Cabanatuan 91 F3 N Philippines
Cabinda 128 B2 NW Angola
Cabinda 128 B3 *Province,* NW Angola
Cabora Bassa, Lake 128 E4 ▧ NW Mozambique
Caborca 105 B2 NW Mexico
Cabot Strait 99 G4 *Strait,* E Canada
Cabrera 57 G4 *Island,* Balearic Islands, Spain
Cáceres 57 C4 W Spain
Cachimbo, Serra do 115 E4 ⛰ C Brazil
Caconda 128 B4 C Angola
Čadca 63 D6 N Slovakia
Cader Idris 39 C3 ▲ NW Wales, UK
Cadiz 91 F4 C Philippines
Cádiz 57 C6 SW Spain
Cádiz, Golfo de *see* Cadiz, Gulf of
Cadiz, Gulf of 57 B6 *Gulf,* Portugal/Spain
Caen 55 C2 N France
Caergwrle 39 E2 N Wales, UK
Caernarfon 39 C2 NW Wales, UK
Caernarfon Bay 39 B2 *Bay,* NW Wales, UK
Caerphilly 39 E7 S Wales, UK
Caerphilly 29 ◐ *Unitary auth.,* S Wales, UK
Caersws 39 E4 C Wales, UK
Caerwent 39 F6 SE Wales, UK
Cafayate 117 B4 N Argentina
Cagayan de Oro 91 F5 Mindanao, S Philippines
Cagliari 61 A6 Sardinia, Italy
Caguas 109 I4 E Puerto Rico
Caha Mountains 31 B7 ⛰ SW Ireland
Caher 31 D6 S Ireland
Caherciveen 31 A6 SW Ireland
Cahore Point 31 E5 *Headland,* SE Ireland
Cahors 55 C6 S France
Cahul 67 D6 S Moldavia
Caicos Bank 40 *Undersea feature,* N Caribbean Sea
Caicos Passage 40 *Strait,* Bahamas/Turks and Caicos Islands
Cairngorm Mountains 33 E4 ⛰ C Scotland, UK
Cairns 133 G2 Queensland, NE Australia
Cairo 122 I2 ● N Egypt
Cajamarca 115 B5 NW Peru
Calabar 124 F5 S Nigeria
Calahorra 57 E2 N Spain
Calais 55 D1 N France
Calama 117 A3 N Chile
Călărași 67 C7 SE Romania
Calatayud 57 E3 NE Spain
Calbayog 91 F4 Samar, C Philippines

CAR Central African Republic   FYR Former Yugoslavian Rebublic   NSW New South Wales   NZ New Zealand   PNG Papua New Guinea   Russ. Fed. Russian Federation   UAE United Arab Emirates   UK United Kingdom   USA United States of America

CALCUTTA

Calcutta 89 G4 NE India
Caldas da Rainha 57 A4 W Portugal
Caldera 117 A4 N Chile
Calderdale 29 ◐ Unitary auth., N England, UK
Caldey Island 39 B6 Island, SW Wales, UK
Caldicot 39 F7 SE Wales, UK
Caledonia 107 C1 N Belize
Caleta Olivia 117 B8 SE Argentina
Calf of Man 35 A4 Island, SW Isle of Man
Calgary 97 G7 Alberta, SW Canada
Cali 115 B3 W Colombia
Calicut 89 D7 SW India
California 103 B3 ◐ State, W USA
California, Gulf of 105 B2 Gulf, NE Mexico
Callabonna, Lake 133 F5 ◎ S Australia
Callan 31 D5 S Ireland
Callander 33 D5 C Scotland, UK
Callao 115 B5 W Peru
Callosa de Segura 57 F5 E Spain
Calne 37 E4 S England, UK
Caloundra 133 H4 Queensland, E Australia
Caltanissetta 61 D8 Sicily, Italy
Caluula 127 G3 NE Somalia
Cam 37 F2 〰 E England, UK
Camabatela 128 B3 NW Angola
Camacupa 128 B4 C Angola
Camagüey 109 D3 C Cuba
Camagüey, Archipiélago de 109 D3 Island group, C Cuba
Camargo 105 D3 N Mexico
Camargue 55 E6 Physical region, SE France
Ca Mau 91 C5 S Vietnam
Cambodia 91 C4 ◆ Republic, SE Asia
Cambrai 55 D1 N France
Cambrian Mountains 39 D4 ⛰ C Wales, UK
Cambridge 135 D3 North Island, NZ
Cambridge 37 G2 E England, UK
Cambridge Bay 97 G4 Victoria Island, NW Terr., NW Canada
Cambridgeshire 29 ◐ County, E England, UK
Camden 29 ◐ London borough, SE England, UK
Cameroon 124 F5 ◆ Republic, W Africa
Cameroon Mountain 124 E5 ✱ SW Cameroon
Camocim 115 H4 E Brazil
Camorta 89 H6 Island, Nicobar Islands, India
Campamento 107 D3 C Honduras
Campbell, Cape 135 D5 Headland, South Island, NZ
Campbell Plateau 15 Undersea feature, SW Pacific Ocean
Campbell River 97 E7 Vancouver Island, British Columbia, SW Canada
Campbeltown 33 C6 W Scotland, UK
Campeche 105 H4 SE Mexico
Campeche, Bay of 105 G4 Bay, E Mexico
Câm Pha 91 C2 N Vietnam
Campina Grande 115 I5 E Brazil
Campinas 115 G7 S Brazil
Campobasso 61 D5 C Italy
Campo de Criptana 57 D4 C Spain
Campo Grande 115 F7 SW Brazil
Campos 115 H7 SE Brazil
Cam Ranh 91 D4 S Vietnam
Canada 93 ◆ Commonwealth Republic, N North America
Canada Basin 139 B3 Undersea feature, Arctic Ocean
Canadian River 103 F4 〰 SW USA
Canadian Shield 99 B3 Physical region, Canada
Çanakkale 79 A2 W Turkey
Cananea 105 B2 NW Mexico
Canarreos, Archipiélago de los 109 B3 Island group, W Cuba
Canary Islands 122 A2 Island group, Spain, NE Atlantic Ocean
Cañas 107 E5 NW Costa Rica
Canaveral, Cape 101 E6 Headland, SE USA
Canavieiras 115 H6 E Brazil
Canberra 133 G6 ● Australian Capital Territory, SE Australia
Cancún 105 I4 SE Mexico
Cangzhou 87 G3 E China
Caniapiscau 99 E2 〰 Québec, E Canada
Caniapiscau, Réservoir de 99 E3 ▣ Québec, C Canada
Canik Dağları 79 E2 ⛰ N Turkey
Çankırı 79 C2 N Turkey
Canna 33 B4 Island, NW Scotland, UK
Cannanore 89 D7 SW India
Cannes 55 F6 SE France
Cannock 35 D6 C England, UK
Canoas 115 F9 S Brazil
Cantabria 57 D1 Cultural region, N Spain
Cantábrica, Cordillera 57 C1 ⛰ N Spain
Canterbury 37 H4 SE England, UK
Canterbury Bight 135 C6 Bight, South Island, NZ
Canterbury Plains 135 C6 Plain, South Island, NZ
Can Tho 91 C4 S Vietnam
Canton 101 E3 Ohio, USA
Cape Barren Island 133 G7 Island, Tasmania, SE Australia
Cape Breton Island 99 G5 Island, Nova Scotia, SE Canada
Cape Coast 124 D5 S Ghana
Cape Cod 99 E6 Bay, Massachusetts, USA
Capel Curig 39 D2 N Wales, UK
Capelle aan den IJssel 50 C4 SW Netherlands
Cape Town 128 C7 ● SW South Africa
Cape Verde 119 ◆ Republic, E Atlantic Ocean
Cape York Peninsula 133 F1 Peninsula, Queensland, N Australia
Cap-Haïtien 109 F4 N Haiti
Capira 107 H6 C Panama
Capitán Arturo Prat 138 A3 Chilean research station, South Shetland Islands, Antarctica
Capitán Pablo Lagerenza 117 C3 N Paraguay
Capri 61 D6 S Italy
Caprivi Strip 128 C4 Cultural region, NE Namibia
Caquetá, Río 115 B3 〰 Brazil/Colombia
Caracal 67 B7 S Romania
Caracaraí 115 E3 W Brazil
Caracas 115 D1 ● N Venezuela
Caratasca, Laguna de 107 E2 Lagoon, NE Honduras
Carballiño 57 B2 NW Spain
Carbonia 61 A6 Sardinia, Italy
Carcassonne 55 D6 S France
Cárdenas 109 C2 W Cuba
Cardiff 39 E7 National region capital, S Wales, UK
Cardiff 29 ◐ Unitary auth., S Wales, UK
Cardigan 39 B5 SW Wales, UK
Cardigan Bay 39 C4 Bay, W Wales, UK
Carey, Lake 133 C5 ◎ Western Australia
Caribbean Sea 109 F6 Sea, W Atlantic Ocean
Carlisle 35 C2 NW England, UK
Carlow 31 E5 SE Ireland
Carlow 29 ◐ County, SE Ireland
Carloway 33 B2 NW Scotland, UK
Carlsbad 103 E5 New Mexico, USA
Carmarthen 39 C6 SW Wales, UK
Carmarthen Bay 39 B6 Inlet, SW Wales, UK
Carmarthenshire 29 ◐ Unitary auth., S Wales, UK
Carmaux 55 D6 S France
Carmel Head 39 B1 Headland, NW Wales, UK
Carmelita 107 B1 N Guatemala
Carmen 105 H5 SE Mexico
Carmona 57 C5 S Spain
Carna 31 B4 W Ireland
Carnarvon 133 A4 Western Australia
Carndonagh 31 D1 NW Ireland
Carnedd Llywelyn 39 D2 ▲ NW Wales, UK
Carnegie, Lake 133 C4 Salt lake, Western Australia
Carn Eige 33 C4 ▲ N Scotland, UK
Car Nicobar 89 H5 Island, Nicobar Islands, India
Carnlough 31 F2 E Northern Ireland, UK
Carno 39 D4 C Wales, UK
Carnoustie 33 E5 E Scotland, UK
Carolina 115 G4 E Brazil
Caroline Island 131 Atoll, Line Islands, E Kiribati
Carpathian Mountains 63 F6 ⛰ E Europe
Carpentaria, Gulf of 133 E1 Gulf, N Australia
Carpi 61 C3 N Italy
Carrara 61 B3 C Italy
Carrauntoohil 31 A6 ▲ SW Ireland
Carrickfergus 31 F2 NE Northern Ireland, UK
Carrickfergus 29 ◐ District, E Northern Ireland, UK
Carrickmacross 31 E3 N Ireland
Carrick-on-Shannon 31 D3 NW Ireland
Carrowmore Lake 31 B3 ◎ NW Ireland
Carson City 103 B3 Nevada, USA
Cartagena 115 B1 NW Colombia
Cartagena 57 F5 SE Spain
Cartago 107 E6 C Costa Rica
Cartwright 99 G3 Newfoundland and Labrador, E Canada
Casablanca 122 C1 NW Morocco
Cascade Range 103 B2 ⛰ NW USA
Cascais 57 A4 C Portugal
Caserta 61 D5 S Italy
Casey 138 E5 Australian research station, Antarctica
Cashel 31 D5 S Ireland
Čáslav 63 C5 C Czech Republic
Casper 103 E2 Wyoming, USA
Caspian Depression 69 B8 Depression, Kazakhstan/Russ. Fed.
Caspian Sea 72 Inland sea, Asia/Europe
Casteggio 61 B2 N Italy
Castelló de la Plana 57 F3 E Spain
Castelnaudary 55 C6 S France
Castelo Branco 57 B4 C Portugal
Castelsarrasin 55 C6 S France
Castelvetrano 61 C8 Sicily, Italy
Castilla-La Mancha 57 E4 Cultural region, NE Spain
Castilla-León 57 C2 Cultural region, NW Spain
Castle Acre 37 G1 E England, UK
Castlebar 31 B3 W Ireland
Castlebay 33 A4 NW Scotland, UK
Castlebellingham 31 E3 NE Ireland
Castleblayney 31 E3 N Ireland
Castlebridge 31 E6 SE Ireland
Castlecomer 31 D5 SE Ireland
Castlecove 31 A6 SW Ireland
Castledawson 31 E2 C Northern Ireland, UK
Castlederg 31 D2 W Northern Ireland, UK
Castle Douglas 33 D7 S Scotland, UK
Castleford 35 E4 N England, UK
Castleisland 31 B6 SW Ireland
Castlemartyr 31 C6 S Ireland
Castlereagh 29 ◐ District, E Northern Ireland, UK
Castletown 35 A4 SE Isle of Man
Castletown Bearhaven 31 B7 SW Ireland
Castletownroche 31 C6 S Ireland
Castricum 50 C3 W Netherlands
Castries 109 K6 ● N Saint Lucia
Castro 117 A7 W Chile
Castrovillari 61 E7 SW Italy
Castuera 57 C4 W Spain
Catacamas 107 D3 C Honduras
Catalan Bay 40 Bay, E Gibraltar
Catalonia 57 G2 Cultural region, N Spain
Cataluña see Catalonia
Catania 61 D8 Sicily, Italy
Catanzaro 61 E7 SW Italy
Catarroja 57 F4 E Spain
Caterham 37 G4 SE England, UK
Cat Island 109 E2 Island, C Bahamas
Catskill Mountains 101 F3 ⛰ New York, USA
Catterick 35 D3 N England, UK
Caucasus 79 G1 ⛰ Georgia/Russ. Fed.
Cavally 124 C5 〰 Ivory Coast/Liberia
Cavan 31 D3 N Ireland
Cavan 29 ◐ County, N Ireland
Cave Point 40 Headland, S Tristan da Cunha
Caviana de Fora, Ilha 115 G3 Island, N Brazil
Caxito 128 B3 NW Angola
Cayenne 115 F2 ○ NE French Guiana
Cayes 109 E4 SW Haiti
Cayman Brac 40 Island, E Cayman Islands
Cayman Islands 40 UK ◇ W West Indies
Cay Sal 109 C2 Islet, SW Bahamas
Cazorla 57 E5 S Spain
Ceará 115 H4 ◐ State, C Brazil
Cébaco, Isla 107 G7 Island, SW Panama
Cebu 91 F4 Cebu, C Philippines
Cecina 61 B4 C Italy
Cedar Rapids 103 G2 Iowa, USA
Cedros, Isla 105 A3 Island, W Mexico
Ceduna 133 E5 S Australia
Cefalù 61 D8 Sicily, Italy
Celbridge 31 E4 E Ireland
Celebes 91 E7 Island, C Indonesia
Celebes Sea 91 E6 Sea, Indonesia/Philippines
Celje 59 E8 C Slovenia
Celldömölk 63 D8 W Hungary
Celle 59 C3 N Germany
Celtic Sea 53 B8 Sea, SW British Isles
Cemaes 39 C1 NW Wales, UK
Cemaes Head 39 B5 Headland, SW Wales, UK
Cenderawasih, Teluk 91 H7 Bay, E Indonesia
Cenon 55 B5 SW France
Central African Republic 124 H5 ◆ Republic, C Africa
Central, Cordillera 109 F4 ⛰ C Dominican Republic
Central, Cordillera 107 G6 ⛰ C Panama
Central, Cordillera 91 F3 ⛰ N Philippines
Central Makran Range 89 B3 ⛰ W Pakistan
Central Pacific Basin 15 Undersea feature, C Pacific Ocean
Central Range 137 A2 ⛰ NW PNG
Central Russian Upland 69 A6 ⛰ C Russ. Fed.
Central Siberian Plateau 76 E3 ⛰ N Russ. Fed.
Central, Sistema 57 D3 ⛰ C Spain
Centre Hills 40 ⛰ C Montserrat
Ceram Sea 91 G7 Sea, E Indonesia
Ceredigion 29 ◐ Unitary auth., W Wales, UK
Cerignola 61 E5 SE Italy
Çerkeş 79 C2 N Turkey
Cernay 55 F3 NE France
Cerrigydrudion 39 D2 N Wales, UK
Cerro de Pasco 115 B5 C Peru
Cervera 57 G2 NE Spain
Cesena 61 C3 N Italy
České Budějovice 63 B6 SW Czech Republic
Český Krumlov 63 B6 SW Czech Republic
Ceuta 57 C6 Spain, N Africa
Cévennes 55 D6 ⛰ S France
Ceyhan 79 D5 S Turkey
Ceylanpınar 79 F5 SE Turkey
Chachapoyas 115 A4 NW Peru
Chad 124 G3 ◆ Republic, C Africa
Chad, Lake 124 G3 ◎ C Africa
Chadron 103 E2 Nebraska, USA
Chagai Hills 89 B2 ⛰ Afghanistan/Pakistan
Chaghcharan 83 E5 C Afghanistan
Chagos Archipelago 40 Island group, British Indian Ocean Territory
Chajul 107 A3 W Guatemala
Chakhansur 83 D6 SW Afghanistan
Chalatenango 107 B3 N El Salvador
Chálki 65 G6 Island, Dodecanese, Greece
Chalkída 65 E5 E Greece
Chalkidikí 65 E4 Peninsula, NE Greece
Challans 55 B4 NW France
Châlons-en-Champagne 55 E2 NE France
Chalon-sur-Saône 55 E4 C France
Chaman 89 B2 SW Pakistan
Chambéry 55 E5 E France
Champagne 55 E2 Cultural region, N France
Champaign 101 D3 Illinois, USA
Champasak 91 C3 S Laos
Champerico 107 A3 SW Guatemala
Champlain, Lake 101 F2 ◎ Canada/USA
Champotón 105 H4 SE Mexico
Chañaral 117 A4 N Chile
Chances Peak 40 ▲ S Montserrat
Chandigarh 89 D2 N India
Chandrapur 89 E5 C India
Changane 128 E5 〰 S Mozambique
Changchun 87 G2 NE China
Chang Jiang see Yangtze
Changsha 87 F5 S China
Changyon 85 A5 SW North Korea
Changzhi 87 F4 C China
Chaniá 65 E7 Crete, Greece
Chañi, Nevado de 117 A3 ▲ NW Argentina
Channel Islands 37 G6 Island group, S English Channel
Channel-Port aux Basques 99 G4 Newfoundland, Newfoundland and Labrador, SE Canada
Channel Tunnel 53 F8 Tunnel, France/UK
Chantada 57 B2 NW Spain
Chaoyang 87 G3 NE China
Chapala, Lago de 105 E5 ◎ C Mexico
Chapan, Gora 83 C3 ▲ C Turkmenistan
Chapayevsk 69 C6 W Russ. Fed.
Chard 37 D5 SW England, UK
Chardzhev 83 E3 E Turkmenistan
Charente 55 C5 Cultural region, W France
Charente 55 C5 〰 W France
Chari 124 H4 〰 CAR/Chad
Charikar 83 F5 NE Afghanistan
Charleroi 50 C7 S Belgium
Charlesbourg 99 E5 Québec, SE Canada
Charles Island 99 D1 Island, NW Terr., NE Canada
Charleston 101 F5 South Carolina, USA
Charleston 101 E4 West Virginia, USA
Charlestown 31 C3 NW Ireland
Charleville 133 G4 Queensland, E Australia
Charleville-Mézières 55 E2 N France
Charlotte 101 E5 North Carolina, USA
Charlotte Amalie 109 I4 ○ Saint Thomas, N Virgin Islands (US)
Charlotte Harbor 101 E7 Inlet, SE USA
Charlottetown 99 G5 Prince Edward Island, SE Canada
Charsk 76 D5 E Kazakhstan
Charters Towers 133 G3 Queensland, NE Australia
Chartres 55 D3 C France
Charus Nuur 87 C2 ◎ NW Mongolia
Chashniki 67 D2 N Belorussia
Châteaubriant 55 B3 NW France
Châteaudun 55 D3 C France
Châteauroux 55 D4 C France
Château-Thierry 55 D2 N France
Châtelet 50 C7 S Belgium
Châtellerault 55 C4 W France
Chatham 37 G4 SE England, UK
Chatkal Range 83 G2 ⛰ Kyrgyzstan/Uzbekistan
Chattahoochee River 101 D6 〰 SE USA
Chattanooga 101 D5 Tennessee, USA
Chatyr-Tash 83 H3 C Kyrgyzstan
Chau Doc 91 C4 S Vietnam
Chaumont 55 E3 N France
Chaves 57 B2 N Portugal
Chaykovskiy 69 D6 NW Russ. Fed.
Cheb 63 A5 W Czech Republic
Cheboksary 69 C5 W Russ. Fed.
Chech, Erg 124 C1 Desert, Algeria/Mali
Cheduba Island 91 A3 Island, W Burma
Cheju-do 85 B8 Island, S South Korea
Cheju Strait 85 B7 Strait, S South Korea
Cheleken 83 B3 W Turkmenistan
Chelkar 76 B5 W Kazakhstan
Chełm 63 G4 SE Poland
Chełmno 63 D2 N Poland
Chelmsford 37 G3 E England, UK
Cheltenham 37 D3 C England, UK
Chelyabinsk 76 C4 C Russ. Fed.
Chemnitz 59 D5 E Germany
Chengde 87 G3 E China
Chengdu 87 E4 C China
Chenzhou 87 F5 S China
Chepstow 39 F6 SE Wales, UK
Cher 55 D4 〰 C France
Cherbourg 55 B1 N France
Cherepovets 69 B4 NW Russ. Fed.
Chergui, Chott ech 70 B5 Salt lake, NW Algeria
Cherkasy 67 E4 C Ukraine
Cherkessk 69 A8 SW Russ. Fed.
Chernihiv 67 E3 NE Ukraine
Chernivtsi 67 C5 W Ukraine
Cherskiy 76 H2 NE Russ. Fed.
Cherskogo, Khrebet 76 G3 ⛰ NE Russ. Fed.
Chesapeake Bay 101 G4 Inlet, NE USA
Chesham 37 F3 C England, UK
Cheshire 29 ◐ County, C England, UK
Chëshskaya Guba 139 E6 Bay, NW Russ. Fed.
Chester 35 C5 C England, UK
Chesterfield 35 E5 C England, UK
Chesterfield, Îles 137 E6 Island group, NW New Caledonia
Chester-le-Street 35 D2 N England, UK
Chetumal 105 I4 SE Mexico
Cheviot Hills 35 C1 Hill range, England/Scotland, UK
Cheviot, The 35 D1 ▲ NE England, UK
Cheyenne 103 E3 Wyoming, USA
Chhapra 89 F3 N India
Chiai 87 H5 C Taiwan
Chiang Mai 91 B3 NW Thailand
Chiapa de Corzo 105 H5 SE Mexico
Chiba 85 G5 S Japan
Chibougamau 99 D4 Québec, SE Canada
Chicago 101 D3 Illinois, USA
Chichester 37 F5 SE England, UK
Chiclayo 115 B5 NW Peru
Chico, Río 117 B7 〰 SE Argentina
Chico, Río 117 A8 〰 S Argentina
Chicoutimi 99 E4 Québec, SE Canada
Chieti 61 D5 C Italy
Chifeng 87 G2 N China
Chihuahua 105 D2 NW Mexico
Chile 117 A4 ◆ Republic, SW South America
Chile Chico 117 A8 W Chile
Chililabombwe 128 D4 C Zambia
Chillán 117 A6 C Chile
Chiloé, Isla de 117 A7 Island, W Chile
Chilpancingo 105 F5 S Mexico
Chiltern Hills 37 F3 Hill range, S England, UK
Chilung 87 H5 N Taiwan
Chimán 107 H6 E Panama
Chimbote 115 B5 W Peru
Chimboy 83 D2 NW Uzbekistan
Chimoio 128 E5 C Mozambique
China 87 C3 ◆ Republic, E Asia
Chinandega 107 C4 NW Nicaragua
Chin-do 85 B7 Island, SW South Korea
Chindwin 91 A1 〰 N Burma
Chingola 128 D4 C Zambia
Chinguetti 124 B2 C Mauritania
Chin Hills 91 A2 ⛰ W Burma
Chioggia 61 D2 NE Italy
Chíos 65 F5 E Greece
Chíos 65 F5 Island, E Greece
Chipata 128 E4 E Zambia
Chippenham 37 D4 S England, UK
Chiquimula 107 B3 SE Guatemala
Chirala 89 E6 E India
Chirchiq 83 F2 E Uzbekistan
Chiriqui Gulf 107 F7 Gulf, SW Panama
Chiriquí, Laguna de 107 F6 Lagoon, NW Panama
Chirk 39 E2 NE Wales, UK
Chirripó Grande, Cerro 107 F6 ▲ SE Costa Rica
Chisec 107 B2 C Guatemala
Chişinău 67 D6 ● C Moldavia
Chita 76 G5 S Russ. Fed.
Chitato 128 C3 NE Angola
Chitina 97 D4 Alaska, USA
Chitose 85 G2 NE Japan
Chitré 107 G7 S Panama
Chittagong 89 H4 SE Bangladesh
Chitungwiza 128 E5 NE Zimbabwe
Chiume 128 C4 E Angola
Chlef 122 D1 NW Algeria
Chodzież 63 C3 NW Poland
Choele Choel 117 B6 C Argentina
Choiseul 137 E2 Island, NW Solomon Islands
Cholet 55 B4 NW France
Choluteca 107 C4 S Honduras
Choluteca, Río 107 D4 〰 SW Honduras
Choma 128 D4 S Zambia
Chomutov 63 A5 NW Czech Republic
Ch'onan 85 B6 W South Korea
Ch'ongjin 85 C3 NE North Korea
Chongju 85 A5 W North Korea
Chongqing 87 E5 C China
Chonos, Archipiélago de los 117 A7 Island group, S Chile
Chorley 35 C4 NW England, UK
Chornobyl' 67 D3 N Ukraine
Chorzów 63 E5 S Poland
Ch'osan 85 A4 N North Korea
Choshi 85 G5 S Japan
Choszczno 63 C3 W Poland
Chota Nagpur 89 E4 Plateau, N India
Choûm 124 B2 C Mauritania
Choybalsan 87 F2 E Mongolia
Christchurch 135 C6 South Island, NZ
Christchurch 37 E5 S England, UK
Chubut, Río 117 B7 〰 SE Argentina
Chucunaque, Río 107 I6 〰 E Panama
Chugoku-sanchi 85 D6 ⛰ Honshu, SW Japan
Chukchi Plain 139 C2 Undersea feature, Arctic Ocean
Chukchi Plateau 139 B2 Undersea feature, Arctic Ocean
Chukchi Sea 76 H1 Sea, Arctic Ocean
Chukot Range 76 H1 ⛰ NE Russ. Fed.
Chulucanas 115 A4 NW Peru
Chulym 76 E5 〰 C Russ. Fed.
Ch'unch'on 85 B5 N South Korea
Ch'ungju 85 B6 C South Korea
Chunya 76 F4 〰 C Russ. Fed.
Chuquicamata 117 A3 N Chile
Chur 59 C8 E Switzerland
Churchill 97 H5 Manitoba, C Canada
Churchill 99 A2 〰 C Canada
Churchill 99 F3 〰 Newfoundland and Labrador, E Canada
Church Stoke 39 E4 C Wales, UK
Church Stretton 35 C6 W England, UK
Churchtown 31 E6 SE Ireland
Chusovoy 69 D5 NW Russ. Fed.
Chuy 117 D5 E Uruguay
Cide 79 C2 N Turkey
Ciechanów 63 E3 C Poland
Ciego de Ávila 109 D3 C Cuba
Cienfuegos 109 C3 C Cuba
Cieza 57 E5 SE Spain
Cihanbeyli 79 C4 C Turkey
Cikobia 137 J4 Island, N Fiji
Cilacap 91 D8 Java, C Indonesia
Cincinnati 101 E4 Ohio, USA
Ciney 50 D8 SE Belgium
Cinto, Monte 55 F7 ▲ Corsica, France
Cipolletti 117 B6 C Argentina
Cirebon 91 C8 Java, S Indonesia
Cirencester 37 E3 C England, UK
Cirò Marina 61 E7 S Italy
Ciudad Bolívar 115 D2 E Venezuela
Ciudad Darío 107 D4 W Nicaragua
Ciudad del Este 117 C4 SE Paraguay
Ciudad Guayana 115 D2 NE Venezuela
Ciudad Guzmán 105 D5 SW Mexico
Ciudad Hidalgo 105 H6 SE Mexico
Ciudad Juárez 105 C1 N Mexico
Ciudad Lerdo 105 D3 C Mexico
Ciudad Madero 105 F4 C Mexico
Ciudad Mante 105 F4 C Mexico
Ciudad Miguel Alemán 105 E3 C Mexico
Ciudad Obregón 105 C3 NW Mexico
Ciudad Real 57 D4 C Spain
Ciudad-Rodrigo 57 C3 N Spain
Ciudad Valles 105 F4 C Mexico
Ciudad Victoria 105 F3 C Mexico
Ciutadella de Menorca 57 H3 Minorca, Spain
Civitanova Marche 61 D4 C Italy
Civitavecchia 61 C5 C Italy
Clackmannan 28 ◐ Unitary auth., C Scotland, UK
Clacton-on-Sea 37 H3 E England, UK
Claerwen Reservoir 39 D4 ▣ E Wales, UK
Clare 29 ◐ County, W Ireland
Clare 31 C4 〰 W Ireland
Clarecastle 31 C5 W Ireland
Claregalway 31 C4 W Ireland
Clare Island 31 A3 Island, W Ireland
Claremorris 31 C3 W Ireland
Clarence 135 C5 South Island, NZ
Clarence 135 C5 〰 South Island, NZ
Clarence Town 109 E2 Long Island, C Bahamas
Clarión, Isla 105 A5 Island, W Mexico
Clark Hill Lake 101 E5 ▣ SE USA
Clarksdale 101 C5 Mississippi, USA
Clarksville 101 D4 Tennessee, USA
Clayton 103 E4 New Mexico, USA
Clear Island 31 B7 Island, S Ireland
Clearwater 101 E7 Florida, USA
Cleethorpes 35 F4 E England, UK
Clermont 133 G3 Queensland, E Australia
Clermont-Ferrand 55 D5 C France
Clevedon 37 D4 SW England, UK
Cleveland 101 E3 Ohio, USA
Clew Bay 31 B3 Inlet, W Ireland
Clifden 31 B4 W Ireland
Clisham 33 B2 ▲ NW Scotland, UK
Clitheroe 35 C4 NW England, UK
Cloghan 31 D4 C Ireland
Cloncurry 133 F3 Queensland, C Australia
Clondalkin 31 E4 E Ireland
Clones 31 D3 N Ireland
Clonmel 31 D6 S Ireland
Cloonboo 31 C4 W Ireland
Cloppenburg 59 B3 NW Germany
Cloud Peak 103 E2 ▲ Wyoming, USA
Clovelly 37 B4 SW England, UK
Cluj-Napoca 67 B6 NW Romania
Clutha 135 B7 〰 South Island, NZ
Clwyd 39 E2 〰 N Wales, UK
Clwydian Range 39 E2 ⛰ N Wales, UK
Clydach 39 D6 S Wales, UK
Clydach Vale 39 E6 S Wales, UK
Clyde 33 D6 〰 W Scotland, UK
Clydebank 33 D5 W Scotland, UK
Clyde, Firth of 33 C6 Inlet, S Scotland, UK
Clyro 39 E5 C Wales, UK
Clywedog, Llyn 39 D4 ▣ E Wales, UK
Coari 115 D4 N Brazil
Coast Mountains 97 E5 ⛰ Canada/USA
Coatbridge 33 D6 S Scotland, UK
Coats Island 97 I4 Island, NW Terr., NE Canada
Coats Land 138 B3 Physical region, Antarctica
Coatzacoalcos 105 G5 E Mexico
Cobán 107 B3 C Guatemala
Cobar 133 G5 NSW, SE Australia
Cobija 117 A1 NW Bolivia
Coburg 59 C5 SE Germany
Cochabamba 117 B2 C Bolivia
Cochin 89 D7 SW India
Cochrane 99 C4 Ontario, S Canada
Cochrane 117 A8 S Chile
Cockburn Harbour 40 South Caicos, S Turks and Caicos Islands
Cockburn Town 109 F3 E Bahamas
Cockburn Town 40 ○ Grand Turk Island, Turks and Caicos Islands
Cockermouth 35 B3 NW England, UK
Coco, Río 107 E3 〰 Honduras/Nicaragua
Cocos Basin 15 Undersea feature, E Indian Ocean
Codfish Island 135 A8 Island, SW NZ
Cody 103 D2 Wyoming, USA
Coedpoeth 39 E2 NE Wales, UK
Coevorden 50 F3 NE Netherlands

◐ Administrative region ◆ Country ● Country capital ◇ Dependent territory ○ Dependent territory capital ⛰ Mountain range ▲ Mountain ✱ Volcano 〰 River ◎ Lake ▣ Reservoir

E

F

Foumban 124 F5 NW Cameroon
Foveaux Strait 135 A8 *Strait*, S NZ
Fowey 37 B5 ☙ SW England, UK
Fox Bay East 40 Falkland Islands
Fox Bay West 40 Falkland Islands
Foxe Basin 97 I3 *Sea*, NW Terr., N Canada
Foxford 31 C3 NW Ireland
Fox Glacier 135 B6 South Island, NZ
Fox Mine 97 H6 Manitoba, C Canada
Fox Point 40 *Headland*, Falkland Islands
Foyle 31 D2 ☙ Ireland/ Northern Ireland, UK
Foyle, Lough 31 D1 *Inlet*, N Ireland
Foynes 31 B5 SW Ireland
Fraga 57 F2 NE Spain
Fram Basin 139 C4 *Undersea feature*, Arctic Ocean
France 55 C4 ◆ *Republic*, W Europe
Franceville 128 B2 E Gabon
Franche-Comté 55 E4 *Cultural region*, E France
Francis Case, Lake 103 F2 ▣ South Dakota, USA
Francisco Escárcega 105 H5 SE Mexico
Francistown 128 D5 North East, NE Botswana
Frankfort 101 E4 Kentucky, USA
Frankfurt am Main 59 B5 SW Germany
Frankfurt an der Oder 59 E4 E Germany
Fränkische Alb 59 C6 ▲ S Germany
Franz Josef Land 76 D1 *Island group*, N Russ. Fed.
Fraserburgh 33 F3 NE Scotland, UK
Fraser Island 133 H4 *Island*, Queensland, E Australia
Fray Bentos 117 C5 W Uruguay
Fredericton 99 F5 New Brunswick, SE Canada
Fredrikstad 49 B5 S Norway
Freeport 109 D1 N Bahamas
Freetown 124 B4 ● W Sierra Leone
Freiburg im Breisgau 59 B7 SW Germany
Fremantle 133 B5 Western Australia
French Guiana 115 F2 *French* ◇ N South America
French Polynesia 131 *French* ◇ S Pacific Ocean
Fresnillo 105 E4 C Mexico
Fresno 103 B3 California, USA
Frías 115 B7 N Argentina
Friedrichshafen 59 B7 S Germany
Frohavet 49 B4 *Sound*, C Norway
Frome 37 D4 SW England, UK
Frome 37 D5 ☙ S England, UK
Frome, Lake 133 F5 *Salt lake*, S Australia
Frongoch 39 D2 NW Wales, UK
Frontera 105 H5 SE Mexico
Frontignan 55 D6 S France
Frøya 49 B4 *Island*, W Norway
Frýdek-Místek 63 D6 SE Czech Republic
Fuengirola 57 D6 S Spain
Fuerte Olimpo 117 C3 NE Paraguay
Fuji, Mount 85 F6 ▲ Honshu, SE Japan
Fukui 85 F6 SW Japan
Fukuoka 85 D7 SW Japan
Fukushima 85 G4 C Japan
Fulda 59 C5 C Germany
Funafuti Atoll 137 J3 *Atoll*, C Tuvalu
Fundy, Bay of 99 F5 *Bay*, Canada/USA
Fürth 59 C6 S Germany
Furukawa 85 G4 C Japan
Fushun 87 G2 NE China
Füssen 59 C7 S Germany
Futuna 137 H5 *Island*, S Vanuatu
Futuna, Île 137 J4 *Island*, S Wallis and Futuna
Fuxin 87 G2 NE China
Fuzhou 87 G6 SE China
Fyn 49 B7 *Island*, C Denmark
Fyne, Loch 33 C5 *Inlet*, W Scotland, UK

G

Gaalkacyo 127 F4 C Somalia
Gabela 128 B3 W Angola
Gabès 122 F2 E Tunisia
Gabès, Golfe de 122 F2 *Gulf*, E Tunisia
Gabon 128 A1 ◆ *Republic*, C Africa
Gaborone 128 D6 ● SE Botswana
Gabrovo 65 F3 C Bulgaria
Gadag 89 D6 W India
Gaeta 61 D5 C Italy
Gaeta, Gulf of 61 C5 *Gulf*, C Italy
Gafsa 122 E2 W Tunisia
Gagnoa 124 C5 C Ivory Coast
Gagra 79 F1 NW Georgia
Gaillac 55 C6 S France
Gainsborough 35 E5 E England, UK
Gairdner, Lake 133 E5 *Salt lake*, S Australia
Galán, Cerro 117 A4 ▲ NW Argentina
Galanta 63 D7 SW Slovakia
Galapagos Islands 115 A7 *Island group*, Ecuador
Galashiels 33 E6 SE Scotland, UK
Galați 67 D7 E Romania
Galicia 57 B1 *Cultural region*, NW Spain
Galle 89 E8 SW Sri Lanka
Gallipoli 61 F6 SE Italy
Gällivare 49 D2 N Sweden
Galloway, Mull of 33 C7 *Headland*, S Scotland, UK
Gallup 103 D4 New Mexico, USA
Galtat-Zemmour 122 B3 C Western Sahara
Galty Mountains 31 C6 ▲ S Ireland
Galveston 103 G5 Texas, USA

Galway 31 C4 W Ireland
Galway 29 ◇ *County*, W Ireland
Galway Bay 31 B4 *Bay*, W Ireland
Gambell 97 C2 Saint Lawrence Island, Alaska, USA
Gambia 124 A3 ◆ *Republic*, W Africa
Gambia 124 B3 ☙ W Africa
Gambier, Îles 131 *Island group*, E French Polynesia
Gamboma 128 B2 E Congo
Gäncä 79 H2 W Azerbaijan
Gandajika 128 C3 S Congo (Zaire)
Gander 99 H4 Newfoundland, Newfoundland and Labrador, SE Canada
Gandhidham 89 C4 W India
Gandía 57 F4 E Spain
Ganges 89 G3 ☙ Bangladesh/India
Ganges, Mouths of the 89 G4 *Delta*, Bangladesh/India
Gangtok 89 G3 N India
Ganzhou 87 F5 S China
Gao 124 D3 E Mali
Gaoual 124 B4 N Guinea
Gap 55 E6 SE France
Gar 87 A4 W China
Garachiné 107 I7 SE Panama
Gara, Lough 31 C3 ☒ N Ireland
Garda, Lake 61 C2 ☒ C Italy
Gardez 83 F5 E Afghanistan
Garforth 35 E4 N England, UK
Garissa 127 E5 E Kenya
Garoowe 127 F3 N Somalia
Garoua 124 G4 N Cameroon
Garron Point 31 F2 *Headland*, E Northern Ireland, UK
Garry Lake 97 H4 ☒ NW Terr., N Canada
Garsen 127 E6 S Kenya
Garth 33 A6 NE Wales, UK
Garwolin 63 F4 E Poland
Gary 101 D3 Indiana, USA
Gascogne see Gascony
Gascony 55 C6 *Cultural region*, France
Gascony, Gulf of 55 B6 *Gulf*, France/Spain
Gascoyne River 133 B4 ☙ Western Australia
Gasmata 137 C2 E PNG
Gaspé 99 F4 Québec, SE Canada
Gaspé, Péninsule de 99 F4 *Peninsula*, Québec, SE Canada
Gatchina 69 A4 NW Russ. Fed.
Gateshead 35 D2 NE England, UK
Gateshead 28 ◇ *Unitary auth.*, NE England, UK
Gatineau 99 D5 Québec, SE Canada
Gatún, Lago 107 G6 ☒ C Panama
Gavbandi 81 E4 S Iran
Gavere 50 B6 W Belgium
Gävle 49 D5 C Sweden
Gawler 133 E6 S Australia
Gaya 89 F3 N India
Gayndah 133 H4 Queensland, E Australia
Gaza 81 G6 NE Gaza Strip
Gaz-Achak 83 D2 NE Turkmenistan
Gazandzhyk 83 C3 W Turkmenistan
Gaza Strip 81 G6 *Disputed region*, SW Asia
Gaziantep 79 E4 S Turkey
Gazimağusa see Famagusta
Gazli 83 E3 C Uzbekistan
Gbanga 124 B5 N Liberia
Gdańsk 63 D2 N Poland
Gdynia 63 D1 N Poland
Gedaref 127 D2 E Sudan
Gediz 79 B3 W Turkey
Gediz Nehri 79 A3 ☙ W Turkey
Geel 50 D6 N Belgium
Geelong 133 F6 Victoria, SE Australia
Geilo 49 B5 S Norway
Gejiu 87 E6 S China
Gela 61 D8 Sicily, Italy
Geldermalsen 50 D4 C Netherlands
Geleen 50 E6 SE Netherlands
Gellinsoor 127 F4 NE Somalia
Gembloux 50 C7 S Belgium
Gemena 128 C1 NW Congo (Zaire)
Gemona del Friuli 61 D2 NE Italy
General Alvear 117 B5 W Argentina
General Eugenio A.Garay 117 B3 S Paraguay
General Santos 91 F5 S Philippines
Geneva 59 A8 SW Switzerland
Geneva, Lake 59 A8 ☒ France/Switzerland
Genève see Geneva
Genk 50 D6 NE Belgium
Gennep 50 E5 SE Netherlands
Genoa 61 B3 NW Italy
Genoa, Gulf of 61 B3 *Gulf*, NW Italy
Genova see Genoa
Gent see Ghent
Geok-Tepe 83 C3 C Turkmenistan
George Island 40 *Island*, S Falkland Islands
Georgetown 40 ◇ NW Ascension Island
George Town 109 D2 C Bahamas
George Town 40 ◇ SW Cayman Islands
Georgetown 115 E2 ● N Guyana
George Town 91 B5 Peninsular Malaysia
George V Land 138 C6 *Physical region*, Antarctica
Georgia 79 G1 ◆ *Republic*, SW Asia
Georgia 101 E5 ◇ *State*, SE USA
Georgian Bay 99 C5 *Lake bay*, Ontario, S Canada

Georg von Neumayer 138 B3 *German research station*, Antarctica
Gera 59 D5 E Germany
Geraldine 135 C6 South Island, NZ
Geraldton 133 B5 Western Australia
Gerede 79 C2 N Turkey
Gereshk 83 D5 SW Afghanistan
Gerlachovský Štít 63 E6 ▲ N Slovakia
Germany 59 B5 ◆ *Federal Republic*, N Europe
Gerpinnes 50 C7 S Belgium
Gerze 79 D2 N Turkey
Getafe 57 D3 C Spain
Gevaş 79 G4 SE Turkey
Ghana 124 D5 ◆ *Republic*, W Africa
Ghanzi 128 C5 W Botswana
Ghardaïa 122 E2 N Algeria
Gharyan 122 F2 NW Libya
Ghazni 83 F5 E Afghanistan
Ghent 50 B6 NW Belgium
Ghijduwon 83 E3 C Uzbekistan
Ghudara 83 G4 SE Tajikistan
Ghurian 83 D5 W Afghanistan
Giannitsá 65 E4 N Greece
Gibbs Hill 40 *Hill*, S Bermuda
Gibraltar 40 *UK* ◇ SW Europe
Gibraltar, Bay of 40 *Bay*, W Gibraltar
Gibraltar Harbour 40 *Harbour*, W Gibraltar
Gibraltar, Strait of 40 *Strait*, Atlantic Ocean/Mediterranean Sea
Gibson Desert 133 C4 *Desert*, Western Australia
Giedraičiai 49 F7 E Lithuania
Giessen 59 B5 W Germany
Giffnock 33 D6 C Scotland, UK
Gifu 85 F6 SW Japan
Gigiga Island 33 B6 *Island*, SW Scotland, UK
Gijón 57 C1 NW Spain
Gilf Kebir Plateau 122 H4 *Plateau*, SW Egypt
Gilford 31 E3 SE Northern Ireland, UK
Gillette 103 E2 Wyoming, USA
Gillingham 37 G4 SE England, UK
Gill Point 40 *Headland*, E Saint Helena
Giluwe, Mount 137 B2 ▲ W PNG
Gilwern 39 E6 SE Wales, UK
Ginger Island 40 *Island*, SE British Virgin Islands
Gingin 133 B5 Western Australia
Giresun 79 E2 NE Turkey
Girne see Kyrenia
Girona 57 H2 NE Spain
Girvan 33 D6 W Scotland, UK
Gisborne 135 E3 North Island, NZ
Gissar Range 83 F3 ▲ Tajikistan/Uzbekistan
Giulianova 61 D4 C Italy
Giurgiu 67 C7 S Romania
Gizo 137 E2 NW Solomon Islands
Gjirokastër 65 D5 ☙ S Albania
Gjoa Haven 97 H3 King William Island, NW Terr., NW Canada
Gjøvik 49 B5 S Norway
Glace Bay 99 G5 Cape Breton Island, Nova Scotia, SE Canada
Gladstone 133 H4 Queensland, E Australia
Gláma 49 B5 ☙ SE Norway
Glasgow 33 D6 S Scotland, UK
Glasgow 28 ◇ *Unitary auth.*, C Scotland, UK
Glaslyn 39 C2 ☙ NW Wales, UK
Glastonbury 37 D4 SW England, UK
Glazov 69 D5 NW Russ. Fed.
Glenamoy 31 B3 NW Ireland
Glen Coe 33 C4 *Valley*, N Scotland, UK
Glengad Head 31 D1 *Headland*, N Ireland
Glengarriff 31 B7 S Ireland
Glenluce 33 C7 SW Scotland, UK
Glen Mor 33 D4 *Valley*, NW Scotland, UK
Glenrothes 33 E5 E Scotland, UK
Glenties 31 C2 NW Ireland
Glin 31 B5 SW Ireland
Glittertind 49 B4 ▲ S Norway
Gliwice 63 D5 S Poland
Głogów 63 C4 W Poland
Glossop 35 D4 C England, UK
Gloucester 137 C2 E PNG
Gloucester 37 D3 C England, UK
Gloucestershire 29 ◇ *County*, C England, UK
Glovers Reef 107 C2 *Reef*, E Belize
Glyn-Neath 39 D6 S Wales, UK
Gniezno 63 D3 C Poland
Gobabis 128 C5 N Namibia
Gobi 87 E3 *Desert*, China/Mongolia
Gobo 85 E7 SW Japan
Godalming 37 F4 SE England, UK
Godavari 89 E5 ☙ C India
Godhra 89 D4 W India
Godoy Cruz 117 A5 W Argentina
Goeree 50 B5 SW Netherlands
Goes 50 B5 SW Netherlands
Goginan 39 D4 W Wales, UK
Goiânia 115 G6 C Brazil
Goiás 15 F5 ◇ *State*, C Brazil
Gojome 85 F3 NW Japan
Göksun 79 E4 C Turkey
Gol 49 B5 S Norway
Golan Heights 81 H5 ▲ SW Syria
Gołdap 63 F2 NE Poland
Gold Coast 133 H5 *Cultural region*, Queensland, E Australia
Golden Bay 135 C4 *Bay*, South Island, NZ
Goleniów 63 B2 NW Poland

Golmud 87 D3 C China
Goma 128 D2 NE Congo (Zaire)
Gombi 124 G4 E Nigeria
Gómez Palacio 105 C3 C Mexico
Gonaïves 109 F4 N Haiti
Gonder 127 D3 NW Ethiopia
Gondia 89 E4 C India
Gongola 124 F4 E Nigeria
Good Hope, Cape of 128 B7 *Headland*, SW South Africa
Goodwick 39 A5 SW Wales, UK
Goole 35 E4 E England, UK
Goondiwindi 133 G5 Queensland, E Australia
Goor 50 F4 E Netherlands
Goose Green 40 East Falkland, Falkland Islands
Göppingen 59 B6 SW Germany
Gorakhpur 89 F3 N India
Goré 124 G5 S Chad
Gore 127 D4 W Ethiopia
Gore 135 B8 South Island, NZ
Gorey 37 I5 E Ireland
Gorey 37 H6 Jersey, Channel Islands
Gorgan 81 E1 N Iran
Gori 79 H1 C Georgia
Gorinchem 50 D5 C Netherlands
Goris 79 I3 SE Armenia
Görlitz 59 E4 E Germany
Goroka 137 B2 C PNG
Gorontalo 91 F6 Celebes, C Indonesia
Gorseinon 39 C6 S Wales, UK
Gorssel 50 E4 E Netherlands
Gort 31 C5 W Ireland
Gorzów Wielkopolski 63 C3 W Poland
Goshogawara 85 F3 C Japan
Gosport 37 E5 S England, UK
Göteborg see Gothenburg
Gotha 59 C5 C Germany
Gothenburg 49 B6 S Sweden
Gotland 49 D6 *Island*, SE Sweden
Goto-retto 85 C8 *Island group*, SW Japan
Gotsu 85 E6 SW Japan
Göttingen 59 C4 C Germany
Gouda 50 C4 C Netherlands
Gouin, Réservoir 99 D4 ☒ Québec, SE Canada
Goulburn 133 G6 NSW, SE Australia
Goundam 124 D3 NW Mali
Gouré 124 F3 SE Niger
Governador Valadares 115 H7 SE Brazil
Govi Altayn Nuruu 87 E2 ▲ S Mongolia
Gower 39 C7 *Peninsula*, S Wales, UK
Gowran 31 D5 SE Ireland
Goya 111 N4 C Argentina
Goz Beïda 124 H4 SE Chad
Gozo 70 A6 *Island*, N Malta
Gradačac 65 C2 N Bosnia and Herzegovina
Gradas, Serra dos 115 F5 ▲ C Brazil
Grafton 133 H5 NSW, SE Australia
Graham Land 138 A4 *Physical region*, Antarctica
Grajewo 63 F2 NE Poland
Grampian Mountains 33 D4 ▲ C Scotland, UK
Granada 107 D5 SW Nicaragua
Granada 57 D5 S Spain
Gran Chaco 117 B3 *Lowland plain*, South America
Grand Bahama Island 109 C1 *Island*, N Bahamas
Grand Caicos 40 *Island*, C Turks and Caicos Islands
Grand Canal 31 C4 *Canal*, C Ireland
Grand Canyon 103 C4 *Canyon*, Arizona, USA
Grand Cayman 40 *Island*, SW Cayman Islands
Grande, Bahía 117 B8 *Bay*, S Argentina
Grande Comore 128 G4 *Island*, NW Comoros
Grande de Matagalpa, Río 107 E4 ☙ C Nicaragua
Grande Prairie 97 F6 Alberta, W Canada
Grand Erg Occidental 122 D2 *Desert*, W Algeria
Grand Erg Oriental 122 E3 *Desert*, Algeria/Tunisia
Grande, Rio 101 F5 ☙ Mexico/USA
Grande Terre 109 K5 *Island*, E West Indies
Grand Falls 99 H4 Newfoundland, Newfoundland and Labrador, SE Canada
Grand Forks 103 F1 North Dakota, USA
Grand Rapids 101 D3 Michigan, USA
Grand Turk Island 40 *Island*, SE Turks and Caicos Islands
Grand Union Canal 37 E2 *Canal*, SE England, UK
Grange 31 C2 N Ireland
Grangemouth 33 D5 C Scotland, UK
Gran Paradiso 61 A2 ▲ NW Italy
Grantham 35 E6 E England, UK
Grantown-on-Spey 33 E3 N Scotland, UK
Granville 55 B3 N France
Graulhet 55 C6 S France
Grave 50 E5 SE Netherlands
Gravesend 37 G4 SE England, UK
Grayling 97 C3 Alaska, USA
Graz 59 E7 SE Austria
Great Abaco 109 D1 *Island*, N Bahamas
Great Artesian Basin 133 F4 *Lowlands*, Queensland, C Australia
Great Australian Bight 133 D5 *Bight*, S Australia
Great Barrier Island 135 D2 *Island*, N NZ

Great Barrier Reef 133 G2 *Reef*, Queensland, NE Australia
Great Basin 103 C3 *Basin*, W USA
Great Bear Lake 97 F4 ☒ NW Terr., NW Canada
Great Belt 49 B7 *Sea waterway*, Denmark
Great Camanoe 40 *Island*, N British Virgin Islands
Great Chagos Bank 40 *Undersea feature*, C Indian Ocean
Great Dividing Range 130 ▲ NE Australia
Greater Antarctica 138 D4 *Physical region*, Antarctica
Greater Antilles 109 E5 *Island group*, West Indies
Great Exhibition Bay 135 C1 *Inlet*, North Island, NZ
Great Exuma Island 109 D2 *Island*, C Bahamas
Great Falls 103 D1 Montana, USA
Great Harbour 40 W British Virgin Islands
Great Hungarian Plain 63 D8 *Plain*, SE Europe
Great Inagua 109 F3 *Island*, S Bahamas
Great Karoo 128 C7 *Plateau region*, S South Africa
Great Khingan Range 87 G1 ▲ NE China
Great Lakes 101 E2 *Lakes*, Canada/USA
Great Malvern 35 D7 W England, UK
Great Man-made River Project 122 F3 ☙ Libya
Great Nicobar 89 H6 *Island*, Nicobar Islands, India
Great Ormes Head 39 D1 *Headland*, N Wales, UK
Great Ouse 35 F6 ☙ E England, UK
Great Rift Valley 117 *Depression*, Asia/Africa
Great Ruaha 127 D7 ☙ S Tanzania
Great Saint Bernard Pass 61 A1 *Pass*, Italy/Switzerland
Great Salt Lake 103 C3 *Salt lake*, Utah, USA
Great Salt Lake Desert 103 C3 *Plain*, Utah, USA
Great Sand Sea 122 H3 *Desert*, Egypt/Libya
Great Sandy Desert 133 C3 *Desert*, Western Australia
Great Slave Lake 97 G5 ☒ NW Terr., NW Canada
Great Tobago 40 *Island*, W British Virgin Islands
Great Torrington 37 B4 SW England, UK
Great Victoria Desert 133 C4 *Desert*, S Australia/Western Australia
Great Wall of China 87 E3 *Ancient monument*, N China
Great Yarmouth 37 H2 E England, UK
Gredos, Sierra de 57 C3 ▲ W Spain
Greece 65 D5 ◆ *Republic*, SE Europe
Greeley 103 E3 Colorado, USA
Green Bay 101 D2 Wisconsin, USA
Green Bay 101 D2 *Lake bay*, N USA
Greencastle 31 E3 S Northern Ireland, UK
Green Islands 137 D2 *Island group*, NE PNG
Greenland 92 *Danish* ◇ NE North America
Greenland Sea 139 C2 *Sea*, Arctic Ocean
Green Mountains 101 G2 ▲ Vermont, USA
Greenock 33 D5 W Scotland, UK
Green River 137 A1 NW PNG
Green River 103 D2 Wyoming, USA
Green River 103 D3 ☙ W USA
Greensboro 101 F4 North Carolina, USA
Greenville 101 E5 South Carolina, USA
Greenwich 29 ◇ *London borough*, SE England, UK
Gregory Range 133 G3 ▲ Queensland, E Australia
Greifswald 59 D2 NE Germany
Grenada 100 J6 ◆ *Commonwealth republic*, SE West Indies
Grenadines, The 109 K6 *Island group*, Grenada/St Vincent and the Grenadines
Grenoble 55 E5 E France
Gretna 33 E7 SW Scotland, UK
Grevenmacher 50 E8 E Luxembourg
Greymouth 135 B6 South Island, NZ
Grey Range 133 F4 ▲ NSW/Queensland, E Australia
Greystones 31 E4 E Ireland
Grimari 124 H5 C CAR
Grimsby 35 F4 E England, UK
Groesbeek 50 E5 SE Netherlands
Grójec 63 F4 C Poland
Groningen 50 F2 NE Netherlands
Groote Eylandt 133 E2 *Island*, Northern Territory, N Australia
Grootfontein 128 C5 N Namibia
Groot Karasberge 128 C6 ▲ S Namibia
Grosseto 61 C4 C Italy
Grossglockner 59 D8 ▲ W Austria
Groznyy 69 B9 SW Russ. Fed.
Grudziądz 63 D2 N Poland
Grums 49 C5 C Sweden
Gryazi 69 B6 W Russ. Fed.
Gryfice 63 C2 NW Poland
Guabito 107 F6 NW Panama
Guadalajara 105 D5 C Mexico
Guadalajara 57 D3 C Spain
Guadalcanal 137 E3 *Island*, C Solomon Islands

Guadalquivir 57 C5 ☙ W Spain
Guadalupe 105 D4 C Mexico
Guadalupe Peak 103 E5 ▲ Texas, USA
Guadarrama, Sierra de 57 E3 ▲ C Spain
Guadeloupe 109 K5 *French* ◇ E West Indies
Guadiana 57 B4 ☙ Portugal/Spain
Guadix 57 D5 S Spain
Guaimaca 107 D3 C Honduras
Gualaco 107 D3 C Honduras
Gualán 107 B3 C Guatemala
Gualeguaychú 117 C5 E Argentina
Guamúchil 105 C3 C Mexico
Guanabacoa 109 B2 W Cuba
Guana Island 40 *Island*, N British Virgin Islands
Guanajuato 105 E4 C Mexico
Guanare 115 C2 N Venezuela
Guangyuan 87 E4 C China
Guangzhou 87 F6 S China
Guantánamo 109 E4 SE Cuba
Guaporé, Rio 115 D5 ☙ Bolivia/Brazil
Guarda 57 B3 N Portugal
Gurumal 107 G7 S Panama
Guasave 105 C3 C Mexico
Guasopa 137 D3 SE PNG
Guatemala 107 A3 ◆ *Republic*, Central America
Guatemala Basin 14 *Undersea feature*, E Pacific Ocean
Guatemala City 107 B3 ● C Guatemala
Guaviare, Río 115 C2 ☙ E Colombia
Guayaquil 115 A4 SW Ecuador
Guayaquil, Golfo de 115 A4 *Gulf*, SW Ecuador
Guaymas 105 B3 NW Mexico
Gubadag 83 D2 N Turkmenistan
Guben 59 E4 E Germany
Gubkin 69 A6 W Russ. Fed.
Gudaut'a 79 F1 NW Georgia
Guéret 55 D4 C France
Guernsey 37 G6 *UK* ◇ NW Europe
Guerrero Negro 105 A3 NW Mexico
Guiana Basin 14 *Undersea feature*, W Atlantic Ocean
Guiana Highlands 115 E3 ▲ N South America
Guider 124 G4 N Cameroon
Guidimouni 124 F3 S Niger
Guildford 37 F4 SE England, UK
Guilin 87 F5 S China
Guimarães 57 B2 N Portugal
Guinea 124 B4 ◆ *Republic*, W Africa
Guinea-Bissau 124 A4 ◆ *Republic*, W Africa
Guinea, Gulf of 124 E6 *Gulf*, E Atlantic Ocean
Guiyang 87 E5 S China
Gujarat 89 C4 *Cultural region*, W India
Gujranwala 89 D2 NE Pakistan
Gujrat 89 D2 E Pakistan
Gulbarga 89 D5 C India
Gulfport 101 C6 Mississippi, USA
Gulf, The 81 D3 *Gulf*, SW Asia
Guliston 83 F2 E Uzbekistan
Gulkana 97 D4 Alaska, USA
Gulu 127 C5 N Uganda
Gümüşhane 79 F2 NE Turkey
Güney Doğu Toroslar 79 F4 ▲ SE Turkey
Gunnbjørn Fjeld 139 A6 ▲ C Greenland
Gunnedah 133 G5 NSW, SE Australia
Gurbantünggüt Shamo 87 C2 *Desert*, NW China
Gurktaler Alpen 59 E8 ▲ S Austria
Gürün 79 E3 C Turkey
Gusau 124 F4 N Nigeria
Gusev 49 E7 W Russ. Fed.
Gushgy 83 D4 S Turkmenistan
Gustavus 97 E5 Alaska, USA
Güstrow 59 D2 NE Germany
Gütersloh 59 B4 W Germany
Guwahati 89 G3 NE India
Guyana 115 F2 ◆ *Republic*, N South America
Güzelyurt see Morfou
Gwadar 89 A3 SW Pakistan
Gwalchmai 39 C1 NW Wales, UK
Gwalior 89 E3 C India
Gwanda 128 D5 SW Zimbabwe
Gweedore 31 C1 NW Ireland
Gwynedd 29 ◇ *Unitary auth.*, NW Wales, UK
Gwytherin 39 D2 N Wales, UK
Gyangzê 87 C5 W China
Gyaring Co 87 C4 ☒ W China
Gympie 133 H4 Queensland, E Australia
Gyomaendrőd 63 F8 SE Hungary
Gyöngyös 63 F7 NE Hungary
Győr 63 D7 NW Hungary
Gyumri 79 G2 W Armenia
Gyzylarbat 83 C4 W Turkmenistan

H

Haacht 50 C6 C Belgium
Haaksbergen 50 F4 E Netherlands
Haarlem 50 C3 W Netherlands
Haast 135 B6 South Island, NZ
Hachijo-jima 85 G7 *Island*, Izu-shoto, SE Japan
Hachinohe 85 G3 C Japan
Hackney 29 ◇ *London borough*, SE England, UK
Haddington 33 E5 SE Scotland, UK
Hadejia 124 F4 N Nigeria
Hadejia 124 F4 ☙ N Nigeria

◆ Administrative region ◆ Country ● Country capital ◊ Dependent territory ○ Dependent territory capital ▲ Mountain range ▲ Mountain ℞ Volcano ≈ River ◎ Lake ◙ Reservoir

L

◆ Administrative region   ◆ Country   ● Country capital   ◊ Dependent territory   ○ Dependent territory capital   ▲ Mountain range   ▲ Mountain   ⛰ Volcano   ☞ River   ○ Lake   ▣ Reservoir

Little Nicobar 89 H6 *Island,*
  Nicobar Islands, India
Little Ouse 37 G2 ⬥ E England, UK
Little Rock 103 G4 Arkansas, USA
Little Saint Bernard Pass 55 F5 *Pass,*
  France/Italy
Little Sandy Desert 133 B4 *Desert,*
  Western Australia
Liuzhou 87 F5 S China
Lively Island 40 *Island,*
  SE Falkland Islands
Liverpool 99 F5 Nova Scotia, SE Canada
Liverpool 35 C5 NW England, UK
Liverpool 28 ◈ *Unitary auth.,*
  NW England, UK
Liverpool Bay 39 E1 *Bay,*
  England/Wales, UK
Livingston 33 E5 West Lothian,
  C Scotland, UK
Livingstone 128 D4 S Zambia
Livingstone Mountains 135 A7
  ▲ South Island, NZ
Livojoki 49 E3 ⬥ C Finland
Livonia 101 E3 Michigan, USA
Livorno 61 B3 C Italy
Lizard Point 37 A6 *Headland,*
  SW England, UK
Ljubljana 59 E8 ● C Slovenia
Ljungby 49 C6 S Sweden
Ljusdal 49 C4 C Sweden
Ljusnan 49 C4 ⬥ C Sweden
Llanaber 39 C5 NW Wales, UK
Llanaelhaearn 39 C2 NW Wales, UK
Llanarth 39 C5 W Wales, UK
Llanbedr 39 C3 NW Wales, UK
Llanbedrog 39 C3 NW Wales, UK
Llanberis 39 C2 NW Wales, UK
Llanbister 39 E4 C Wales, UK
Llanbrynmair 39 D3 C Wales, UK
Llandeilo 39 D6 S Wales, UK
Llandovery 39 D5 S Wales, UK
Llandrindod Wells 39 E5 E Wales, UK
Llandudno 39 D1 N Wales, UK
Llandybie 39 C6 S Wales, UK
Llandysul 39 C5 S Wales, UK
Llanelli 39 C6 S Wales, UK
Llanerchymedd 39 C1 NW Wales, UK
Llanes 57 D1 N Spain
Llanfachraeth 39 B1 NW Wales, UK
Llanfaelog 39 C2 NW Wales, UK
Llanfair Caereinion 39 E3 C Wales, UK
Llanfair Talhaiarn 39 D2 N Wales, UK
Llanfihangel-nant-Melan 39 E5
  C Wales, UK
Llanfyllin 39 E3 C Wales, UK
Llangadfan 39 E3 C Wales, UK
Llangadog 39 D6 S Wales, UK
Llangefni 39 C1 NW Wales, UK
Llangoed 39 C1 NW Wales, UK
Llangollen 39 E2 NE Wales, UK
Llangurig 39 D4 C Wales, UK
Llanharan 39 E7 S Wales, UK
Llanidloes 39 D4 C Wales, UK
Llanilar 39 D4 W Wales, UK
Llanllyfni 39 C2 NW Wales, UK
Llanon 39 C4 W Wales, UK
Llanos 115 C2 *Physical region,*
  Colombia/Venezuela
Llanrhaeadr-ym-Mochnant 39 E3
  C Wales, UK
Llanrhidian 39 C6 S Wales, UK
Llanrhystud 39 C4 W Wales, UK
Llanrwst 39 D2 N Wales, UK
Llansteffan 39 C6 S Wales, UK
Llantrisant 39 E7 S Wales, UK
Llantwit Major 39 E7 S Wales, UK
Llanuwchllyn 39 D3 NW Wales, UK
Llanwrda 39 D5 S Wales, UK
Llanwrtyd Wells 39 D5 C Wales, UK
Llanybydder 39 C5 S Wales, UK
Lleida 57 F2 NE Spain
Lleyn Peninsula 39 C2 *Peninsula,*
  NW Wales, UK
Llucmajor 57 H4 Majorca, Spain
Llwyngwril 39 C3 NW Wales, UK
Llyn Brianne Reservoir 39 C5 ◎
  E Wales, UK
Llyswen 39 E5 C Wales, UK
Lobatse 128 D6 SE Botswana
Löbau 59 E4 E Germany
Lobito 128 B4 W Angola
Locarno 59 B8 S Switzerland
Lochboisdale 33 A4 NW Scotland, UK
Lochdon 33 C5 W Scotland, UK
Lochem 50 E4 E Netherlands
Lochgilphead 33 C5 W Scotland, UK
Lochinver 33 C2 N Scotland, UK
Lochmaddy 33 B3 NW Scotland, UK
Lochnagar 33 E4 ▲ C Scotland, UK
Lochy, Loch 33 C4 ◎ N Scotland, UK
Lockerbie 33 E7 S Scotland, UK
Lodja 128 C2 C Congo (Zaire)
Lodwar 127 D5 NW Kenya
Łódz 63 E4 C Poland
Lofoten 49 C2 *Island group,* C Norway
Logan, Mount 97 E5 ▲ Yukon Territory,
  W Canada
Logroño 57 E2 N Spain
Loibl Pass 59 E8 *Pass,* Austria/Slovenia
Loire 55 C3 ⬥ W France
Loja 115 B4 S Ecuador
Lokitaung 127 D4 NW Kenya
Lokoja 124 E5 S Nigeria
Lolland 49 B7 *Island,* S Denmark
Lom 65 E2 NW Bulgaria
Lomami 128 D2 ⬥ C Congo (Zaire)
Lomas de Zamora 117 C5 E Argentina
Lombardia *see* Lombardy
Lombardy 61 C2 *Cultural region,* N Italy
Lombok, Pulau 91 E8 *Island,*
  Nusa Tenggara, C Indonesia
Lomé 124 D5 ● S Togo

Lomela 128 C2 C Congo (Zaire)
Lommel 50 D6 N Belgium
Lomond, Loch 33 D5 ◎ C Scotland, UK
Lomonosov Ridge 139 C4 *Undersea*
  feature, Arctic Ocean
Łomza 63 F2 NE Poland
Loncoche 117 A6 C Chile
London 99 E5 Ontario, S Canada
London 37 G4 ● SE England, UK
London, City of 29 ◆ *London borough,* SE
  England, UK
Londonderry 31 D2
  NW Northern Ireland, UK
Londonderry 29 ◆ *District,* NW
  Northern Ireland, UK
Londonderry, Cape 133 C1 *Headland,*
  Western Australia
Londrina 115 F7 S Brazil
Long Bay 101 F5 *Bay,* E USA
Long Beach 103 B4 California, USA
Longbluff 40 *Headland,*
  SW Tristan da Cunha
Long Eaton 35 E6 C England, UK
Longford 31 D4 C Ireland
Longford 29 ◆ *County,* C Ireland
Long Island 109 E2 *Island,* C Bahamas
Long Island 101 G3 *Island,*
  New York, USA
Long Island Sound 101 G3 *Sound,*
  NE USA
Longlac 99 B4 Ontario, S Canada
Longreach 133 G3 Queensland,
  E Australia
Long Strait 76 H1 *Strait,* NE Russ. Fed.
Long Swamp 40 ◆ British Virgin Islands
Longview 103 B1 Washington, USA
Longwood 40 C Saint Helena
Longyan 87 G5 SE China
Longyearbyen 139 C5 ◎ Spitsbergen,
  W Svalbard
Lons-le-Saunier 55 E4 E France
Loop Head 31 A5 *Headland,* W Ireland
Lop Nur 87 C3 *Seasonal lake,* NW China
Loppersum 50 F2 NE Netherlands
Lorca 57 E5 S Spain
Lorengau 137 B1 Manus Island, N PNG
Loreto 105 B3 W Mexico
Lorient 55 B3 NW France
Lorn, Firth of 33 B5 *Inlet,*
  W Scotland, UK
Lörrach 59 B7 S Germany
Lorraine 55 F2 *Cultural region,*
  NE France
Los Amates 107 B3 E Guatemala
Los Ángeles 117 A6 C Chile
Los Angeles 103 B4 California, USA
Lošinj 65 A2 *Island,* W Croatia
Los Mochis 105 C3 C Mexico
Los Roques, Islas 109 H7 *Island group,*
  N Venezuela
Lossiemouth 33 E3 NE Scotland, UK
Los Testigos 109 J7 *Island,* NE Venezuela
Lot 55 C5 *Cultural region,* C France
Lot 55 C6 ⬥ S France
Lotagipi Swamp 127 D4 *Wetland,*
  Kenya/Sudan
Louangphabang 91 B3 N Laos
Loudéac 55 B2 NW France
Loudi 87 F5 S China
Louga 124 A3 NW Senegal
Loughborough 35 E6 C England, UK
Loughrea 31 C4 W Ireland
Louisburgh 31 B3 NW Ireland
Louisiade Archipelago 137 D3
  Island group, SE PNG
Louisiana 103 G4 ◆ *State,* S USA
Louisville 101 D4 Kentucky, USA
Louisville Ridge 14 *Undersea ridge,*
  SW Pacific Ocean
Lourdes 55 C5 S France
Louth 31 E3 NE Ireland
Louth 35 F5 E England, UK
Louth 29 ◆ *County,* NE Ireland
Loutrá 65 E4 N Greece
Louvain-la Neuve 50 C7 C Belgium
Louviers 55 D2 N France
Lovosice 63 B5 NW Czech Republic
Lóvua 128 C3 NE Angola
Lower California 105 B3 *Peninsula,*
  NW Mexico
Lower Hutt 135 D5 North Island, NZ
Lower Lough Erne 31 D2 ◎
  SW Northern Ireland, UK
Lower Red Lake 103 G1 ◎
  Minnesota, USA
Lower Tunguska 76 E4 ⬥ N Russ. Fed.
Lowestoft 37 H2 E England, UK
Loyauté, Îles 137 G6 *Island group,*
  S New Caledonia
Lualaba 128 D2 ⬥ SE Congo (Zaire)
Luanda 128 B3 ● NW Angola
Luangwa 128 E4 ⬥
  Mozambique/Zambia
Luanshya 128 D4 C Zambia
Luarca 57 C1 N Spain
Lubaczów 63 G5 SE Poland
Lubań 63 B4 SW Poland
Lubango 128 B4 SW Angola
Lubao 128 D2 C Congo (Zaire)
Lübben 59 E4 E Germany
Lübbenau 59 E4 E Germany
Lubbock 103 F4 Texas, USA
Lübeck 59 C2 N Germany
Lubelska, Wyżyna 63 F4 *Plateau,*
  SE Poland
Lubin 63 C4 W Poland
Lublin 63 F4 E Poland
Lubliniec 63 D5 S Poland
Lubny 67 E4 NE Ukraine
Lubsko 63 B4 W Poland
Lubumbashi 128 D3 SE Congo (Zaire)
Lucan 31 E4 E Ireland

Lucano, Appennino 61 E6 ▲ S Italy
Lucapa 128 C3 NE Angola
Lucca 61 C3 C Italy
Luce Bay 33 C7 *Inlet,* SW Scotland, UK
Lucena 91 F3 Luzon, N Philippines
Lucena 57 D5 S Spain
Lučenec 63 E7 S Slovakia
Lucknow 89 E3 N India
Luda Kamchiya 65 F3 ⬥ E Bulgaria
Lüderitz 128 B6 SW Namibia
Ludhiana 89 D2 N India
Ludlow 35 C6 W England, UK
Ludvika 49 C5 C Sweden
Ludwigsburg 59 B6 SW Germany
Lüdwigsfelde 59 D4 NE Germany
Ludwigshafen 59 B6 W Germany
Ludwigslust 59 D3 N Germany
Ludza 49 F6 E Latvia
Luena 128 C3 E Angola
Lufira 128 D3 ⬥ SE Congo (Zaire)
Luga 69 A4 NW Russ. Fed.
Lugano 59 B8 S Switzerland
Luganville 137 G4 C Vanuatu
Lugenda, Rio 128 F4 ⬥ N Mozambique
Lugnaquillia Mountain 31 E5 ▲
  E Ireland
Lugo 57 B1 NW Spain
Lugoj 67 A6 W Romania
Luhans'k 67 G5 E Ukraine
Lukenie 128 C2 ⬥ C Congo (Zaire)
Łuków 63 F4 E Poland
Lukuga 128 D3 ⬥ SE Congo (Zaire)
Luleå 49 D3 N Sweden
Luleälven 49 D3 ⬥ N Sweden
Lulimba 128 D2 E Congo (Zaire)
Lulonga 128 C1 ⬥ NW Congo (Zaire)
Lumbo 128 F4 NE Mozambique
Lumi 137 A1 NW PNG
Lumsden 135 B7 South Island, NZ
Lund 49 C7 S Sweden
Lundy 37 B4 *Island,* SW England, UK
Lüneburg 59 C3 N Germany
Lungué-Bungo 128 C4 ⬥
  Angola/Zambia
Luninyets 67 C3 SW Belorussia
Lunteren 50 D4 C Netherlands
Luoyang 87 F4 C China
Lurgan 31 E2 S Northern Ireland, UK
Lúrio 128 F4 NE Mozambique
Lúrio, Rio 128 F4 ⬥ NE Mozambique
Lusaka 128 D4 ● SE Zambia
Lut, Dasht-e 81 E2 *Desert,* E Iran
Luti 137 E2 NW Solomon Islands
Luton 37 F3 E England, UK
Luton 29 ◆ *Unitary auth.,* C England, UK
Lutselk'e 97 G5 NW Terr., W Canada
Luts'k 67 C4 NW Ukraine
Lützow-Holm Bay 138 D3 *Bay,*
  Antarctica
Luuq 127 E4 SW Somalia
Luwego 127 D7 ⬥ S Tanzania
Luxembourg 50 E8 ● S Luxembourg
Luxembourg 50 E8 ◆ *Monarchy,*
  NW Europe
Luxor 122 J3 E Egypt
Luza 69 C4 NW Russ. Fed.
Luzern 59 B8 C Switzerland
Luzon 91 F3 *Island,* N Philippines
Luzon Strait 91 F3 *Strait,*
  Philippines/Taiwan
L'viv 67 B4 W Ukraine
Lycksele 49 D3 N Sweden
Lyepyel' 67 D2 N Belorussia
Lyme Bay 37 C5 *Bay,* S England, UK
Lyme Regis 37 D5 S England, UK
Lymington 37 E5 S England, UK
Lynton 37 C4 SW England, UK
Lyon 55 E5 E France
Lysychans'k 67 G4 E Ukraine
Lytham St Anne's 35 C4
  NW England, UK
Lyttelton 135 C6 South Island, NZ

M

Maamturk Mountains 31 B4 ▲
  W Ireland
Maaseik 50 E6 NE Belgium
Maastricht 50 E6 SE Netherlands
Mablethorpe 35 F5 E England, UK
Macao 87 G6 *Portuguese* ◇ E Asia
Macapá 115 F3 N Brazil
Macbride Head 40 *Headland,*
  Falkland Islands
Macclesfield 35 D5 C England, UK
Macdonnell Ranges 133 D3 ▲
  Northern Territory, C Australia
Macduff 33 F3 NE Scotland, UK
Macedonia 65 D4 ◆ *Republic,*
  SE Europe
Maceió 115 I5 E Brazil
Macgillycuddy's Reeks 31 B6 ▲
  SW Ireland
Machala 115 A4 SW Ecuador
Machanga 128 E5 E Mozambique
Machilipatnam 89 E5 E India
Machynlleth 39 D3 C Wales, UK
Mackay 133 G3 Queensland,
  NE Australia
Mackay, Lake 133 D3 *Salt lake,*
  Northern Territory/Western Australia
Mackenzie 97 F4 ⬥ NW Terr.,
  NW Canada
Mackenzie Bay 138 E4 *Bay,* Antarctica
Mackenzie Mountains 97 E4 ▲
  NW Terr., NW Canada
Macleod, Lake 133 A4 ◎
  Western Australia
Macomer 61 A6 Sardinia, Italy
Macon 101 E4 Georgia, USA
Mâcon 55 E4 C France

Macroom 31 B6 SW Ireland
Macuspana 105 H5 SE Mexico
Ma'daba 81 A2 NW Jordan
Madagascar 128 G5 ◆ *Republic,*
  W Indian Ocean
Madang 137 B2 N PNG
Made 50 C5 S Netherlands
Madeira, Rio 115 E4 ⬥ Bolivia/Brazil
Madeleine, Îles de la 99 F4 *Island group,*
  Québec, E Canada
Madhya Pradesh 89 E4 *Cultural region,*
  C India
Madison 101 D2 Wisconsin, USA
Madiun 91 D8 Java, C Indonesia
Madras 89 E6 S India
Madre de Dios, Río 117 A1 ⬥
  Bolivia/Peru
Madre del Sur, Sierra 105 F5 ▲
  S Mexico
Madre, Laguna 105 F3 *Lagoon,*
  NE Mexico
Madre Occidental, Sierra *see* Western
  Sierra Madre
Madre Oriental, Sierra
  see Eastern Sierra Madre
Madrid 57 D3 ● C Spain
Madrid 57 D3 *Cultural region,* C Spain
Madurai 89 D7 S India
Madura, Pulau 91 E8 *Island,* C Indonesia
Maebashi 85 G5 S Japan
Mae Nam Nan 91 B3 ⬥ NW Thailand
Maentwrog 39 D2 NW Wales, UK
Maesteg 39 D6 S Wales, UK
Maewo 137 G4 *Island,* C Vanuatu
Mafia 127 E7 *Island,* E Tanzania
Magadan 76 H3 E Russ. Fed.
Magarida 137 C3 SW PNG
Magdalena 105 B2 NW Mexico
Magdalena 117 B1 N Bolivia
Magdalena, Isla 105 B4 *Island,*
  W Mexico
Magdalena, Río 115 B3 ⬥ C Colombia
Magdeburg 59 D4 C Germany
Magee, Island 31 F2 *Island,*
  E Northern Ireland, UK
Magelang 91 C8 Java, C Indonesia
Magellan, Strait of 117 B9 *Strait,*
  Argentina/Chile
Magerøya 49 D1 *Island,* N Norway
Maggiore, Lake 61 B1 ◎
  Italy/Switzerland
Maghera 31 E2 C Northern Ireland, UK
Magherafelt 29 *District,*
  C Northern Ireland, UK
Maglie 61 F6 SE Italy
Magnitogorsk 76 C4 C Russ. Fed.
Magta' Lahjar 124 B3 SW Mauritania
Mahajanga 128 G4 NW Madagascar
Mahakam, Sungai 91 E6 ⬥
  C Indonesia
Mahalapye 128 D5 SE Botswana
Mahanadi 89 F4 ⬥ E India
Maharashtra 89 D5 *Cultural region,*
  W India
Mahbubnagar 89 D5 C India
Mahia Peninsula 135 E4 *Peninsula,*
  North Island, NZ
Mahilyow 67 D2 E Belorussia
Mahmud-e Raqi 83 F3 NE Afghanistan
Mahón 57 H3 Minorca, Spain
Maidenhead 37 F3 S England, UK
Maidens, The 31 F2 *Island group,*
  E Northern Ireland, UK
Maidstone 37 G4 SE England, UK
Maiduguri 124 G4 NE Nigeria
Main 59 C5 ⬥ C Germany
Mai-Ndombe, Lac 128 C2 ◎
  W Congo (Zaire)
Maine 101 H2 ◆ *State,* NE USA
Maine 55 C2 *Cultural region,* NW France
Maine, Gulf of 101 H2 *Gulf,* NE USA
Mainland 33 F1 *Island,* NE Scotland, UK
Mainland 33 A6 *Island,*
  NE Scotland, UK
Mainz 59 B5 SW Germany
Maitri 138 C3 *Indian research station,*
  Antarctica
Maizhokunggar 87 C4 W China
Majorca 57 H4 *Island,*
  Balearic Islands, Spain
Makarov Basin 139 C4 *Undersea feature,*
  Arctic Ocean
Makassar Strait 91 E7 *Strait,*
  C Indonesia
Makeni 124 B4 C Sierra Leone
Makhachkala 69 B9 SW Russ. Fed.
Makiyivka 67 G5 E Ukraine
Makkovik 99 F3 Newfoundland and
  Labrador, NE Canada
Makó 63 F8 SE Hungary
Makoua 128 B2 C Congo
Makran Coast 81 F4 *Coastal region,*
  SE Iran
Makrany 67 B3 SW Belorussia
Makurdi 124 F5 C Nigeria
Malabo 124 E5 ● Isla de Bioco,
  NW Equatorial Guinea
Malacca, Strait of 91 B6 *Strait,*
  Indonesia/Malaysia
Malacky 63 C7 W Slovakia
Maladzyechna 67 C2 C Belorussia
Málaga 57 D6 S Spain
Malahide 31 E4 E Ireland
Malaita 137 F3 *Island,*
  N Solomon Islands
Malakal 127 C5 S Sudan
Malang 91 D8 Java, C Indonesia
Malanje 128 B3 NW Angola
Mälaren 49 D5 ◎ C Sweden
Malatya 79 E4 SE Turkey
Malawi 128 E4 ◆ *Republic,* S Africa

Malay Peninsula 91 B5 *Peninsula,*
  Malaysia/Thailand
Malaysia 91 C5 ◆ *Monarchy,* SE Asia
Malbork 63 E2 N Poland
Malchin 59 D2 N Germany
Maldives 89 ◆ *Republic,*
  N Indian Ocean
Malden Island 131 *Atoll,* E Kiribati
Maldives 89 ◆ *Republic,*
  N Indian Ocean
Malegaon 89 E4 *Cultural region,*
  C India
Male' 89 C6 ● Maldives
Malheur Lake 103 ◎ Oregon, USA
Mali 124 D3 ◆ *Republic,* W Africa
Mali Kyun 91 A4 *Island,* Mergui
  Archipelago, S Burma
Malin 31 D1 N Ireland
Malindi 127 E6 SE Kenya
Malin Head 31 D1 *Headland,*
  NW Ireland
Mallaig 33 C4 N Scotland, UK
Mallawi 122 I3 C Egypt
Mallorca *see* Majorca
Mallow 31 C6 SW Ireland
Mallwyd 39 D3 NW Wales, UK
Malmberget 49 D2 N Sweden
Malmédy 50 E7 E Belgium
Malmö 49 C7 S Sweden
Małopolska 63 F5 *Plateau,* S Poland
Malozemel'skaya Tundra 69 D3
  Physical region, NW Russ. Fed.
Malta 61 ◆ *Republic,* C
  Mediterranean Sea
Malta Channel 61 D9 *Strait,* Italy/Malta
Malton 35 E4 N England, UK
Maluku *see* Moluccas
Malung 49 C5 C Sweden
Malvern Hills 35 C7 *Hill range,*
  W England, UK
Mamberamo, Sungai 91 I7 ⬥
  E Indonesia
Mamonovo 49 D7 W Russ. Fed.
Mamoré, Rio 117 B1 ⬥ Bolivia/Brazil
Mamou 124 B4 W Guinea
Mamoudzou 128 G4 ◇ Mayotte
Mamuno 128 C5 W Botswana
Manacor 57 H4 Majorca, Spain
Manado 91 F6 Celebes, C Indonesia
Managua 107 D5 ● W Nicaragua
Managua, Lake 107 D4 ◎ W Nicaragua
Manakara 128 G5 SE Madagascar
Manama 81 C4 ● N Bahrain
Mananjary 128 G5 SE Madagascar
Manapouri, Lake 135 A7 ◎
  South Island, NZ
Manas, Gora 83 F2 ▲
  Kyrgyzstan/Uzbekistan
Manau 137 C2 S PNG
Manaus 115 E4 NW Brazil
Manavgat 79 C5 SW Turkey
Manbij 81 B1 N Syria
Manchester 101 G2
  New Hampshire, USA
Manchester 35 D5 NW England, UK
Manchester 28 ◆ *Unitary auth.,*
  NW England, UK
Mandalay 91 A2 C Burma
Mand, Rud-e 81 D3 ⬥ S Iran
Mandurah 133 B5 Western Australia
Manduria 61 F6 SE Italy
Mandya 89 D6 C India
Manfredonia 61 E5 SE Italy
Mangai 128 C2 W Congo (Zaire)
Mangalmé 124 H4 SE Chad
Mangalore 89 D6 W India
Mangerton Mountain 31 B6 ▲
  SW Ireland
Mangoky 128 F5 ⬥ W Madagascar
Manicouagan, Réservoir 99 E4 ◎
  Québec, E Canada
Manihiki 131 *Atoll,* N Cook Islands
Manila 91 F4 ● Luzon, N Philippines
Manisa 79 A3 W Turkey
Manitoba 97 H6 ◆ *Province,* S Canada
Manitoba, Lake 97 H6 ◎ Manitoba,
  S Canada
Manitoulin Island 99 C5 *Island,*
  Ontario, S Canada
Manizales 115 B2 W Colombia
Manjimup 133 B6 Western Australia
Manlleu 57 G2 NE Spain
Manmad 89 D3 SE Congo (Zaire)
Manono 128 D3 SE Congo (Zaire)
Manorbier 39 B6 SW Wales, UK
Manorhamilton 31 C3 NW Ireland
Manosque 55 E6 SE France
Mansa 128 D3 N Zambia
Mansel Island 97 I4 *Island,*
  NW Terr., NE Canada
Mansfield 35 E5 C England, UK
Mansfield 101 E3 Ohio, USA
Mantova 61 C2 NW Italy
Manurewa 135 D2 North Island, NZ
Manus Island 137 B1 *Island,* N PNG
Manzanares 57 D4 C Spain
Manzanillo 109 D3 E Cuba
Manzanillo 105 D5 SW Mexico
Manzhouli 87 F1 N China
Mao 124 G3 W Chad
Maoke, Pegunungan 91 I7 ▲
  E Indonesia
Maoming 87 F6 S China
Maputo 128 E5 ● S Mozambique
Maraa 137 A6 W French Polynesia
Marabá 115 G4 NE Brazil
Maracaibo 115 C1 N Venezuela
Maracaibo, Lake 115 B2 *Inlet,*
  NW Venezuela
Maradah 122 G3 N Libya
Maradi 124 F3 S Niger
Maragheh 81 C1 NW Iran

Marajó, Baía de 115 G3 *Bay,* N Brazil
Marajó, Ilha de 115 F3 *Island,* N Brazil
Maranhão 115 G4 ◆ *State,* E Brazil
Marañón, Río 115 B4 ⬥ N Peru
Marathon 99 B4 Ontario, S Canada
Marbella 57 D6 S Spain
Marble Bar 133 B3 Western Australia
Marburg an der Lahn 59 B5
  W Germany
March 37 G2 E England, UK
Marche 55 D4 *Cultural region,* C France
Marche-en-Famenne 50 D8 SE Belgium
Mar Chiquita, Laguna 117 B5 ◎
  C Argentina
Mardan 89 C1 N Pakistan
Mar del Plata 117 C6 E Argentina
Mardin 79 F4 SE Turkey
Maré 137 G6 *Island,* Îles Loyauté,
  E New Caledonia
Mareeba 133 G2 Queensland,
  NE Australia
Maree, Loch 33 C3 ◎ N Scotland, UK
Margarita, Isla de 115 D1 *Island,*
  N Venezuela
Margate 37 H4 SE England, UK
Margherita, Lake 127 D4 ◎ SW Ethiopia
Margow, Dasht-e 83 D6 *Desert,*
  SW Afghanistan
Mari 137 A3 SW PNG
María Cleofas, Isla 105 C5 *Island,*
  C Mexico
Maria Island 133 G7 *Island,* Tasmania,
  SE Australia
María Madre, Isla 105 C4 *Island,*
  C Mexico
María Magdalena, Isla 105 C4 *Island,*
  C Mexico
Mariana Islands 15 *Island group,*
  Guam/Northern Mariana Islands
Mariana Trench 15 *Undersea feature,*
  W Pacific Ocean
Mariánské Lázně 63 A5
  W Czech Republic
Maribor 59 F8 NE Slovenia
Maridi 127 B4 SW Sudan
Marie Byrd Land 138 B5 *Physical region,*
  Antarctica
Marie-Galante 109 K5 *Island,*
  SE Guadeloupe
Mariental 128 C6 SW Namibia
Mariestad 49 C6 S Sweden
Marília 115 F7 S Brazil
Marín 57 B2 NW Spain
Maringá 115 F7 S Brazil
Mariscal Estigarribia 117 C3
  NW Paraguay
Maritsa 65 F3 ⬥ SW Europe
Mariupol' 67 G5 SE Ukraine
Marka 127 F5 S Somalia
Market Harborough 35 E6
  C England, UK
Markham, Mount 138 C5 ▲ Antarctica
Markounda 124 H5 NW CAR
Marktredwitz 59 D5 E Germany
Marmande 55 C5 SW France
Marmara, Sea of 79 A2 *Sea,* NW Turkey
Marmaris 79 A5 SW Turkey
Marne 55 E2 *Cultural region,* N France
Marne 55 E2 ⬥ N France
Maro 124 H4 S Chad
Maroantsetra 128 G4 NE Madagascar
Maromokotro 128 G4 ▲ N Madagascar
Maroni River 115 F2 ⬥
  French Guiana/Surinam
Maroua 124 G4 N Cameroon
Marquises, Îles 131 *Island group,*
  N French Polynesia
Marrakech 122 C2 W Morocco
Marrawah 133 F7 Tasmania,
  SE Australia
Marree 133 E5 S Australia
Marsá al Burayqah 122 G3 N Libya
Marsabit 127 D5 N Kenya
Marsala 61 C8 Sicily, Italy
Mars Bay 40 *Bay,* Ascension Island,
  C Atlantic Ocean
Marsberg 59 B4 W Germany
Marseille 55 E7 SE France
Marshall Islands 15 ◆ *Republic,*
  W Pacific Ocean
Marsh Harbour 109 D1 Great Abaco,
  W Bahamas
Martigues 55 E6 SE France
Martin 63 E6 NW Slovakia
Martinique 109 K5 *French* ◇,
  E West Indies
Martinique Passage 109 K5 *Channel,*
  Dominica/Martinique
Marton 135 D4 North Island, NZ
Martos 57 D5 S Spain
Mary 83 D4 S Turkmenistan
Maryborough 133 H4 Queensland,
  E Australia
Maryland 101 F4 ◆ *State,* NE USA
Masai Steppe 127 D6 *Grassland,*
  NW Tanzania
Masaka 127 C5 SW Uganda
Masasi 127 D7 SE Tanzania
Masaya 107 D5 W Nicaragua
Maseru 128 D6 ● W Lesotho
Mashhad 81 F1 NE Iran
Masindi 127 C5 W Uganda
Masira, Gulf of 81 F5 *Bay,* E Oman
Mask, Lough 31 B4 ◎ W Ireland
Masqat *see* Muscat
Massa 61 B3 C Italy
Massachusetts 101 G3 ◆ *State,* NE USA
Massawa 127 D2 E Eritrea

OLDENZAAL

Nagykörös 63 E8 C Hungary
Naha 85 A8 Okinawa, SW Japan
Nahariyya 81 H5 N Israel
Nahuel Huapi, Lago 117 A7 ◎ W Argentina
Nain 99 F2 Newfoundland and Labrador, NE Canada
Nairn 33 D3 N Scotland, UK
Nairobi 127 D5 ● S Kenya
Najin 85 C3 NE North Korea
Najran 81 C6 S Saudi Arabia
Nakamura 85 E7 Shikoku, SW Japan
Nakatsugawa 85 F6 SW Japan
Nakhodka 76 H6 SE Russ. Fed.
Nakhon Ratchasima 91 B3 E Thailand
Nakhon Sawan 91 B3 W Thailand
Nakhon Si Thammarat 91 B5 SW Thailand
Nakuru 127 D5 SW Kenya
Nal'chik 69 A8 SW Russ. Fed.
Nalut 122 F2 NW Libya
Namangan 83 G3 E Uzbekistan
Nam Co 87 C4 ◎ W China
Nam Dinh 91 C2 N Vietnam
Namhae-do 85 B7 *Island*, S South Korea
Namib Desert 128 B5 *Desert*, W Namibia
Namibe 128 B4 SW Angola
Namibia 128 B5 ◆ *Republic*, S Africa
Nam Ou 91 B2 ~ N Laos
Namp'o 85 A5 SW North Korea
Nampula 128 F4 NE Mozambique
Namsan-ni 85 A4 NW North Korea
Namsos 49 C3 C Norway
Namur 50 D7 SE Belgium
Namwon 85 B6 S South Korea
Nanaimo 97 E7 Vancouver Island, British Columbia, SW Canada
Nanchang 87 F5 S China
Nancy 55 F3 NE France
Nandaime 107 D5 SW Nicaragua
Nanded 89 D5 C India
Nandyal 89 E6 E India
Nangnim-sanmaek 85 B4 ⛰ C North Korea
Nanjing 87 G4 E China
Nanning 87 F6 S China
Nanping 87 G5 SE China
Nansen Basin 139 D4 *Undersea feature*, Arctic Ocean
Nansen Cordillera 139 C4 *Undersea feature*, Arctic Ocean
Nanterre 55 D2 N France
Nantes 55 B3 NW France
Nantwich 35 C5 W England, UK
Nanumaga 137 I2 *Atoll*, NW Tuvalu
Nanumea Atoll 137 I2 *Atoll*, NW Tuvalu
Nanyang 87 F4 C China
Napier 135 E4 North Island, NZ
Naples 61 D6 S Italy
Napoli *see* Naples
Napo, Río 115 B3 ~ Ecuador/Peru
Naracoorte 133 F6 S Australia
Narberth 39 B6 SW Wales, UK
Narbonne 55 D7 S France
Nares Strait 97 H1 *Strait*, Canada/Greenland
Narew 63 F3 ~ E Poland
Narowlya 67 D3 SE Belorussia
Närpes 49 D4 W Finland
Närpiö *see* Närpes
Narrabri 133 G5 NSW, SE Australia
Narrogin 133 B5 Western Australia
Narva 49 F5 NE Estonia
Narvik 49 D2 C Norway
Nar'yan-Mar 69 D3 NW Russ. Fed.
Naryn 83 H2 C Kyrgyzstan
Nashik 89 D5 W India
Nashville 101 D4 Tennessee, USA
Näsijärvi 49 E4 ◎ SW Finland
Nassau 109 D2 ● New Providence, N Bahamas
Nasser, Lake 122 J4 ◎ Egypt/Sudan
Nata 128 D5 NE Botswana
Natal 115 I4 E Brazil
Natchez 101 C5 Mississippi, USA
Natitingou 124 D4 NW Benin
Natuna, Kepulauan 91 C6 *Island group*, W Indonesia
Nauru 137 G1 ◆ *Republic*, W Pacific Ocean
Navan 31 E4 E Ireland
Navapolatsk 67 D1 N Belorussia
Navarra 57 E2 *Cultural region*, N Spain
Navassa Island 109 D4 *US* ◇ C West Indies
Navojoa 105 C3 NW Mexico
Navolat 105 C3 C Mexico
Nawabshah 89 B3 S Pakistan
Nawoiy 83 E3 C Uzbekistan
Naxcivan 79 H3 SW Azerbaijan
Náxos 65 F6 *Island*, Cyclades, Greece
Nayoro 85 G1 NE Japan
Nazareth 81 H5 N Israel
Nazca Ridge 14 *Undersea feature*, E Pacific Ocean
Naze 85 B7 SW Japan
Nazilli 79 A4 SW Turkey
Nazret 127 D3 C Ethiopia
N'Dalatando 128 B3 NW Angola
Ndélé 124 H4 N CAR
Ndendé 128 A2 S Gabon
Ndindi 128 A2 S Gabon
Ndjamena 124 G4 ● W Chad
Ndola 128 D4 C Zambia
Neagh, Lough 31 E2 ◎ E Northern Ireland, UK
Neápoli 65 E6 S Greece
Neápoli 65 D4 N Greece
Neath 39 D6 S Wales, UK
Neath Port Talbot 29 ◐ *Unitary auth.*, S Wales, UK
Nebaj 107 A3 W Guatemala
Nebitdag 83 B3 W Turkmenistan
Neblina, Pico da 115 C3 ▲ NW Brazil
Nebraska 103 F2 ◐ *State*, C USA
Neckar 59 B6 ~ SW Germany
Necochea 117 C6 E Argentina
Neder Rijn 50 D4 ~ C Netherlands
Nederweert 50 E6 SE Netherlands
Neede 50 F4 E Netherlands
Neerpelt 50 D6 NE Belgium
Neftekamsk 69 D6 W Russ. Fed.
Nefyn 39 B2 NW Wales, UK
Negele 127 E4 S Ethiopia
Negev 81 G6 *Desert*, S Israel
Negombo 89 E8 SW Sri Lanka
Negotin 65 D2 E Yugoslavia
Negra, Punta 115 A4 *Headland*, NW Peru
Negro, Río 117 B6 ~ E Argentina
Negro, Rio 115 D3 ~ N South America
Negros 91 F5 *Island*, C Philippines
Neijiang 87 E5 C China
Nellore 89 E6 E India
Nelson 135 C5 South Island, NZ
Nelson 35 D4 NW England, UK
Nelson 97 H6 ~ Manitoba, C Canada
Nelson Island 40 *Island*, N British Indian Ocean Territory
Néma 124 C3 SE Mauritania
Neman 49 E7 ~ NE Europe
Nemours 55 D3 N France
Nemuro 85 H1 NE Japan
Nenagh 31 C5 C Ireland
Nendö 137 G3 *Island*, Santa Cruz Islands, E Solomon Islands
Nene 37 G2 ~ E England, UK
Nepal 89 E3 ◆ *Monarchy*, S Asia
Nepean 99 D5 Ontario, SE Canada
Nephin 31 B3 ▲ W Ireland
Neretva 65 C2 ~ Bosnia and Herzegovina/Croatia
Neringa 49 E7 SW Lithuania
Neris 67 C2 ~ Belorussia/Lithuania
Nerva 57 C5 S Spain
Neryungri 76 G4 NE Russ. Fed.
Neskaupstadhur 49 B1 E Iceland
Ness, Loch 33 D4 ◎ N Scotland, UK
Néstos 65 E4 ~ Bulgaria/Greece
Netanya 81 G6 C Israel
Netherlands 50 D3 ◆ *Monarchy*, NW Europe
Netherlands Antilles 109 G7 *Dutch* ◇ S Caribbean Sea
Nettilling Lake 97 I3 ◎ Baffin Island, NW Terr., N Canada
Neubrandenburg 59 D3 NE Germany
Neuchâtel 59 A8 W Switzerland
Neuchâtel, Lac de 59 A8 ◎ W Switzerland
Neufchâteau 50 D8 SE Belgium
Neumünster 59 C2 N Germany
Neunkirchen 59 A6 SW Germany
Neuquén 117 A6 SE Argentina
Neuruppin 59 D3 NE Germany
Neusiedler See 59 F7 ◎ Austria/Hungary
Neustadt an der Weinstrasse 59 A6 SW Germany
Neustrelitz 59 D3 NE Germany
Neu-Ulm 59 C7 S Germany
Neuwied 59 B5 W Germany
Nevada 103 C3 ◐ *State*, W USA
Nevers 55 D4 C France
Nevinnomyssk 69 A8 SW Russ. Fed.
Nevşehir 79 D4 C Turkey
Newala 127 D7 SE Tanzania
New Amsterdam 115 E2 E Guyana
Newark 101 G3 New Jersey, USA
Newark-on-Trent 35 E5 C England, UK
Newborough 39 C2 NW Wales, UK
Newbridge 31 C4 W Ireland
Newbridge 39 E6 S Wales, UK
Newbridge on Wye 39 E5 C Wales, UK
New Britain 137 C2 *Island*, E PNG
New Brunswick 99 F5 ◐ *Province*, SE Canada
Newbury 37 E4 S England, UK
Newbury 29 ◐ *Unitary auth.*, S England, UK
New Caledonia 137 D5 *French* ◇ SW Pacific Ocean
Newcastle 133 G5 NSW, SE Australia
Newcastle 31 F3 SE Northern Ireland, UK
Newcastle Emlyn 39 C5 S Wales, UK
Newcastle-under-Lyme 35 D5 C England, UK
Newcastle upon Tyne 35 D2 NE England, UK
Newcastle upon Tyne 28 ◐ *Unitary auth.*, NE England, UK
Newcastle West 31 B5 SW Ireland
New Delhi 89 D3 ● N India
New England 101 G2 *Cultural region*, NE USA
New Forest 37 E5 *Physical region*, S England, UK
Newfoundland 99 G4 *Island*, Newfoundland and Labrador, SE Canada
Newfoundland and Labrador 99 G3 ◐ *Province*, E Canada
New Georgia 137 E2 *Island*, New Georgia Islands, NW Solomon Islands
New Georgia Islands 137 D3 *Island group*, NW Solomon Islands
New Glasgow 99 G5 Nova Scotia, SE Canada
New Guinea 137 A2 *Island*, Indonesia/PNG
Newham 29 ◐ *London borough*, SE England, UK
New Hampshire 101 G2 ◐ *State*, NE USA
New Hanover 137 C1 *Island*, NE PNG
Newhaven 37 G5 SE England, UK
New Haven 101 G3 Connecticut, USA
New Ireland 137 C1 *Island*, NE PNG
New Island 40 *Island*, W Falkland Islands
New Jersey 101 G3 ◐ *State*, NE USA
Newman 133 B3 Western Australia
Newmarket 37 G2 E England, UK
Newmarket on Fergus 31 C5 W Ireland
New Mexico 103 D4 ◐ *State*, SW USA
New Orleans 103 H5 Louisiana, USA
New Plymouth 135 D4 North Island, NZ
Newport 37 E5 S England, UK
Newport 39 F7 SE Wales, UK
Newport 39 B5 SW Wales, UK
Newport 29 *Unitary auth.*, SE Wales, UK
Newport Bay 39 B5 *Bay*, SW Wales, UK
Newport News 101 F4 Virginia, USA
Newport Pagnell 37 F3 SE England, UK
New Providence 109 D1 *Island*, N Bahamas
Newquay 37 A5 SW England, UK
New Quay 39 C5 SW Wales, UK
New Ross 31 E6 SE Ireland
Newry 31 E3 SE Northern Ireland, UK
Newry and Mourne 29 ◐ *District*, S Northern Ireland, UK
New Siberian Islands 76 F2 *Island group*, N Russ. Fed.
New South Wales 133 F5 ◐ *State*, SE Australia
Newton Abbot 37 C5 SW England, UK
Newton Stewart 33 D7 S Scotland, UK
Newtown 31 C6 S Ireland
Newtown 39 E4 E Wales, UK
Newtownabbey 31 E2 E Northern Ireland, UK
Newtownabbey 29 ◐ *District*, E Northern Ireland, UK
Newtown St Boswells 33 E6 S Scotland, UK
Newtownstewart 31 D2 W Northern Ireland, UK
New York 101 G3 New York, USA
New York 101 F3 ◐ *State*, NE USA
New Zealand 135 A5 ◆ *Commonwealth Republic*, SW Pacific Ocean
Neyland 39 B6 SW Wales, UK
Neyveli 89 E7 SE India
Ngangze Co 87 B4 ◎ W China
Ngaoundéré 124 G5 N Cameroon
N'Giva 128 B4 S Angola
Ngo 128 B2 SE Congo
Ngoko 124 G6 ~ Cameroon/Congo
Ngourti 124 G3 E Niger
Nguigmi 124 G3 SE Niger
Nguru 124 F4 NE Nigeria
Nha Trang 91 D4 S Vietnam
Nhulunbuy 133 E1 Northern Territory, N Australia
Niagara Falls 99 D6 Ontario, S Canada
Niagara Falls 101 F2 New York, USA
Niagara Falls 101 E3 *Waterfall*, Canada/USA
Niamey 124 E3 ● SW Niger
Niangay, Lac 124 D3 ◎ E Mali
Nia-Nia 128 D1 NE Congo (Zaire)
Nias, Pulau 91 A6 *Island*, W Indonesia
Nicaragua 107 D4 ◆ *republic*, C America
Nicaragua, Lake 107 E5 ◎ S Nicaragua
Nice 55 F6 SE France
Nicholls Town 109 D1 NW Bahamas
Nicobar Islands 89 H6 *Island group*, India, E Indian Ocean
Nicosia 70 C6 ● C Cyprus
Nicoya 107 D6 W Costa Rica
Nicoya, Golfo de 107 E6 *Gulf*, W Costa Rica
Nicoya, Península de 107 D6 *Peninsula*, NW Costa Rica
Nidzica 63 E2 N Poland
Nieuw-Bergen 50 E5 SE Netherlands
Nieuwegein 50 D4 C Netherlands
Nieuw Nickerie 115 E2 NW Surinam
Niğde 79 D4 C Turkey
Niger 124 E3 ◆ *Republic*, W Africa
Niger 124 E4 ~ W Africa
Niger Delta 118 *Delta*, S Nigeria
Nigeria 124 E4 ◆ *Federal Republic*, W Africa
Niger, Mouths of the 124 E5 *Delta*, S Nigeria
Niigata 85 F4 C Japan
Niihama 85 E7 Shikoku, SW Japan
Niihau 103 A5 *Island*, Hawaii, USA
Nii-jima 85 G6 *Island*, E Japan
Nijkerk 50 D4 C Netherlands
Nijlen 50 C6 N Belgium
Nijmegen 50 E4 SE Netherlands
Nikel' 69 B2 NW Russ. Fed.
Nikiniki 91 F8 S Indonesia
Nikopol' 67 F5 SE Ukraine
Nikšić 65 C3 SW Yugoslavia
Nile 122 I3 ~ N Africa
Nile Delta 122 I2 *Delta*, N Egypt
Nîmes 55 E6 S France
Nine Degree Channel 89 C7 *Channel*, India/Maldives
Ninetyeast Ridge 15 *Undersea feature*, E Indian Ocean
Ningbo 87 G4 SE China
Ninigo Group 137 A1 *Island group*, N PNG
Nioro 124 B3 W Mali
Niort 55 C4 W France
Nipigon 99 B4 Ontario, S Canada
Nipigon, Lake 99 B4 ◎ Ontario, S Canada
Niš 65 D2 SE Yugoslavia
Nisko 63 F5 SE Poland
Nísyros 65 G6 *Island*, Dodecanese, Greece
Nith 33 D6 ~ S Scotland, UK
Nitra 63 D7 SW Slovakia
Nitra 63 D7 ~ W Slovakia
Niue 131 *Self-governing* ◇ S Pacific Ocean
Niulakita 137 J3 *Atoll*, S Tuvalu
Niutao 137 J2 *Atoll*, NW Tuvalu
Nivernais 55 D4 *Cultural region*, C France
Nizamabad 89 D5 C India
Niznekamsk 69 C6 W Russ. Fed.
Nizhnevartovsk 76 D4 C Russ. Fed.
Nizhniy Novgorod 69 B5 W Russ. Fed.
Nizhniy Odes 69 D4 NW Russ. Fed.
Nizhyn 67 E4 NE Ukraine
Njombe 127 D7 S Tanzania
Nkayi 128 B2 S Congo
Nkongsamba 124 F5 W Cameroon
Nmai Hka 91 B1 ~ N Burma
Nobeoka 85 D8 SW Japan
Noboribetsu 85 F2 NE Japan
Nogales 105 B2 NW Mexico
Nokia 49 E5 SW Finland
Nokou 124 G3 W Chad
Nola 124 G5 SW CAR
Nolinsk 69 C5 NW Russ. Fed.
Nome 139 B1 Alaska, USA
Noord-Beveland 50 B5 *Island*, SW Netherlands
Noordwijk aan Zee 50 C4 W Netherlands
Nora 49 C5 C Sweden
Norak 83 F3 W Tajikistan
Norddeutsches Tiefland 63 A2 *Plain*, N Germany
Norden 59 B3 NW Germany
Norderstedt 59 C3 N Germany
Nordfriesische Inseln *see* North Frisian Islands
Nordhausen 59 C4 C Germany
Nordhorn 59 A3 NW Germany
Nordkapp *see* North Cape
Nore 31 D5 ~ S Ireland
Norfolk 101 G4 Virginia, USA
Norfolk 29 ◐ *County*, E England, UK
Norfolk Island 131 *Australian* ◇ SW Pacific Ocean
Noril'sk 76 E3 N Russ. Fed.
Norman 103 F4 Oklahoma, USA
Normandie *see* Normandy
Normandy 55 C2 *Cultural region*, France
Norman Island 40 *Island*, S British Virgin Islands
Normanton 133 F2 Queensland, NE Australia
Norrköping 49 C6 S Sweden
Norrtälje 49 D5 C Sweden
Norseman 133 C5 Western Australia
Norsup 137 G5 Malekula, C Vanuatu
Northallerton 35 E3 N England, UK
Northam 133 B5 Western Australia
North America 92 *Continent*
North American Basin 14 *Undersea feature*, W Sargasso Sea
Northampton 37 F2 C England, UK
Northamptonshire 29 ◐ *County*, C England, UK
North Andaman 89 H4 *Island*, Andaman Islands, India
North Arm 40 Falkland Islands
North Ayrshire 28 ◐ *Unitary auth.*, W Scotland, UK
North Bay 99 D5 Ontario, S Canada
North Berwick 33 E5 SE Scotland, UK
North Caicos 40 *Island*, NW Turks and Caicos Islands
North Cape 135 C1 *Headland*, North Island, NZ
North Cape 49 E1 *Headland*, N Norway
North Carolina 101 E5 ◐ *State*, SE USA
North Channel 33 B6 *Strait*, Northern Ireland/Scotland, UK
North Dakota 103 F1 ◐ *State*, N USA
North Down 29 ◐ *District*, E Northern Ireland, UK
North East Bay 40 *Bay*, Ascension Island, C Atlantic Ocean
North East Lincolnshire 29 ◐ *Unitary auth.*, N England, UK
Northeim 59 C4 C Germany
Northern Cook Islands 131 *Island group*, N Cook Islands
Northern Dvina 69 C4 ~ NW Russ. Fed.
Northern Ireland 29 *Political division*, Northern Ireland, UK
Northern Mariana Islands 131 *US* ◇ W Pacific Ocean
Northern Sporades 65 E5 *Island group*, E Greece
Northern Territory 133 D2 ◐ *Territory*, N Australia
North Esk 33 E4 ~ E Scotland, UK
North European Plain 44 *Plain*, N Europe
North Foreland 37 H3 *Headland*, SE England, UK
North Frisian Islands 59 B2 *Island group*, N Germany
North Geomagnetic Pole 139 A4 *Pole*, Arctic Ocean
North Island 135 B2 *Island*, N NZ
North Korea 85 C4 ◆ *Republic*, E Asia
North Lanarkshire 28 ◐ *Unitary auth.*, C Scotland, UK
Northland 135 C1 *Cultural region*, North Island, NZ
North Lincolnshire 29 ◐ *Unitary auth.*, N England, UK
North Little Rock 103 G4 Arkansas, USA
North Mole 40 *Harbour wall*, NW Gibraltar
North Platte River 103 E2 ~ C USA
North Point 40 *Headland*, Ascension Island, C Atlantic Ocean
North Pole 139 C4 *Pole*, Arctic Ocean
North Ronaldsay 33 F1 *Island*, NE Scotland, UK
North Saskatchewan 97 G6 ~ S Canada
North Sea 44 *Sea*, NW Europe
North Siberian Lowland 76 E3 *Lowlands*, N Russ. Fed.
North Sound 40 *Sound*, W Cayman Islands
North Sound 31 B4 *Sound*, W Ireland
North Sound, The 33 E1 *Sound*, N Scotland, UK
North Taranaki Bight 135 C3 *Gulf*, North Island, NZ
North Tyne 35 D2 ~ N England, UK
North Tyneside 28 ◐ *Unitary auth.*, NE England, UK
North Uist 33 A3 *Island*, NW Scotland, UK
Northumberland 29 ◐ *County*, N England, UK
North West Bluff 40 *Headland*, N Montserrat
North West Highlands 33 C3 ⛰ N Scotland, UK
Northwest Pacific Basin 15 *Undersea feature*, NW Pacific Ocean
North West Somerset 29 ◐ *Unitary auth.*, SW England, UK
Northwest Territories 97 F4 ◐ *Territory*, NW Canada
Northwich 35 C5 C England, UK
Northwind Plain 139 B2 *Undersea feature*, Arctic Ocean
North York Moors 35 E3 *Moorland*, N England, UK
North Yorkshire 29 ◐ *County*, N England, UK
Norton Sound 97 C3 *Inlet*, Alaska, USA
Norway 49 A4 ◆ *Monarchy*, N Europe
Norwegian Sea 49 A4 *Sea*, NE Atlantic Ocean
Norwich 37 H2 E England, UK
Noshiro 85 F3 C Japan
Nossob 128 C6 ~ E Namibia
Noteć 63 D3 ~ NW Poland
Nottingham 35 E5 C England, UK
Nottingham 29 ◐ *Unitary auth.*, C England, UK
Nottinghamshire 29 ◐ *County*, C England, UK
Nouâdhibou 124 A2 W Mauritania
Nouakchott 124 A2 ● SW Mauritania
Nouméa 137 G6 ○ S New Caledonia
Nova Gorica 59 E8 W Slovenia
Nova Iguaçu 115 G7 SE Brazil
Novara 61 B2 NW Italy
Nova Scotia 99 F5 ◐ *Province*, SE Canada
Novaya Sibir', Ostrov 76 G2 *Island*, NE Russ. Fed.
Novaya Zemlya 69 E1 *Island group*, N Russ. Fed.
Novgorod 69 A4 W Russ. Fed.
Novi Sad 65 D1 N Yugoslavia
Novoazovs'k 67 G5 E Ukraine
Novocheboksarsk 69 C6 W Russ. Fed.
Novocherkassk 69 A7 SW Russ. Fed.
Novodvinsk 69 C3 NW Russ. Fed.
Novokazalinsk 76 B5 SW Kazakhstan
Novokuznetsk 76 E5 S Russ. Fed.
Novolazarevskaya 138 C3 *Russian research station*, Antarctica
Novo Mesto 59 E9 SE Slovenia
Novomoskovs'k 67 F5 E Ukraine
Novomoskovsk 69 B6 W Russ. Fed.
Novorossiysk 69 A8 SW Russ. Fed.
Novoshakhtinsk 69 A7 SW Russ. Fed.
Novosibirsk 76 D5 C Russ. Fed.
Novotroitsk 69 D7 W Russ. Fed.
Novyy Buh 67 E5 S Ukraine
Novyy Uzen' 76 B5 W Kazakhstan
Nowogard 63 C2 NW Poland
Nowy Dwór Mazowiecki 63 E3 C Poland
Nowy Sącz 63 F6 S Poland
Nowy Tomyśl 63 C3 W Poland
Noyon 55 D2 N France
Ntomba, Lac 128 B2 ◎ NW Congo (Zaire)
Nubian Desert 127 C1 *Desert*, NE Sudan
Nueva Gerona 109 B3 S Cuba
Nueva Guinea 107 E5 SE Nicaragua
Nueva Ocotepeque 107 B3 W Honduras
Nueva Rosita 105 E2 NE Mexico
Nuevitas 109 D3 E Cuba
Nuevo Casas Grandes 105 C2 N Mexico
Nuevo, Golfo 117 B7 *Gulf*, S Argentina
Nuevo Laredo 105 E2 NE Mexico
Nui Atoll 137 I2 *Atoll*, W Tuvalu
Nuku'alofa 131 ● Tongatapu, S Tonga
Nukufetau Atoll 137 J2 *Atoll*, C Tuvalu
Nukulaelae Atoll 137 J3 *Atoll*, E Tuvalu
Nukumanu Islands 137 E1 *Island group*, NE PNG
Nukus 83 D2 W Uzbekistan
Nullarbor Plain 133 D5 *Plateau*, S Australia/Western Australia
Nuneaton 35 E6 C England, UK
Nunivak Island 97 B3 *Island*, Alaska, USA
Nunspeet 50 E4 E Netherlands
Nuoro 61 A6 Sardinia, Italy
Nuremberg 59 C6 S Germany
Nurmes 49 F4 E Finland
Nürnberg *see* Nuremberg
Nurota 83 E3 C Uzbekistan
Nusaybin 79 G4 SE Turkey
Nyagan' 76 D3 N Russ. Fed.
Nyainqentanglha Shan 87 C4 ⛰ W China
Nyala 127 B3 W Sudan
Nyamtumbo 127 D7 S Tanzania
Nyandoma 69 B4 NW Russ. Fed.
Nyantakara 127 C6 NW Tanzania
Nyasa, Lake 128 E4 ◎ E Africa
Nyeri 127 D5 C Kenya
Nyima 87 C4 W China
Nyíregyháza 63 F7 NE Hungary
Nykøbing 49 B7 SE Denmark
Nyköping 49 D6 S Sweden
Nylstroom 128 D6 NE South Africa
Nyngan 133 G5 NSW, SE Australia
Nyurba 76 F4 NE Russ. Fed.
Nzega 127 C6 C Tanzania
Nzérékoré 124 B5 SE Guinea
N'Zeto 128 B3 NW Angola

O

Oahu 103 B5 *Island*, Hawaii, USA
Oakham 35 E6 C England, UK
Oakland 103 B3 California, USA
Oamaru 135 B7 South Island, NZ
Oa, Mull of 33 B6 *Headland*, W Scotland, UK
Oaxaca 105 F5 SE Mexico
Ob' 76 D3 ~ C Russ. Fed.
Oban 33 C5 W Scotland, UK
Ob, Gulf of 76 D3 *Gulf*, N Russ. Fed.
Obihiro 85 G2 NE Japan
Obo 124 I5 E CAR
Obock 127 E3 E Djibouti
Oborniki 63 C3 W Poland
Ocaña 57 D3 C Spain
Occidental, Cordillera 117 A2 ⛰ Bolivia/Chile
Ocean Falls 97 E6 British Columbia, SW Canada
Oceanside 103 C4 California, USA
Och'amch'ire 79 G1 W Georgia
Ochil Hills 33 E5 ⛰ C Scotland, UK
Ocotal 107 D4 NW Nicaragua
Ocozocuautla 105 G5 SE Mexico
October Revolution Island 76 F2 *Island*, N Russ. Fed.
Ocú 107 G7 S Panama
Odate 85 G3 C Japan
Ödemiş 79 A4 SW Turkey
Odense 49 B7 C Denmark
Oder 59 E3 ~ C Europe
Oderhaff 63 B2 *Bay*, Germany/Poland
Odesa 67 E6 SW Ukraine
Odessa 103 F5 Texas, USA
Odienné 124 C4 NW Ivory Coast
Odoorn 50 F2 NE Netherlands
Of 79 F2 NE Turkey
Ofanto 61 E6 ~ S Italy
Offaly 29 ◐ *County*, C Ireland
Offenbach 59 B5 W Germany
Offenburg 59 B7 SW Germany
Ogaden 127 F4 *Plateau*, Ethiopia/Somalia
Ogaki 85 F6 SW Japan
Ogbomosho 124 E5 W Nigeria
Ogden 103 D3 Utah, USA
Ohio 101 E3 ◐ *State*, N USA
Ohio River 101 D4 ~ N USA
Ohrid, Lake 65 D4 ◎ Albania/FYR Macedonia
Ohura 135 D3 North Island, NZ
Oirschot 50 D5 S Netherlands
Oise 55 D2 ~ N France
Oita 85 D7 Kyushu, SW Japan
Ojinaga 105 D2 N Mexico
Ojos del Salado, Cerro 117 A4 ▲ W Argentina
Okaihau 135 C1 North Island, NZ
Okara 89 D2 E Pakistan
Okavango 128 C5 ~ S Africa
Okavango Delta 128 C5 *Wetland*, N Botswana
Okayama 85 E6 SW Japan
Okazaki 85 F6 C Japan
Okeechobee, Lake 101 E7 ◎ SE USA
Okehampton 37 C5 SW England, UK
Okhotsk 76 H3 E Russ. Fed.
Okhotsk, Sea of 76 H4 *Sea*, NW Pacific Ocean
Okhtyrka 67 F4 NE Ukraine
Okinawa 85 A8 SW Japan
Okinawa-shoto 85 A8 *Island group*, SW Japan
Oki-shoto 85 D6 *Island group*, SW Japan
Oklahoma 103 F4 ◐ *State*, C USA
Oklahoma City 103 F4 Oklahoma, USA
Oko, Wadi 127 D1 ~ NE Sudan
Oktyabr'skiy 69 D6 SW Russ. Fed.
Okushiri-to 85 F2 *Island*, NE Japan
Öland 49 D7 *Island*, S Sweden
Olavarría 117 C6 E Argentina
Oława 63 D4 SW Poland
Olbia 61 B5 Sardinia, Italy
Oldebroek 50 E3 E Netherlands
Oldenburg 59 B3 NW Germany
Oldenburg 59 C2 N Germany
Oldenzaal 50 F4 E Netherlands

CAR Central African Republic FYR Former Yugoslavian Rebublic NSW New South Wales NZ New Zealand PNG Papua New Guinea Russ. Fed. Russian Federation UAE United Arab Emirates UK United Kingdom USA United States of America

◈ *Administrative region*   ◆ *Country*   ● *Country capital*   ◇ *Dependent territory*   ○ *Dependent territory capital*   ▲ *Mountain range*   ▲ *Mountain*   ▲ *Volcano*   ✦ *River*   ⊚ *Lake*   ▣ *Reservoir*

◆ Administrative region   ◆ Country   ● Country capital   ◇ Dependent territory   ◎ Dependent territory capital   ▲ Mountain range   ▲ Mountain   ⛰ Volcano   ✍ River   ◎ Lake   ▣ Reservoir

SUNDA, SELAT

Serengeti Plain 127 C6 *Plain*, N Tanzania
Serenje 128 D4 E Zambia
Sérifos 65 E6 *Island*, Cyclades, Greece
Serov 76 C4 C Russ. Fed.
Serowe 128 D5 SE Botswana
Serpukhov 69 A5 W Russ. Fed.
Sesto San Giovanni 61 B2 N Italy
Sète 55 D6 S France
Setesdal 49 B5 *Valley*, S Norway
Sétif 122 E1 N Algeria
Setté Cama 128 A2 SW Gabon
Settle 35 D4 N England, UK
Setúbal 57 A4 W Portugal
Setúbal, Baía de 57 A5 *Bay*, W Portugal
Seul, Lac 99 A4 ◎ Ontario, S Canada
Sevan 79 H2 C Armenia
Sevan, Lake 79 H2 ◎ E Armenia
Sevastopol' 67 F7 S Ukraine
Sevenoaks 37 G4 SE England, UK
Severn 99 B3 ~ Ontario, S Canada
Severn 37 D3 ~ England/Wales, UK
Severnaya Zemlya 76 E2 *Island group*, N Russ. Fed.
Severn, Mouth of the 39 F7 *Estuary*, England/Wales, UK
Severnyy 69 E3 NW Russ. Fed.
Severodvinsk 69 C3 NW Russ. Fed.
Severomorsk 69 C2 NW Russ. Fed.
Sevilla *see* Seville
Seville 57 B5 S Spain
Seychelles 118 ◆ *Republic*, W Indian Ocean
Seydhisfjördhur 49 B1 E Iceland
Seydi 83 E3 E Turkmenistan
Sfântu Gheorghe 67 C6 C Romania
Sfax 122 F2 E Tunisia
's-Gravenhage *see* The Hague
's-Gravenzande 50 C4 W Netherlands
Sgurr Na Lapaich 33 C3 ▲ NW Scotland, UK
Shache 87 A3 NW China
Shackleton Ice Shelf 138 E5 *Ice shelf*, Antarctica
Shaftesbury 37 D4 S England, UK
Shahany, Ozero 67 D6 ◎ SW Ukraine
Shahrak 83 E5 C Afghanistan
Shahr-e Kord 81 D2 C Iran
Shahrud 81 E1 N Iran
Shanghai 87 G4 E China
Shangrao 87 G5 S China
Shannon 31 C5 W Ireland
Shannon 31 B5 ~ W Ireland
Shannon Erne Waterway 31 D3 *Canal*, N Ireland
Shannon, Mouth of the 31 A5 *Estuary*, W Ireland
Shan Plateau 91 B2 *Plateau*, E Burma
Shantou 87 G5 S China
Shaoguan 87 F5 S China
Shapinsay 33 E1 *Island*, NE Scotland, UK
Sharjah 81 E4 NE UAE
Shark Bay 133 A4 *Bay*, E Indian Ocean
Shashe 128 D5 ~ Botswana/Zimbabwe
Shchëkino 69 A6 W Russ. Fed.
Shchors 67 E3 N Ukraine
Shchuchinsk 76 C5 N Kazakhstan
Shchuchyn 67 B2 W Belorussia
Shebekino 69 A6 W Russ. Fed.
Shebeli 127 E4 ~ Ethiopia/Somalia
Sheberghan 83 E4 N Afghanistan
Shebshi Mountains 124 F4 ▲ E Nigeria
Sheelin, Lough 31 D3 ◎ C Ireland
Sheerness 37 G4 SE England, UK
Sheffield 35 E5 N England, UK
Sheffield 29 ◐ *Unitary auth.*, N England, UK
Shelekhov Gulf 76 H3 *Gulf*, E Russ. Fed.
Shendi 127 C2 NE Sudan
Shenyang 87 G2 NE China
Shepherd Islands 137 H5 *Island group*, C Vanuatu
Shepparton 133 F6 Victoria, SE Australia
Shepton Mallet 37 D4 SW England, UK
Sherbrooke 99 E5 Québec, SE Canada
Shereik 127 C1 N Sudan
's-Hertogenbosch 50 D5 S Netherlands
Shetland Islands 33 A7 *Island group*, NE Scotland, UK
Shetland Islands 28 ◐ *Unitary auth.*, NE Scotland, UK
Shevchenko *see* Aktau
Shiant Islands 33 B3 *Island group*, NW Scotland, UK
Shibetsu 85 G1 NE Japan
Shibushi-wan 85 D8 *Bay*, SW Japan
Shihezi 87 C2 NW China
Shijiazhuang 87 F3 E China
Shikarpur 89 C3 S Pakistan
Shikoku 85 E7 *Island*, SW Japan
Shilabo 127 F4 SE Ethiopia
Shildon 35 D3 N England, UK
Shiliguri 89 G3 NE India
Shilka 76 G5 ~ S Russ. Fed.
Shillelagh 31 E5 E Ireland
Shillong 89 G3 NE India
Shimbiris 127 F3 ▲ N Somalia
Shimoga 89 D6 W India
Shimonoseki 85 D7 Honshu, SW Japan
Shinano-gawa 85 F5 ~ Honshu, C Japan
Shindand 83 D5 W Afghanistan
Shingu 85 F7 Honshu, SW Japan
Shinjo 85 G4 Honshu, C Japan
Shin, Loch 33 D2 ◎ N Scotland, UK
Shinyanga 127 C6 NW Tanzania
Shiraz 81 D3 S Iran
Shivpuri 89 D3 C India
Shizugawa 85 G4 NE Japan
Shizuoka 85 F6 Honshu, S Japan
Shkodër 65 D3 NW Albania
Shoreham-by-Sea 37 F5 SE England, UK
Shostka 67 E3 NE Ukraine
Shreveport 103 G4 Louisiana, USA
Shrewsbury 35 C6 W England, UK
Shropshire 29 ◐ *County*, W England, UK
Shu 76 C6 SE Kazakhstan
Shumen 65 F2 NE Bulgaria
Shuqrah 81 C7 SW Yemen
Shymkent 76 B6 S Kazakhstan
Sialum 137 B2 C PNG
Šiauliai 49 E7 N Lithuania
Sibay 69 D7 W Russ. Fed.
Siberia 76 E4 *Physical region*, Russ. Fed.
Siberut, Pulau 91 A6 *Island*, Kepulauan Mentawai, W Indonesia
Sibi 89 B2 SW Pakistan
Sibiti 128 B2 S Congo
Sibiu 67 B6 C Romania
Sibolga 91 B6 Sumatra, W Indonesia
Sibu 91 D6 East Malaysia
Sibut 124 H5 S CAR
Sibuyan Sea 91 F4 *Sea*, W Pacific Ocean
Sichon 91 B5 SW Thailand
Sichuan Pendi 87 E4 *Basin*, C China
Sicilia *see* Sicily
Sicily 61 C8 *Island*, Italy
Sicily, Strait of 61 B8 *Strait*, C Mediterranean Sea
Siderno 61 E8 SW Italy
Sîdi Barrâni 122 H2 NW Egypt
Sidi Bel Abbès 122 D1 NW Algeria
Sidlaw Hills 33 E5 ▲ E Scotland, UK
Sidley, Mount 138 B5 ▲ Antarctica
Sidmouth 37 C5 SW England, UK
Siedlce 63 F3 E Poland
Siegen 59 B5 W Germany
Siemiatycze 63 G3 E Poland
Siena 61 C4 C Italy
Sieradz 63 D4 C Poland
Sierpc 63 E3 C Poland
Sierra Leone 124 A5 ◆ *Republic*, W Africa
Sierra Madre 107 A3 ▲ Guatemala/Mexico
Sierra Morena 70 B4 ▲ SW Spain Europe
Sierra Nevada 57 D6 ▲ S Spain
Sierra Nevada 103 B3 ▲ W USA
Sífnos 65 E6 *Island*, Cyclades, Greece
Sigli 91 A5 Sumatra, W Indonesia Asia
Siglufjördhur 49 A1 N Iceland
Signy 138 A3 *UK research station*, South Orkney Islands, Antarctica
Siguatepeque 107 C3 W Honduras
Siguiri 124 B4 NE Guinea
Siilinjärvi 49 F4 C Finland
Siirt 79 G4 SE Turkey
Sikasso 124 C4 S Mali
Siklós 63 D9 SW Hungary
Silchar 89 H3 NE India
Silesia 63 D4 *Physical region*, SW Poland
Silifke 79 D5 S Turkey
Siling Co 87 C4 ◎ W China
Silisili 137 A4 ▲ C Samoa
Silistra 65 F2 NE Bulgaria
Šilutė 49 E7 W Lithuania
Silvan 79 F4 SE Turkey
Silverek 79 F4 SE Turkey
Simav 79 B3 W Turkey
Simav Çayı 79 A3 ~ NW Turkey
Simeto 61 D8 ~ Sicily, Italy
Simeulue, Pulau 91 A6 *Island*, NW Indonesia
Simferopol' 67 F7 S Ukraine
Simpelveld 50 E6 SE Netherlands
Simplon Pass 59 B8 *Pass*, S Switzerland
Simpson Desert 133 E4 *Desert*, Northern Territory/South Australia
Sinai 122 J2 *Physical region*, NE Egypt
Sincelejo 115 B2 NW Colombia
Sind 89 B3 *Cultural region*, SE Pakistan
Sindelfingen 59 B6 SW Germany
Sines 57 A5 S Portugal
Singapore 91 C6 ● SE Asia
Singapore 91 C6 ◆ *Republic*, SE Asia
Singen 59 B7 S Germany
Singida 127 D6 C Tanzania
Singkawang 91 D6 C Indonesia
Siniscola 61 B5 Sardinia, Italy
Sinmi-do 85 A5 *Island*, NW North Korea
Sinoie, Lacul 67 D7 *Lagoon*, SE Romania
Sinop 79 D2 N Turkey
Sinp'o 85 B4 E North Korea
Sinsheim 59 B6 SW Germany
Sint-Michielsgestel 50 D5 S Netherlands
Sint-Niklaas 50 C6 N Belgium
Sint-Pieters-Leeuw 50 B7 C Belgium
Sintra 57 A4 W Portugal
Sinuiju 85 A4 W North Korea
Sinujiif 127 F3 NE Somalia
Sion 59 A8 SW Switzerland
Sion Mills 31 D2 W Northern Ireland, UK
Sioux City 103 F2 Iowa, USA
Sioux Falls 103 F2 South Dakota, USA
Siping 87 G2 NE China
Siple, Mount 138 A5 ▲ Siple Island, Antarctica
Siquirres 107 F6 E Costa Rica
Siracusa 61 D8 Sicily, Italy
Sir Edward Pellew Group 133 E2 *Island group*, Northern Territory, NE Australia
Siret 67 C6 ~ Romania/Ukraine
Sir Francis Drake Channel 40 *Channel*, E Caribbean Sea
Sirikit Reservoir 91 B3 ◎ N Thailand
Sirjan 81 E3 S Iran
Şırnak 79 G4 SE Turkey
Sirte, Gulf of 122 G2 *Gulf*, N Libya
Sisimiut 139 A5 S Greenland
Sitges 57 G3 NE Spain
Sittang 91 A3 ~ S Burma
Sittard 50 E6 SE Netherlands
Sittwe 91 A2 W Burma
Siuna 107 E3 NE Nicaragua
Sivas 79 E3 C Turkey
Sivers'kyy Donets' 67 F4 ~ Russian Federation/Ukraine
Siwa 122 H3 NW Egypt
Six-Fours-les-Plages 55 E7 SE France
Siyäzän 79 J2 NE Azerbaijan
Sjælland 49 B7 *Island*, E Denmark
Skagerrak 49 B5 *Channel*, N Europe
Skalka 49 D2 ◎ N Sweden
Skegness 35 F5 E England, UK
Skellefteå 49 D3 N Sweden
Skellefteälven 49 D3 ~ N Sweden
Skerries 31 E4 E Ireland
Ski 49 B5 S Norway
Skiddaw 35 C3 ▲ NW England, UK
Skikda 122 E1 NE Algeria
Skipton 35 D4 N England, UK
Skokholm Island 39 A6 *Island*, SW Wales, UK
Skomer Island 39 A6 *Island*, SW Wales, UK
Skopje 65 D3 ● N FYR Macedonia
Skovorodino 76 G5 SE Russ. Fed.
Skrīveri 49 E6 S Latvia
Skull 31 B7 SW Ireland
Skye, Isle of 33 B3 *Island*, NW Scotland, UK
Skýros 65 F5 *Island*, Vóreioi Sporádes, Greece
Slagelse 49 B7 E Denmark
Slane 31 E4 E Ireland
Slaney 31 E5 ~ SE Ireland
Slatina 67 B7 S Romania
Slavonski Brod 65 C1 NE Croatia
Sławno 63 C2 NW Poland
Sleaford 35 F5 E England, UK
Sleat, Sound of 33 C4 *Strait*, NW Scotland, UK
Sliema 70 B6 N Malta
Slieve Gamph 31 C3 ▲ N Ireland
Slieve League 31 C2 ▲ N Ireland Europe
Slieve Mish Mountains 31 B6 ▲ SW Ireland
Slievenamon 31 D6 ▲ S Ireland
Sligo 31 C3 NW Ireland
Sligo 29 ◐ *County*, NW Ireland
Sligo Bay 31 C2 *Inlet*, NW Ireland
Sliven 65 F3 E Bulgaria
Slough 37 F3 S England, UK
Slough 29 ◐ *Unitary auth.*, S England, UK
Slovakia 63 E6 ◆ *Republic*, C Europe
Slovenia 59 E8 ◆ *Republic*, SE Europe
Slovenské Rudohorie 63 E6 ▲ C Slovakia
Slov"yans'k 67 G4 E Ukraine
Słubice 63 B3 W Poland
Sluch 67 C4 ~ NW Ukraine
Słupsk 63 D1 NW Poland
Slutsk 67 C3 S Belorussia
Slyne Head 31 A4 *Headland*, W Ireland
Smallwood Reservoir 99 F3 ◎ Newfoundland and Labrador, S Canada
Smara 122 B3 N Western Sahara
Smederevo 65 D2 N Yugoslavia
Smederevska Palanka 65 E2 C Yugoslavia
Smøla 49 B4 *Island*, W Norway
Smolensk 69 A5 W Russ. Fed.
Snaefell 35 A3 ▲ C Isle of Man
Snake River 103 C2 ~ NW USA
Snake River Plain 103 D2 *Plain*, Idaho, USA
Sneek 50 E2 N Netherlands
Sneem 31 B6 SW Ireland
Sněžka 63 C5 ▲ N Czech Republic
Snina 63 F6 E Slovakia
Snowdon 39 C2 ▲ NW Wales, UK
Snowdonia 39 C2 ▲ NW Wales, UK
Sobradinho, Represa de 115 G5 ◎ E Brazil
Sochi 69 A8 SW Russ. Fed.
Society Islands 131 *Island group*, W French Polynesia
Socorro, Isla 105 B5 *Island*, W Mexico
Socotra 81 D7 *Island*, SE Yemen
Socuéllamos 57 E4 C Spain
Sodankylä 49 E2 N Finland
Söderhamn 49 D5 C Sweden
Södertälje 49 D5 C Sweden
Sodiri 127 B2 C Sudan
Sofia 65 E3 ● W Bulgaria
Sofiya *see* Sofia
Sogamoso 115 C2 C Colombia
Sognefjorden 49 A5 *Fjord*, NE North Sea
Sohag 122 I3 C Egypt
Sokch'o 85 B5 N South Korea
Söke 79 A4 SW Turkey
Sokhumi 79 F1 NW Georgia
Sokodé 124 D4 C Togo
Sokol 69 B4 NW Russ. Fed.
Sokolov 63 A5 W Czech Republic
Sokone 124 A3 W Senegal
Sokoto 124 E4 NW Nigeria
Sokoto 124 E4 ~ NW Nigeria
Solapur 89 D5 W India
Sol, Costa del 57 D6 *Coastal region*, S Spain
Solec Kujawski 63 D3 W Poland
Solihull 35 D6 C England, UK
Solihull 29 ◐ *Unitary auth.*, C England, UK
Solikamsk 69 D5 NW Russ. Fed.
Sol'-Iletsk 69 D7 W Russ. Fed.
Solingen 59 A4 W Germany
Sollentuna 49 D5 C Sweden
Solomon Islands 137 F2 ◆ *Commonwealth Republic*, W Pacific Ocean
Solomon Sea 137 C2 *Sea*, W Pacific Ocean
Soltau 59 C3 NW Germany
Sol'tsy 69 A4 W Russ. Fed.
Solva 39 A6 SW Wales, UK
Solway Firth 35 B3 *Inlet*, England/Scotland, UK
Solwezi 128 D4 NW Zambia
Soma 85 G4 C Japan
Somalia 127 F4 ◆ *Republic*, E Africa
Somali Plain 15 *Undersea feature*, W Indian Ocean
Sombrero 109 J4 *Island*, N Anguilla
Someren 50 E5 SE Netherlands
Somerset 40 W Bermuda
Somerset 29 ◐ *County*, SW England, UK
Somerset Island 40 *Island*, W Bermuda
Somerset Island 97 H2 *Island*, Queen Elizabeth Islands, NW Terr., NW Canada
Somme 55 D1 ~ N France
Somotillo 107 D4 NW Nicaragua
Somoto 107 D4 NW Nicaragua
Songea 127 D7 S Tanzania
Songkhla 91 B5 SW Thailand
Sonoran Desert 103 C4 *Desert*, Mexico/USA
Sonsonate 107 B4 W El Salvador
Sopot 63 D2 N Poland
Sopron 63 C7 NW Hungary
Sorgues 55 E6 SE France
Sorgun 79 D3 C Turkey
Soria 57 E2 N Spain
Sorong 91 G6 E Indonesia
Sørøya 49 D1 *Island*, N Norway
Sortavala 69 A3 NW Russ. Fed.
Sotkamo 49 F3 C Finland
Soufriére Hills 40 ▲ E Montserrat
Sŏul *see* Seoul
Sourpi 65 E5 C Greece
Sousse 122 F1 NE Tunisia
South Africa 128 C7 ◆ *Republic*, S Africa
South America 117 *Continent*
Southampton 37 E4 S England, UK
Southampton 29 ◐ *Unitary auth.*, S England, UK
Southampton Island 97 I4 *Island*, NW Terr., NE Canada
South Andaman 89 H5 *Island*, Andaman Islands, India
South Australia 133 D4 ◐ *State*, S Australia
South Ayrshire 29 ◐ *Unitary auth.*, W Scotland, UK
South Bend 101 D3 Indiana, USA
South Bruny Island 133 G7 *Island*, Tasmania, SE Australia
South Caicos 40 *Island*, S Turks and Caicos Islands
South Carolina 101 E5 ◐ *State*, SE USA
South China Sea 91 E3 *Sea*, SE Asia
South Dakota 103 E2 ◐ *State*, N USA
South Downs 37 F4 *Hill range*, SE England, UK
Southeast Indian Ridge 15 *Undersea feature*, Indian Ocean/Pacific Ocean
South East Point 40 *Headland*, SE Ascension Island
South East Point 133 F7 *Headland*, Victoria, S Australia
Southend-on-Sea 37 G3 E England, UK
Southend-on-Sea 29 ◐ *Unitary auth.*, SE England, UK
Southern Alps 135 B6 ▲ South Island, NZ
Southern Cook Islands 131 *Island group*, S Cook Islands
Southern Cross 133 B5 Western Australia
Southern Indian Lake 97 H5 ◎ Manitoba, C Canada
Southern Ocean 14 *Ocean*, Atlantic Ocean/Indian Ocean/Pacific Ocean
Southern Uplands 33 D6 ▲ S Scotland, UK
South Esk 33 E4 ~ E Scotland, UK
South Foreland 37 H4 *Headland*, SE England, UK
South Geomagnetic Pole 138 C5 *Pole*, Antarctica
South Georgia 138 A2 *Island*, South Georgia and the South Sandwich Islands, SW Atlantic Ocean
South Gloucestershire 29 ◐ *Unitary auth.*, W England, UK
South Goulburn Island 133 E1 *Island*, Northern Territory, N Australia
South Indian Basin 15 *Undersea basin*, S Indian Ocean
South Island 135 C6 *Island*, S NZ
South Korea 85 A6 ◆ *Republic*, E Asia
South Lanarkshire 28 ◐ *Unitary auth.*, C Scotland, UK
South Molton 37 C4 SW England, UK
South Orkney Islands 138 A3 *Island group*, Antarctica
South Point 40 *Headland*, S Ascension Island
South Pole 138 C5 *Pole*, Antarctica
Southport 35 C4 NW England, UK
South Ronaldsay 33 E1 *Island*, NE Scotland, UK
South Sandwich Islands 138 A2 *Island group*, SE South Georgia and South Sandwich Islands
South Sandwich Trench 138 B2 *Undersea feature*, SW Atlantic Ocean
South Shetland Islands 138 A3 *Island group*, Antarctica
South Shields 35 E2 NE England, UK
South Sound 40 E British Virgin Islands
South Sound 31 B5 *Sound*, W Ireland
South Taranaki Bight 135 C4 *Bight*, SE Tasman Sea
South Town 40 Little Cayman, C Cayman Islands
South Tyne 35 C2 ~ N England, UK
South Tyneside 28 ◐ *Unitary auth.*, NE England, UK
South Uist 33 A3 *Island*, NW Scotland, UK
Southwark 29 ◐ *London borough*, SE England, UK
South West Cape 135 A8 *Headland*, Stewart Island, NZ
Southwest Indian Ridge 15 *Undersea feature*, SW Indian Ocean
Southwest Pacific Basin 14 *Undersea feature*, SE Pacific Ocean
South West Point 40 *Headland*, SW Saint Helena
Southwold 37 H2 E England, UK
Soweto 128 D6 NE South Africa
Spain 57 C3 ◆ *Monarchy*, SW Europe
Spalding 35 F6 E England, UK
Spanish Town 40 E British Virgin Islands
Spanish Town 109 D4 C Jamaica
Spárti 65 E6 S Greece
Speedwell Island Settlement 40 S Falkland Islands
Spencer Gulf 133 E6 *Gulf*, S Australia
Spennymoor 35 D3 N England, UK
Spey 33 E3 ~ NE Scotland, UK
Spijkenisse 50 C4 SW Netherlands
Spin Buldak 83 E6 S Afghanistan
Spitsbergen 139 C5 *Island*, NW Svalbard
Split 65 B2 S Croatia
Spokane 103 C1 Washington, USA
Spot Bay 40 NE Cayman Islands
Spratly Islands 91 D4 *Disputed* ◇ SE Asia
Spree 59 E4 ~ E Germany
Springfield 101 D3 Illinois, USA
Springfield 103 G3 Missouri, USA
Springfield 101 D3 Ohio, USA
Spring Point 40 Falkland Islands
Springs Junction 135 C5 South Island, NZ
Springsure 133 G4 Queensland, E Australia
Spruce Knob 101 E4 ▲ West Virginia, USA
Spurn Head 35 F4 *Headland*, E England, UK
Sri Aman 91 D6 East Malaysia
Sri Jayawardanapura 89 E8 W Sri Lanka
Srikakulam 89 F5 E India
Sri Lanka 89 D8 ◆ *Republic*, S Asia
Srinagar 89 D1 N India
Stabroek 50 C5 N Belgium
Stack Skerry 33 D1 *Island*, N Scotland, UK
Stade 59 C3 NW Germany
Stadskanaal 50 F2 NE Netherlands
Stafford 35 D6 C England, UK
Staffordshire 29 ◐ *County*, C England, UK
Staines 37 F4 SE England, UK
Staithes 35 E3 N England, UK
Stakhanov 67 G4 E Ukraine
Stalowa Wola 63 F5 SE Poland
Stamford 35 F6 E England, UK
Stamford 101 G3 Connecticut, USA
Stanhope 35 D3 N England, UK
Stanley 40 ○ Falkland Islands
Stanley 35 D2 N England, UK
Stanthorpe 133 H5 Queensland, E Australia
Staphorst 50 E3 E Netherlands
Starachowice 63 F4 SE Poland
Stara Zagora 65 F3 C Bulgaria
Starbuck Island 131 *Island*, E Kiribati
Stargard Szczeciński 63 B2 NW Poland
Starobil's'k 67 G4 E Ukraine
Starogard Gdański 63 D2 N Poland
Starominskaya 69 A7 SW Russ. Fed.
Start Bay 37 C6 *Bay*, SW England, UK
Start Point 37 C6 *Headland*, SW England, UK
Staryy Oskol 69 A6 W Russ. Fed.
Stavanger 49 A5 S Norway
Stavropol' 69 A8 SW Russ. Fed.
Steenwijk 50 E3 N Netherlands
Steinkjer 49 C4 C Norway
Stendal 59 D3 C Germany
Sterlitamak 69 D6 W Russ. Fed.
Stevenage 37 F3 E England, UK
Stewart Island 135 A8 *Island*, S NZ
Steyr 59 E7 N Austria
Stickford 35 F5 E England, UK
Stirling 33 D5 C Scotland, UK
Stirling 28 ◐ *Unitary auth.*, C Scotland, UK
Stjørdal 49 B4 C Norway
Stockach 59 B7 S Germany
Stockholm 49 D5 ● C Sweden
Stockport 35 D5 NW England, UK
Stockport 28 ◐ *Unitary auth.*, NW England, UK
Stockton 103 B3 California, USA
Stockton-on-Tees 35 E3 N England, UK
Stockton-on-Tees 28 ◐ *Unitary auth.*, NE England, UK
Stoke-on-Trent 35 D5 C England, UK
Stoke-on-Trent 29 ◐ *Unitary auth.*, C England, UK
Stone 35 D6 C England, UK
Stonehaven 33 F4 NE Scotland, UK
Stonyhill Point 40 *Headland*, S Tristan da Cunha
Støren 49 B4 S Norway
Stornoway 33 B2 NW Scotland, UK
Storsjön 49 C4 ◎ C Sweden
Storuman 49 D3 N Sweden
Storuman 49 C3 ◎ N Sweden
Stour 37 D4 ~ E England, UK
Stour 37 H3 ~ S England, UK
Stourport-on-Severn 35 D7 W England, UK
Stowmarket 37 G2 E England, UK
Strabane 31 D2 W Northern Ireland, UK
Strabane 29 ◐ *District*, W Northern Ireland, UK
Stradbally 31 D5 C Ireland
Strakonice 63 B6 SW Czech Republic
Stralsund 59 D2 NE Germany
Strangford Lough 31 F3 *Inlet*, E Northern Ireland, UK
Stranraer 33 C7 S Scotland, UK
Strasbourg 55 F3 NE France
Stratford 135 D4 North Island, NZ
Stratford-upon-Avon 35 D7 C England, UK
Strathy Point 33 D2 *Headland*, N Scotland, UK
Straubing 59 D6 SE Germany
Strehaia 67 B7 SW Romania
Strelka 76 E4 C Russ. Fed.
Strickland 137 A2 ~ SW PNG
Stromboli 61 D7 ▲ Isola Stromboli, SW Italy
Stromeferry 33 C3 N Scotland, UK
Stromness 33 E1 N Scotland, UK
Strömstad 49 B6 S Sweden
Strömsund 49 C4 C Sweden
Stronsay 33 E1 *Island*, NE Scotland, UK
Stroud 37 D3 C England, UK
Strumble Head 39 A5 *Headland*, SW Wales, UK
Strymónas 65 E4 ~ Bulgaria/Greece
Stryy 67 B5 NW Ukraine
Studholme 135 B7 South Island, NZ
Stuttgart 59 B6 SW Germany
Stykkishólmur 49 A1 W Iceland
Styr 67 C4 ~ Belorussia/Ukraine
Suakin 127 D1 NE Sudan
Subotica 65 D1 N Yugoslavia
Suceava 67 C5 NE Romania
Suck 31 C4 ~ C Ireland
Suckling, Mount 137 C3 ▲ S PNG
Sucre 117 B3 ● S Bolivia
Sudan 127 B3 ◆ *Republic*, N Africa
Sudbury 99 C5 Ontario, S Canada
Sudbury 37 G2 E England, UK
Sudd 127 B4 *Swamp region*, S Sudan
Sudeten 63 C5 ▲ Czech Republic/Poland
Sue 127 B4 ~ S Sudan
Sueca 57 F4 E Spain
Suez 122 I2 NE Egypt
Suez Canal 122 I2 *Canal*, NE Egypt
Suez, Gulf of 70 J6 *Gulf*, NE Egypt
Suffolk 29 ◐ *County*, E England, UK
Sugar Loaf Point 40 *Headland*, N Saint Helena
Suğla Gölü 79 B4 ◎ SW Turkey
Suhar 81 E4 N Oman
Sühbaatar 87 E1 N Mongolia
Suhl 59 C5 C Germany
Suir 31 D6 ~ S Ireland
Sujawal 89 B3 SE Pakistan
Sukabumi 91 C8 Java, C Indonesia
Sukagawa 85 G5 C Japan
Sukhona 69 C4 ~ NW Russ. Fed.
Sukkur 89 C3 SE Pakistan
Sukumo 85 E7 Shikoku, SW Japan
Sulaiman Range 89 C2 ▲ C Pakistan
Sula, Kepulauan 91 F7 *Island group*, C Indonesia
Sulawesi *see* Celebes
Sule Skerry 33 D1 *Island*, N Scotland, UK
Sullana 115 A4 NW Peru
Sulu Archipelago 91 F5 *Island group*, SW Philippines
Sulu Sea 91 E5 *Sea*, SW Philippines
Sulyukta 83 F3 SW Kyrgyzstan
Sumatra 91 B6 *Island*, W Indonesia
Sumba, Pulau 91 E8 *Island*, Nusa Tenggara, C Indonesia
Sumba, Selat 91 E8 *Strait*, Nusa Tenggara, S Indonesia
Sumbawanga 127 C7 W Tanzania
Sumbe 128 B3 W Angola
Sumburgh 33 A7 NE Scotland, UK
Sumburgh Head 33 A7 *Headland*, NE Scotland, UK
Sumeih 127 B3 S Sudan
Summer Isles 33 C3 *Island group*, NW Scotland, UK
Summit 40 ▲ C Gibraltar
Sumqayit 79 J2 E Azerbaijan
Sumy 67 F4 NE Ukraine
Sunch'on 85 B7 S South Korea
Sunda, Selat 91 C7 *Strait*, Java/Sumatra, SW Indonesia

CAR Central African Republic **FYR** Former Yugoslavian Rebublic **NSW** New South Wales **NZ** New Zealand **PNG** Papua New Guinea **Russ. Fed.** Russian Federation **UAE** United Arab Emirates **UK** United Kingdom **USA** United States of America 157

◆ Administrative region ◆ Country ● Country capital ◊ Dependent territory ○ Dependent territory capital ▲ Mountain range ▲ Mountain ☈ Volcano ↗ River ● Lake ◲ Reservoir

U

V

W

◆ *Administrative region* ◆ *Country* ● *Country capital* ◇ *Dependent territory* ○ *Dependent territory capital* ▲ *Mountain range* ▲ *Mountain* ⛰ *Volcano* ≈ *River* ◎ *Lake* ⊠ *Reservoir*

NORTH AMERICA

 CANADA UNITED STATES OF AMERICA MEXICO BELIZE COSTA RICA EL SALVADOR GUATEMALA HONDURAS

SOUTH AMERICA

 GRENADA HAITI JAMAICA ST KITTS & NEVIS ST LUCIA ST VINCENT & THE GRENADINES TRINIDAD & TOBAGO COLOMBIA

AFRICA

 URUGUAY CHILE PARAGUAY ALGERIA EGYPT LIBYA MOROCCO  TUNISIA

 LIBERIA MALI MAURITANIA NIGER NIGERIA SENEGAL SIERRA LEONE TOGO

 BURUNDI DJIBOUTI ERITREA ETHIOPIA KENYA RWANDA SOMALIA SUDAN

EUROPE

 SOUTH AFRICA  SWAZILAND ZAMBIA ZIMBABWE DENMARK FINLAND ICELAND NORWAY

 MONACO ANDORRA PORTUGAL SPAIN ITALY SAN MARINO VATICAN CITY AUSTRIA

 BOSNIA & HERZEGOVINA CROATIA MACEDONIA YUGOSLAVIA (SERBIA & MONTENEGRO) BULGARIA GREECE MOLDAVIA ROMANIA

ASIA

 ARMENIA AZERBAIJAN GEORGIA TURKEY IRAQ ISRAEL JORDAN LEBANON

 IRAN  KAZAKHSTAN KYRGYZSTAN TAJIKISTAN TURKMENISTAN UZBEKISTAN AFGHANISTAN PAKISTAN

 SOUTH KOREA TAIWAN JAPAN BRUNEI INDONESIA MALAYSIA SINGAPORE BURMA

AUSTRALASIA & OCEANIA

 MAURITIUS  SEYCHELLES AUSTRALIA  NEW ZEALAND PAPUA NEW GUINEA SOLOMON ISLANDS MARSHALL ISLANDS MICRONESIA